Brazil

NATIONS OF THE MODERN WORLD: LATIN AMERICA

Ronald M. Schneider, *Series Editor*

---

†*Brazil: Culture and Politics in
a New Industrial Powerhouse,* Ronald M. Schneider

Colombia: Democracy Under Assault,
Second Edition, Harvey F. Kline

†*Cuba: Dilemmas of a Revolution,*
Third Edition, Juan M. del Aguila

Bolivia: Land of Struggle, Waltraud Queiser Morales

†*The Dominican Republic: A Caribbean Crucible,*
Second Edition, Howard J. Wiarda and Michael J. Kryzanek

Nicaragua: The Land of Sandino,
Third Edition, Thomas W. Walker

Venezuela: Tarnished Democracy, Daniel C. Hellinger

Paraguay: The Personalist Legacy,
Riordan Roett and Richard Scott Sacks

Haiti: The Breached Citadel, Patrick Bellegarde-Smith

Mexico: Paradoxes of Stability and Change,
Second Edition, Daniel Levy and Gabriele Székely

FORTHCOMING

Peru, Gregory D. Schmidt

†Available in hardcover and paperback

BRAZIL

*Culture and Politics
in a New Industrial
Powerhouse*

RONALD M. SCHNEIDER

WestviewPress

A Division of HarperCollins*Publishers*

Nations of the Modern World: Latin America

Copyright © 1996 by Westview Press, Inc., A Division of HarperCollins Pubishers, Inc.

Published in 1996 in the United States of America by Westview Press, Inc., 5500 Central Avenue,
Boulder, Colorado 80301-2877, and in the United Kingdom by Westview Press, 12 Hid's Copse Road,
Cumnor Hill, Oxford OX2 9JJ

Library of Congress Cataloging-in-Publication Data
Schneider, Ronald M.
    Brazil : culture and politics in a new industrial powerhouse /
Ronald Schneider.
        p.   cm. — (Nations of the modern world. Latin America)
    Includes index.
    ISBN 0-8133-2436-X (HC) — ISBN 0-8133-2437-8 (PB)
    1. Brazil.   I. Title.   II. Series.
    F2508.S33   1996
    981—dc20   95-37942
                                                                               CIP

The paper used in this publication meets the requirements of the American National Standard for
Permanence of Paper for Printed Library Materials Z39.48-1984.

10   9   8   7   6   5   4   3   2   1

Contents

List of Tables and Illustrations   ix
Preface   xi
List of Acronyms   xv

1 THE SEVERAL BRAZILS   1

The Heartland, 4
The South, 12
The Center-West, 17
The North, 21
The Northeast, 28

2 FROM DISCOVERY THROUGH OLIGARCHICAL REPUBLIC: BRAZIL TO 1930   35

From Colony to Kingdom, 35
Consolidation and Nation Building, 38
Establishment of the Republic, 44
Transition to Civilian Rule, 48
Politics Without Parties, 1906–1922, 51
Tenentismo and the Road Toward Revolution, 54

3 FROM REVOLUTION TO REVOLUTION: BRAZIL 1930–1964   58

The 1930 Revolution and Vargas's Rise, 58
The Vargas Regime, 62
The Democratic Interregnum and Vargas Again, 67
The Quest for Development and Democracy: 1955–1960, 73
Crises, Compromise, and Radicalization: 1961–1962, 80
Dissensus, Decay, and Disaster: 1963–1964, 84

4 FROM MILITARY RULE THROUGH DEMOCRATIC TRANSITION: BRAZIL 1964–1989

Castelo Branco and the Arbiter-Ruler Dilemma, 88
Dominance by the *Duros,* 91
The Road Back Under Geisel, 95
Figueiredo: Political Opening and Economic Difficulties, 1979–1984, 99
The Sarney Government: Transition Under a Caretaker, 104
Consolidating the Transition, 109

5 POLITICS AND GOVERNMENT POLICIES IN THE 1990S

The First Year: Shakedown Cruise to the Doldrums, 114
The Second Year: Stemming the Slide and Regaining Momentum, 117
The Third Year: Disaster for Collor, Opportunity for Franco, 120
1993: Muddling Through, 122
Overhauling the Constitution and Choosing a President, 123
Composition and Orientation of the Cardoso Administration, 127
Political Organizations and Machinery of Government, 130
Soldiers, Property Owners, and Workers, 132

6 THE ECONOMY AND FINANCES

Brazilian Growth: Demographic and Economic, 137
Industrialization, Modernization of Agriculture, and Natural Resources, 141
Infrastructure: Energy, Transportation, Communications, and Financial
   Institutions, 147
Shadows on Development: Inflation, the Public Sector, and Paying the Bills, 152
External Factors: Debt, Balance of Payments, Investment, and Trade, 157

7 SOCIETY AND SOCIAL PROBLEMS

Workforce, Income Distribution, and Social Mobility, 170
Social Conditions and Problems, 173
Education, 178
Racial Factors and Race Relations, 182
Religion, 187

8 CULTURE AND BRAZILIAN WAYS 191

Cultural Traits and the Media, 192
The Written Word, 195
Music and Theater, 197
Cinema and Electronic Media, 199
Art and Architecture, 202

9 BRAZIL IN THE WORLD 204

From Object to Actor, 205
The Once-Special U.S.-Brazilian Relationship, 207
Brazil's Neighbors Become More Special, 213
Worldview and Foreign Policy Making, 214

Notes   219
About the Book and Author   237
Index   239

Tables and Illustrations

TABLES

1.1 Metropolitan regions and major cities   3
1.2 Characteristics and rank of Brazil's states   6
6.1 Economic performance 1971–1994   162

MAPS

Brazil's political divisions   2
Heartland   5
South   13
Center-west   17
North   22
Northeast   29

PHOTOGRAPHS

Downtown São Paulo   7
Botofogo District of Rio de Janeiro   10
Foz de Iguaçu   14
Germanic architecture in Blumenau   15
The Pantanal   19
The Amazon River   23
Deforestation in the Amazon   24
Reforestation   24
Brazilian congressional building   76
Student demonstrations in the 1970s   94
Lula da Silva addressing striking metal workers, 1979   101
Congress voting on Collor's impeachment, September 1992   121
Inauguration of Fernando Henrique Cardoso, January 1, 1995   127
Fiats (automobiles) awaiting export   142
Soybean fields   146
Itaipú Dam   149
Children playing in the interior of Brazil   174
Locals fish on a northeastern river   175
Street children huddle together for warmth in São Paulo   176
Family from a typical small town in the Brazilian interior   181

Preface

Ours is a preponderantly, indeed lopsidedly, Northern Hemisphere–oriented world. Even South and Southeast Asia lie almost exclusively above the equator, and only two of the world's twenty-five most populous countries are located in the southern half of the globe: Brazil in the western quadrant and Indonesia in the eastern. With 157 million inhabitants, Brazil ranks fifth in the world in both population and territory, and its GDP, exceeding $560 billion, makes the country the globe's ninth largest economy. Making up nearly half the South American landmass—being twice the size of Mexico—Brazil constitutes most of the vast Amazon basin; it also anchors the Southern Cone and borders all but two of the Andean countries. Not only is Brazil territorially almost the size of the United States or China, and its Amazon by far the world's greatest river, but it also has an extremely diverse resource base, including most of the minerals required by modern industry; produces a wide variety of agricultural crops; and comes close to being world leader in livestock. Moreover, Brazil possesses much potentially productive farmland that has not yet been put to the plow and could double its agricultural output by 2005.

Brazil's vastness is matched by its diversity. Its population of at least partial African descent (roughly 70 million) is substantially greater than that found in North America including the Caribbean or that of any African country save Nigeria. Yet at nearly 90 million, European-descended Brazilians match the population of Mexico. Brazil has two of the world's largest cities, São Paulo and Rio de Janeiro, lying in close proximity to each other. In the entire Southern Hemisphere these are rivaled in size only by Buenos Aires and Jakarta; globally they are in a league with Tokyo, London, New York, and Mexico City. But huge as they are, these megametropolises account for but one-sixth of the country's population; Brazil also has another eighteen urban centers of between 780,000 and 3.8 million inhabitants.

Brazil has undergone wrenching transformations since the 1950s—analogous in many ways to Britain during the industrial revolution or Germany in the latter half of the nineteenth century. Individuals by the tens of millions have been uprooted from rural areas and small towns to swell the population of great and intermediate cities. In the process, serious social problems have spread and intensified, giving rise to the lamentable situation of thousands of homeless street children who frequently slip into a life of crime and too often become victims of brutal repression by "death squads" of renegade police. International media seize upon such instances as well as conflicts between outlaw prospectors and Brazil's small surviving indigenous population to project an essentially negative image of Brazil. This, along with extremely skewed income distribution, masks substantial progress made on a wide variety of fronts. I have closely observed Brazil for four decades, have examined five centuries of its history, and am familiar with other nations of Latin America, and I am convinced that Brazil's vitality and the virtues of much of its population outweigh its imperfections.

Brazil's progress has been retarded by frustratingly dysfunctional features of its politics. For historical reasons analyzed in this book, Brazil's modern and forward-looking regions have held the presidency for but a very small part of the past sixty-five years—a situation that was changed only at the beginning of 1995. Moreover, its most developed state, São Paulo, a nation within a nation, is grotesquely underrepresented in Congress. Resolution of glaring social inequities is blocked by grievous shortcomings of the political system, which in recent years have also retarded economic development. Yet only gross political malperformance can prevent dreams of past generations of Brazilians from becoming reality during the lifetime of present youth. But the most backward regions of this vast country will not soon catch up with advanced states; their persistent fundamental problems have so far eluded effective solutions. Fortunately, Brazil may be reaching a watershed with the election to the presidency of Fernando Henrique Cardoso, a cosmopolitan, world-renowned social scientist whose political tilt is social democratic—just as sustained economic growth has again been achieved.

This book is the result of an adult lifetime of study and observation. Since the early 1950s I have become painfully aware of Brazil's flaws yet impressed by the progress it has made and its great potential. I have tried to present a portrait of this diverse country that is critically understanding as well as informative. To this end, the first chapter demonstrates the enormous variations in the regions, states, and cities of Brazil. This is done by means of a clockwise swing around the country with attention to geographic features, demographic considerations, and economic activities. Given the immensity of Brazil, a survey of its parts is essential before beginning to view it as a whole—particularly since until quite recently Brazil was distinctly not a single, integrated entity.

The book then examines the historical development of Brazil, starting with Portuguese settlement at the beginning of the 1500s along the northeastern coastal region. The essential events and trends of the colonial era (to 1822), the nineteenth-century Brazilian monarchy (1822–1889), and the elite-dominated early republican era (1889–1930) are sketched. A less broad historical brush is used in Chapter 3 to portray developments from the 1930 revolution through the crisis of populist "democracy" in the early 1960s that led to the military's seizure of power. Chapter 4 focuses on the 1964–1984 period and on the transitional civilian government from 1985 through 1989. Together these chapters lay out the country's fundamental features and its development into a semimodern, substantially urban and industrial nation. Chapter 5 concentrates on politics, policies, and governmental processes in the 1990s. It includes informed speculation concerning possible winds of change and future developments worth keeping an eye on while following Brazil down the road that leads to the challenges of the new century. It provides guideposts as to what might well happen under the new government that took office at the beginning of 1995. Chapter 6 analyzes the economy, focusing on the present but spotlighting significant trends to provide perspective on critical current issues. Chapter 7 discusses the evolution of Brazilian society, including the complex and perplexing question of race relations. Chapter 8 provides an overview of Brazilian culture and the arts, crucial because Brazil in these respects is not just a variation of Spanish America. Finally, Chapter 9 is devoted to a discussion of Brazil's place in the world.

An enterprise of this scope involves input from many individuals. Eric Alan Schneider spurred me toward the goal of a book in which a young Brazilian-American might take pride—once old enough to read it. Ricardo P. Schneider aided greatly with the maps, photos, and tables, and Frank McCann perceptively commented on preliminary drafts. Half the photos are from *Abril Imagens* courtesy of *Editora Abril* through the cooperation of Susana Camargo, chief of its department of documentation, and Eurípedes Alcantara, its representative/correspondent in New York. Most of the rest are a result of the good will of the Brazilian Foreign Ministry and the head of its press office, Minister Vera Machado. At Westview Press, Barbara Ellington made this a better book by her many useful editorial suggestions. The sensitive editing of Ida May Norton contributed significantly to clarity and precision. The guiding through production by Jennifer Blandford and Scott Horst as well as the indexing by Doug Easton were appreciated. None of these midwives is responsible for the work's remaining flaws; these are reflections of my own limitations and the problem of portraying a nation undergoing profound changes in a world itself being transformed.

Ronald M. Schneider

Acronyms

ADEP   Democratic Parliamentary Action and
   Popular Democratic Action
ARENA   National Renovating Alliance
AL   Liberal Alliance
ANL   National Liberating Alliance ·
BNDE   National Economic Development Bank
BNDES   National Economic and Social Development Bank
CEB   ecclesial base community
CEBRAP   Brazilian Center of Analysis and Planning
CGT   General Workers Center and
   General Workers Command
CNBB   National Conference of Brazilian Bishops
CNI   National Confederation of Industries
CNTI   National Confederation of Industrial Workers
CONCLAT   National Conference of the Working Class
CSN   National Steel Company
CUT   Single Workers Center
CVRD   Vale do Rio Doce Company
EAP   economically active population
ESG   National War College
EU   European Union
FEB   Brazilian Expeditionary Force
FPN   Nationalist Parliamentary Front
FMP   Popular Mobilization Front
FS   Força Sindical
IADB   Inter-American Development Bank
IBAD   Brazilian Institute of Democratic Action
IBRD   International Bank for Reconstruction and Development (World Bank)
IMF   International Monetary Fund
IPES   Institute for Social Research and Studies
LIBOR   London interbank offered rate
MDB   Brazilian Democratic Movement
NIC   newly industrialized country
PAEG   Program of Government Economic Action
PCB   Brazilian Communist Party

PCdoB   Communist Party of Brazil
PDC   Christian Democratic Party
PDS   Democratic Social Party
PDT   Democratic Workers' Party
PFL   Liberal Front Party
PL   Liberator Party and
   Liberal Party
PMDB   Party of the Brazilian Democratic Movement
PP   Popular Party
PPR   Progressive Renovating Party
PPS   Popular Socialist Party
PRC   Conservative Republican Party
PRF   Federal Republican Party
PRN   National Renovation Party
PRONA   National Reconstruction of Order Party
PSB   Brazilian Socialist Party
PSD   Social Democratic Party
PSDB   Brazilian Social Democracy Party
PSP   Social Progressive Party
PT   Workers' Party
PTB   Brazilian Labor Party
SNI   National Intelligence Service
UDN   National Democratic Union

1

THE SEVERAL BRAZILS

B RAZIL IS A VAST, triangular country facing the Atlantic Ocean on the east, bounded on the west and south by five neighbors and by five others to the north (see Map 1). At nearly 3.3 million square miles, its area is 48 percent of the landmass of the South American continent and could almost contain Europe. Its 4,600-mile shoreline is exceeded by 9,800 miles of land borders. Although Brazil nearly equals the United States in size, only an area equivalent to France lies in the temperate zone, with by far the greater part falling into the tropical or subtropical climes. Its continental dimensions lead to a wide range of regional variations, for the country runs 2,700 miles both north-south and east-west. It lies fully to the east of Philadelphia, extending out to a point past the middle of the North Atlantic. Its northern extreme is even with such central African cities as Accra and Lagos; its southern end is on a line with the tip of Africa.

Altitude differences are less important than in many South American countries, since Brazil contains no major mountain range. But well over half the country is situated on the Brazilian highlands, and the coastal escarpment southward from Salvador averages 2,600 feet, with many mountains of 7,000 to 8,000 feet and a few peaks in the 9,000-foot range. Moreover, the Guiana Highlands in the north are composed of stumps of eroded mountains that in places rise to nearly 10,000 feet. Three-eighths of the country is plateaus with the rest mainly plains. In terms of vegetation, the narrow coastal belt is chiefly deciduous forest, the Amazon basin is rain forests, the northeast is largely scrub woodlands, and the central highlands are chiefly grasslands, often mixed with trees. The country's southern portion includes temperate mixed forests, prairie areas, and tropical deciduous forests.[1]

Brazil is so diverse that generalizations about it run serious risk of being either bland platitudes of the lowest-common-denominator-variety or averages that mask great variations. Hence Brazilian society, economy, and political processes must be viewed against a backdrop of the distinctive characteristics of the major sections of this vast country. This perspective is provided through a tour that begins at the nation's core and moves around the periphery. Before I outline such a

Brazil's Political Divisions

trip, however, a few fundamental facts must be borne in mind: First, Brazil is a federal nation in which the states enjoy considerable autonomy and are potent political actors. Since a good number of Brazilian states are not only larger but also more populous than many Latin American countries, it is necessary to differentiate among them. Second, Brazil is increasingly a highly urban country. Whereas it was 36 percent urban in 1940 and 56 percent by 1970, the 1991 census designated nearly 76 percent urban—a very high sustained rate of urbanization. Now 85.5 million persons—over 54 percent of its population—reside in cities of 100,000 or more. As documented in Table 1.1, in excess of one in three Brazilians, some 53.7 million persons, live in fifteen metropolitan regions of over 1 million inhabitants, with nearly half of these in greater São Paulo and Rio de Janeiro. An additional 22.2 million inhabit urban centers in the 200,000–970,000 range, and

TABLE 1.1 Metropolitan Regions and Major Cities

Metropolitan Region / Major City	Population[a]	Metropolitan Region / Major City	Population[a]
São Paulo	16.350	Juiz de Fora	0.420
Rio de Janeiro	9.970	Campos	0.410
Belo Horizonte	3.820	Volta Redonda/Barra Mansa	0.405
Porto Alegre	3.320	Joinville	0.395
Recife	3.070	Imperatriz	0.385
Salvador	2.780	Porto Velho	0.365
Fortaleza	2.610	Campina Grande	0.360
Curitiba	2.190	Petrolina/Juazeiro	0.350
Federal District (Brasília)	1.780	Santarém	0.350
Belém	1.480	Ipatinga	0.340
Goiânia	1.450	Crato/Juazeiro do Norte	0.325
Manaus	1.340	São José do Rio Preto	0.325
Campinas	1.220	Caxias do Sul	0.320
Santos	1.170	Piracicaba	0.310
Vitória	1.150	Pelotas	0.305
São Luís	0.970	Bauru	0.290
Natal	0.870	Ilhéus	0.275
Teresina/Timon	0.840	Montes Claros	0.275
João Pessoa	0.790	Franca	0.270
Maceió	0.780	Luziania	0.270
Cuiabá	0.740	Maringá	0.270
Campo Grande	0.690	Anápolis	0.265
Aracajú	0.620	Petrópolis	0.265
Florianópolis	0.570	Mogi Mirim/Mogi Guaçu	0.255
Sumaré/Americana	0.570	Ponta Grossa	0.255
Sorocaba	0.520	Governador Valadares	0.245
São José dos Campos	0.515	Limeira	0.245
Jundiaí	0.480	Vitória da Conquista	0.245
Ribeirão Preto	0.480	Rio Branco	0.235
Londrina	0.460	Blumenau	0.230
Feira de Santana	0.455	Caruaru	0.230
Uberlândia	0.425	Santa Maria	0.230

[a]Millions of inhabitants

more than 25.7 million dwell in cities of 50,000 to 199,999.[2] An understanding of Brazil's national life requires familiarity with the most important of its cities.

It is also essential to remember that there is no other country where rivers so define the regions of a near-continental landmass. The mighty Amazon with its 1,100 tributaries is supplemented by other major systems, several of which are themselves among the hemisphere's largest. Brazil's rivers supply the world's greatest hydroelectric generating potential and are being incorporated into the country's transportation system. Pollution of them may constitute a more serious environmental peril for Brazilians than the far more publicized destruction of rain forests—a matter of greater concern to Northern Hemisphere industrialized nations. Moreover, Brazil's coast has played a crucial role in shaping the country. A majority of state capitals are ports, and there are a half dozen other important ports serving inland capitals. These essentially were the country for much of the colonial period, and even today the finest collection of harbors in the world constitutes a major asset for a Brazil increasingly integrated into the global economy.

The Heartland

Clearly all regions of Brazil are not of equal importance. São Paulo, Rio de Janeiro, Minas Gerais, and little Espírito Santo contain the greatest concentration of population—over 66 million persons, heavily urbanized—and of economic activity. With 11 percent of the country's area, the southeast has 42 percent of the nation's population as well as nearly 62 percent of GDP and over 70 percent of its industry. As shown in Table 1.2, São Paulo boasts nearly half the country's industry, furnishes over 35 percent of GDP, provides 34.0 percent of Brazil's exports, and is the source of half the tax on industrial products and nearly as high a proportion of income tax receipts. Minas Gerais supplies 12.5 percent of GDP and is second in exports; next is Rio de Janeiro with 11 percent of GDP and sixth place in exports slightly ahead of Espírito Santo. Clearly this is the dominant region of the country. To the degree that it foreshadows future changes in other parts of the country—which it clearly does—the southeast affords a strong basis for hope.

Country Within a Country

São Paulo with 34.0 million inhabitants—equal to Argentina or Colombia—is the state par excellence of cities, industry, and commercialized agriculture. Half are to be found in sprawling São Paulo city, which has as its chief components the municipality of that name (with 9.9 million inhabitants) plus the state's third, fourth, fifth, and sixth most populous localities.[3] If Rio de Janeiro is a challenger for the title of the world's most beautiful city, São Paulo is a contender for that of most dynamic megacity. The metropolitan region alone has 16 million residents, and within a radius of sixty miles there are six other urban centers, two with populations of over 1 million and four with 480,000–570,000. This is the heartland's

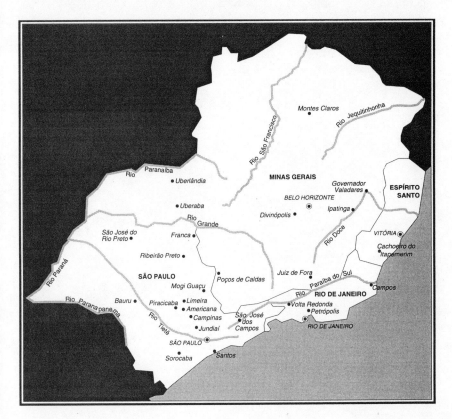

Heartland

heartland; it includes the country's equivalent of Wall Street as well as of Detroit and St. Louis and has the number one port. The urban region's economically active population nearing 9 million, one-eighth of the nation's workforce, produces a quarter of the country's GDP.

Centered between the Tietê and Pinheiros Rivers and lying on the tropic of Capricorn, this teeming metropolis spills across these borders in all directions. Although 3.6 million persons live in one type of slum or another—from tenements in the old center regions to shanties in the industrial suburbs—São Paulo also has a large middle class and the country's greatest concentration of rich and near-rich. This affluent elite is highly visible in the luxury apartments of the Gardens neighborhoods and the walled mansions of Morumbí. Choked with vehicular traffic, São Paulo now boasts a modern subway, and along Avenida Paulista are some of the world's most striking office buildings. In all parts of the sprawling city are found large modern shopping centers and fast-food franchises. As befits a world-level industrial and commercial center, it is served by a network of express highways running out in every direction complemented by railroads.

TABLE 1.2 Characteristics and Rank of Brazil's States

State	Area[a]	Population[b]	Share of GDP	Share of Exports	Ranking in Industry[c]	Ranking in Agriculture[c]	Ranking in Livestock[d]
São Paulo	95,870	34.0	35.6%	34.3%	1	1	2
Minas Gerais	226,550	16.7	12.5%	13.1%	2	4	1
Rio de Janeiro	16,860	13.2	12.5%	5.4%	3	15	14
Bahia	218,960	12.8	4.5%	3.8%	7	5	8
Rio Grande do Sul	108,390	9.6	6.6%	12.5%	4	3	3
Paraná	76,980	8.7	6.1%	7.4%	5	2	6
Pernambuco	39,010	7.5	2.6%	1.0%	8	12	15
Ceará	56,270	6.7	1.5%	0.8%	11	14	13
Pará	481,510	5.8	1.3%	4.4%	13	11	12
Maranhão	127,270	5.3	1.2%	1.5%	18	13	11
Santa Catarina	36,810	4.9	3.0%	5.6%	6	7	9
Goiás	131,370	4.4	2.1%	0.8%	12	8	4
Paraíba	20,840	3.4	0.7%	0.2%	14	16	16
Espírito Santo	17,660	2.8	1.9%	5.2%	10	6	17
Alagoas	11,240	2.7	0.7%	0.6%	15	17	20
Piauí	97,040	2.7	0.4%	0.2%	22	18	18
Rio Grande do Norte	20,530	2.6	0.7%	0.2%	16	20	21
Amazonas	605,520	2.4	1.3%	0.5%	9	23	23
Mato Grosso	348,120	2.4	0.6%	1.1%	21	9	7
Mato Grosso do Sul	138,050	1.9	1.8%	0.7%	17	10	5
Federal District	2,240	1.8	1.4%	0.0%	20	27	27
Sergipe	8,440	1.6	0.4%	0.1%	19	21	19
Rondônia	92,060	1.5	0.3%	0.1%	23	19	22
Tocantins	107,100	1.0	0.1%	0.0%	24	22	10
Acre	59,980	0.5	0.2%	0.0%	26	24	24
Amapá	54,980	0.4	0.1%	0.1%	25	26	26
Roraima	86,900	0.3	0.1%	0.0%	27	25	25

[a]In square miles   [b]Millions   [c]By value of production   [d]By value including poultry and fish

Downtown São Paulo (photo courtesy of the Brazilian Foreign Ministry)

Only in the early 1990s was attention finally given to pollution of the Tietê, which rises high in the Serra do Mar behind Santos and flows through the capital westward across the state into the Paraná.

Many other Paulistas live in the corridor running southeast to the country's leading port, Santos (435,000 inhabitants, plus another 735,000 in the rest of its metropolitan region). Several million more dwell in the urban belt extending northwestward to the state's second city, Campinas, with a population of 1.22 million and a diversified industrial base. Yet dominant as are these great urban conglomerations, there are thirteen other cities of from 200,000 to well over 500,000 population scattered around the rest of the state—as well as an additional fifty-three cities between 50,000 and 199,999 inhabitants. Their polyglot population reflects the influx of Italian and Japanese immigrants brought in to work coffee plantations during the half century 1880–1930. Equally apparent are the millions of residents, many dark-skinned, resulting from the sustained heavy flow of internal migration from Brazil's overcrowded northeast, a shift that has characterized the post–World War II period.

The "locomotive" state of Brazil begins with a narrow coastal lowland, overshadowed by a towering escarpment leading to a plateau on which is found the basin containing the capital city at an altitude of 2,500 feet. West of a mild mountain range just inland from São Paulo city, the land falls away in the form of a wide depression until reaching a third stretch of highlands from which it slopes downward to its western extreme at the Paraná River. Almost two-thirds of the state lies in its basin. In the upper eastern corner the Paraíba Valley runs east-northeast with the jagged range of the Serra da Mantiqueira as its backdrop—features extending up into the state of Rio de Janeiro. São José dos Campos (515,000 inhabitants), center of this northeastward extension, is the hub of the country's high-tech aviation, armaments, and space industries. The São Paulo suburb of São Bernardo do Campo is the site for much of Brazil's automotive industry.

Between São Paulo and Campinas lies Jundiaí, an industrial city of 480,000 that serves as fulcrum for a fruit-growing region. A little to the south and west is Piricicaba (310,000 residents), while a short ride along the northwestward axis lie the twin cities of Sumaré/Americana (570,000 inhabitants) and a series of closely spaced industrial cities in the 150,000–245,000 bracket serving an area producing sugarcane, citrus fruits, and livestock on a large scale. Ribeirão Preto (480,000 inhabitants) is an industrial and commercial center dominating the rich north-central part of the state with its bountiful harvests of sugarcane, coffee, corn, and soybeans. Around it are produced a third of all Brazil's alcohol and 90 percent of its orange juice.

Fifty miles farther north is Franca (population 270,000), an internationally important focus of the shoe industry. São José de Rio Preto (325,000 residents) centers the northwestern sector between the Grande and Tietê Rivers. The diversified crops and livestock of this region include rice, cotton, coffee, corn, oranges, cattle, and hogs. To the west, sugarcane also becomes prominent as the Paranapanema River separates São Paulo from Paraná. Most visible in this corner of the state are the more than 2 million cattle grazing there. Railroad hub Bauru (290,000) anchors the agricultural region of the state's center-south with its temperate-zone crops. Burgeoning Sorocaba (520,000) is the industrial fulcrum of the area directly west of the capital.

Thus, São Paulo still includes Brazil's richest farmlands, but industry has increasingly come to be the backbone of its essentially first-world economy, and factories dominate the landscape of the eastern part of the state. During the process that produced this industrialization, São Paulo lost its place as the world's key coffee-growing area—as coffee first moved southward into Paraná, then northward to Minas Gerais and Espírito Santo. Yet sparked by sugarcane and oranges—it leads the country in both by a wide margin—the interior of São Paulo is still one of the world's most productive agricultural areas. Thus, São Paulo provides well over 20 percent of the nation's agricultural production, including more than 6 million tons of grains as well as 38 million hens and 12.5 million head of cattle. The link between agriculture and industry in this richest area of all Latin America is made evident by the large number of distilleries spread across nearly half the state busily converting the vast fields of sugarcane into alcohol to fuel a large share of the automobiles produced around the great capital. Indeed, three-fifths of the country's annual production of 13 billion liters of alcohol is produced in this state.

An Impressive Number Two

Minas Gerais, with a population over 16.7 million in an area equal to France and Belgium combined, stretches northward from São Paulo for more than 600 miles and measures an equal distance east to west at its widest point. There the "Minas Triangle" extends in the extreme southwest as a wedge between São Paulo and Goiás bounded by the Grande and Paranaíba Rivers. And here around the cities of Uberlândia (population 425,000) and Uberaba (215,000) there is a prosperous livestock region complemented by cultivation of rice, coffee, corn, soy, and pineapples and by some titanium mining. This fertile area helps Minas Gerais follow closely on São Paulo's heels with nearly 6 million tons of grain harvested in a normal year.

Blessed with abundant power from the Furnas and Tres Marias hydroelectric projects, the center-south portion of the state lies on the Brasília–Rio de Janeiro railroad and highway lines and near the Brasília–São Paulo transportation axis. Its hub is Brazil's third city, Belo Horizonte, boasting a metropolitan region population in excess of 3.8 million. With steel mills and Fiat's automobile factory as its backbone, greater Belo Horizonte has become an impressive industrial pole—trailing only São Paulo and Rio de Janeiro in this regard. Located in a deep circular basin watered by a series of small rivers dammed up into beautiful Lake Pampulha, it is in the middle of what was in the 1600s and much of the 1700s the continent's richest mining area. Now it produces massive exports of iron ore as well as 36 percent of the country's steel. Indeed, this central region with Belo Horizonte as its hub is often still referred to as the "iron quadrangle." Its western edge lies west of Divinópolis, a city of 165,000 with substantial textile and clothing industries. The northeastern edge of the central region, featuring steel and livestock, revolves around Ipatinga (340,000) and contains such world-class steel mills as Usiminas, Mannesmann, and Belgo-Mineiro.

Also quite developed, albeit on a lesser industrial scale, is the state's southeastern quadrant. Here Juiz da Fora (population 420,000) has closer ties to Rio de Janeiro than to its own capital. A southern salient protruding into São Paulo contains many popular lake resorts and mineral spas; Poços de Caldas (115,000), located in the crater of a long-extinct volcano, also is a focus of uranium mining and enriching.

Most of the southern and central regions of Minas Gerais range between hilly and near-mountainous, with elevations of 2,600–2,800 feet common and higher crests quite frequent. Indeed, Pico da Bandeira on the border with Espírito Santo reaches nearly 9,500 feet and is part of the same Serra da Mantequeira found as the northeastern boundary of São Paulo. These topographical features extend into the gemstone region in the eastern part of the state around Governor Valladares (population 245,000) on the Rio Doce. Farther north is the Jequitinhonha Valley—the state's poorest region—stretching through the northeastern portion of Minas Gerais into the very bottom of Bahia. Near there the Serra do Espinhaço runs northward from the Serra da Mantequeira at elevations of 3,600 to 4,200 feet, occasionally surpassing 5,500 feet. More to the north it softens into the hilly tablelands of the Chapada Diamantina (which extends well up into Bahia).

Behind this watershed divide, where the streams on the eastern side flow toward the Atlantic and those beyond the crest into the São Francisco River, lies the vast expanse of the north of Minas. Although still underdeveloped, it compares favorably with the neighboring southern quadrant of Bahia. Montes Claros, with 275,000 inhabitants, is a rapidly growing provincial city with biomedical and cement industries. The surrounding area is used for extensive grazing, cultivation of sugarcane, and commercial forestry for industrial fuel. Although large expanses are quite flat, there are areas of rolling hills as well as many hogbacks rising to over 5,000 feet. A short distance to the west is the São Francisco Valley, a farming area beginning to benefit from large-scale irrigation. To the east of this long north-south depression can be found extensive stretches of *caatinga* (semiarid scrub brushlands), and west of it are *cerrados* (dry grasslands with scattered trees) like those of Goiás and Mato Grosso, broken by *chapadões* (tablelands). Because the long dry season regularly runs from April through September, irrigation is essential if agriculture is to become profitable.

Despite the mineral wealth of Minas Gerais, agriculture and livestock are the most obvious activities, and it is for these it was famed during the nineteenth century through the 1960s. It still holds first place in coffee and is third in both corn and rice. Industrialization came only after the first major hydroelectric projects were in place, yet the region has already overtaken Rio de Janeiro in industrial production.

The Reality of Rio

The size of Switzerland and Denmark together, with a population pushing 13.2 million, Rio de Janeiro has never fully adjusted to no longer being the nation's

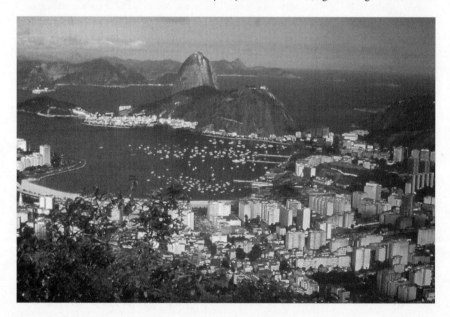

Botofogo District of Rio de Janeiro (photo courtesy of the Brazilian Foreign Ministry)

capital. The city of Rio de Janeiro is still in many ways the country's cultural capital, and with its world-famous white beaches and Miami-like climate it is clearly the center of Brazil's multibillion-dollar tourist industry. Containing masses of urban poor, who are concentrated not only in its colorful hillside *favelas* but also in the sprawling belt of industrial suburbs that surround the city proper to the north and west, it is also the seat of a large bureaucratic middle class. Its commerce and industrial employment fluctuate with the national economic situation. A boom-and-bust shipbuilding industry is vital in a region where petrochemicals, textiles, and light manufactures do not generate a similar multiplier effect. As a port, Rio de Janeiro lags far behind Santos, but Sepetiba down the coast is steadily growing.

The metropolitan region of Rio de Janeiro surrounding Guanabara Bay has nearly 10 million residents, including those in the city itself and in the ring of largely working-class suburbs forming a horseshoe around it.[4] Several of these have populations in the 400,000 to over 1 million range. Along the sea to the south of the city are the new luxury apartment areas, veritable cities in themselves, which are favored by the wealthy and the upper middle class as a refuge from the overcrowding and violence of the urban center. There are 3 million residents living in substandard housing, 1.2–1.5 million of them contained in the nearly 600 *favela* neighborhoods. The bay itself is horribly polluted; the formidable task of cleaning it up barely started in 1993.

Southwest of this great city the sea comes ever closer to the escarpment, greatly reducing the area of the narrow coastal lowlands. Inland the Paraíba Valley extends up from São Paulo through the urban industrial conglomerate formed by the almost adjoining cities of Volta Redonda and Barra Mansa (405,000 inhabitants). The former houses the National Steel Company, the ninth largest steel mill in the world. On the western side of the valley the peaks of the Serra da Mantiqueira rise to heights of over 8,000 feet with Agulhas Negras (Black Needles) soaring above 9,100 feet. The Itatiaia park of which it is part centers on a volcanic extension of nearly 450 square miles—the world's second largest. Inland off the Paraíba River there are valleys so deep as to approximate canyons with bare rock cliffs sometimes exceeding 1,000 feet, whereas the coastal Serra do Mar contains seas of hills with their wavelike peaks extending farther than one can see.

Bordering the high plateau north of the city of Rio de Janeiro, the escarpment of the Serra do Orgãos (an extension of the Serra do Mar running up the middle of the state) often crests near 5,000 feet, sometimes in spectacular "sugar loafs" and occasionally more needlelike formations. Behind it the old winter capital of Petrópolis (262,000 inhabitants) serves as the pole of a tourist region. The major upstate center, however, is Campos (410,000 residents), located where the Paraíba River turns eastward toward the ocean. In an area in which coffee coexists with sugarcane, it is the hub for supplying the great offshore oil fields that have spelled an end to Brazil's long dependence upon imported oil. Between Campos and Rio de Janeiro flat coastal plains are fairly extensive. The state produces 24 percent of Brazil's steel and accounts for 11.5 percent of the turnover tax. Its economically active population is distributed 63 percent in the service sector, 35 percent in industry, and only 2 percent in agriculture.

The Odd Man Out

The little sister in the heartland region, albeit still the size of the Dominican Republic, is the state of Espírito Santo, nestled with its back to Minas Gerais, its feet to Rio de Janeiro, and its front facing the sea. Two-fifths of its 2.8 million inhabitants live in greater Vitória, a region that includes the deepwater port of Tubarão, outlet for the heaviest tonnage of Brazil's exports, chiefly iron ore, and Serra, seat of a 3-million-ton-capacity steel mill. Espírito Santo is also site of the country's largest cellulose company and is in second place in coffee production with 5 million sacks yearly. The coastal half of the state enjoys income levels at or above the national average, but the interior and northern parts lag well behind, which has caused tens of thousands to flee to the slums of the metropolis. Cachoeira de Itapemirim (155,000 inhabitants), a center of marble quarrying and grazing, functions as the fulcrum of the southern third of the state. North of the capital marshy lowlands with sand deposits along the coast contrast with the proximity of the escarpment to the shore elsewhere.

The South

Three states in which 15 percent of the country's population inhabit less than 7 percent of its area but produce 16.7 percent of the nation's wealth lie fully below the tropic of Capricorn. These sit on the southern plateau, beginning in the east with the fairly high escarpment of the Serra do Mar, which in some places comes right down to the sea and in others falls short to create a narrow coastal lowland that becomes broader in the extreme south. The first plateau behind these uplands may drop off to around 1,800 feet. This ends with a lower range of hills followed by a second plateau at a lower elevation, which in turn leads to a third belt of hills. The final plateau then descends gradually toward the Paraná River, which marks the border for this narrowest part of the country. Rainfall throughout the south is about fifty to sixty inches distributed around the year with freezing temperatures occasionally experienced in June, July, and August.

An Agricultural Powerhouse

Even in the shadow of dominant São Paulo, Paraná itself is impressive. More than the size of Syria and Lebanon combined, with an enterprising population of 8.7 million, it is the country's number two agricultural producer with nearly 20 percent of the national total—including 16 million tons of grains—and fourth in value of exports. First in wheat and corn; second in soy, cotton, and peanuts; third in beans; and fourth in coffee, it also has nearly 9 million of Brazil's cattle and is the leading

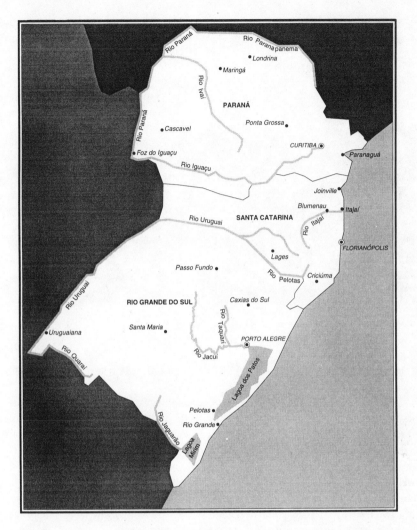

The following place names appear on the map:

Rio Paraná · Rio Paranapanema · Londrina · Maringá · Rio Ivaí · PARANÁ · Rio Paraná · Cascavel · Ponta Grossa · CURITIBA · Paranaguá · Foz do Iguaçu · Rio Iguaçu · Joinville · Blumenau · Itajaí · Rio Uruguai · SANTA CATARINA · Rio Itajaí · FLORIANÓPOLIS · Lages · Passo Fundo · Rio Pelotas · Criciúma · Rio Uruguai · RIO GRANDE DO SUL · Caxias do Sul · Rio Taquari · Santa Maria · PORTO ALEGRE · Uruguaiana · Rio Jacuí · Lagoa dos Patos · Rio Quaraí · Pelotas · Rio Grande · Rio Jaguarão · Lagoa Mirim

South

producer of hogs. Yet its population is more than two-thirds urban. The north of the state is geographically an extension of southern São Paulo. It centers around the cities of Londrina (with a population of 452,000) and Maringá (263,000). Below this region, toward the eastern edge of the Paraná plateau at an altitude of 3,000 feet, is Curitiba, the capital, a rapidly growing city of over 2.1 million. Almost free of slum areas, this clean and modern metropolis—with its near-record fifty-one square meters of parklands per resident, one of the world's best bus systems, and an unmatched network of bicycle paths—has a broadening industrial base grounded in lumber and furniture. The port of Paranaguá (116,000)

Foz de Iguaçu (photo courtesy of the Brazilian Foreign Ministry)

serves not only the state but Paraguay as well and in 1988 had over 8 million tons of exports valued at above $2.6 billion.

Less than seventy miles inland from Curitiba lies Ponta Grossa (248,000 inhabitants), center for an area of mixed agriculture and livestock. It is the doorway to the ultrafertile Ivaí Valley in the state's northwest, still a major coffee-growing area. In the extreme west is the booming city of Foz de Iguaçu (209,000), near the dramatic waterfalls of that name—truly one of the world's natural marvels—as well as the globe's largest hydroelectric complex at Itaipu. The falls, actually a complex of 275 cataracts falling over 200-foot-high cliffs, include the awe-inspiring Devil's Throat (Garganta de Diabo), just upstream from where the Paraná leaves Brazil to enter Argentina. Here tourism and contraband from Paraguay are sources of prosperity, as is agriculture in a belt running eastward past Cascavel (210,000 inhabitants), south of which is the locus of the country's leading lumbering industry (softwoods). Around São Mateus do Sul is a large area of oil-bearing shale that is finally being exploited.

A Little Piece of Germany

Wedged in below Paraná and above Rio Grande do Sul is the state of Santa Catarina. The size of Hungary or Portugal, it contains a population of 4.9 million. Its coastal region, which includes the island capital of Florianópolis (nearly 570,000 inhabitants) and mainland suburbs, is important for textiles and clothing—on the strength of which it ranks fifth among Brazil's states in value of exports. Its gleaming beaches attract tourists, nearly 400,000 of them from Argentina in the peak summer months. Also along the coast with its fine bays are Joinville (population 395,000) in the extreme north, Brazil's center of refrigerator and compressor manufacturing, with 9 million units of the latter a year constituting 12 percent of world output, and Itajaí (135,000 residents), which serves as outlet for the valley of that name—Latin America's leading textile center. A short distance upriver is the industrial city of Blumenau (population 230,000), hub of Germanic settlement—still apparent in its architecture and cultural life, including an Oktoberfest. Here the coastal plain is wide—the Serra do Mar lies well inland—and hence Itajaí peak at over 4,200 feet appears even higher in contrast to its low-lying surroundings.

The southern part of the coastal belt, revolving around Criciúma (population 165,000), is the nation's main source of coal, high in sulfur and ash content. This is also the base for Brazil's tile and ceramic flooring industry, which has an annual production of over 62 million square meters. Northward along the coast is a narrow strip of sand and lagoons, and inland behind the Serra Geral's 2,700-foot heights is the plateau of the upper Uruguay River, where raising pigs, chickens, and turkeys is a major activity. The state grows three-fifths of Brazil's apples, leads the country in pork and fowl, and contributes 35 percent of tobacco production. Beyond Lages (160,000 inhabitants) are impor-

Germanic architecture in Blumenau (photo courtesy of the Brazilian Foreign Ministry)

tant lumbering operations, the country's largest meatpacking plants, and significant coal deposits. Santa Catarina is seventh in foodstuffs production, is responsible for 3.2 percent of Brazil's GDP, and has one of the country's lowest infant mortality rates.

Twice an Uruguay

Brazil's fifth state in population at 9.6 million and fourth in GDP with nearly 7 percent is Rio Grande do Sul, which ranks third in exports. More important, it is responsible for over 15 percent of the country's agricultural production—leading in soy and rice and ranking second in corn. It has over half the country's sheep as well as 14 million cattle. Not only is its population double that of neighboring Uruguay, but with an area equal to that of Italy, it dwarfs it as well. Along its northern edge extending inland toward the upper tributaries of the Uruguay River is an area of diversified farming and grazing. This river, which constitutes the border with Santa Catarina before becoming Brazil's boundary with Argentina, drains over half the state through a web of tributaries that stretch eastward almost to the Atlantic. Below it the coastal region is well served by several smaller rivers flowing down from the first range of hills into the ocean. Farther west is the country's major wine region with Caxias do Sul (population 320,000) as its commercial hub. Here the plateau lies at about 2,400 feet. In the north-central region, where Passo Fundo (160,000) is the transportation fulcrum, Rio Grande do Sul is much like the neighboring region of Santa Catarina, with livestock, fruits, and vegetables mixed with corn, wheat, and soy. Up in the very northwest timber predominates, and some coal is present.

Porto Alegre, a third of the way down the state, is Brazil's largest city south of São Paulo. With a population over 3.3 million (including in an array of satellite cities), it has a diversified industrial base featuring steel, petrochemicals, cellulose, clothing, textiles, leather goods, and some consumer durables. Porto Alegre is also the hub of the state's excellent network of railroads and highways. A port although well inland from the ocean, it sits between where the junction of the Jacuí and Taquari Rivers form the broad Guaíba and the latter disappears in the 200-mile Lagoa dos Patos (Duck Lagoon) that runs for two-thirds the length of the state before entering the sea.

Rio Grande (population 185,000) at the mouth of the Lagoa dos Patos is a deepwater port handling $3 billion a year in exports, and Pelotas (305,000) is a major food-processing center for rice, soy, and fruits. Inland lies the belt of grain farms and ranches bordering Uruguay along the Jaguarão and Quaraí Rivers and home to meatpacking centers. Santa Maria (230,000) is railroad and highway hub for the central section of the state on a line straight west from Porto Alegre, and Uruguaiana (125,000) anchors the extreme southwest salient. Between them much of the nation's rice is grown.

The Center-West

Inland from the economic and demographic heartland of Brazil there is a fast-developing region comprising just over one-fourth of the country's area but with less than one-twelfth of its population and 6.3 percent of GDP. This vast expanse is Brazil's rough equivalent of the U.S. Great Plains. Its eastern and southern fringes are becoming much like the bordering portions of the heartland; farther west and north it is still raw frontier. Larger than Mexico, this region stretches from the edge of Brazil's southern plateau up into the lower portion of the Amazon basin. Its river systems make it geologically and topographically diverse. Much of it is covered by *cerrados*. Near where it abuts the heartland at the São Paulo–Minas Gerais border, a number of streams originating much farther north come together to form the Paraná River, which is fed by the Tietê, Paranapenema, Iguaçu, and Uruguay and flows into the River Plate estuary that reaches oceanic

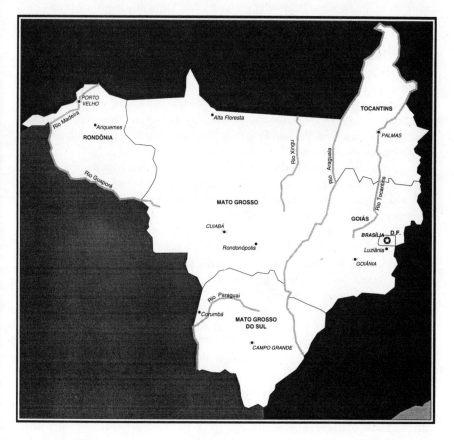

Center-west

status between Montevideo and Buenos Aires, capitals of Brazil's southern neighbors.

More Center Than West

This region's northeastern third, the size of Poland and Hungary combined, is made up of Goiás and Tocantins—the latter separated from the former in late 1988. Goiás has a population of 4.4 million in addition to the nearly 1.8 million residing in the Federal District, an enclave in its southeastern corner where live some 700,000 in Brasília and over 1 million in working-class satellite cities. Its rapid growth and development during the past quarter century was catalyzed by the inauguration of the new capital at the end of the 1950s.[5] At the heart of the state is the Goiás Massif, on whose southern part lies Goiânia, a city of 1.45 million. An urbanized belt runs eastward through Anápolis (258,000 population) to Brasília and its surrounding towns. Most of Goiás's rivers run north, but those in the southern third drain into the Paraná and hence on to the La Plata. Beginning at about 3,500 feet altitude at the Minas Gerais border, the land slopes gently in alternate levels of hilly plateaus, scrub grass flatlands, and tropical riverbeds. This is not strikingly different from the rolling plains alternating with chains of small mountains that mark much of western Minas Gerais.

Goiás is Brazil's third-ranking cattle state at close to 19 million head, is second in rice and fourth in soy, has substantial amounts of corn and beans among its 6- to 7-million-ton annual grain harvest, and is fourth in mineral production (most of it nonmetallic). Only 45,000 hectares (110,000 acres) are irrigated at present, chiefly in the east near the São Francisco. One of the state's major advantages is the strong network of roads and railroads centering on Brasília.

Tocantins, the former northern third of Goiás and with a population nudging 1 million, contains no nationally significant cities. Tucked between the backsides of Pará and Maranhão, it sees poverty still prevail amid an often chaotic frontier environment—with disputes over land often having violent outcomes. Its backbone is the Belém-Brasília highway and the Tocantins River, which originates between the capital and Goiânia and leads up into the Amazon. In the southwestern part of the state, within the Araguaia River, is the fascinating wildlife refuge on the great island of Bananal—270 miles long by 65 miles wide. The new state's nearly 5 million head of cattle add to its pronounced wild west appearance. Unlike the situation in the United States, where Indian tribes are found in major industrial states, it is here that in our tour of Brazil we first encounter them as anything but a minuscule trace in a sea of European- and Afro-Brazilians, and then only in terms of a few hundreds spilling across from Pará in the northern part of the state.

The Mature Frontier

The country's main agricultural frontier has moved up and inland from Paraná and São Paulo to the area between Goiás and Bolivia. Mato Grosso do Sul, with an area equal to Yugoslavia and Hungary combined but only 1.9 million inhabitants, has a rich strip of commercial rice, beans, soy, corn, and wheat producing 4 mil-

lion tons of grain yearly. This is accompanied by extensive grazing in the fertile
south and along the Paraná River in the east, areas in which two-fifths of the population dwell. Family farms abound in the eastern and northeastern regions bordering São Paulo and Goiás, where coffee and sugarcane enrich the crop mix. As
in the rest of the center-west region, annual rainfall is an ample fifty to seventy
inches.

Dynamic Campo Grande in the center of the state has a burgeoning population
nearing 690,000. To its west and northwest huge cattle ranches dominate the low,
damp Pantanal, the seasonally flooded alluvial plain some 400 miles in its north-
south extension by 200 miles in width along the Paraguay River. To the east the
land rises to the Pé da Serra foothills (altitude 500 feet) before joining the tablelands (1,000 feet) extending west from São Paulo. Corumbá in the northwest, a
river port of 100,000 inhabitants on the western fringe of the Pantanal, stagnates
in spite of having half of Brazil's plentiful manganese reserves as well as substantial deposits of iron ore, since these are also available nearer domestic users and
ocean ports. Agreements with Bolivia regarding a gas pipeline, steel mill, and
thermoelectric plant centered on Corumbá's twin city of Puerto Suarez, Bolivia,
bode well for this frontier region. Even now the state ranks third nationally in soy,
a fast-rising second in cattle (on Minas Gerais's heels with 20 million head), and
seventh as a producer of rice. Scattered in small groups through the area stretching southward along the Paraguayan border from Corumbá into the extreme

The Pantanal (photo by Júlio Bernardes, courtesy of Abril Imagens)

northwest corner of Paraná are some 5,000 Terêna and 3,000 Kaiwá Indians not yet subject to full acculturation and assimilation.

The Rawer West

Mato Grosso, a vast area nearly the size of Venezuela but with a population a bit over 2.4 million, lies directly west of Goiás. From east to west the land climbs to a plateau from the Araguaia River before beginning its descent near Rondonópolis, a farming center of 145,000 inhabitants. Farther north lie large expanses of savanna grasslands crossed by meandering rivers. The state's northeastern third is made up of the basins of the Araguaia and Xingu Rivers as they head north toward the Amazon; its northwestern third is the Mato Grosso Massif cut by many smaller rivers. The Pantanal extends up into its southwestern sector as the Paraguay River's headwaters are found not far from the capital, Cuiabá, which along with its suburbs contains 740,000 inhabitants. Located on the river of the same name that flows south, the capital lies just below the headwaters of the rivers that help form the Tapajós—one of the Amazon's most important tributaries—as well as near the beginning of the Xingu and the Rio das Mortes, which later joins the Araguaia. Yet it is the cities of the northeastern part—above the Chapada dos Guimarães that divides the Amazon and Paraguay river basins—that are expanding at a dizzying rate.

Up in Alta Floresta, the salient in the state's extreme north between Amazonas and Pará, there are rich deposits of alluvial gold. The most significant Indian presence is in the northeastern corner where the Xingu national park is home to the majority of 1,800 Kayapó Indians and perhaps an equal number of others in small tribal groups spreading up into Pará. Some 1,600 Xavántes are found farther east near Bananal. In this part of Brazil hunting is still quite good, as is fishing in rivers not yet polluted by the mercury prospectors use or by the sewage and industrial waste of cities that is a scourge of more urbanized and developed regions.

Landholdings in Mato Grosso tend to be large with extensive ranching and farming, but a few efficiently operated agroindustrial operations have attained productivity far above the national average—especially for rice, corn, and soy (in which it holds third place). The state's grain production surpasses 7 million tons yearly and is rapidly rising. With half the state still covered with forests and only 10 percent of the land productively utilized, this area is the most capable of absorbing the country's future demographic pressures. In many ways it is today what Goiás was a short time ago.

The Wild West

Conventionally considered part of the north, Rondônia is in reality more a portion of the western frontier region. As large as the United Kingdom, its population is nearing 1.5 million, compared to a 1970 figure of only 117,000. Porto Velho, in the extreme west on the Congo-like Madeira River as it heads toward its rendezvous with the Amazon, has grown from 85,000 in 1970 to 365,000. Ariquemes has burgeoned from a sleepy village to a city of 115,000 inhabitants—

largely due to cassiterite mining. Although the state is rich in minerals, including substantial quantities of this raw material of tin, it lacks electrical energy for industrialization. Better transportation links to the southeast are badly needed, but even now Rondônia underscores that development of the interior of the South American continent is no longer an unrealizable dream.[6]

Unfortunately, Rondônia's proximity to Bolivia, Peru, and Colombia has made it a major area of drug commerce with all the problems that social cancer brings. Senator Olavo Pires, top finisher in the 1990 governorship balloting, was murdered, which led to the third-place contender being elected in a runoff, and several of its congressmen, apparently with close ties to foreign cocaine cartels, have been censured and expelled for corruption. Although it is the center of Brazil's belt of rapid deforestation, chiefly for pasture, land use has improved in the 1990s. Hundreds of Cinta Larga Indians extending into the state from Mato Grosso enjoy a reputation as the most warlike in the country, and the state is home to perhaps 2,000 other Indians.

The North

Above the western frontier lies the immense north with two-fifths of Brazil's area but less than 6 percent of its population and producing 3.0 percent of GDP. Dominated by the Amazon River, it contains a few important urban centers, but these are widely spaced. This sprawling region extends in the north to the Guiana Highlands and in the west beyond Bolivia far enough to make a deep dent into Peru. Imperial more than just majestic, the Amazon spans the entire width of Brazil and runs up the Peruvian and Ecuadorean slopes to a height of 18,000 feet. With a length of 4,200 miles—slightly longer than the Nile—and more than 200 major tributaries, the Amazon drains an area double that of the Mississippi-Missouri's 1.4 million square miles and two and a half times that of the Nile. The navigable parts of the Amazon and its feeders total 31,000 miles, more than half again that of their North American rival. Its estuary sprawls to a width of 200 miles, and for much of the Amazon's course it is bounded by a fifty-mile-wide flood plain. Its maximum flow of 100,000 cubic meters per second sends freshwater 100 miles out into the Atlantic. Indeed, its volume is eight times that of the Congo and fourteen times that of the Mississippi, and it provides a fifth of the freshwater flow into the world's oceans. Between February and June it may crest as much as thirty to fifty feet over its low season.

Three-fifths of the nearly 3-million-square-mile Amazon basin is in Brazil, where it covers 57 percent of the country's territory (1.85 million square miles). Fed from Peru and Colombia, the great river is known as the Solimões until where it merges with the Rio Negro just below Manaus and becomes the region's major route for transportation of people and products. Extending 800 miles north to south in its western part, the basin narrows as it approaches the Guiana Highlands, then widens as it nears the ocean. Tropical rain forests abound, but the

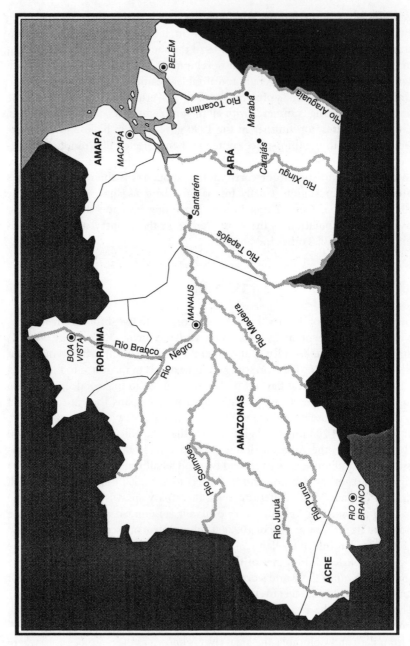

North

The Amazon River (photo courtesy of the Brazilian Foreign Ministry)

lower reaches of the vast basin have flat grasslands spotted with scrub forest, much of which is usable for grazing and some for commercial agriculture. In it are found some 80 percent of the country's 350,000 professional prospectors as well as two-thirds of Brazil's 246,000 surviving Indians. Although much international concern surrounds the preservation of the Amazon's rain forests, Brazil currently destroys 0.3 percent of its forests yearly—a rate far below that for deforestation in Peru (chiefly for the cultivation of coca leaf) or Ecuador and only a fraction of that prevailing in Brazil during the 1980s. Yet because this region contains two-fifths of the world's remaining tropical humid forests, close attention will continue to be paid to the policies for a rational balance of development and conservation pledged by the national government inaugurated January 1, 1995. Fernando Henrique Cardoso is a world-famous sociologist who has written about the region, whose roots are in Brazil's developed heartland, and who has served as foreign minister. Hence it is unlikely that there will be abandonment of the more responsible environmental and conservation policies of recent years—much less return to the shortsighted and predatory policies followed in the 1970s and 1980s.

Acre, to the west of Rondônia, is a relatively stagnant area the size of Denmark and Switzerland together but with a population of only 470,000. Tucked in a corner between the most remote and undeveloped parts of Peru and Bolivia, it has never recovered from the end of the short-lived rubber boom occasioned by World War I.[7] Rio Branco in the extreme southeast is a provincial center (235,000 inhabitants) that relies on the bloated governmental payroll to keep limping along. Without roads or railroads, its transportation is limited to rivers and airplanes, much as in the desolate stretches of Bolivia and Peru nearby. The

Deforestation in the Amazon (photo by Andre Penner, courtesy of Abril Imagens*)*

Reforestation (photo by Marcelo Carnaval, courtesy of Abril Imagens*)*

brutal murder here of rubber gatherers leader Chico Mendes in December 1988 focused attention upon the struggle over land reminiscent of the U.S. Southwest more than a century earlier. In May 1992 Governor Edmundo Pinto—elected over candidates backed by large landowners and the radical Left—was murdered; suspicion was divided between drug traffickers and corrupt contractors. Half the state's forests are protected as Indian reservations, mineral reserves, and state and national park, yet experience in both the United States and Brazil demonstrates that profit-oriented elements will continue to seek a way to get around such obstacles.

The Heart of the Amazon

Although much of the vast expanse of Amazonas has poverty-line subsistence as its salient characteristic, this changes when one reaches its northeast corner and the metropolis of Manaus—over a thousand miles from the Atlantic yet only twenty feet above sea level. The state has an area nearly that of Iran, but its population is only 2.3 million, half of whom live in greater Manaus, where the $7 billion industry of the Free Zone makes the city responsible for the vast preponderance of the state's economy. Just downstream from the metropolis the light blue-green water of the Solimões blends with the dark blackish-green Rio Negro to give the Amazon its pale muddy-brown hue.[8]

Large natural gas reserves have been found at Juruá in the west, and oil wells are beginning to produce farther south. Although considerable tin exists in the state's northeastern corner, and there is perhaps a majority of the world's niobium in the northwestern area, Amazonas's development will depend heavily upon other parts of the country becoming so settled that its less hospitable spaces become the demographic escape valve—a condition still far in the future. Yet the potential for settlement and colonization is there, particularly as thought is given to connecting the river systems to provide inland water transportation from the Venezuelan coast to the La Plata estuary. A short distance from the rivers feeding into the Paraná and hence on to the South Atlantic run other rivers heading north toward the Amazon and merging along the way to form larger rivers. In the east in Pará state is the Tocantins, accompanied farther inland by the Araguaia until they join together near Carajás. More toward the center of the continent is the Xingu, paralleled by the group of rivers that eventually form the Tapajós. Farther to the west rivers beginning in Bolivia and Peru run up into Amazonas's Madeira, Purus, and Juruá Rivers.[9] Yet the headwaters of the southward-flowing Paraguay River lie above the fifteenth parallel with its tributaries running like interlocked fingers between streams heading north to the Tapajós and Xingu. Moreover, northern tributaries of the Amazon come very close to connecting with rivers leading to Venezuela's Orinoco and hence to the North Atlantic.

Settlement of the vast expanses of Amazonas state would impact heavily upon its widely dispersed native population. In the north along the Rio Negro (which in volume and flow exceeds the Congo, considered number two in the world in this respect), there are some 3,500 Baníwa and Tariána Indians. Two to three times that number of Tukúno live farther west near the Colombian and Peruvian border; fishing is a crucial facet of their existence. The southern part of the state is home to a score of tribes totaling perhaps 3,000 individuals around the Purus and Juruá Rivers. In the east between the Madeira and Tapajós there are some 2,000 Mawé, 1,500 Mundaukú, and 1,000 Kayabí as well as upward of 2,000 in a congeries of smaller tribal groupings.

The military functions as the chief developer of enclave settlements along the extensive border with Peru, Colombia, and Venezuela—mainly because of activity by the international drug trade in these remote areas but also because of lingering suspicion that industrial powers have designs to use this underpopulated area as a dumping ground for the rapidly growing excess population of the Asian world.[10] The boundary area is mountainous; Pico de Neblina reaches 9,850 feet and Mt. Roraima rises to over 9,400 feet. The base for the army's activity is Boa Vista in the new state of Roraima, a city of 195,000 (in a state of only 260,000 inhabitants) tucked between the most neglected parts of Venezuela and Guyana (and bigger than Guyana) in an area containing unmapped mineral wealth including gold, diamonds, silver, copper, cassiterite, zinc, and bauxite. This has led to a population increase of 150 percent since 1985 as prospectors have overrun Indian lands and spilled across into Venezuela. With more than half the state set aside for Indian or ecological reserves, the region has replaced southern Pará as the chief focus of conflict among groups giving zealous priority to resource development, environmental concerns, and security considerations. Because population density of the 9,900 seminomadic Yanomanis is only 0.1 per square kilometer of their Portugal-sized reserves, and the land of the 4,000 or so Macuxi is rich in cassiterite, local politicians and officials continue to favor encroachment and resource exploitation. Since prospectors are the largest segment of their electorates, this is a natural albeit far from salutary basic fact of political life—one highly analogous to the situation in many parts of the United States during settlement and consolidation of frontier areas.

From Rags to Riches?

Pará, the size of Peru with a population above 5.8 million, contrasts with its western neighbors. Located much closer to the coast and reached from the south by the Belém-Brasília highway, its mineral riches are being developed on a massive scale. This is particularly true of Carajás in the southeastern corner, which holds the world's greatest iron ore deposits (18 billion tons, much of it with a 66 percent iron content), 62 million tons of manganese, 47 million tons of nickel, and 40 million tons of bauxite as well as the gold of nearby Serra Pelada. Over 35 million tons of iron ore and other minerals are being moved out annually by railroad through the neighboring state of Maranhão, and 3 million tons a year of bauxite from Trombetas (in the northwest of the state where over 2.5 billion tons of this mineral are known to exist) feed the alumina and aluminum factories of Alunorte/Albras near the capital. These draw power from the Tucuruí hydroelectric facility (on the Tocantins above its juncture with the Araguaia), already fifth in the world at 4 million kilowatts and scheduled for substantial expansion. With copper, silver, tin, molybdenum, and zinc also abundant in the Carajás region, growth of Belém, Pará's capital, will continue beyond the present 1.45 million. There is some development around Santarém, a city of 350,000 about 800 miles upriver from the capital at the juncture with the wide, blue, and clear Tapajós River. Marabá, where the Carajás railroad crosses the Tocantins River, has burgeoned to 170,000 as multitudes tarry there coming from or going to Carajás.

In contrast to this ongoing development in the northeastern portion of Pará, the other four-fifths is in much the same sad condition as most of Amazonas, and land conflicts are prevalent in the south. Bico de Papagaio (Parrot's Beak), which includes the upper tip of Tocantins as well as the southeast of Maranhão, is a mecca of hired guns—as was Texas in the 1870s. Over a thousand killings since 1982 have yielded only seventeen convictions because it is thought that powerful ranching interests are responsible for the killing of small farmers or union activists. Chiefs of the more than 2,000 Kayapó Indians have amassed fortunes as great as $8 million for gold, mahogany, and cosmetic oils from their extensive reserves—including 7.7 million acres at Gorotire on the southern part of the Xingu River. Along with the new Mekragnote reservation between them and Xingu National Park near the river's headwaters in Mato Grosso, this provides a significant Indian corridor through the middle of the state. In Pará's northwestern corner on the Trombetas there are 1,200 Paankotō-Tiriyós; stretching westward into Amazonas are 1,500 Parukotó-Charúmas and myriad smaller tribal groups. In the east of the state can be found 1,000 Taulipáng with related tribal settlements stringing across into neighboring Maranhão.

It is clear that much of Pará will experience dramatic transformation in the coming decades, but the northern part will have to wait upon increased world demand for its hardwoods—already a major export—and for future development of the mineral resources up near the Guyana border; these are neither needed nor economical to develop as long as Carajás is still expanding. Meanwhile, Brazilian entrepreneurs have proved the viability of the multibillion-dollar Jari pulpwood-cellulose-mining-agricultural project started in the 1960s by Daniel Ludwig along the shore of the Amazon on the border with Amapá.[11]

Wedged in between the Jari River and French Guiana is the state of Amapá; the capital, Macapá (on the north bank of the Amazon estuary), has 210,000 inhabitants (60 percent of the state's total population). Although large-scale manganese mining is the most important economic activity—the ore at Serra do Navio is 42–50 percent pure—grazing and fishing provide much more employment. Copper deposits just over the border in Pará reinforce belief that other minerals exist in promising quantities. Its estimated 1,500 Indians are concentrated near the border with French Guiana. As is true for tribes near Colombia, Peru, and Venezuela, international frontiers have little or no meaning to these native peoples, who are accustomed to moving freely across the poorly demarcated borders.

The Northeast

Covering 18 percent of the country's area with its 45 million inhabitants (nearly 29 percent of the nation's population), this nine-state region was once the heart of colonial Brazil but has long been sunk in depression brought on by outdated agriculture combined with periodic droughts.[12] Indeed, it contributes under 13 percent of Brazil's GDP and has but 6 percent of the country's industry to go along with 20 percent of its agriculture. Although since 1970 its economy has grown 1.2 percent a year more than the rest of the country, this is not enough to keep it from lagging behind in absolute terms. Over a longer span there has been some progress: In 1955 its per capita consumption of electricity was only 7 percent of the national average but is now pushing 60 percent. As recently as 1960 the region's per capita GDP was only 43 percent of the national average but has risen to 60 percent. Although 2.2 million of its inhabitants migrated southward in the 1960s, the number fell to 1.5 million during the 1970s and appears to have declined further during the 1980s. In very recent years it has begun to benefit from the world's longest continuous belt of beaches that stretch some 2,000 miles. In 1993 it received nearly a half million foreign tourists during the November to February summer season.

Three-fifths of the region is semiarid *sertão* receiving only twenty-five inches of rain in a normal year and covered by a thorn-forest vegetation *caatinga* composed largely of giant cacti, mimosas, and scrub brush with some wax-producing *carnaúba* palms in oasis areas. Most of the population centers are found in the narrow coastal belt called the "Zona da Matta" for the stretch south from the bulge and the "area of *carnaúba*" and the salt and *babaçu* region (*babaçu* is a nut used as an important source of vegetable oil) for the long stretches running northwestward to the edge of the equatorial forests in Maranhão. At its northern end this region is only about fifteen miles wide; it broadens to fifty miles in Alagoas and narrows again below the mouth of the São Francisco River. Between this relatively humid coastal belt and the dry *sertão* (similar in a general way to the Australian outback) is a transitional region called the *agreste* where annual rainfall is fairly reliable and runs around thirty-five inches, enough for crops such as cotton but not for the sugarcane that is so salient nearer the coast.

The immense *sertão*, a parched wilderness of scrub growth ribbed with rocky ridges and bare stone mountains, is an eroded area of crystalline plateaus at altitudes of 1,300 to 1,900 feet above sea level with a seven- to nine-month normal

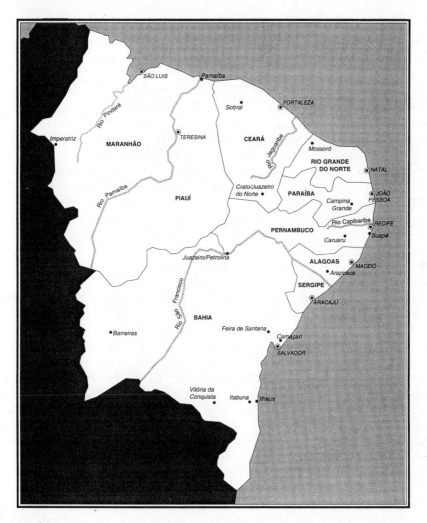

Northeast

dry season and frequent droughts. It includes the southern half of Ceará, the southeastern half of Piauí, the interior half of Rio Grande do Norte, the western two-thirds of Paraíba, a larger proportion of Pernambuco, the western quarters of Alagoas and Sergipe, and the interior two-thirds of Bahia. Fortunately there are some humid pockets where agriculture is possible, as parts of the *sertão* are cut through by river systems allowing farming along the valleys (between droughts) as well as grazing near any of the feeder streams that still have water at the height of the dry season.

North or Northeast?

The northernmost state of this underdeveloped and relatively overpopulated region is Maranhão, the size of Norway and with a population of 5.3 million. Its capital, São Luis, founded at the beginning of the 1600s, is a city of 970,000 inhabitants located on an island in the large bay of São Marcos where several rivers come together, the most important of which is the Pindaré. Still bearing strong architectural signs of having once been the center of French influence in South America, São Luis with its heavy metallurgical industry is beginning to transform the coastal region. A 500-mile railroad constructed from those mountains of metallic ores to the newly inaugurated deepwater port facilities capable of handling ships of 300,000 tons displacement is turning São Luis into an industrial city. In addition to the Alumar project of Alcoa and Shell, there will soon be a steel mill with 3 million tons capacity to catalyze industrial development.

Even this nucleus of heavy industry may not be enough to enable the state as a whole to break out of the stultifying stagnation that in the past has characterized it even more than many of its neighbors. These belated massive infrastructural investments still leave the vast majority of Maranhenses—perhaps as many as 80 percent of them—living near or in poverty, and 450,000 families subsist as itinerant harvest laborers. Sale of huge land areas to Rio de Janeiro and São Paulo companies, which in most cases have not yet implanted the promised agrobusiness operations, has led to the absurdity of a state that was long the country's second-ranking producer of rice having dropped to but 800,000 tons a year. Livestock herds have greatly decreased for the same reason. The one finished stretch of the north-south railroad has enabled Imperatriz (population 385,000) in the extreme west of the state near the junction of the Tocantins and Araguaia Rivers to become a second-line development pole, albeit it is marred by violence. The state's Indian population has at its core perhaps 3,000 living in thirty-five villages in the western region near Pará.

Maranhão is geographically atypical of the northeast, since its western part is made up of equatorial forests and the rest composed of the *babaçu* area that has precipitation adequate for livestock and agriculture and that extends into Piauí, although it gets less rainfall. This elongated state, the size of the United Kingdom but with a population of only 2.7 million, suffers from having a very short coastline and from having half its territory to the south fall within the drought areas of the *sertão*; hence it fails to produce enough foodstuffs for its population. Teresinha, with 840,000 inhabitants, is located well inland on the Parnaíba River, which marks the state's western boundary, and is its most productive agricultural region. The port of Parnaíba (135,000 residents), lying on the beautiful 2,700-square-kilometer delta where the river ends its meandering journey of some 900 miles, is the only other major city.

A Future Australia?

With a population exceeding 6.7 million and an area equal to that of Nicaragua, Ceará has its northern part in the semiarid area of *carnaúba* and salt. This coastal region, characterized by dunes, is best suitable for cultivation of cashew nuts (these provide 45 percent of the state's exports) cotton (in which the state ranks third nationally), and bananas and coconuts (in which it is the leader). Toward the eastern part is Fortaleza, a port city of 2.61 million that has undergone recent industrialization, much of it linked to textiles; this development has created a belt of hundreds of small factories as well as vast sprawling lower-class suburbs on the flatlands extending inward from the sea. Yet even in Fortaleza and again around Sobral (population 135,000), fulcrum of the northwestern region, handicraft industries still predominate—albeit some textiles are factory produced. Extensive grazing and subsistence agriculture mark the interior, and the state is second to Bahia among northeast livestock producers. This can be seen clearly in the southern region around the twin cities of Crato and Juazeiro do Norte (population 325,000).

Through a rational approach to development provided by a new generation of modernizing business and political leadership that wrested control of the state from the traditional machines in 1982, Ceará has moved forward dramatically, attracting considerable international attention and significant investment. Over the past ten years its economy grew 50 percent compared to but 20 percent for the rest of the country, and infant mortality was cut in half to below that for Uruguay. In the last few years Fortaleza's sewer system was expanded to cover 80 percent of the city, up from a mere 15 percent. Ceará's only mineral resource is uranium, and although it has nearly half the country's reserves, this provides precious little employment. As in the case of other northeastern states, irrigation is a pressing need; the Jaguaribe River, arising in the southeastern corner and paralleling the state's border, is the chief available source of water for this purpose.

Most of Ceará sits on the Borborema Plateau, an old complex of crystalline rocks extending down from Ceará and Piauí as a dominant feature of the topography of the states of the Brazilian bulge. Lying at an altitude generally between 1,600 and 3,300 feet, it slopes up from the coast quite gradually in Ceará. It is separated from Piauí by the Serra Grande, also known as the Serra dos Cariris Novos, an eastward-facing escarpment behind which lies the sandstone-covered plateau that constitutes the biggest part of the *sertão*. Running out in an eastward direction from this mini-cordillera and dividing the extreme southwest of Ceará from the interior tail of Pernambuco is the Chapada de Araipe, a high tableland. Some 100 miles long and forty miles wide, it juts into the Borborema Plateau.

The Brazilian Bulge

Rio Grande do Norte, with a population over 2.6 million, was once noted as a producer of cotton and still ranks fourth in this respect. Like neighboring Paraíba, it has come to depend more heavily upon sugarcane. A bit larger than Jordan, Rio Grande do Norte produces some 2.8 million tons of salt yearly, roughly 70 percent of the country's total. This industry is beginning to produce a surplus for sale abroad, and the state has a modest production of petroleum, much in the form of natural gas. Natal (a city of 870,000 surrounded by giant sand dunes) sits at the juncture of the *carnaúba* zone to the west and the Zona da Matta to its south; the state's northern coast is geographically an extension of Ceará, and its eastern coast below Cabo São Roque begins the type of humid coastal belt that runs south along the ocean. In the northeastern corner of the state, Mossoró, on the river of the same name, is Rio Grande do Norte's second city, boasting a population of 220,000 and noted for oils and melons. Inland from the small tip of the *agreste* behind Natal more than half the state is essentially *sertão*.

Paraíba, a bit bigger than Costa Rica with nearly 3.4 million inhabitants, enjoys a very small sliver of the Zona da Matta, one that contains the capital of João Pessoa (population 790,000 and endowed with fine beaches) as well as a larger region of *agreste* and a *sertão* located as a salient between Ceará and Pernambuco. On the border between these two inland zones, where the Borborema Plateau rises with a suddenly looming escarpment, is the city of Campina Grande (360,000), center of the country's sisal production. Elsewhere in Paráiba's interior the crying need can be summed up in a single word—irrigation.

Pernambuco, larger than Portugal, is the region's second most populous state at 7.5 million. Once the country's key province, it has struggled for generations against the mounting irrelevancy of its outdated agriculture. Overconcentration on the cultivation of sugarcane, in which it is now a distant second to São Paulo, has forced Pernambuco to import most of its foodstuffs—although the coastal area is blessed with rainfall of sixty inches per year. The creation of a host of sub-sidized industries around the swollen urban center of Recife (population almost 3.1 million within its eleven satellite municipalities, including historic Olinda and industrial Jabotão) has only led to an increased flow of migrants from the interior. Called the Venice of Brazil because of the rivers that cut it into islands, Recife has become a focus for misery with its slums built on stilts above the marshy areas bordering the rivers; the slums house 900,000 persons. Hordes of abandoned children and legions of prostitutes coexist with the Boa Viagem district with its mansions, luxury apartments, and five-star tourist hotels lining the glistening white sand beaches protected by the reef from which the city gets its name.

West of the capital along the Capibaribe River in the *agreste*, where the land gradually rises, is the city of Caruaru (population 230,000) around which corn and beans are the leading crops. Farther inland the chief means of transportation, the São Francisco River, comes up from Bahia and goes on to Alagoas and Sergipe. Marijuana has emerged as the most profitable crop in areas of the *sertão* where lack of water and distance to markets are handicaps to such cash crops as onions, corn, beans, and tomatoes. Here in isolated pockets are found perhaps 7,000 Pankararú, Fulnio, Xukurú, and Uamué Indians. Traces of remote Indian ancestry can be discerned in the facial features of a fairly significant proportion of the rural working class. Pernambuco will remain for some time an agricultural state, and the future of its *sertão*, like that of the other northeastern states, lies largely in irrigation. The fishing port of Suapé remains unfinished, but this industry has potential for aiding the millions who live near the verge of starvation.

With a population of 2.7 million in an area equal to Haiti, Alagoas has only its western tip in the *sertão*. Maceió is a burgeoning city of 780,000 with spectacular ocean beaches featuring coral-reefed pools just offshore on two sides and a lagoon on a third. It also has the beginnings of a chemical industry. Income levels are low, illiteracy runs near 65 percent, and infant mortality remains at a high 125 per 1,000. Alagoas trails only São Paulo and Pernambuco as a sugar producer and is also third in the nation in cultivation of tobacco, much of it near the state's second city, Arapiraca (population 180,000).

Squeezed between Alagoas and giant Bahia, Sergipe has 1.6 million inhabitants in an area bigger than Israel. As the country's third-ranked petroleum producer, it seems the main hope for the petrochemical industry. Over a billion dollars has been invested in a "chlorochemical pole." Like Alagoas, Sergipe has only its tail in the *sertão*, and they share the mouth of the São Francisco River with its promise of abundant power from the massive Xingô dam—when its 5 million kilowatts come on line. Aracajú, a city of 620,000, contains a high proportion of the state's population.

The Old Dominion

The dominant state of the northeast is its most southern one, Bahia. Larger than France and with a population of 12.8 million, Bahia is the heartland of Afro-Brazilian culture. Its capital, Salvador (population 2.78 million including suburbs), still reflects the era when it was colonial Brazil's capital and ranks only behind Rio de Janeiro as a tourist attraction. Its scores of colonial-era churches, the irresistible beaches of one of the world's most beautiful bays, and the excitement of its folkloric dances with their sensuality and hints of Afro-Brazilian religious mysteries attract even greater numbers of Europeans than North Americans. Some 2 million tourists a year bring in roughly $475 billion. The old lower city of wharves and markets is connected to the upper city some 250 feet above by an elevator tower, and the restored old part of the latter, Pelourinho, has become part of the background for a number of North American and European films.

A short ride from Salvador leads to the Southern Hemisphere's premier concentration of petrochemical industry at Camaçari. To the north and slightly inland is the Recôncavo, a low-lying bowl-shaped area in which are located the country's major on-land oilfields as well as the state's second city, Feira de Santana (population 455,000), the focus for a region of mixed farming and animal husbandry. Copper is also produced in this part of the state, but oil is the chief factor—at least indirectly through the petrochemical industry—and Bahia contributes 4 percent to Brazil's exports.

In contrast to the relative development of this part of Bahia is the poverty of the interior, chiefly made up of *sertão*, which limits the state's contribution to the country's GDP to only 4.5 percent. Industry contributes 30 percent of Bahia's economy but only 5 percent of its employment; agriculture produces 50 percent of jobs but only 15 percent of GDP. In southeastern Bahia cocoa is king, with 90 percent of Brazil's production of this until recently billion-dollar crop centered in the deep red soils around the twin cities of Ilhéus and Itabuna (populations 265,000 and 200,000 respectively). Inland from this area made famous by the writings of Brazil's leading novelist, Jorge Amado, semiintensive livestock raising prevails in the narrow band of the *agreste*. Vitória da Conquista (245,000 residents) is the major city in the southern border area near Minas Gerais. Ahead even of Ceará in livestock, with 12 million cattle and 10 million hens, Bahia needs to replace extensive grazing with more modern techniques and to develop intensive agriculture in the interior to raise income levels to the national average. In this respect the hope for the millions of subsistence farmers lies in irrigation from the São Francisco River and its tributaries. Encouraging beginnings have been made around Barreiras in the northwest, a remote area with deep soils and some usable supplies of subsoil water.

At the top of the state the 210-mile-long lake created by the Sobradinho dam provides hope, and other irrigation projects exist farther east around Paulo Affonso where the São Francisco drops sharply over the escarpment in a series of falls and a great gorge. Juazeiro (population 140,000) across the river from Petrolina, Pernambuco (210,000), is the hub of a region producing fruits and vegetables in abundance. The Itaparica dam has created a 100-mile-long lake, but the sparsely populated southwestern corner of the state, distant from these hydroelectric complexes and all but forgotten by the government in distant Salvador, has a much lower priority for the heavy investments required for irrigation.

The São Francisco River is vital to a country within Brazil. Draining a basin of nearly 250,000 square miles, it encompasses over 10 million people, few of whom could survive without the irrigation, power, transportation, and fish it provides. Beginning at 47 degrees west longitude and 20 degrees south latitude, it ascends to the proximity of 8 degrees south before entering the Atlantic at 36 degrees west. This is the equivalent to the distances between Bismarck, North Dakota, well up on the Missouri River, to Memphis, Tennessee, on the lower reaches of the Mississippi. A new link at the extreme west of Pernambuco to waterways in the interior of northeastern states will benefit some 9 million persons through large-scale irrigation projects.

To Bear in Mind

The images of these several Brazils—varying from the First World heartland centered on the São Paulo–Rio de Janeiro–Belo Horizonte triangle through the developing south and the dynamic western frontier on to the vast north and finally the Third World backwardness of much of the northeast—must be borne in mind when looking at the national picture. Only in this way will totals and averages for the country not mask either the more developed and modern Brazil that is emerging or the multiple laggard sectors retarding this progress.

2

FROM DISCOVERY THROUGH OLIGARCHICAL REPUBLIC: BRAZIL TO 1930

B RAZIL'S DEVELOPMENT AS a nation has been essentially evolutionary with few sharp breaks or drastic discontinuities.[1] The chain of events begins in 1500 when maritime-oriented Portugal, then a leading European nation engaged in a spirited rivalry with Spain in transoceanic discovery and colonization, dispatched Pedro Álvares Cabral to reach Asia by sailing west. Along the way his flotilla landed on the Brazilian coast, to which Portugal had established an a priori claim through the Treaty of Tordesillas with Spain in 1494. Trading posts were quickly set up, and permanent colonization came in 1531. Short on population and capital, the Portuguese crown made large land grants to aristocratic entrepreneurs responsible for implanting settlements and organizing trade.[2] As the burden of defense against French and Indian attacks added to the large investments required, most of the original donees failed to make a go of this enterprise. Thus, in 1549 the crown bought back Bahia at the midpoint of Brazil's long seacoast and sent Tomé de Souza there as governor general.

From Colony to Kingdom

With the governor general also came reinforcement of the Catholic Church's position as well as the first rudimentary elements of a military establishment—institutions that would be the first to take on national scope and that, in the face of sharply defined regionalism, would play key political roles in Brazil's life down to the present. In the absence of a significant permanent army, large landowners were obliged to maintain private military forces from among their retainers and dependents. These evolved into organized militia units under the control of the most powerful regional figures, who not only were responsible for maintaining law and order in the hinterlands but, given the lack of regular officials in these rural areas, often performed additional governmental tasks. So began the phenomenon of *coronelismo,* a system of rural political bosses and their machine politics that still persists in remote interior areas.[3]

Brazil Begins to Take Shape

Consolidation of Portuguese presence progressed slowly in the second half of the seventeenth century. Native females served the Portuguese as sexual partners, and these relationships gave rise to a sizable number of *mamelucos* or *caboclos,* mixed-blood offspring with European fathers and indigenous mothers. Because Indians could easily escape into the vast interior, landowners needed a new source of labor not easily able to survive without the protection and security of the *engenhos* and *fazendas* (plantations and large ranches). This led to importation of African slaves, already common in Portugal, totaling 250,000 by 1650 and exceeding 600,000 by the end of the century. Thus, the three major components of future Brazilian society were present and mixing through widespread miscegenation early in the colonial period.[4] Unfortunately, Brazil's indigenous population would be reduced (largely through disease but also by interbreeding, assimilation, and in some cases violence) by 1 million a century until there were only 250,000 natives by the 1970s. As they retreated into the vast interior to survive and preserve their ways of life, these predominantly hunting and fishing tribes left very little mark upon Brazil's national culture—a stark contrast with the heritage of the Aztecs in Mexico or of the Incas in Peru.

By the seventeenth century sugar was firmly established as Brazil's chief export, one so profitable that it attracted heavy attention from Portugal's European rivals. England, France, and the Netherlands each sought to seize control of inviting portions of the Portuguese domains. In 1630 the Dutch successfully seized all of Pernambuco; the Portuguese counteroffensive culminated in January 1654 when the beleaguered Dutch surrendered Recife.

Meanwhile the Portuguese had begun to move inland beyond the intimidating escarpment. Based increasingly in the city of São Paulo, which was founded by the Jesuits in 1554 on the plateau inland from São Vicente, expeditions called *bandeiras* brought back large numbers of native slaves from as far away as Paraguay. Subsequently the *bandeirantes* turned their attention to the quest for mineral riches and were rewarded in the 1690s by major discoveries of gold in the region north of São Paulo, an area soon labeled "General Mines" (Minas Gerais). This resulted in Minas becoming a province in 1720. In 1694 the Pernambuco planters, aided by armed detachments from the south, finally destroyed the large community of escaped slaves (Quilombo) that for several decades had flourished at Palmares.[5] This brutal repression was rooted in the conviction that its continued survival would encourage insubordination among the rapidly growing and increasingly valuable slave population.

The eighteenth century was crucial for defining Brazil's borders with surrounding Spanish domains—generally by force, on occasion smoothed by diplomacy. More important, from the middle of the seventeenth century on, Brazil faced relentless competition from the British, French, and Dutch—all of whom came to produce sugar efficiently on their Caribbean possessions. With sugar revenues cut drastically, Brazil's salvation lay in its becoming the world's leading source of gold and, after 1729, diamonds as well. But as gold production dropped off sharply in the 1760s and sugar remained in the doldrums, the Brazilian economy stagnated.

During the third quarter of the eighteenth century, Portugal was run in the name of a weak king by Sebastião José de Carvalho e Mello, the marquês de Pombal. In addition to expelling the Jesuits from Brazil in 1759, this towering figure partially centralized Portugal's South American colonies and placed the overall capital in Rio de Janeiro. The Brazil of this period had changed substantially since the beginning of the century.[6] Not only had many thousands of colonists abandoned their agricultural pursuits and rushed to Minas Gerais in quest of wealth for themselves or their masters, but this El Dorado also served as a magnet for immigration from Portugal as well as other European countries. Although mulattoes had become a significant social element on the coast, it was in Minas Gerais during the first half of the 1700s that African-European miscegenation turned them into an element more numerous than the Indian-European mamelucos.

The Road to Independence

The latter part of the eighteenth century brought events that would have a powerful effect upon the course of Brazilian affairs. First came the establishment of an independent and republican United States and then the French Revolution following on its heels. Some Brazilians already resentful of restraints on trade other than with Portugal were further alienated by a 1785 decree prohibiting manufacturing in Brazil. Subversive talk was rife in urban centers, and in 1789 an unsuccessful conspiracy known as the Inconfidência Mineira and still celebrated as the harbinger of independence was broken up.[7] Its leader, Joaquim José da Silva Xavier, known as "Tiradentes" (Toothpuller), was executed as a warning to other discontented elements.

The Minas conspiracy was followed by chain-reaction counterparts in Rio de Janeiro (1794), Bahia (1798), and Pernambuco (1801). Although these were quickly repressed, they reflected a dangerous degree of alienation that would be augmented in the years just ahead by the Spanish American wars of independence. First, however, Napoleon's invasion of Portugal would give rise to important changes. In November 1807 the royal family, accompanied by the civil and military bureaucracies, set sail under British naval escort for Rio de Janeiro. During a brief stopover at Salvador, the prince regent (the future King João VI) opened Brazil's ports to trade with Britain and other countries—as much a price for British support as a sop to the colonists. Manufacturing was permitted, institutions of higher education were founded, and naval and military academies were established. Most important in the long run, a new army composed of a mixture of Portuguese troops and local recruits was created. To co-opt local elites, in 1815 Brazil was accorded status of a kingdom formally coequal with Portugal.

By the end of the Napoleonic Wars, the colony was fast outgrowing its mother country. The Portuguese Liberals convoked a legislature in which they enjoyed a safe majority. Not surprisingly, measures to reestablish most of Portugal's previous domination catalyzed separatist sentiment in Brazil.[8] Thus when the king was required to return home in April 1821, he advised his twenty-two-year-old son Pedro, who was staying behind as prince regent, to head the independence movement should it appear to be getting out of control. Indeed, Pedro soon had cause to heed his father's advice. In the midst of clashes between Brazilian-born elements and Portuguese troops, he rejected an order of the Portuguese Côrtes to return to Lisbon. This *fico* (I'm staying) of January 9, 1822, was followed by appointment of a cabinet headed by native Brazilian José Bonifácio de Andrada e Silva. Efforts by Lisbon to tighten its hold over Brazil resulted in Pedro's dramatic cry of "Independence or death!" on September 7, 1822—commemorated as Brazil's Independence Day. Within ninety days of this challenge, he was crowned (on his twenty-fourth birthday) "constitutional emperor and perpetual defender of Brazil."[9]

Consolidation and Nation Building

Commencing national life under the rule of the individual who had been governing in the name of the mother country enabled Brazil to avoid the vacuum of legitimate authority that plagued most of its neighbors, whose path to independence combined rupture with Spain and adoption of a radically different and untried political regime—a republic. Moreover, compared to the protracted wars and large-scale civil strife through which Spanish American countries had won their independence, Brazil's emancipation was quick, albeit not peaceful. There were repeated skirmishes and prolonged confrontations with provincial authorities and Portuguese troops loyal to João VI and the Lisbon government.

The First Emperor and Regency

While these conflicts were still continuing in the north, efforts to establish a viable governmental structure were under way in the capital. Brazil's first constituent assembly began to function on May 3, 1823, but after six months of executive-legislative conflict, Pedro used the army to close it down. A constitution drawn up by a hand-picked commission of experts was promulgated by imperial decree on March 25, 1824. The emperor could both convene and dissolve the

General Assembly as well as appoint the presidents of the provinces. Members of the Senate were chosen by him from lists submitted by the provinces and served for life, and the lower house was indirectly elected by a severely limited suffrage.

Reaction to the closing of the assembly and the establishment of a centralized regime was widespread and violent. Yet of lasting importance was that ultimately Brazil's territorial integrity was preserved. Liberal rebels in the north sought in 1824 to form a Confederation of the Equator. Troops under General Francisco de Lima e Silva reestablished order with a heavy hand. Tensions between native-born Brazilians and Portuguese combined with regionalist uprisings were problems enough for the new nation, but the emperor also engaged in an expensive and unsuccessful adventure that led to war with the United Provinces of the Rio de La Plata (modern Argentina) over what would become Uruguay.

By the end of the decade, the stiff-necked, impulsive, and short-tempered emperor found himself in an untenable position. The ouster of French King Charles X by the July 1830 revolution had a sharp impact upon elite opinion, and the intensifying legislative-executive conflict, which the army had decided in 1823 in favor of the monarch, was replayed with the military leaning in the opposite direction. Pedro's response was to abdicate on April 7 in favor of his five-year-old son. Although a victory for the Brazilians over the Portuguese elements at the national level, the abdication left scars that were not to be healed for many years.[10] In the tripartite regency that emerged, General Lima e Silva functioned as the president and swingman. Nonetheless, with the hand of the legislators reinforced vis-à-vis the executive by the recent course of events, he was not in a position to block the establishment of a national guard as a counterweight to the army. Diogo Antônio Feijó, who as minister of justice would supervise the newly created guard, thus saw his position vastly strengthened.

The regency period was marked by separatist and republican revolts as well as frequent troop mutinies. The Additional Act of August 1834 modified the governmental system in the direction of decentralization, including powers for the provincial legislative assemblies, although not nearly to the degree the advanced Liberals desired. The following April, Feijó, their spokesman, was elected single regent by a slim margin of 2,826 to 2,251 and assumed office in October. A new wave of regionalist revolts would, however, provide a springboard for Lima e Silva's son to emerge as a dominating figure—for Colonel Luís Alves de Lima e Silva, the future duke of Caxias, would jump-start a rapid rise by "pacifying" Maranhão with 8,000 troops in 1841.

Faced with a resurgence of Conservative strength, Feijó resigned as regent in September 1837. Pedro de Araújo Lima—the future marquês de Olinda—won the narrowly based direct election in April of the following year. Back in power these regressive elements curbed provincial autonomy through the Interpretive Law of 1839. Stung deeply, the Liberals engineered a parliamentary *golpe* (coup) that brought Pedro II to the throne in July 1840—at the ripe age of fourteen.

The Monarchy at Its Prime

The country had managed to hold together under the regency; it would be consolidated during the early years of Pedro II's long reign. Caxias's role in maintaining internal security for the empire had only begun with the success in Maranhão. By now a baron as well as a brigadier general, Caxias crushed a Feijó-led São Paulo revolt in 1842. He could then turn to the War of the Farrapos, or Farroupilha Revolution, which had ignited in Rio Grande do Sul in mid-1835. As the one case in which many large landowners did not back the central government, the insurrection had greater staying power. However, once the other regional revolts had been put down, Caxias restored order by 1845. Repression of a final regional revolt in Recife then ushered in a period of nearly four decades of internal peace and order. Thus by midcentury the causes of thirty years of instability were sharply curbed. The chief conflict, centralism versus decentralization, was resolved in favor of the former by force—a portent of future development of the armed forces into the arbiter of national politics.

The domestic stability achieved by 1850 was accompanied by the proliferation and expansion of law schools during that decade, and many sons of the provincial elite turned in the direction of governmental careers as a springboard to more rapid advancement than was possible in an increasingly professionalized army. This emergence of the *bacharel* as intermediary between the local *coroneis* and the growing imperial bureaucracy temporarily reduced the political role of the military, which was even more deeply undercut by central government control and "aristocratization" of the national guard—a trend that involved eliminating dark-skinned officers.

By 1850, then, the elements were in place that would allow Brazil to enjoy over a third of a century of political stability and internal order accompanied by modest economic development and limited social progress. Brazil's economy and society had undergone important changes since the end of the colonial era. Population had risen to around 7.5 million from just over 5.3 million in 1830, and Rio de Janeiro had grown to a city of some 250,000. When British pressure finally brought an end to the slave trade at the beginning of the 1850s, more than 2.5 million slaves made up one-third of the country's population. Nevertheless, by 1872 over 85 percent of Brazilians were free (8.6 million out of 10.1 million), and 1.5 million were slaves.[11] Although the main stream of immigration was still ahead, recent European arrivals were already a key component of the population in Rio Grande do Sul and Santa Catarina.

Economic growth had averaged 1.6 percent annually between 1822 and 1849, but industrialization remained in low gear. Although its great expansion was still to come, coffee already provided half of the country's exports—twice that accounted for by sugar, which it had first surpassed during the 1830s. Centered in the Paraíba River Valley of northwestern São Paulo and southern Rio de Janeiro, coffee growing would soon move to the interior of São Paulo with a consequent fundamental shift in the center of economic power—a shift reflected first in the emergence of the coffee nobility as a social force but eventually having profound political ramifications. In the 1830s Brazil supplied 30 percent of the world's coffee; this rose during the next decade to 40 percent and to 50 percent from the

1850s through the 1870s. As a consequence, by midcentury per capita income levels in the southeast had passed those of the northeast, and this trend would continue far into the future. The prime years of the empire would also see the beginnings of railroad construction, badly needed to tie coastal ports to interior producing areas in the center-south.

During the monarchy's heyday, Brazil's stability would be bolstered by a fairly homogeneous political "class" oriented to national unity. The large landowners and export producers enjoyed considerable political power, but there was significant scope for autonomous action by middle-sector political-bureaucratic elements occupying the higher echelons of the centralized state administrative apparatus. The elite's ability to co-opt emerging urban elements rested upon the *cartorial* state with appointments exchanged for electoral support and public employment used to provide positions in response to the clientelistic political needs of the elite. Away from the capital, decentralized but politically potent power was exercised by the provincial landed class. Given the great distances and poor communications involved, the Brazilian state—even at the apogee of the monarchy—had to recognize the existence of powerful local interests. These could constrain policy choices of the national government, though not force it to follow their preferred course of action.[12] In the final analysis, the emperor remained the balance wheel of the system.

Pedro II's fairly subtle exercise of the "moderating power"—which gave him authority to change ministers when in his judgment this was needed to maintain balance between assembly and cabinet—took the edge off legislative-executive friction. Elections were indirect with a progressively stringent scale of income requirements for first-stage voters (who had a say only in local elections), provincial electors, and those eligible to be elected. First-stage voters reached 1.1 million by 1872, but the 1881 law eliminating the indirect process also toughened income requirements and reduced the electorate to 117,000 in 1886.

The Conservative Party, formed in 1836—backed up by the national guard and often manipulated by the emperor—along with the Liberal Party constituted the linchpin of a system in which controlled elections for the national legislature were a means of legitimizing a ministry that in fact had already been chosen by the emperor in his exercise of the moderating power. Eleven times during his long reign, Pedro II alternated the parties in power, dissolving the lower house and gaining support for his new cabinet through elections whose outcomes were never really in doubt. Yet behind the scenes an intricate political game of intraelite interests and ambitions was at play—one the monarch understood very well, as he did the maneuverings by notables at the provincial level to build patronage structures and establish ties with influential figures in the capital.

Until the beginning of the monarchy's decline, the emperor enjoyed the collaboration—in political as well as military matters—of the individual who had already done so much to hold the country together: Caxias. By then a marquis, General Luís Alves de Lima e Silva was named war minister in June 1855, succeeding to the premiership in 1856. He became war minister and president of the council of ministers again in March 1861 and retained these dual posts until the Liberals came to office in May 1862. Until his death in 1880 this combination military leader and Conservative statesman functioned also as the chief guarantor of the army's loyalty to the emperor.[13]

Although it contributed to a prolonged period of internal peace and stability, this system had negative implications for political development because parties lost any capacity to serve as vehicles for modernization and change—a situation prevailing to the present. The relative disassociation of economic and political power found at the heyday of the monarchy diminished after industrialization got under way, yet during the political decay of the empire in the 1880s the limited political influence of the new economic interests would be a salient factor.

The Liberals returned to power in 1862, but before they could more than hesitantly attack the country's developmental needs, they had to turn their efforts instead to a major international war. The conflict strained the nation's resources to the limit and allowed the Conservatives to regain control of the central government in time to garner the credit for its eventual successful outcome. Uruguay's independence had brought little stability to the River Plate region, and during the early 1860s Brazil intervened to aid the Colorado Party (Conservatives) in its struggle with the Blancos (Liberals), who turned to Paraguayan dictator Francisco Solano López for help. Small, but highly militarized, Paraguay at the end of 1864 sent forces across Argentinian and Brazilian soil to reach Uruguay.

The Paraguayan War

With a population in excess of 9 million and at least the beginnings of an industrial plant, the empire had significant material advantages over its warlike neighbor. Yet at the outbreak of hostilities, Paraguay had 64,000 men under arms and Brazil only 18,000. It would take time for the monarchical regime to mobilize its manpower resources and bring them to bear on a distant and inaccessible front. With the Liberals in power, Caxias first turned down an invitation to command the Brazilian army. But when the allies' forces of over 65,000 troops—including some 57,000 Brazilians—stalled in front of the fortifications at Humaitá, he took command in the field. In a development that would establish a dangerous precedent and in response to the hero's "either him or me" ultimatum in February 1868, the emperor found the ministry of Zacarias de Góes e Vasconcelos to be expendable. Thus, with the Conservatives back in power, Caxias could concentrate upon winning the war. Humaitá was taken in August, and the capital fell at the beginning of 1869.

During the more than five years the conflict lasted, Brazil mobilized nearly 200,000 men, sent a total of 139,000 to the war zone, and suffered at least 30,000 casualties. The burdensome financial cost to Brazil fed inflation and forced the government to increase its foreign debt substantially. Moreover, the national guard was largely absorbed into the army. In many ways the political system never fully recovered from the dislocations and strains intensified by the war. Upset at having been ousted abruptly from power, the Liberals initiated a decade in opposition by issuing a reform manifesto in 1869 calling for electoral reform, elimination of the moderating power, disbanding of the national guard, and even abolition of slavery. In 1870 disenchanted Liberals formed the Republican Party, whose ranks would gradually grow as the Liberals endured their longest period ever out of office.

Development, Dissent, and Discontent

The attack upon slavery gained impetus through the war and led to the Rio Branco legislation in September 1871 declaring that children born to slave mothers would be free at twenty-one. By 1884 slaves had declined to 1.24 million, and a law then freed all over sixty years of age. By 1887, 723,000 slaves constituted only 5 percent of Brazil's population.[14]

As in the societal realm, change in the economy was significant yet circumscribed. Under Pedro II, the government came to intervene in the nation's economic life to subsidize a wide variety of activities such as coastal steamboats, railroad construction, modernization of the sugar industry, and European immigration. Yet only after 1870 did economic development receive as much as 20 percent of the central government's expenditures; the proportion reached 33 percent by 1889. All through the empire, taxes on foreign trade continued to be the major source of government revenue. Failure of agricultural production to generate sufficient income was the major restraint on industrialization. The problem of a small domestic market for manufactured goods was aggravated by high internal transportation costs stemming from the long distances involved.[15] Yet by the end of the empire, manufacturing establishments had risen from 50 at midcentury to 636 and were concentrated in textiles. Meanwhile, the land law of 1850, which had benefited the coffee producers and allowed continuation of latifundia, remained the basis of a land tenure system that would prove resistant to change even a century later.

If the abolitionists and Republicans presented the geriatric monarchy with an increasingly divisive political agenda, a similar situation of discontent prevailed within the armed forces. A series of reform measures passed in 1873 and 1874 temporarily satisfied much of the officer corps but whetted the appetites of more radical figures. Those officers who wished vigorous reform of their service felt misunderstood, as efforts toward modernization met with indifference at best. The civilian elite, lulled into complacency by the absence of political adventures by the army during the long Caxias era, perceived no risk in taking the military for granted. Thus the horizon was already clouded when economic depression was aggravated by a coffee crisis after 1880.

The landmark 1881 Saraiva law made parliamentary elections direct by a single class of electors that included for the first time non-Catholics, freedmen, and naturalized citizens.[16] The subsequent October elections dealt the first electoral reverse to the party in power in the nation's history, as the emperor maintained an unaccustomed posture of impartiality. Yet the establishment adapted rapidly to this modification of the rules of the electoral game, and clientelism at least partially replaced coercion in maintaining the essence of the old electoral politics—manageability. Indeed, the elections of August 1889, just months before the empire's demise, were manipulated much as before this reform. More of a threat to the system was the "new" military. Marshal Manuel Luíz Osório, the Liberals' leading military figure, died in 1879; within a year so did Caxias, who during the period 1875–1878 had headed the war ministry and the council of ministers for the third time. These prestigious old-school figures had helped contain discontent within the armed forces, but their heirs in the military leadership would ride this wave to power instead of seeking to stem it.

A growing divorce between the political elite and the military contributed to acceptance by a majority of the office corps of a coup engineered by a small radicalized faction drawn chiefly from the post–Paraguayan War generation. The government failed to realize that military leaders could provide a quite different type of opposition from what churchmen had mounted in the 1870s on the "religious question" when the state clashed with the upper clergy over prerogatives. Military officers possessed different power capabilities from those of the Catholic hierarchy, which had been quite divided during this crisis. They could also subordinate partisan inclinations and personal rivalries to a prickly sense of corporate pride and strong institutional interests, as civilian governments, both Liberal and Conservative, provided issues that united rather than divided them.[17]

Establishment of the Republic

The impact of abolition was most strongly felt through involvement of the younger generation of the military in the abolitionist campaigns. The slavery issue provided common cause for an alliance of change-oriented civilian and military elements.

The Military Takes Charge

With the abolition of slavery on May 13, 1888, the monarchy gained a modicum of renewed popular support but at the price of alienation of provincial landowners who were still important in the Conservative Party. Republican leaders, their party having been credited with less than one-seventh of the vote in the 1889 elections, realized their need for a prestigious military figure at the head of their movement. Oppositionist activity by the Military Club featured Marshal Manuel Deodoro da Fonseca's nephew, thirty-four-year-old Hermes Rodrigues da Fonseca. The last scruples of Deodoro were overcome by his being named to head the revolutionary government, and he brought Floriano Peixoto into the picture. When Floriano's 2,000 troops joined the 600-man rebel column headed by Deodoro and Benjamin Constant on November 15, the prime minister's resignation was not enough. The empire was at an end.

For the first time in the nation's history, a dictatorship was in control, legitimized only by its monopoly of force and significant but far from overwhelming popular support for a republic. The crucial factor for the future course of Brazil's political development was that the Republicans had turned to the armed forces as the one institution that could put an end to the monarchy without precipitating drastic change in the distribution of power among contending social groups; Republicans wanted only an alteration in the framework of government to accommodate the economic and social changes that had already occurred. Coffee provided two-thirds of the country's exports (almost 5.6 million 132-pound sacks in 1889), and the ascendant coffee producers and their mercantile associates sought greater say in national policy than the monarchy with its ties to ossifying parties provided. Serving in the last parliament of the empire were two Republican Party deputies elected from São Paulo in 1884 who would soon become the nation's first civilian presidents: Prudente José de Morais Barros (1894–1898) and Manuel Ferraz de Campos Salles (1898–1902).

Contrary to the expectations of many of those who had worked hard to bring it about, the replacement of the monarchy by a republic proved to be only a political regime change and did not usher in any sharp break in economic policy or new departures in the social realm.[18] The provisional government that found itself suddenly in office on November 15, 1889, was not agreed upon what kind of a republic should be installed. Historical Republicans, Jacobin army officers, and traditional notables seeking to salvage what they could from the sinking of the empire all vied for office and influence.[19] Headed by a conservative militarist who had never believed in republicanism, the new government after a short period of turmoil and strife saw the old local and regional elites reassert their control over all but the most urban and industrializing parts of the country.

The outlines of significant features of contemporary Brazil can be discerned at the beginning of the republican era: The military had emerged to assume an arbiter role in the nation's political life, the racial composition of the country was rapidly changing as European immigrants were flowing in even faster than had African slaves in earlier periods, and the indigeneous population had declined precipitously (to under 1.5 million by 1750, only 800,000 by 1819, and a mere half million by 1867). Overall, however, population had risen to 14.3 million from 11.8 million in 1880 with over two-fifths still living in the economically declining northeast region. Yet the economic heart of the country had shifted southward into São Paulo; its 1890 population of 1.4 million would more than triple to 4.6 million by 1920, largely as a result of immigration. Still, just 11 percent of Brazilians lived in cities of over 10,000 population, and industry accounted for only 10 percent of GDP. But urbanization was on the increase, albeit as much from immigration as from industrialization.

Immigration was beginning to change the face of Brazilian society, as the flow from Europe—which had been about 10,000 a year through the 1850s and 1860s and double that during the 1870s—jumped from 55,000 in 1887 to over 132,000 in 1888 on the way to a record 215,000 in 1891. But this immigration had—and would continue to have—a chilling effect upon the lot of the rural masses. By fill-ing the workforce needs of the developing coffee areas, immigration served to keep the former slave population fixed at about where this group was before emancipation—at the bottom of the social pyramid. Moreover, the abundance of labor helped keep wages down.[20] Although only 14 percent of school-age children were enrolled, this was an improvement over the early 1850s when there were 61,700 primary school students in all of Brazil and only 3,700 enrolled at the sec-ondary level. Literacy rates reflected this lack of educational opportunity; they were 19 percent for males and just a little over 10 percent for females. Thus the ex-tension of suffrage to all literate males by the republican regime did not lead to anything like mass political participation.

The industrial genesis of Brazil is found during the 1886–1894 period bridg-ing the demise of the monarchy and the inception of the republican regime. Textile factories, flour mills, breweries, and light metallurgical works increased in number during the 1880s and accelerated after 1886 on the crest of ex-panded exports, which allowed for capital accumulation by the agroexporting sector and its mercantile allies. By 1894 the rail network nearly doubled to 6,900 miles and exceeded 9,950 miles by the turn of the century. British capital played a major part in this expansion through loans in the earlier period and subsequently by means of direct investments.[21] Even before 1888 the Brazilian government had modestly helped finance agricultural loans to adjust from credits partially secured by slaves as collateral. But more important was the law enacted at the end of 1888 permitting banks to issue paper money. It led to in-flation and rampant stock market speculation, but it also resulted in significant real growth.

Ruy Barbosa as the republic's first finance minister implemented a moderate degree of protectionism, considering this to be politically crucial for consolida-tion of the new regime. At the same time, banks emitted so much currency that the money supply almost doubled in 1890 and expanded by just over 50 percent the next year. Administrative discontinuity in the economic sphere was extreme at the inception of the Old Republic; there were nine finance ministers during the first seven years.

Deodoro, Floriano, and Civil War

Shadows of these economic and social changes could be discerned in the political realm. Although some planters had supported the Republican Party, from November 1889 to 1894 control of the government was more in the hands of pre-dominantly urban-oriented individuals, chiefly military, who took some steps in-imical to the planters' interests. The nation's center of gravity had moved to the center-south, with Minas Gerais, the country's most populous state at 3.1 million in 1890, occupying a pivotal position as link between the former heartland and the soon-to-be dominant region.

The provisional regime not only abolished the monarchy but also dissolved the Chamber of Deputies and eliminated the life tenure of Senate members. Deodoro assumed the title "chief of the provisional government," and military men governed a majority of states. Floriano Peixoto wielded great power even before he assumed the post of war minister at the end of April 1890; he replaced Ruy Barbosa as first deputy chief less than four months later. When the constituent assembly elected on September 15, 1890, met in November, the administration presented it with a draft constitution.[22] The resulting basic charter was promulgated on February 24, 1891, and the following day Deodoro was chosen president over Prudente by a vote of 129 to 97. Floriano, however, was elected vice president by a larger majority (153–57). As constitutional president, Deodoro was in a substantially weaker position than when chief of the provisional government. He had difficulty in dealing with a hostile Congress that was now his constitutional equal. Unable to stand what he viewed as unjustified congressional obstruction, the thin-skinned president dissolved the legislature in November 1891. A revolt broke out in Rio Grande do Sul, and Admiral Custódio de Melo incited most of the fleet to revolt.[23] Recognizing the weakness of his position, Deodoro resigned.

Those who overthrew him fared little better at governing the infant republic and narrowly avoided institutionalizing recourse to force and violence as a means for deciding the control of political power. In the absence of channels for resolving elite differences, the military remained arbiter. Devious where his predecessor was direct, impassive instead of emotional, distrustful rather than open, and cautiously calculating in contrast to Deodoro's impulsiveness, Floriano managed to arouse extremes of feeling. If Deodoro had established the republic, Floriano was faced with the task of consolidating the new regime. Caught between monarchical sentiment in the navy and support on the part of some officers for the deposed president, but impelled as well by his authoritarianism, Floriano was far from a democratic executive.

Admiral Custódio de Melo, who considered himself "father" of the November 23 coup, interfered in government affairs beyond the normal scope of navy minister and president of the Military Club. He broke with Floriano in April 1893, and when the Federalists invaded Rio Grande do Sul from Uruguay, a major revolt of the fleet followed on September 6. De Melo was disappointed in his belief that battleships could force Floriano to quit—the United States and European powers blocked this ploy.[24]

As the 1890s wore on, the constitutionalist reaction to a half decade of military rule spread to elements of the armed forces who came to feel that professionalism had suffered, unity had been sacrificed, and the ability to act as the moderating power had been compromised. Thus, they came to consider the advisability of disengaging from the direct control of government.

Transition to Civilian Rule

Although the naval revolt and protracted civil war could not dislodge Floriano, they did guarantee that he would leave office at the end of his term. While the chief executive was preoccupied with the survival of his government, the São Paulo civilian elites were able to establish a basis for the election to the presidency of one of their spokesmen. They achieved this by furnishing state troops to keep the rebels bottled up in the south and by leading the government's support in Congress. Yet the new political order they inaugurated turned out to be almost as distant from parliamentary democracy as was the military interregnum, since in the end much of the patriarchal society was preserved, and local and regional oligarchies not only survived but actually found their hand strengthened—at least at home—against the new political forces that had begun to challenge their domination. The survival of *coronelismo* was rooted in the fact that the foundation of the republic did not alter basic conditions in the traditional rural areas, especially in the northeast and north. There the societal props of the old political system remained firm. The rural patriarchal society had produced an authoritarian paternalism that provided a continuing basis for patrimonial politics.

Co-optation of the middle sectors was the urban counterpart of the maintenance of rural machines. Product of urbanization that preceded industrialization, the Brazilian middle class during the nineteenth century exceeded the country's limited needs for technical and administrative personnel. Many bargained with the ruling stratum of plantation owners and export-import merchants for bureaucratic posts in exchange for political support. This style of clientelistic politics existed at all levels. With the *cartorial* state functioning as both product of clientelistic politics and vehicle for its perpetuation, the oligarchy was able to stage a strong and rapid political comeback within a few years after the elimination of the monarchy to which they had appeared to be wed.

At the beginning of the republic, the São Paulo elites had been most concerned over influencing economic policy. Closest to their hearts—and to their wallets— was the issue of exchange rates and money supply. Devaluation served to protect the income of the coffee producers, since their sales were overwhelmingly for export. At the same time, however, it caused inflation and fed government budget deficits. Moreover, a drop in tax receipts led to renewed foreign borrowing with a consequent rise in the cost of servicing the increased foreign debt that already required nearly all the hard-won trade surplus. Concerned with financial stability, obtaining foreign credits, and European immigration, São Paulo coffee growers and businessmen did their best to take advantage of Floriano's difficulties to gain his approval of their preferred policies. Their ultimate goal was a civilian government headed by one of their experienced statesman-administrators with the armed forces back in the barracks.

The São Paulo Dynasty, 1894–1906

Civilian supporters of the government pressed Floriano in spite of the continuing civil war to hold presidential elections on March 1, 1894. The rebels were on the offensive in the south and in control of Rio de Janeiro's harbor, and the government could ill afford to alienate the two richest provinces, so Floriano reluctantly accepted the victory of Federal Republican Party (PRF) nominee Prudente de Morais, who received 277,000 votes compared to only 38,000 for Afonso Augusto Moreira Pena. With Prudente's inauguration, representatives of the São Paulo elites came to occupy the presidency for twelve consecutive years. Yet the armed forces continued to exert influence on national political life. Since their predominant orientation was neither clearly in support of those opposing all change nor in favor of the still weak radical forces in Brazilian society, they tended to blend in with the political currents of the day. Much of their image as disinterested watchdogs of national welfare resulted from the fact that there was no real competition in Brazil between national parties. The dominant coalition of state elites centered in São Paulo and Minas Gerais would select the next president with only grumbling by the smaller states.

Under these circumstances, Prudente's government enjoyed success in dealing with the military. Cautious, persistent, tenacious, and experienced, the new chief executive was aided by the cessation of hostilities in mid-1895. Yet to many of Floriano's supporters, this taciturn representative of the São Paulo aristocracy seemed to represent reactionary interests. The relative freedom granted to monarchist groups, contrasted to their repression under the military presidents, made Prudente suspect in the eyes of exalted Republicans and militant military Jacobins.

The tragic affair of Canudos soon provided them with an opportunity to exploit the weaknesses of his position. Only in an atmosphere of extreme political passions could the existence of a small colony of impoverished religious fanatics in the backlands be seen as a monarchist plot and a threat to the existence of the republic. Yet cynical manipulation of this situation created a politico-military crisis.[25] Antônio Conselheiro, a primitive mystic, had founded a community in an inaccessible spot in the interior of Bahia. The belief soon spread in the capital that this was a monarchical conspiracy supported from abroad. Bahian officials and embarrassed army spokesmen found in this a convenient explanation for the inability of three successive expeditions to defeat the mob they had grossly underestimated. National public uproar exploded in March 1897 after a federal force of 1,300 trained troops accompanied by artillery was all but wiped out.

Aware that the various military factions, whose differences and rivalries had allowed him to govern, might unite now that the army's reputation was on the line, the president sent a new war minister into the field with 10,000 men. He methodically laid siege to the fortified shantytown, which had grown to a city of some 25,000 inhabitants. On October 5, Canudos was completely demolished and its defenders were annihilated. Thus with a loss of some 5,000 lives on the government side and of at least 15,000 humble, uneducated peasants the traumatizing affair was ended.

Election of fifty-seven-year-old São Paulo chief executive Campos Salles as Brazil's second civilian president took place in an atmosphere of comparative calm with the winner receiving 420,000 votes to 39,000 for his opponent. Described as "moderate, opportunist, and vigilant against the excesses of the multitude," the new president was a successful agriculturalist. Campos Salles is often considered as the restorer of Brazil's shattered finances and credit; reversing the policy of his predecessors, he ceased to be preoccupied with maintaining supporters in power at the provincial level, preferring instead to accept whoever won the power struggle in each state as long as their representatives in Congress lent him their support. Under the "politics of the governors," electoral fraud and coercion by state machines were tolerated and victories by their opponents not recognized by the Chamber of Deputies. In turn the governors extended local elites a similar deal of patronage and services for votes. This arrangement strengthened the municipalities as a basic political unit but in such a way as to reinforce the hold of the regional oligarchies and local clientelistic machines.

Thus in the context of insufficient institutionalization and the persistence of a traditional sociopolitical order in the rural areas making up most of the country, the introduction of formal democracy through extension of the franchise worked not so much for change as to bolster the entrenched elites. There was in fact a reestablishment of duality between centralized power over national matters in the hands of the federal executive and local autonomy, often bordering on license, in "lesser" matters—although these were often of life or death import to the bulk of the population. Under these circumstances politically active military elements concentrated on attempts to hold eroding positions at the provincial level; they met with greatest success on the periphery of the country. Undercut by the political tactics of Campos Salles, as followed by a successor they viewed less favorably, the military "modernizers" would subsequently begin to focus on regaining control of the central government.[26]

Ingenious as it appeared, Campos Salles's effort to enable the president to stay above the dispute of shifting factions with little programmatic content bought temporary equilibrium at the expense of future crises. Virtually eliminating any possibility of peaceful alternation at the state level, it set up tensions that would burst through after 1910. Rooted in absence of real national political parties, the president's policy had the effect of further weakening feeble party structures that did exist. A chaotic scene of shifting factional alliances predominated, based on the interplay of center-state, interstate, and intrastate maneuvering.

In this environment of domestic peace—despite economic troubles—combined with manipulable political competition, Campos Salles chose as successor the incumbent president of São Paulo, fifty-four-year-old Francisco de Paula Rodrigues Alves. He had served as finance minister for both Floriano and Prudente and was admirably prepared for the presidency. His election in 1902 by a vote of 316,000 to 25,000 showed that the system of succession by agreement among the heads of key states was working smoothly. In office Rodrigues Alves continued the shift toward a condominium of Conservative oligarchies. Given these circumstances, it is not surprising that at the midpoint of his term he was faced with a revolt as proponents of a positivist military dictatorship sought to escalate popular dissatisfaction into a coup. The November 1904 uprising was firmly put down. All cadets were transferred to Rio Grande do Sul, where they would come in contact with young Gaúcho student politicians who were subsequently to organize the 1930 revolution.

Economy and Society in the New Century

Economically and, to some extent, socially as well, Brazil had moved ahead during these dozen years of relative peace and stability. Population at the turn of the century passed 17 million as immigration during the 1890s had risen sharply, despite civil war and economic ups and downs, to over 1.2 million, some 690,000 of whom came from Italy. Factory workers by 1900 totaled 160,000, and GDP, which had grown only 16 percent from 1889 through 1899, climbed by 4.2 percent a year during the 1900–1909 period. From 1898 through 1910 coffee accounted for 53 percent of exports; rubber rose to 26 percent.[27] Indeed, coffee production exploded in the early years of the republic, from 5.6 million sacks in the 1890–1891 harvest to 16.3 million sacks in 1901–1902.

The Rodrigues Alves years marked the beginning of the economic *reerguimento* characterized by tight monetary policies having recessive effects offset by amplified public works programs stressing rail and port facilities and sewer and water systems for the capital city, which boasted a population exceeding 800,000. At this juncture the presidents of São Paulo, Minas Gerais, and Rio de Janeiro met in February 1906 at Taubaté and developed a scheme to stabilize coffee prices to be financed by a £15 million loan contracted by São Paulo with federal government approval. By the time this occurred in midyear, a new chief executive had been elected in March—Afonso Pena of Minas Gerais—thus ending the twelve-year hold of São Paulo on the presidency. Since Minas Gerais had by 1896 replaced Rio de Janeiro as the country's second leading coffee state, the shift to a president from Minas Gerais did not signify any major change in the distribution of power away from the influential, although not fully hegemonic, coffee elite.

Politics Without Parties, 1906–1922

The 1906 succession witnessed the emergence of a new balance wheel to the politics of the governors. The shift partially accommodated but, more important, co-opted and channeled the interests of states other than São Paulo and Minas Gerais, because in August 1905 Rio Grande do Sul Senator José Gomes Pinheiro

Machado had launched his career as kingmaker by masterfully articulating Pena's candidacy.

One for Minas Gerais and One for the Army

As Minas Gerais was number one in population, electorate, and congressional seats, elevation of its former chief executive to the presidency was logical, even overdue. Essentially unopposed, Pena received over 288,000 votes to fewer than 5,000 for his token opponent. Well aware of the realities of the situation, Pena prudently chose as his war minister Marshal Hermes da Fonseca, the legalist hero of the 1904 crisis. Hermes was relatively slow to develop presidential ambitions, but disunity and intransigence among the civilian elites would create a vacuum he could readily be convinced to fill. In the eyes of opposition politicians, Hermes appeared a capable administrator who would be amenable to their influence, if not subject to their management. To important elements of the armed forces, he seemed to combine the best qualities of his uncle Deodoro with Floriano's virtues.

To combat this resurgence of Florianism, Ruy Barbosa launched his own "civilist" candidacy and received the backing of São Paulo, Bahia, and Rio de Janeiro. Although the champion of civilism carried the cities of the south, the combination of state machines and military support was decisive in the interior. The official figures registered a win for Hermes by 404,000 to 223,000—a record-low margin of victory (with just over 57 percent of the valid vote compared to 84 percent in 1894, 91 percent in 1898, 92 percent in 1902, and 98 percent in 1906). Despite the fact that these figures were inflated, Hermes was inaugurated November 15, 1910, as Brazil's third military chief executive; Minas Gerais's Wenceslau Bráz Pereira Gomes took office as vice president amid a series of local uprisings. Of greatest significance for the future was that for the first time in a presidential election, the candidate supported by São Paulo failed to win.

Following the precedent of Deodoro and Floriano rather than the live-and-let-live stance of the intervening civilian presidents, Hermes strove to overthrow provincial administrations hostile to his policies. Influenced by a new alliance of middle-class military with civilianists, during 1911 he unleashed a series of political "salvations." Targeted were oligarchical machines of local political chiefs and powerful landholding families allied with Pinheiro Machado and his embryonic Conservative Republican Party (PRC). They were difficult targets that needed to be attacked because of the high degree of political and administrative autonomy that gave the governors nearly complete control of political life in their states. This was implemented and maintained through clientelistic appointments and nepotism; electoral corruption bordering on the absurd; and, in the ultimate resort, violence pure and simple. Such a system of well-mounted political machines consolidated leadership of the regional chief in the states and of the colonel in the municipalities in such a way that the peasantry was practically "feudalized." This situation undercut the emergence of national political parties capable of disciplining legislative politics. Only in São Paulo, Minas Gerais, and Rio Grande do Sul did strong, coherent Republican Parties exist. Thus, Hermes obtained but a partial rotation of oligarchical elites. In Rio Grande do Sul the partnership of Antônio Augusto Borges de Medeiros (its strongman since 1903) and Pinheiro Machado withstood the central administration. But efforts to make the PRC into a real national party were effectively undermined.[28]

During the latter stages of his administration, Hermes was plagued with internal security problems. A Canudos-type situation with major political implications had developed in the contested area (Contestado) between the provinces of Paraná and Santa Catarina. In a period rife with corruption, unemployment, and speculation, Miguel Lucena Boavista built up a following among the superstitious poor before being killed in October 1912. The same mistakes were made by the government as at Canudos, so not until 1915 was the last resistance crushed, an effort that required a field army of over 7,000 men. Government troops lost over 300 men with perhaps twenty times that number of rebels killed—almost all of them humble people participating in an essentially spontaneous protest movement by those marginalized by the existing social order and political process.[29]

Minas Again and a Chance for the Northeast

Before the end of the Contestado campaign, Hermes was succeeded by forty-six-year-old Wenceslau Bráz, who polled 92 percent of the small vote in the March 1914 elections. In September 1915 Pinheiro Machado was murdered; his death led to the collapse of the PRC. With World War I in progress, the nomination and election of Rodrigues Alves for a second stint as president aroused little opposition. In keeping with the pattern of "coffee with milk" politics, an alliance of São Paulo and Minas Gerais, Mineiro chief executive Delfim Moreira was chosen as his running mate, and the official slate polled 99 percent of a turnout of 400,000.

Mortally ill, Rodrigues Alves died in January 1919; the vice president was also in very poor health. The compromise choice for the resulting special election fell upon fifty-four-year-old Epitácio Pessoa—who had headed Brazil's delegation to the Versailles peace conference but who would normally have been barred from consideration because he came from the small northeastern state of Paraíba. On April 19 he received 71 percent of the fewer than half million votes cast; Ruy Barbosa in his last hurrah was credited with 119,000 votes to the victor's 341,000.

This first civilian president from outside the center-south was called upon to govern a Brazil that had changed significantly since the early 1900s. Its population had passed the 22 million mark in 1910 on the way to 30.6 million by 1920. Rio de Janeiro was by now a city of nearly 1.2 million. The economy, which had expanded some 77 percent from 1900 to 1913 and led to an increase in per capita GDP of 35 percent, had slowed to a modest 2.4 percent annual growth rate between 1914 and 1918. Although coffee still accounted for over 47 percent of the nation's exports in the 1914–1918 period, this was below its nearly 62 percent share during the Hermes years. Rubber, source of 20 percent of Brazil's foreign sales during that period, declined to 12 percent in Bráz's term. Immigration had fallen off during the first decade of the century, but a total of 650,000 was substantial, and between 1910 and 1919 the flow rose again to 820,000. Life expectancy by 1920 was up to thirty-two years, and the labor force had reached 9.2 million. With 29 percent of school-age children enrolled, compared to 20 percent in 1907, literacy rates by 1920 reached 29 percent for males and 20 percent for females.

World War I clearly focused the attention of both elites and government on the need for diversifying industrial production so as not to be caught short in any future international crisis. Consequently, during the 1920s the government provided incentives and extended subsidies to certain priority industries. Since 1906 the Taubaté pact had protected the coffee sector but at the cost of disorganizing the market as a guide to investments. Moreover, although by mid-1913 São Paulo had repaid the £15 million loan contracted in 1908, there was still a demand for price support that further fed the high inflation of the wartime years, and a more than 27 percent fall in coffee revenues in 1920 led to further reliance upon keeping prices up through loans and expansion of the money supply.

Political passions ran high through Pessoa's truncated tenure. Although nomination of Minas Gerais chief executive Artur da Silva Bernardes for the 1922–1926 term was agreed upon by the nation's political leaders in early 1921, Rio Grande do Sul under Borges de Medeiros joined with Rio de Janeiro, Bahia, and Pernambuco in the "Republican Reaction." Hermes da Fonseca, returning from six years in Europe to find that his absence had indeed made him fonder to the hearts of many Brazilians, threw his support to this opposition slate, which already enjoyed the backing of young military reformists and even the venerable Ruy Barbosa. The March 1922 balloting saw the government candidate win as always. But with intellectual sectors sensitized by the centennial of independence, the Republican Reaction refused to accept the announced results as valid, and Hermes—presiding over the Military Club—called for a "tribunal of honor" to verify the electoral results. When Bernardes was proclaimed president-elect on June 7 with the lowest margin yet (only 56 percent of the vote, or 467,000 to 318,000), Hermes, once again in the presidency of the Military Club, reacted with a seditious declaration. This led to his arrest.

Tenentismo and the Road Toward Revolution

The reaction of Hermes's supporters was a revolt designed to bring the armed forces back to power. The uprising was articulated on short notice by romantic young officers, and the failure of Marshal Hermes to make it more than a gallant but futile gesture would be the epitaph for Florianism. But out of their heroic behavior a more potent force—*tenentismo*—was born as a modern movement freed from the shackles of seeking to emulate successes of an earlier era.[30]

The First Angry Shots and the Prestes Column

In the perspective of 1922, however, the young military rebels looked to be anything but the wave of the future. Indeed, the July 5 revolt involved only a small part of the troops in the Rio de Janeiro area. Fort Copacabana, under Captain Euclides Hermes da Fonseca, son of the marshal, rebelled in the early morning hours of July 5, but these gallant rebels soon found themselves in isolated resistance against the full forces of the government. Under heavy fire, a group of the most militant young officers decided to embark on a suicidal sally against the ground forces besieging them; the seriously wounded Antônio de Siqueira Campos and Eduardo Gomes survived to become national heroes.

Inaugurated on November 15, 1922, Bernardes was to enjoy little respite from crises during his four years in office. A bloody civil war broke out in Rio Grande do Sul over the disputed outcome of the November 25 gubernatorial voting. Old scores remaining from earlier armed struggles were settled by acts of violence often crossing the line into barbarism. The Pact of Pedras Altas of December 14, 1923, provided for an eventual end to Borges's stranglehold on the governorship. Long before the civil strife ended in Rio Grande do Sul, plans for a new revolt against the increasingly repressive Bernardes government were going forward under leaders with greater skill and coherence. Launched on the second anniversary of the 1922 revolt, it met with initial success, and the rebels controlled São Paulo city for eighteen days. Yet by July 27, as government planes began aerial warfare against São Paulo, a strategic withdrawal to the interior was in order.

Luís Carlos Prestes had by this time managed to instigate fighting in the chronic powder keg of Rio Grande do Sul. After two months his column marched northward to join with the São Paulo rebels, a feat achieved in April 1925. With Prestes as chief of staff, the rebels undertook a more than 15,000-mile campaign. They fought fifty battles and skirmishes before going into exile in Bolivia in February 1927 and in the process caught the country's imagination and succeeded in outlasting the target of their hatred, President Bernardes. Significantly, the regular army left most of the task of combating the insurgents to militia or even the private armies of the interior colonels.

Times were changing. The revolts of 1922 and 1924 were harbingers of these changes, and the Prestes column was their catalyst. A new civilian-military coalition was emerging—one that within a short time would be capable of pushing aside the decaying structures of the past four decades much as the military Jacobins, Deodoro, and the Republican Party had done away with the empire.

Breakdown of the Old Republic

The presidential succession of 1926 was one of the smoothest the republic had yet experienced. The government candidate was São Paulo chief executive Washington Luís Pereira de Souza; his Minas Gerais counterpart was running mate. The official results of 688,000 to 1,116 gave a grossly misleading impression of national consensus. By the second half of 1927 dissident oligarchies began to take shape. Large coffee planters, São Paulo professionals, and the newer generation of the traditional middle class formed the Democratic Party in February 1926 to challenge the long-entrenched Paulista Republican Party.[31] At the same time, Antônio Carlos Ribeiro da Andrada achieved the presidency of Minas Gerais. In Rio Grande do Sul the elements that had formed the Liberationist Alliance in 1922 and 1923 formally constituted the Liberator Party (PL) in March 1928. Tory reformism was finally under way, but the situation was slipping past the point at which this might be enough because by 1928 the oligarchic republican regime had reached a point of deterioration similar to the decay of the empire by the mid-1880s. Institutions and processes perhaps suitable for the first years of republican government had failed to evolve beyond an amalgam with traditional practices carried over from the monarchy. The electoral process was highly fraudulent, national parties simply did not exist, and protests against the inequities of the established order were met with repression rather than compromise and evolutionary reform.

As long as elections might lead to change, there was no strong popular base for revolution, but the Brazilian people were aware that never in the history of the republic had the government's candidate lost. Thus, the presidential succession of 1930 was to be the last chance for the old system to demonstrate a significant capacity to adapt.

The original core of the revolutionary movement that eventually triumphed in October 1930 was composed of the *tenentes*. The successful revolution became possible, however, only after they formed an alliance with a broad coalition of political forces possessing a power base in key states. Yet unless assured of widespread military adhesions, the quite prudent political leaders would not have risked a revolutionary venture. The spread of insurrectionist sentiment among the military, for its part, coincided with the increasing alienation of urban progressive groups from a political establishment unresponsive to the desire by middle sectors for a significant say in policymaking and indisposed to yield to demands for any type of reforms, including the electoral realm. Dissension within the political elite over presidential succession combined with the impact of the world economic crisis made the regime vulnerable and catalyzed formation of a revolutionary coalition capable of overthrowing the established order. This time, in contrast to the termination of the monarchy four decades earlier, nationwide mobilization and substantial fighting were required to topple the old regime.

As the 1920s drew to a close, Brazil's population had passed 35 million. Rio de Janeiro was a city of 1.5 million, and São Paulo was nearing 900,000. After stagnating in 1924 and 1925, economic expansion recovered to 11 percent a year for 1927 and 1928—but on a fragile basis. This relative prosperity was highly mortgaged to coffee, responsible for over 72 percent of export earnings from 1924 through 1929. GDP growth for 1929 was a nearly imperceptible 1.2 percent. Between September and December coffee prices fell by one-third, and by the second half of 1930 they were down an additional 70 percent under the burden of a massive harvest.

The revolutionary movement that took form during 1930 was a heterogeneous amalgam of groups desiring sweeping political changes, if not a new social order, with elements violently opposed to the incumbent administration's control of presidential succession but devoid of any wish for more than moderate political and administrative reforms. In both its civilian and military components, the movement was almost exclusively bourgeois in nature. Indeed, the Communists refused to participate or even endorse the October 1930 revolt. Presidential succession served as the issue around which the fragmented opposition forces coalesced into a movement cohesive insofar as its immediate objective—attainment of power—was concerned. By 1929 it was already apparent that the president's choice was São Paulo chief executive Júlio Prestes, and Antônio Carlos was determined to thwart the imposition of the younger Paulista politician. In this venture he required the cooperation of Rio Grande do Sul, which had long awaited an opportunity for a favorite son to become president.

In January 1928 that state came under the administration of Getúlio Dornelles Vargas, a forty-four-year-old politician from the interior who had already served as the country's finance minister under Washington Luís.[32] Vargas had had a brief army career, which was to facilitate his dealings with the armed forces during his first fifteen-year stint as the nation's chief executive. Clearly possessing unusual leadership talents, he was successful as a law school politician and was quickly co-opted into the Borges de Medeiros machine. Elected to the state legislature in 1909, he rose to be its majority leader before moving on to Congress. Named finance minister in 1926, he went home to govern the Gaúcho state in November 1927.

Vargas's conciliatory policies made possible cooperation between the bitterly antagonistic Libertadores and the Republicans in the quest to capture the presidency for Rio Grande do Sul. The organization of the Liberal Alliance (AL) on a national basis went forward because some of its leaders saw it as a means of pressuring the president into making either Vargas or the Minas Gerais leader the official candidate. Although Minas Gerais and Rio Grande do Sul together gave Vargas nearly 600,000 votes, he was credited with only 200,000 votes in the rest of the country, whereas the government candidate was given a national total of nearly 1.1 million. In any case, the country knew that no opposition candidate had ever before run nearly this strongly: Although the winner's announced share of the vote was under 58 percent, this was two and a half times the number of opposition ballots counted only eight years earlier. Yet despite more than a year of contingency planning, the civilians and military who would soon mobilize the most extensive revolutionary movement in Brazil's history—and very possibly that of all Latin America—were still wary and distrustful of each other.

3

FROM REVOLUTION TO REVOLUTION: BRAZIL 1930–1964

B Y THE LATE 1920s Brazil's political system was in a state of debilitating disarray and heading for outright decay, as had been the monarchy in the mid-1880s. This deterioration was a function of a lack of flexibility and capacity to modernize by political structures and processes as well as an accelerating pace of economic change and resultant societal tensions. Urban middle classes—including the military—took a leading part in the 1930 revolution but lacked independence to formulate a political program or establish autonomy from dissident oligarchies who also participated in the movement or quickly aligned with the new regime. These emerging elements realized that electoral democracy under the existing socioeconomic system would result in a return to power of the class of landowners and export merchants whose dependents greatly exceeded the urban middle-class vote. Thus, the new groups submerged their liberal ideas and accepted a regime without parties or elections but one in which they could play a major role in a rapidly expanding bureaucracy.[1]

The 1930 Revolution and Vargas's Rise

In 1930, as in 1889, the army was the vehicle for dissident elites and the middle class to overturn old governmental institutions. When the military returned to the barracks, civilian middle sectors could not hold on to political power in a still essentially patrimonial society, yet they could reap individual benefits from the clientelistic-*cartorial* system by again agreeing to be co-opted. Hence, instead of a pluralist democracy, the populist authoritarian regime of Getúlio Vargas emerged and built up the urban working class as a potential power factor under a corporative institutional structure. Most critical to the failure of the 1930 revolution to develop into a rupture with the past was the fact that the *tenentes,* the cutting edge of the movement for political reform, had no consensus view of a more appropriate role for the working class.[2] However, during the fifteen years of Vargas's rule, hegemony of traditional agricultural elites would be broken, with new industrial elements coming to exert a significant influence on national policy and the middle class taking on political muscle. Under stop-and-go government sponsorship, the urban working class would emerge from the wings and assume a position on the political stage—albeit no closer to the focus of action than upstage left.

Ousting the Old Regime

Catalyzing the decision to raise the banner of revolt was the assassination of vice-presidential candidate João Pessoa on July 26.[3] Forty-year-old Lieutenant Colonel Pedro Aurélio de Góes Monteiro emerged as the movement's chief of staff. While attending military school in Porto Alegre from 1906 to 1909 he was in contact with law student leaders there. He studied at the command and general staff school during the 1922 and 1924 revolts and later gained combat experience on the legalist side against the Prestes column. Launched on October 3, the revolt quickly swept aside or drew into its wake the powerful 14,000-man federal force in Rio Grande do Sul. By the end of the first week the rebel column was preparing for a showdown with legalist forces massed in southern São Paulo. Meanwhile, in the northeast, the revolution scored a series of successes, and by October 23 rebel forces were on the verge of breaking through from Minas Gerais into Rio de Janeiro. Senior generals in Rio de Janeiro forced the resignation of Washington Luís and on October 24 a "pacifying junta" took power. A month after the revolution was launched, Vargas assumed office, promising a program of "national reconstruction," an amalgam of the Liberal Alliance program with a laundry list of demands of the diverse groups that had supported the revolt.

The Provisional Government

Through moves more heavy-handed than those adopted in 1889 by Deodoro, the provisional government established itself as a dictatorship with vast discretionary authority. Representative bodies were dissolved, and *interventors* appointed by Vargas had nearly total power in the states. (An *interventor* was a figure appointed by the president to replace an elected governor when the federal government "intervened" in a state to take over.) Large numbers of politicians associated with the ousted government were arrested. A large proportion of senior military chiefs had viewed Vargas only as a lesser evil than an extensive civil war, and this did not provide a firm basis for continued cooperation, for they had little sympathy for his program. Relations with the new regime were further strained by tension with the *tenentes,* whom they viewed as politically ambitious upstarts. Historical revolutionaries mistrusted senior officers and midgrade legalists as opportunists whose loyalty to revolutionary goals was suspect. The issue of prolonged rule by the provisional government versus rapid reconstitutionalization further separated the two groups. *Tenentes* and dissident oligarchies had allied only as events moved from the electoral arena to armed revolt. Their marriage of necessity was complemented by one of convenience with military groups joining at the last moment.

Far from homogeneous in their political orientation, the *tenentes* generally shared several common attitudes that set them apart from the civilian liberal constitutionalists. They were mistrustful of politicians as a class and more concerned with the substance of vaguely articulated social and economic reforms than with democratic forms. Many of them professed a general and often ill-defined socialist leaning, but they also manifested an elitist approach toward "national regeneration" from the top that frequently shaded into an authoritarian nationalism. Then, too, certain elements of corporativist thought had begun to take root in the minds of those *tenentes* who were concerned about a programmatic basis for their movement. Over time different factions of *tenentes* allied with differing civilian elements, diluting the possible impact of *tenentismo*.[4] Although the Communists and other radical movements were quite weak, both old elites and emerging middle sectors manifested a near obsession with the proletarian threat. Creation of a labor ministry was designed to provide an effective instrument for government control of the union movement. Force was used against labor when its demands appeared too great or its political action excessively direct, but under Vargas manipulative paternalism came to constitute the federal government's preferred strategy in this field.

Since the common denominator of the Liberal Alliance was opposition to the Washington Luís government more so than a hostile attitude toward the established order, intramural divisions came to the surface soon after victory. The dissident oligarchies as represented by São Paulo Democrats and Minas Gerais Republicans wished for little more than narrow political reforms. For these moderately conservative to liberal elements, a formal system of representative democracy would work suitably once the power of the rural oligarchical machines could be curbed by eliminating their ability to manipulate election results. Even less reform-minded were opposition groups in various smaller states that had joined the Liberal Alliance only as a vehicle for achieving power; all they wished was to receive the same type of favors from the new government as the local machines they replaced had enjoyed under the old regime. In contrast, for more reformist elements, the Liberal Alliance platform represented but the first steps in a program of national reorganization and restructuring of the social order.[5] Thus, the coalition of forces that overthrew the Old Republic was so heterogeneous that there was no real chance of welding it into a coherent party or movement.

The São Paulo Revolt

The São Paulo uprising, which was to spur the disaggregation of the revolutionary forces, quickly erupted in good part because João Alberto Lins de Barros, placed in charge there by Vargas, was an outsider to this nation within the nation. When João Alberto established the Revolutionary Legion in São Paulo, the Democratic Party broke with the government. Vargas sought to stave off the coming revolt by announcing elections for a constituent assembly to be held in May 1933. Yet by May 1932 Brazil found itself on the brink of civil war. Flôres da Cunha in Rio Grande do Sul remained loyal to Vargas and thus doomed the revolt. Minas Gerais sent state militia against São Paulo, and there was no military uprising in Rio de Janeiro—from where instead waves of reinforcements left for the front, bolstered by troops sent by the *tenente interventors* in the north and northeast.

Although São Paulo put nearly 40,000 armed men into the field, well over half were poorly trained civilian volunteers. By contrast, government forces eventually totaled at least 75,000 on the three main fronts. On October 2 the São Paulo government resigned, ending a valiant struggle against overwhelming odds. Vargas had played skillfully upon memories of São Paulo domination to arouse hostility toward the province believed by many to harbor separatist proclivities. Then, too, the elites there failed to enlist the effective support of the working class—fear of whose greater political role was a cause of attrition with Vargas.

The Constitutional Interlude

In spite of opposition from the *tenentes,* who felt reconstitutionalization was still premature, Vargas chose to honor commitments assumed with the governments of Minas Gerais and Rio Grande do Sul—which had weighed heavily in their not joining the Paulistas. This policy of conciliation served to undercut efforts for a new revolt, but it also opened the door for a political resurgence of the pre-1930 elites. Elections held in May 1933 for a National Constituent Assembly were marked by the participation of a confusingly large number of new parties existing solely at the state level, most of which represented old established political interests and leaders. The victors included many political notables and relatively few representatives of the various *tenente*-backed reformist movements. To strengthen the government's hand in the new legislative body, 40 "class" representatives were added to the 214 members elected on May 3.

Over vocal opposition from *tenentes,* the São Paulo government was entrusted in October to Armando de Sales Oliveira. Vargas had decided to gain the support of his old political enemies even at the cost of alienating some of his earliest allies so that, unlike Deodoro, he would not be faced with unified Paulista opposition to his presidential bid. The assembly was engaged in approving a new constitution and preparing to elect a president for the 1934–1938 term, and Vargas found himself in a strengthened position on both the military side and in the political realm. Senior officers had been retired, and the luster of the *tenentes* was dimmed by the 1933 politicking. Officers loyal to the government in 1932 by now occupied key positions in the command structure. Under these circumstances, an overwhelming majority of Brazil's political leaders saw no real alternative, much less rival or threat, to Vargas in the presidential sweepstakes. Accordingly, in July Vargas was chosen constitutional president by a very comfortable margin. Within the limits of a conveniently ambivalent constitution, he was free to continue with his work of gradual modernization of the Brazilian nation.

The contradictions within the constitution reflected divisions within a body politic in which slightly renovated rural oligarchic structures and liberal constitutionalist movements representing urban bourgeois aspirations coexisted with disparate emerging middle-class elements that had not yet translated their aspirations into viable programs, ideologies, or movements. The core of the 1891 charter and its classical republican institutions were preserved, but grafted on were political reforms dear to the liberal constitutionalists and socioeconomic guarantees demanded by the *tenentes* and their reformist civilian counterparts. Powers of the Senate were curbed—to reduce the influence of small traditional states—and the basis for representation in the Chamber of Deputies was designed to restrict dominance of São Paulo and Minas Gerais. The states' great influence in the legislative branch would lead Vargas to turn to the military as his allies in a struggle to strengthen the national government vis-à-vis state oligarchies.

Transition from dictator to constitutional president meant that Vargas, who had been following a centrist course since coming to office, would need to pay greater attention to the claims of organized political groups. Since he was ineligible to succeed himself, maneuvering for 1938 began with the 1934 congressional balloting and the subsequent indirect election of governors critical to the ambitions of the several aspirants. In all major states the forces supporting the *interventors* emerged on top.

The Vargas Regime

Constitutional government soon fell victim to polarization, which gave Vargas an opportunity to rule Brazil. By 1935 emergence of strong ideological political movements on the Left and Right overshadowed the contest between oligarchical forces and *tenente* reformism that had characterized the politics of the early 1930s. Benefiting from a situation in which Vargas showed no inclination toward building a national party, the Left began to develop the beginnings of a mass base; in reaction a militant ideological movement emerged on the Right. Indeed, the Communist Party and the incipient Brazilian fascist movement possessed ideological underpinnings and potentially charismatic leadership that the *tenentes* lacked. Luís Carlos Prestes and Plínio Salgado by 1935 were capturing the attention of the urban populace. Although Salgado's Integralists were gathering strength during 1934 and 1935, their enemies on the Left were preparing even more rapidly to make a bid for power. In March 1935 the National Liberating Alliance (ANL) was launched as a united front of radical leftist forces including the illegal Brazilian Communist Party (PCB), the radical wing of *tenentism,* and alienated liberal democrats.[6]

The PCB's plans for armed struggle in the name of the ANL were based upon an unrealistic assessment of the situation and undercut by unwillingness of many middle-class radical politicians to undertake such an extreme and risky step. Thus, instead of a mighty explosion, the November 1935 revolt erupted more as a string of firecrackers—a series of local military uprisings easily subdued by the regime. Brief as was the Communist-led revolt of 1935, it would leave an anti-Communist legacy on the part of most of the Brazilian officer corps still highly operative a generation later. Its immediate effects were to strengthen Vargas's hand and to induce a majority of the officer corps to close ranks against the "subversive" Left. It also brought the Catholic Church and propertied interests into alliance with the military to combat all progressive forces that could be viewed as allies of the Communists. Thus, the abortive revolt enabled Vargas to lay the groundwork for his own coup and the establishment of a long-term dictatorship.[7]

The Estado Novo

The year 1937 was the most momentous for Brazil since 1930. While the public's attention was focused upon the contest for Vargas's successor, to be chosen in January 1938, crucial developments were largely behind the scenes, where the president skillfully carried to fruition his undermining of political rivals and creation of a favorable situation among the military. At the end of 1936 he had installed General Eurico Gaspar Dutra as war minister, and soon after Goés Monteiro became army chief of staff. Both the presidential campaign and Vargas's conspiracy to abort it went into high gear in mid-1937 with nominations of Sales and José Américo de Almeida. The former was portrayed by opponents as a Paulista oligarch, the latter as dangerously demagogic. Hence much of the political elite and a growing number of the middle class were susceptible to the idea that the elections should be postponed if a suitable unity candidate could not be found.

Vargas moved astutely to engineer a controlled escalation of the crisis. Polarization was fostered by encouragement of Integralism on the one hand and reactivation of the specter of Communist subversion on the other—through the so called Cohen Plan—replete with vivid detail on the liquidation of anti-Communists, burning of churches, and other violent acts. Although a rank forgery, it induced an atmosphere of near hysteria. On November 10 Congress was closed and the new constitution declared to be in effect. The eight-year run of the "New State" had begun. Its early weeks were filled with initiatives reminiscent of the first moves of the provisional government seven years earlier. Astutely, Vargas portrayed himself as the reluctant dragon who would bring Brazil a "strong government of peace, justice, and work." In reality, he had been aiming toward this moment ever since reconstitutionalization had been forced upon him by the 1932 revolt. He had used *tenentes,* the senior military, the new civilian elites, the old oligarchical machines, the Integralists, and even radical leftists dedicated to his overthrow as he quietly and effectively mobilized discontent against the constitutional system, diverting it away from himself. Thus, he was able in November 1937 to assume the stance of a unifying symbol in a situation where polarization provided salience to both communism and fascism, whereas those rejecting radicalism were divided between the traditional constitutionalism of Sales and the fundamental, often incoherent populism of José Américo.

The 1937 constitution's articles concerning representation and legislation never went into effect. Instead Vargas continued to enjoy complete decree powers augmented by those pertaining to a permanent state of national emergency. The "Communist threat" laid to rest, the only challenge to Vargas's new order came in May 1938 when Integralists joined with some liberal constitutionalist conspirators in a poorly executed coup attempt. Even after this abortive coup, Vargas continued to govern without a political party and made no effort to channel his support into any type of an organized movement. Suspicious that parties might prove a vehicle for the rise of rivals, he also viewed parties as electoral trappings irrelevant to his needs and objectives. His basic political technique of manipulative paternalism shifting toward personalistic populism did not call for new intermediary structures. In this respect Vargas was not innovative, preferring to turn existing forces to his use and destroying those he could not utilize. He also preferred to exploit personal rivalries among leading figures, often turning yesterday's opponents into today's allies rather than coping with institutionalized power contenders.

Vargas did not significantly change his political style or the institutional structure of the Estado Novo during the seven years following the elimination of the Integralists, but Brazil was changing and he adapted pragmatically to altered conditions. The processes of industrialization and urbanization, though not achieving the rate they would in the post–World War II period, were modifying the societal foundations of the polity. As the moratorium on normal political life continued into wartime, shifts in the composition of the electorate, changes in their orientation, or new alliance patterns were not readily apparent but were definitely occurring in reaction to external as well as internal stimuli.

National integration continued to progress, and the federal executive developed capabilities far beyond those of an earlier era. An array of administrative agencies was established to deal with matters previously outside the scope of public policy but now of concern to the centralized, increasingly interventionist state under Vargas. Moreover, a wide variety of government corporations and mixed capital enterprises came into being to play an ever more important role in economic development—along with a network of organizations designed to tie urban workers more closely to the government through both the dependent union movement and a rudimentary social welfare system.

Social and Economic Change Under Vargas

By 1940 the country's population had grown to over 41 million (on its way to 52 million by 1950) with São Paulo surpassing Minas Gerais. Urbanization had progressed in cities: Rio de Janeiro had a population of 1.9 million and São Paulo 1.3

million. During the Vargas period there was a sustained surge of import-substitution industrialization. By 1945 industry's share of GDP was up to 28 percent; agriculture had declined to under 29 percent but still provided nearly two-thirds of employment. Yet with expansion of the incipient intermediate goods industry, by the time of Vargas's departure from power, internal economic activity had replaced external demand as the principal determinant of the accumulation of industrial capital. As a result of these developments, hegemony of the traditional coffee bourgeoisie came to an end as the obverse side of the rise of the new urban, industry-related bourgeoisie. Indeed, diversification was taking place in agriculture as coffee fell from 48 percent of the value of Brazil's agricultural output in the late 1920s to 30 percent for the 1932–1936 period and only a bit over 16 percent between 1939 and 1943.

In contrast to simplicity of the central government during the federalist Old Republic, institutes, autonomous agencies, and consultative councils proliferated. This remained a rather ramshackle and jerry-built structure lacking mechanisms for effective coordination short of the presidency. Yet these agencies fulfilled their primary political purpose, that of "transferring the conflict among the different dominant groups to within the State bureaucracy itself through self-representation of interests in these technical organs."[8] There were multiple interests seeking to influence public policy but after 1937 no legislative arena and no opportunity to mobilize electoral support and bring it to bear upon the executive. Vargas was an astute political balancer, conciliator, and manipulator, and he could concern himself only with the most important matters. In this context there was need to develop structures for linking state and society. With parties ruled out, the answer was a network tying together the Vargas-appointed *interventors*, the growing array of governmental agencies, and the sectoral organizations fostered by the basically corporativist design of the Estado Novo. This arrangement, as ably orchestrated by Vargas, provided a means for accommodating emerging interests while at the same time easing the decline of traditional elites by continuing to provide them with opportunity to influence decisions most vital to their economic interests. Centralization was made more palatable by furnishing a widening variety of groups with new avenues of access to policymaking and implementation above the working level. The resulting system of co-optative clientelism enhanced the viability of the Vargas-designed system by channeling concerns of politically relevant elements into narrow struggles over policy in particular areas—hence away from questions of the regime's basic orientation and underlying priorities.

Governmental capabilities of the executive grew from 1930 through 1937 and on to 1945—accompanied by increasing penetration of at least the urban, modernizing sectors of society. As the central government came to affect the lives of a larger proportion of the population directly, more frequently, and in a wider variety of ways, the regime built a multiclass base, even if this was not reflected in the sphere of political organization. Hence, although there was very little mobilization, the foundation for a future move in this direction was laid.

World War II, however, was the most important factor in Vargas's maintenance of effective power and authority vis-à-vis the armed forces. It not only enabled him to channel military energies into the war effort while rallying popular support in the name of national defense but also provided opportunity for sending many of the more activist officers to the United States for training and, subsequently, to combat in Italy. Furthermore, the armed forces were satisfied with the new equipment they received from the United States and the favorable position relative to Argentina that Brazil came to enjoy. This would be jeopardized by any move against Vargas, who skillfully exploited the image of President Roosevelt's valued ally in the hemisphere.

The War and Vargas's Fall

World War II was to have a profound impact upon the Brazilian armed forces, especially officers of the *tenente* generation. Among the key figures undergoing shift from a position of sympathy for Hitler's Germany to being proponents of hemispheric solidarity and eventually champions of liberal democracy were both Dutra and Góes Monteiro.[9] The first phase of this transformation accompanied that of Vargas himself; the second carried them to the point of joining the movement to oust the dictator from power—in part to negate the danger of being dragged down with him in the face of growing opinion that a return to representative government was overdue. The Brazilian Expeditionary Force (FEB) also had a profound influence in reshaping the outlook of a major portion of the Brazilian military. A reinforced division that arrived in Italy in 1944 sustained over 450 combat deaths. Its heroic reputation would give its veterans leverage in the political maneuvering that characterized the second half of 1945. In alliance with important civilian groups, one wing of them would be instrumental in forcing Vargas from office within a few months of their return home.

By 1943 Vargas was aware that the Estado Novo could not carry over into the postwar era without major modifications. In the wake of Allied victory, pressures for return to competitive politics might well be irresistible. Hence the regime would need a political organization capable of mobilizing public support for an eventual contest at the polls. Building upon the foundation of amplified social programs for urban workers and the government's close control over their unions, Vargas began to organize a machine that could rapidly be transformed into a party. At the same time, the dictator's public pronouncements took on an increasingly populist tone mixed with nationalist exhortations. Industrialization became the touchstone of a diffuse program designed to appeal to workers, urban commercial and entrepreneurial interests, government employees, and—of course—the military.

Vargas hoped he would be able to ride out the growing pressures toward ending his arbitrary rule and retain power as he had when faced by demands for constitutionalization in 1932 and again when the question of presidential succession arose in 1937. But the introduction of military contenders destroyed the parallel with 1937, as Dutra could not be used and pushed aside as easily as had been the case with José Américo, and Gomes possessed great support in the armed forces and popular prestige that Sales had sorely lacked. Determined that if he could not hold on to power directly, it must pass to his allies and supporters rather than to his critics, Vargas demonstrated resourcefulness in playing out his losing hand. Through adroit maneuvering he retained a great deal of initiative over the course of affairs until the very end and left office in a way that maximized his possibilities for mounting a political comeback.

On April 7 representatives of all political currents opposed to Vargas had founded the National Democratic Union (UDN).[10] The next day the Social Democratic Party (PSD) was launched, and the *interventors* took up the work of organizing the state political establishments into branches of the new party. At the end of May, Vargas convoked elections for December 2 for president and Congress. Nominated by the PSD on July 17, Dutra stepped down as war minister shortly thereafter and was succeeded by Góes Monteiro. Vargas's chief interest came to focus upon the newly formed Brazilian Labor Party (PTB), a vehicle for channeling support from the government-controlled unions. By yielding to the irresistible, Vargas was able to depart from office with honor and dignity and, even more important for his political future, without having opened an irreparable breach with the armed forces. Thus, Supreme Court head José Linhares assumed the presidency on October 30. The Estado Novo was at its end.

The Democratic Interregnum and Vargas Again

Whereas corporatism had been woven deeply into the fabric of the Brazilian nation between 1930 and 1945, the subsequent decade would bring the development of populism, nationalism, and developmentalism. Vargas would continue to be the central figure in the events of this period, both in person and through his legacy and political heirs, continuing to cast a long shadow over Brazilian politics. Even the 1946–1950 period would be more a pause than a sharp change of course, in large part because of the carryover momentum of the processes of economic and social change stimulated during Vargas's fruitful 1930–1945 stewardship. Indeed, Vargas's ouster in 1945 was largely a reaction by the old landowning and mercantile elite in alliance with the middle class against this process of change, which threatened to undermine the viability of continued conservative dominance of politics and use of the state to further their interests. The middle class itself was undergoing a transformation at this juncture with entrance of a new generation of technical and administratively oriented personnel and a "new intelligentsia" concerned with development problems. These insecure elements of the middle class feared the possibility of losing their recent gains as a consequence of the rise of the working class and extension of expensive social benefits to them.

Governments from the reelection of Vargas in 1950 through the overthrow of João Goulart in 1964 would be based upon a loose coalition of industrialists, the commercial sectors linked to the internal market, the technical elements of the middle class, and the organized sector of the urban working class. But it would be the military—with the support of the more traditional component of the middle class as well as conservative interests—who would intervene repeatedly when the process of development threatened to bring significant socioeconomic changes. Progressive forces failed to create a new party, resting instead upon the inadequate basis of the Vargas-forged alliance between the PSD, strong in Congress, and the PTB, which had popular support in urban areas. The middle class, more concerned with its patronage positions than with radical changes in the system, had failed to fulfill a revolutionary role in the 1930s, and in the post-war period it permitted consolidation of democratic forms without social contents.

Even after hounding him to his grave in 1954, Vargas's opponents could only engineer a temporary detour, and a brief year and a half later his political heirs would reclaim control and resume headway along the course Vargas had charted 1930–1945 and refined during the early 1950s. Yet they would meet a hard wall: the continued obstruction of any progress in rural Brazil by determined political elements closely linked to the old agrarian interests and entrenched in the governmental machinery. The intransigent Right was greatly aided by the gross overrepresentation of the less developed rural states and the increasingly grotesque underrepresentation of states that were most advanced economically and socially and politically progressing—especially São Paulo. Thus land tenure remained virtually unchanged, and the rural working population was excluded from effective political participation and the benefits of a limited welfare state.

Dutra and the Conservative Republic

Brazil's return to constitutional ways began, as had the republic and the post-1930 experiments, with civilian political groups indebted to the military for having ousted the "decadent" regime. Moreover, Dutra's election depended more upon the durability of forces entrenched in control of the majority of states plus the urban masses responsive to Vargas's populist appeals than upon anything the nominee said or did. Hence when the December 2 results were tabulated, Dutra had defeated the UDN's Eduardo Gomes by better than three to two (3.3 million to 2 million) with the Communist nominee trailing far behind with a respectable 570,000 votes. Dutra was a majority choice of the quite restricted electorate, but over three-fifths of his margin came from Rio Grande do Sul and São Paulo with much of the rest run up in Minas Gerais.

Dutra, a sixty-year-old career officer experienced in the intraregime politics of the Vargas era, took office on January 31, 1946, as Brazil's first popularly elected chief executive in over fifteen years. Owing to his cautious nature, Brazil failed to receive strong or imaginative presidential leadership during this crucial period of transition from a relatively closed discretionary regime toward an open, competitive, and representative system. Meeting with constituent powers on February 8, Congress took until mid-September to produce a constitution designed to curb the executive's powers and to guarantee the preservation of federalism while providing an institutional framework for continued national integration and development. Most significant in the January 1947 state election was the victory in São Paulo of Adhemar de Barros, who had engineered the merger of three small splinter movements into the Social Progressive Party (PSP).

During Dutra's term parties were still in their infancy, and thus schisms, mergers, and realignments were routine occurrences. At the same time, Vargas's continuation as the potentially dominant figure for two of the three major parties drastically inhibited their development along modern programmatic lines or into institutionalized vehicles for political mobilization. Anti-Vargism was the unifying factor and guiding principle of the UDN; the power-oriented PSD remained tied to the former dictator. Thus policy differences would be subordinated to emotional issues of Vargism, and divisions stemming from Estado Novo days would override class and interest similarities between much of the UDN and the PSD—keeping the latter in increasingly uneasy alliance with the PTB.

The PSD, preeminently the party of the political "ins," supplied the majority in the 1946–1950 Congress, occupied most executive positions in Dutra's cabinet, and controlled the greater proportion of state administrations. Essentially non-ideological, it combined dominant rural machines of the post-1930 period with businessmen and industrialists who had benefited from Vargas's increasing orientation toward objectives of economic development. A high proportion of the new bureaucratic elite whose numbers multiplied through the expansion of government activities during the Vargas era also leaned toward the PSD, whose ranks were swelled by those seeking advantage from being associated with the administration party in Brazil's patronage-oriented *cartorial* state. These groups wanted more of what they had been receiving from Vargas, and they pressed Dutra for favors and increased support for programs beneficial to their interests.

In its early years the UDN was almost as distinctively an alliance of political "outs" as the PSD was a coalition of the holders of power. With bifactionalism by far the predominant pattern on the local level in rural areas, the UDN label was often adopted in 1945 by the political chief of the clan that was not linked to the state *interventor*'s power structure—which at times brought the largest and most reactionary landowners into the UDN. Moreover, in the cities the UDN was supported heavily by commercial-industrial interests and contained especially high proportions of bankers, administrators of large companies, and offspring of prestigious families. The PSD attracted middle-class voters tied to the expanding government bureaucracy; the UDN recruited heavily from among the professional men and white-collar employees of the private sector. Initially strong among intellectuals and students, in the larger cities the UDN represented a classically liberal tendency, but on social and economic issues it came increasingly under the influence of its conservative rural constituents.

At the beginning of Dutra's term, the PTB was more significant for its potential than its existing strength; it was an effective electoral force only in the major industrial centers. Yet few politicians could be blind to the fact that with the continued mobilization of urban groups and the development of the working class, it would almost surely continue to grow.

Governing with little opposition from the UDN, Dutra strove to establish the basis for long-term stability. In his eyes the threat to order came from the Communists, so the PCB was ruled illegal, the Brazilian Workers' Confederation (CTB) was closed down, and diplomatic relations with the Soviet Union were severed. Thus, the Dutra years were a period of lost opportunities for lasting consolidation of the transition from authoritarian rule. Many of the vices of the Estado Novo were eliminated, but its virtues were also lost, and some of the least desirable features of the pre-Vargas system reemerged. Instead of liberal democracy being legitimized by its achievements, its shortcomings were underscored by a policy of drift and accommodation with retrograde forces.

Indeed, return to regular elections and a functioning Congress enabled the old agricultural interests through their controlled voters to regain much of the power they had held before 1937—if not before 1930. Hence the "conservative" republic turned out to be marked by immobility. Large agriculturalists and associated mercantile interests strove to preserve an economic order based on export of agricultural products and unhindered access to imported manufactured goods, whereas business, banking, and an emerging industrial sector demanded fiscal policies promoting industrialization and tariff protection for their products. Despite unimaginative government policies, the annual real GDP increase under Dutra averaged 6 percent, fully double the rate of population growth.

The conservative character of the Dutra government reflected the dominant orientation of senior officers during the late 1940s, an outlook that was increasingly out of step with the more nationalist and developmentalist views of many of the younger military generation. Heavily imbued with a legalist tradition, in contrast with the political activism of the *tenentes* immediately preceding them, officers who had gone through the military academy in the late 1920s and early 1930s frequently took Captain Henrique Duffles Teixeira Lott as their model nonpolitical career soldier. A few years later this role came to be filled by Major Humberto de Alencar Castelo Branco. The 1950 Military Club elections centered on an issue parallel to one in the concurrent presidential campaign, economic nationalism—a theme upon which Vargas was placing increasing emphasis in his quest to mobilize popular support for a return to power as constitutional president. In the realities of Brazilian politics, the attitude of the armed forces was as important as that of the electorate, since the former could effectively veto Vargas's candidacy. The victory of the nationalist slate removed this threat to Vargas's comeback.

Vargas's Encore

On April 19, 1950, his sixty-seventh birthday, Vargas accepted a PTB draft, having already reached a bargain with Adhemar de Barros for PSP support. Thoroughly understanding the PSD politicians, most of whom had been his collaborators during the Estado Novo, Vargas used his influence within the PSD to assure the selection of a weak candidate with an appeal limited to the same sectors as that of the UDN standard-bearer. Moreover, capitalizing upon the appeal of his name to their constituents, Vargas made deals with PSD legislative and gubernatorial candidates for PTB votes in return for their support in the presidential balloting. His chief agent in this work was the young and little known João Goulart, destined to become Vargas's protégé and successor as leader of the PTB. Although PSD candidates were victorious in most of the country, Vargas carried seventeen states plus the Federal District with 3.9 million votes (nearly 49 percent) to 2.3 million (almost 30 percent) for Gomes and fewer than 1.7 million (better than 21 percent) for the demoralized PSD nomineee.[11]

The marriage of the predominantly rural-based traditionalist PSD and the largely urban, development-oriented PTB that Vargas constructed would survive, albeit with mutual infidelity and bickering, until the 1964 revolution. The blend of clientelistic and populist politics inaugurated by Vargas shaped the PTB and deeply affected the PSD despite repeated efforts to introduce programmatic or ideological content into these parties. The proportions of the mix were to vary as the PTB grew in strength relative to the PSD and developmentalists and reformers increased within their ranks.

Accustomed to governing relatively free from restraints, Vargas was not comfortable operating within an institutional structure designed to minimize his freedom of action. Moreover, Dutra's narrow interpretation of presidential powers created a situation in which each move by Vargas to provide strong presidential leadership was criticized as an indication of "dictatorial" proclivities. Thus, although his administration got off to a good start during 1951, tensions subsequently built up, with the opposition suspicious of the motives behind Vargas's every initiative. In turn the president was impatient with shortsighted obstruction of policies designed to modernize the nation and attacks upon his evolutionary approach to social welfare for the urban working class.

As he entered the presidency for his final term, Vargas wished to function as the manipulator of existing political interests as well as mediator between these and emergent groups. Preferring to let contending political forces articulate issues and policy alternatives, he remained the resourceful conciliator but found himself obliged to pursue an ambivalent policy. Vargas began his presidency in a relatively favorable economic situation, but this would soon deteriorate. He had catered during the campaign to a wide variety of regional economic interests and was faced with the task of making industrialization and diversification common denominators for national economic policy. Aided by the demand for Brazilian exports spurred by the Korean War, he was able to win reasonably broad acceptance of a return to a more active economic role for the state, including a significant degree of government planning.

Given the Truman administration's willingness to provide technical assistance for basic planning studies, Vargas initially accepted the established rules of the international economic system, turning a deaf ear to radical nationalists. At the same time, he maintained his populist stance by advocating measures of economic nationalism. Near the end of 1951 Vargas submitted a bill to Congress creating a mixed capital corporation to explore and exploit Brazil's oil resources. Thus, the military's running debate on the oil question came to center around the administration's proposal, making this a divisive issue within the armed forces.

Even during this period of moderate and democratic behavior by Vargas, important leaders outside the regime's power scheme launched a strong campaign against its military pillars. In 1951 the alignment within the three services shifted markedly over the question of Brazil's stance toward the Korean conflict. This impingement of international considerations led to serious deterioration in Vargas's military *dispositivo*, which was built upon the leftist nationalist faction of the army. The dominant military faction advocated cooperation with the United States and was sensitive to the freedom the Communists seemed to be enjoying.

Discord and Polarization

Radicalization of political life took place during the latter half of 1953. The armed forces not only once again suspected Vargas of harboring continuist objectives, but this time felt he had the backing of Argentine strongman Juan Perón.[12] Spearheaded by the biting press and radio attacks of UDN Congressman Carlos Lacerda, Vargas's opponents lambasted the government for its reopening of the labor movement to Communist penetration as well as incompetence and corruption.[13] As would again be the case in the early 1960s, inflation served as the catalyst of social tensions and raised dilemmas of financial policy the administration had sought to avoid, which made it necessary to disappoint groups Vargas was seeking to court. Wage restraints and credit restrictions, essential for economic reasons, undercut Vargas's efforts to build up political support among labor and the new industrialists. The cost of living in 1952 had risen 21 percent—nearly double the rate in preceding years—and was threatening to go higher. The middle class was squeezed by the hike in prices, and labor called for more substantial wage increases rather than kind words. Thus, wage policy was to prove a critical factor in the collapse of Vargas's conciliatory strategy and the replacement of compromise by confrontation during 1954.

Vargas's problems were accentuated by change of administrations in the United States. Willingness to use public funds to aid Brazil's development was replaced by a policy of insisting that U.S. private investment would do the job if the Brazilian government would only create a sufficiently attractive climate. Opposition to the Petrobrás law was openly expressed as private U.S. interests attacked it as Communist-inspired. Vargas reacted by increasing the nationalistic tenor of his pronouncements. Such a tactic of attributing Brazil's economic troubles to external forces made political sense in diverting resentment stemming from austerity. Yet this stress on nationalism, which struck a responsive chord among the urban workers and middle sectors, did not prove to be the unifying force its advocates expected.

By the end of 1953 there was a propaganda war going on between rightist opponents of the government and those on the other side of the spectrum who hoped to turn anti–foreign capital sentiment against the domestic capitalist system. Conservatives for their part strove to drive a wedge between the urban middle sectors and the working class by depicting the political rise of the latter as a threat to the former and by grossly exaggerating the extent of the Communist menace. The backbone of the anti-Vargas movement was an alliance of the UDN with the strongly anti-Communist wing of the armed forces. At the beginning of 1954 the military was divided much as it would be a decade later, with attitudes on legalism partially crosscutting those on nationalism. Events of the ensuing eight months would move the armed forces closer to consensus on the need to exercise the moderating power once again, but not resolved were differences on major questions of national policy, particularly in the economic and social realms.[14]

An institution that brought civilian politicians, journalists, and businessmen together with officers of all the services, the National War College (ESG) was the arena for development of a doctrine of national security that saw Brazil's future as firmly allied with the Western Christian world in its confrontation with the Communist bloc. Among the ESG students in 1954 was Lacerda, who there cemented his close ties with a group of rising young anti-Communist officers and who would emerge as detonator of the fatal crisis. An August 5 attempt on his life unleashed a process that would instead cost the president his life. A military-run investigation traced the attempt to individuals linked to the presidency, in the process giving the public a look at some of the unsavory types found there as well as uncovering a wide variety of shady dealings in which Vargas's cronies and advisers were involved.

When leading generals rejected his offer to take a temporary leave, Vargas responded by shooting himself. At his bedside was found a brief document roundly condemning the "international economic and financial groups" that had thwarted his efforts to emancipate the Brazilian nation and brought irresistible pressure upon the Brazilian economy. Vargas had avoided the final humiliation of a second deposition through his suicide and the shrewdly designed political testament. From a tragic failure he was immediately transformed into a patriotic martyr. Instead of mass demonstrations against his regime, the country was swept by a wave of attacks upon his enemies and symbols of U.S. imperialism.

The Quest for Development
and Democracy: 1955–1960

Even after the 1945 reestablishment of representative politics, personalities continued to take precedence over programs. Alongside still relatively effective clientelistic politics, new types of populist leaders were called forth by the situation, filling the vacuum resulting from the elimination of the one ideological party of the Left, the PCB. The basically conservative orientation of the major political parties and the heavy, if not predominant, rural influence in their leadership prevented any close identification of urban voters with them. Hence, the masses turned instead to a direct link between their votes and a political leader with some significant degree of charisma. Clientelism continued as the basis for holding the middle class to established political leadership and existing parties in terms of an exchange of votes for employment or favors. But it could not work for the urban masses as the electorate ballooned beyond the patronage potential of the *cartorial* state. From 1 million in 1908 and 2.7 million for the 1934 balloting, the electorate passed 7.4 million by 1945—and would grow even faster thereafter.

With Vargas gone from the stage he had dominated for a quarter century, the peculiarly Brazilian form of populism, combining features of urban machine politics with personalism, emotional appeals, and effective performance in the material realm, assumed several distinct forms. In addition to the labor-oriented nationalism of Vargas less aptly carried on by Goulart, there was the crusading anti-Communist zeal of Lacerda and his mystique of intransigent oppositionism in a system where opportunism and accommodation predominated. Centered in São Paulo was the conservative brand of Adhemar de Barros, whose style blended massive public works expenditures with demagogic campaigning and exploitation of graft and patronage for electoral ends. Its antithesis was the moralistic messianism of Jânio Quadros, the ascetic giant-killer capitalizing on popular desires for an end to the corruption and controversy of Vargism and Adhemarism. Although Juscelino Kubitschek—greatest of the post-Vargas leaders—relied more upon developmentalism and nationalism than populism, the period of his administration (1956–1960) witnessed the introduction of new varieties of populism to fill the vacuum left by Vargas's death. Leonel Brizola modernized the *trabalhista* (appeal to workers) line by adding a more ideological brand of nationalism and, like Lacerda, effectively exploiting the new medium of television to transcend the limitations of communication with the masses on the basis of personal appearances. These strains of populism shared an appeal to the poorly assimilated mass urban population being fed by heavy migration from the countryside and plagued by the insecurities of city life as well as dissatisfaction with its level of living in the midst of sustained, dramatic development. Restless, but largely nonradical, the middle sectors also gave substantial support to populist politicians.

The Café Filho Government and Return to Normalcy

Tension between pro- and anti-Vargas forces dominated the political scene. Vice President João Café Filho's administration, composed of a mixture of nearly all non-Vargist political forces including the Dutra wing of the PSD, assumed a caretaker role. This was in keeping with the country being in the advanced stages of campaigning for October 1954 legislative and partial gubernatorial elections and the presidential balloting only a little over a year away. Most of Café Filho's military scheme was composed of officers active in Vargas's ouster; Lott was brought in as war minister. The outcome of the October 3 elections, held only forty days after Vargas's death, was surprisingly normal, with results a stand-off between Vargas heirs and foes. In many states the PTB and UDN allied as if Vargas's blood was not between them, in disregard of the PSD-PTB coalition in Congress. As usual, the chief concern of politicians was winning, and national issues took a back seat to local questions and alliances of convenience. When the dust settled, the PSD held on to its dominant position with 114 Chamber of Deputies seats, the PTB edged up to 56, and the UDN slipped to 74. Thus Café Filho and his successors would have to govern until February 1959 with a Congress little changed from that elected with Vargas in 1950.

Brazil was to have no respite from campaigning; maneuvering was already under way for the next year's presidential sweepstakes. Once the PTB allied with the PSD behind Kubitschek on the basis of Goulart for vice president, ranking *tenente* Juarez do Nascimento Fernandes Távora accepted nomination by the Christian Democratic Party (PDC) with the UDN as the long leg of the coalition. With Adhemar de Barros also making a determined bid, the elections gave a slim plurality to Kubitschek and Goulart with the former receiving nearly 3.1 million votes—almost 470,000 more than Juarez Távora. Kubitschek's home-state victory in Minas Gerais by some 430,000 votes nearly equaled his national plurality; overall, "Juscelino" (as Kubitschek was known) received only 34 percent of the total presidential vote cast—a record 9.1 million votes.

Lott had by this time become the dominant army figure. On November 8 the military ministers were informed of Café Filho's intention, owing to a mild heart attack, to turn the presidential office over temporarily to Carlos Luz—presiding officer of the Chamber of Deputies and a rival of Kubitschek within Minas Gerais politics. Lott seized control of the government on the assumption that an anti-Kubitschek conspiracy was afoot. Reaction to this smoothly executed military action was minimal, and on November 11 the PSD-PTB majority in Congress voted Luz's "impediment." Senate presiding officer Nereu Ramos accepted the figurehead presidency.

Juscelino Kubitschek de Oliveira, the grandson of a Czech immigrant, earned a unique place in Brazilian history by enjoying greater popularity at the end of his mandate than at the beginning. His successes caught most observers by surprise.[15] But Kubitschek brought to the tasks of reestablishing stability and putting the country squarely on the road to development all the legendary facility for political maneuvering and compromise of an experienced Mineiro politician. This was coupled with a solid background of experience as mayor of Brazil's third city and governor of its second state. He also possessed both a penchant for building and a blueprint for the construction of a modern Brazilian nation.

His Program of Goals (Programa de Metas) set ambitious targets, promising "fifty years' progress in five" and emphasizing transportation, energy, manufacturing, and construction of a new capital in the sparsely settled interior. It offered something to nearly every relevant group, with its long-run effect one of consolidating Brazil's industrialization by building up the requisite infrastructure while implanting heavy industry—especially automotive—and fostering a capital goods sector. Essentially a dynamic and pragmatic centrist, Kubitschek gave economic development marked priority over social welfare measures.

This prototype of the Brazilian "amiable man," whose political centrism and conciliatory style made few enemies, carefully avoided the kind of confrontation that had cost Vargas his office and life. In tacit alliance with landowning forces so powerful within his PSD, he left their economic and political interests untouched in exchange for a free hand in promoting industry and some steps toward modernization of urban society. But the painless economic growth of Kubitschek's years could not be duplicated—owing to the limits reached on import-substitution industrialization and the high level of inflation that was the negative side of his legacy. Hence, successor administrations faced hard and politically divisive choices that he was able to avoid.

Lott constituted a strong bulwark against the continued refusal of some UDN elements to accept the new administration as legitimate, but he also infringed upon the president's authority and freedom of action. Yet Kubitschek managed progressively to exert his leadership within the government during the course of 1957. Emphasis upon growth, moderate nationalism, and conciliation did much to dispel lingering suspicions among the centrist majority of the officer corps. Kubitschek's infectious enthusiasm for Brazil's future disarmed all but the most hardened of his opponents and moved the country closer to a national consensus on many basic issues than had existed since before the 1920s. Even the construc-

Brazilian congressional building (photo courtesy of the Brazilian Foreign Ministry)

tion of a new capital, Brasília, on the interior plateau a thousand miles northwest of Rio de Janeiro contributed to the new national psychology and caught the imagination of a large proportion of the military as well as of the civilian populace. Criticism by the far Left removed much of the lingering distrust on the part of conservative elements stemming from his alliance with Goulart as well as his Communist support in the 1955 campaign.

Development, Democracy, and Resistance to U.S. Pressure

The Kubitschek period, apex of reasonably functioning representative politics down to the present, was not without controversy and an active and often effective opposition. But in contrast with what was to come as well as with the past, this was kept within the bounds of normal political competition. The UDN finally settled down into routine criticism and minor obstructionism; radical leftist and ultranationalist elements were generally unable to mobilize strong opposition. Repeatedly Kubitschek assumed a stance just nationalistic enough to take some of the wind from their sails, and the high rate of economic growth—around 7 percent each year—allowed for substantial wage concessions to the urban working class without disturbing the highly satisfactory profits of the business and industrial sectors. Stabilization efforts were aimed at pulling inflation back to tolerable levels without even seriously sacrificing development. A master in use of patronage as a means of political persuasion, Kubitschek dealt with all but the most radical extremes of Left and Right as potential allies and collaborators rather than confirmed opponents.

Congressional elections of October 1958 (with gubernatorial balloting in half the states) came at a time when financial problems that were to plague the administration for the rest of its term were not yet out of hand. The 326-member Chamber of Deputies chosen to serve for the last two years of Kubitschek's term and the first years of his successor's was little changed from that elected four years earlier. The outcome of state races had important implications for the future, particularly the election of Leonel Brizola as governor of Rio Grande do Sul and the defeat of Adhemar de Barros by Quadros's candidate in São Paulo.[16]

After the elections a new phase opened characterized by marked progress toward fulfillment of Kubitschek's development goals, an ever-increasing rate of inflation (which brought with it international complications and domestic social tensions), adoption of a more active foreign policy, and the beginnings of maneuvering with regard to succession. Influenced by the rising cost of living and Fidel Castro's coming to power in Cuba, the Nationalist Parliamentary Front (FPN), the supraparty within Congress founded in 1957 by a majority of the PTB deputies and the leftist elements of other parties, came to play an important role in setting the tone for consideration of economic and foreign policy matters.

In this changed environment, the stiffening of the attitudes of U.S. and international financial institutions led to tensions in U.S.-Brazilian relations that foreshadowed disagreements that were to mark the subsequent Goulart period. A high rate of investment and economic growth did not prove compatible with price stability, and the structuralist-monetarist controversy, which had been previewed under Vargas and sidestepped by the Café Filho administration, was joined full force: The Brazilian government feared possible stagnation; the sources of financial assistance, particularly the U.S. government, stressed the overriding dangers of inflation.

The situation in mid-1959 was aggravated by failure of the United States to respond positively to Kubitschek's proposal, first formulated in May 1958, for a joint crusade against underdevelopment in the hemisphere. Kubitschek viewed this Operation Pan-American as a statesmanlike initiative to meet Latin America's obvious priority problems and to undercut communism by eliminating its breeding ground. Kubitschek was unwilling to back away from his commitment to industrialization and was concerned over attacks from the Left. Hence he was not inclined to take further steps insisted upon by the U.S. government and the International Monetary Fund (IMF). Instead he opted for continued development at all costs, blaming foreign obstructionism for the upsurge in inflation that followed. Thus, U.S. policy, which called for providing only enough external assistance to maintain Brazil on a fairly even keel, ran up against far greater determination on Kubitschek's part than had been foreseen. Inside Brazil the consensus on developmental nationalism that had been skillfully built up in the 1956–1958 period began to disintegrate in the face of political polemics between economic liberals' advocacy of orthodox fiscal measures and radical nationalists' attacks on foreign capital and external influences.

This shift toward a more Vargas-like policy was sealed in June 1959 when Kubitschek broke off negotiations with the IMF. From a pragmatic political viewpoint, he had little choice, for following the tough stabilization line insisted upon by the IMF would almost surely have brought him to the end of his term without having fulfilled his promises in the development field. This would have left his successor to benefit from the country's sanitized finances at the expense of Kubitschek's ambitions for a second term in 1965. The dramatic strategy he adopted, in contrast, rallied support around the goal of development, depicted the rising cost of living as the result of U.S. unwillingness to accord Brazil the consideration it merited, and projected him as a fearless patriot.

Presidential Succession

Such a forceful assertion of independence clearly suited the new and more nationalistic mood that was a by-product of Kubitschek's successful campaign to demonstrate to his compatriots that they were capable of determining their own destiny. Indeed, the president's prestige and personal popularity remained high and may well even have continued to grow during his last year in office because the Brazil Kubitschek prepared to hand over had changed a great deal since the end of World War II and the Estado Novo. Population was up to 70 million with over 31 million classified as urban dwellers. Life expectancy was nearing fifty-three (compared to under forty-three around 1940), and infant mortality had dropped from 145 per 1,000 live births in the 1940s to around 117. The doubling of industrial production during his term was reflected in the presence of 2.9 million employees of industry in the labor force of more than 22.7 million—a significant rise from 1.6 million in 1940. By 1960 industry accounted for 25 percent of GDP, compared to 23 percent for agriculture.[17] Total nonagricultural employment had shot up from 6.7 million in 1950 to over 10.3 million—twice the increase in agricultural employment.

Income was still unevenly distributed with nearly 40 percent going to the highly favored top one-tenth of the population, 36 percent to the next 30 percent, and only 25 percent to the bottom three-fifths of the social pyramid. But Kubitschek had done much to build a base for development on a scale assuring that in the future there would be something more adequate to distribute. Growth in GDP had slowed in 1956 to only 2.9 percent, chiefly as a result of the drift and hesitation during the latter part of 1955. Over the next five years—the span of Kubitschek's responsibility—the economy expanded in real terms at an annual rate of 8.3 percent, for a per capita gain above 5 percent a year.

In the process, Kubitschek doubled iron production to 7.5 million tons a year; raised steel-making capacity from less than 1.2 million to over 2.5 million tons; expanded oil production from a token 5,500 to 82,000 barrels a day; and upped refining from 108,000 to 308,000 barrels daily (by 1961). He increased installed electrical generating capacity from 3,000 to 4,750 megawatts, had projects under construction that would bring this to 8,500 by 1965, and built from scratch an automotive industry that produced 321,000 vehicles in 1960. Thus, the Kubitschek years did mark consolidation of industrialization in Brazil and provide a foundation for the post-1967 economic takeoff. First, however, three years of poor management of the economy in the midst of renewed political instability would lead to overturning of the political system Kubitschek's adroitness and economic successes had bolstered.

By 1960 the balance in the PSD-PTB alliance had shifted to a point where the latter demanded a greater say in picking the presidential candidate, with his nationalist credentials of key importance. But the candidate selected—Lott—lacked popular appeal. Hence the electorate's hopes came to rest upon Quadros, a new and exciting type of populist politician who promised to reform or dismantle the system rather than manipulate it. Viewed by many as a political messiah, he pledged to sweep out the accumulated corruption and inefficiency of three decades of the Vargas succession while setting Brazil's administrative house in order, maintaining the momentum of development, and remembering the little people whose interests had been largely neglected by Kubitschek's emphasis upon infrastructual growth over social development. Disappointment bordering on betrayal of these hopes when the providential man fled from the challenge after a few short months lent depth to the crises of the 1962–1964 period and contributed to a pernicious radicalization as some sought in doctrinaire programs or ideology the remaking of institutions and practices that the demagogic populist leader so roundly failed to deliver.

Before being catapulted to national prominence by his upset victory over Adhemar de Barros in the 1954 São Paulo governorship contest, Quadros had risen from the obscurity of a secondary-school teacher in only a few brief years. In sharp contrast to Kubitschek's step-by-step rise through the PSD machine, Quadros relied upon a charismatic appeal and highly unorthodox campaign techniques in which he frequently changed party labels in order to build an image and a following transcending the lines of Brazil's fragmented political organizations. The October 3, 1960, voting carried him into the presidency with nearly 5.6 million votes to Lott's fewer than 3.8 million and Adhemar de Barros's distant third of almost 2.2 million. In amassing a record plurality, he carried all of Brazil's major states—something neither Dutra, Vargas, nor Kubitschek had been able to accomplish.[18] At the same, time Goulart narrowly achieved reelection as vice president.

Crises, Compromise, and Radicalization: 1961–1962

The positive heritage left by Kubitschek was dissipated by his successors, which paved the way for the most dismal decade in Brazil's life as a nation—1963 to 1973. Underlying the political decay of the early 1960s was tension between modernizing sectors of Brazilian society and those opposed to fundamental change in the patrimonial order—rooted in clientelism, co-optation, and the *cartorial* state—that had successfully withstood both the 1930 revolution and the postwar "reestablishment of democracy." The progressives were concentrated in the center-south; conservative traditional forces were still dominant in the northeast and north. This cleavage proved resistant to efforts to bridge it through formulas for accommodation and compromise and resulted in polarization as direct popular election of the president gave more advanced sectors a major voice in choosing the executive, but the continued gross overrepresentation of the most backward states guaranteed at least veto group power for traditional conservative forces.

In short, economic development had by the early 1960s so transformed urban Brazilian society that old rules of the patrimonial political game no longer applied. But these changes had not yet reached the hinterlands, still the locus of power because of the grotesque congressional underrepresentation of the most populous states. At the local and state level of the northeast, north, and center-west, the patrimonial political structures proved resistant to the limited reflections there of the ongoing economic and social transformation of the area below the eighteenth parallel. Moreover, co-optation, rather than true representation, was rooted in the fact that strong governmental structures had been established before mobilization of social groups. From this stemmed repeated electoral victories at the state level that enabled these rural-based conservative elites to exert heavy influence, if not always control, within the decentralized national structures of the UDN and PSD. Thus, at the national level patronage politics survived in the face of sustained economic growth and modernizing influences in society. With parties incapable of representing group interests, the latter expressed themselves through their respective "class" organizations, unions, and commercial associations. Inadequately organized, the middle classes would come to view the army as defender of their basic interests, a shift leading to a breakdown of the developmentalist coalition of forces that had functioned effectively during the Kubitschek era.

In this context, political issues, particularly those with deep social and economic roots, proved highly divisive during the Quadros presidency and became positively indigestible through the Goulart years. Agrarian interests demonstrated ability to find allies in Congress for efforts to thwart executive initiatives; when in 1963 and 1964 they found themselves dislodged from the levers of political power and facing the prospect of major changes for the rural sector becoming law, they responded by doing away with electoral and legislative processes that no longer served their purposes. To accomplish this they needed to convince centrist elements of the desirability of putting an end to "demagogic" politics by force. Their allies within the armed forces did the same vis-à-vis moderates in that decisive institution because there was a well-defined military nucleus frustrated by the fact that every time they had pushed Vargas and his heirs out of power (1945, 1954, and 1960), the "misguided" electorate quickly opened the door for their return (1950, 1955, and 1961).

The Quadros Regime: A Peaceful Revolution Fails

Quadros emphasized gravity of financial problems and woeful state of the administrative machinery. Knowing that his measures would encounter strong opposition from entrenched interests and offend some of his backers, Quadros realized that he needed to develop new links between his government and the people whose hopes were deposited in him. He had little idea, however, of how to accomplish this task. When he moved into the field of pressing economic and financial measures, Quadros encountered the dilemma of arousing the ire of important interests without gaining more public support. Congress, accustomed to the concern for its interests and sensibilities shown by Kubitschek, resented Quadros's technique of neglecting it, appealing over its head to the public, and chastising it for obstructionism.

The issue that precipitated the August 1961 crisis was a foreign policy matter only indirectly involving the Congress. Aware that his economic policies would prove highly unpopular with the Left and organized labor in particular, Quadros set out to offset this and partially neutralize the opposition leaning of these groups by following a dramatically nationalist, independent line in foreign affairs. But as it worked out in his short seven-month tenure in office, the Third World aspects of Quadros's international policy cost him much of his conservative support without gaining significant new strength from the Left.

The crisis that brought Brazil perilously close to civil war began on the night of August 18 with a highly unsatisfactory encounter between Lacerda and the president. In a dramatic twist on August 24, Lacerda revealed that the president intended to close Congress and implement a series of institutional reforms that would subsequently be legitimized by means of a plebiscite. This denunciation exploded like a bombshell in Brasília, where Quadros insisted on seeing a congressional plot to undermine the presidency. Determined to avoid the dead end in which Vargas had found himself seven years earlier, he chose to take the initiative, subsequently claiming that to govern Brazil effectively he required powers similar to those held at the end of the 1950s by Charles de Gaulle. These he knew Congress would not grant him, so a way had to be found to bypass that body. But once his plans were exposed by Lacerda's denunciation, Quadros opted for an all-out gamble.

Aware that the military and most conservative elements would not accept Goulart, Quadros hoped that the dilemma would be resolved in his favor. Extraordinary powers for him would be a lesser evil in the eyes of many of these elements than the rise of Goulart and the PTB to power or a breakdown of constitutional order and establishment of a military regime. His miscalculations lay in underestimating the Congress he scorned and in assuming that the armed forces high command could impose its will on the entire military establishment. While the military leaders continued to grope for a way out of the impasse in which Quadros had placed them, the president's August 25 resignation letter patterned along the lines of Vargas's suicide note heaped fuel on the fire.

As Goulart slowly wended his way back from a state visit to China, a compromise was hammered together to avoid civil war. On September 2 Congress instituted a parliamentary form of government, and on September 7 João Belchior Marques Goulart took the oath of office. The next day the parliamentary experiment began as the Chamber of Deputies approved a Council of Ministers headed by Tancredo de Almeida Neves—who also held the Justice Ministry. The disaster of civil war had been avoided without resort to a rupture of legality and implantation of military rule. But this would prove to be only a stay of execution, not a permanent reprieve.

The Parliamentary Regime and the 1962 Elections

Brief as was the Goulart government—albeit it lasted four times as long as that of Quadros—crucial events occurred during it that carried Brazil down the slippery road to a crisis of the system, not just of the regime. The first stage was a period of impasse; the latter part was a tragic case of political mobilization leading to a preemptive counterrevolution instead of the structural reforms that were its banners. During this time a real breakdown of democracy took place, one involving an abject failure of the Brazilian knack for compromise and conciliation that had been recently demonstrated during the Quadros resignation crisis.

Both intransigence of the conservative elements and detachment from reality on the part of the extreme Left were important factors in the triumph of polarization following the evaporation of the flimsy consensus achieved in the Kubitschek years. The far Right was, as usual, very shortsighted in its opposition to further change, and the Left let wishful thinking run rampant in 1963 and early 1964 until it turned into suicidal self-delusion reminiscent of the ANL militants in 1935.

Each extreme bore a heavy share of responsibility for the lamentable events of 1964–1973. The failure of the parliamentary regime to function in even a minimally adequate manner—in large part owing to the weakness fundamental to Brazil's political parties—started matters down the path of decline. Although the situation would have been difficult for any chief executive, Goulart's shortcomings aggravated the crisis and brought on its unfortunate denouement; Goulart proved to be a poor student of what Vargas had tried to teach. Yet dilemmas inherent in the situation of the early 1960s would have severely tested the mettle of even Vargas or Kubitschek. Radicalization, fragility and instability of political coalitions, fragmentation of power resources, and high turnover in key governmental positions were major elements in this process of decay.

As was natural given the coerced nature of the 1961 compromise, which was reluctantly accepted by both sides as a lesser evil, the year following Goulart's inauguration was marked by increasing conflict between Congress and the president. Central was the latter's efforts to prove the new system unworkable so as to engineer a return to presidentialism. Although the Brazilian gift for compromise, as often postponing a showdown as avoiding it, brought the country through several potentially serious crises during 1962, the price was steep in terms of economic and social problems left unattended and a legacy of deepening mistrust and mutual suspicion. The tension was aggravated by a polarizing legislative election campaign in which the clash between Right and Left was greatly intensified.

By mid-1962 Goulart was preoccupied with the possibility of being outflanked on the left by Brizola. Hence he adopted a more leftist tack, strongly criticizing Congress and seeking early recovery of full presidential powers. With campaigning under way, the anti-Goulart militants of Democratic Parliamentary Action (ADEP), an anti-Communist ideological supraparty bloc, came out in an aggressive manner against all presidential policies. Through links to the Brazilian Institute of Democratic Action (IBAD) and ADEP's network of Popular Democratic Action (also ADEP) groups, this U.S.-supported movement sought to offset the influence of the emerging National Liberation Front of Brizola, Recife Mayor Miguel Arraes, and Peasant Leagues organizer Francisco Julião. So by midyear the forces for polarization and radicalization of Brazilian political life again outweighed efforts toward conciliation.

Still shaken by stiff military opposition to his becoming president, Goulart scrupulously avoided conflicts or even significant policy differences with the armed forces during his initial year in office. Yet with the end of the semiparliamentary system, Goulart was to find increasing difficulty in avoiding friction with the military without losing his support from the Left. As during the 1954 crisis Vargas had faced a Military Club controlled by his enemies, Goulart would feel the weight of its increasing hostility. In this the anti-Goulart officers would have militant and well-organized allies, as the Institute for Social Research and Studies (IPES) was organized by elements of the commercial and industrial classes following the 1961 crisis.[19]

As the situation became increasingly tense following a series of cabinet crises, 15 million Brazilians—of 18.5 million registered—cast their votes on October 7 for a Chamber of Deputies (to hold office until February 1967), two senators from each state (with terms expiring only in early 1971), and in half the states, new governors (for the next four years).[20] In the great urban centers electoral battles polarized sharply around the antithetical themes of "basic reforms" and "Communist menace." With patronage, personalism, and local political disputes determining the outcome in most of the interior, the overall results were very mixed. The Left and Right each experienced victories and defeats in majority elections, and legislative balloting under Brazil's peculiar form of proportional representation returned most incumbents to Congress along with a heterogeneous array of newcomers. All but a few governorships remained in the hands of moderates, a fact that was to have important ramifications in the 1964 crisis. On the far Left, Brizola consolidated his position by polling a record vote for Congress, and he transferred his political base to Guanabara (the state including Rio de Janeiro city).

Congressional balloting, which was to give rise to investigations of corruption and economic abuses by both the IBAD-backed anti-Communists and the many leftists who benefited from administration favors and assistance, resulted in a Chamber in which the PSD, PTB, and UDN possessed relatively equal strength with 119, 104, and 97 seats respectively—for a total of 320 to only 89 for the other ten parties. Party strength in the Senate was proportional to these results, so maintenance of a PTB-PSD alliance provided the prospect of a viable congressional base for the administration if Goulart could walk a line between insistent demands for reforms coming from the majority component of the PTB and the conservatism of the rural-based core of the PSD.

Dissensus, Decay, and Disaster: 1963–1964

The early months of 1963 were the highwater mark of Goulart's government as the January 6 plebiscite favored return to presidentialism by 9.5 million votes to but 2 million opposed. By interpreting the five-to-one margin as an overwhelming vote of confidence and personal mandate, Goulart miscalculated his position. Opposition rose rapidly as he began to push for policies injurious to the interests of the established power structure.

Presidentialism and Polarization

Wary of losing support of his original political base, Goulart wavered during early 1963 with respect to implementing policies his cabinet had just formulated and adopted. Indeed, the series of crises that led almost directly to the March 1964 overthrow of the existing regime germinated almost a year earlier as the last major effort at conciliation foundered. Instead of moderation, the most dramatic development of the year was growth and increasing assertiveness of the nationalist Left as manifested through a network of political, labor, and student groups enjoying close ties to Brizola. Finance Minister Francisco Clementino de San Thiago Dantas proved unable to retool as a populist leader, and neither he nor Planning Minister Celso Furtado, who lacked a political base, was sufficiently adept at manipulation of politicians to prevail over the more radical forces. As Goulart abandoned their Three-Year Plan under political pressures, the balance sheet for 1963 showed a decrease in per capita GDP and a cost of living rise of over 80 percent. Since even in troubled 1961 growth had been 7.9 percent, compared to 1963's 2.8 percent, and inflation had been half that of 1963, the government was highly vulnerable to charges of economic mismanagement.

Extremists of both Left and Right were more concerned with the power implications of the government's proposed reforms than with their economic soundness or social justice. Radicals viewed essentially moderate measures as inadequate or designed as palliatives to deaden revolutionary impulses; reactionaries saw the same proposals as dangerous entering wedges for more drastic changes that would upset the social order and shift political power perilously far to the Left. Hence the acerbic polemic of the 1962 election campaign persisted. The opposition continued to portray Goulart as in agreement with Brizola and the other PTB radicals supporting "Communistic" measures, and these elements strove to pull Goulart to the Left and to transform his administration into a "nationalist and popular" regime.

Although party lines had come to have little significance by this time, division of centrist forces as a result of traditional partisan disputes hamstrung efforts at conciliation. Rival presidential aspirations on the part of key figures impeded cooperation in support of a program of economic recovery and development accompanied by moderate reforms. In contrast, formidable radicalizing forces existed on both Left and Right. Within the UDN, Lacerda headed a faction as determined to oust the president as they had been a decade earlier when they had begun maneuvering to bring about Vargas's downfall. The power struggle within the PTB turned in favor of the radical wing. To maintain their support, Goulart sacrificed Dantas and Furtado.

Within the PTB of the early 1960s, Goulart represented a center position. His brand of patronage-oriented, paternalistic populism was devoid of ideological content. A true disciple of Vargas in this respect, he felt uncomfortable without room to maneuver and was most at ease in a fluid bargaining situation where he could play competing interests off against each other and follow a zig-zag course toward his objectives. In contrast, the forty-year-old Brizola, a political speaker matched only by Lacerda, enjoyed far greater appeal to the urban working class than did the president. By mid-1963 he had Goulart on a string, since the president worried about Brizola capturing the leadership of labor and moved leftward to head this off. Moreover, conservatives held Goulart responsible for his brother-in-law's revolutionary pronouncements, but in reality he had no control over firebrand Brizola.

As of mid-1963, neither the extreme Right nor radical Left wished to see moderate reforms enacted, an unfortunate situation clearest in the crucial struggle over agrarian reform—the pivotal issue upon which the prospects for political peace through accommodation rested. In mid-September the degree to which leftist agitation within the military had undermined discipline became dramatically apparent as a sizable group of air force and naval noncoms briefly seized control of Brasília. The revolt was contained within the Federal District, but the appearance at rebel headquarters of leaders of the Nationalist Parliamentary Front pushed a significant number of dismayed officers into the ranks of the anti-Goulart conspiracy. Indeed, concern over government efforts to undermine discipline now extended from the high command to the junior officers in most immediate contact with the troops. Goulart's October 4 request to Congress for a countrywide state of siege was ill-conceived and self-defeating. Sheepishly withdrawing the request in the face of a lack of support within his own party, Goulart again appeared ineffective to both extremes. Moreover, this cost his government the support of a very large proportion of the legalist-democratic majority in the officer corps, upon whose constitutionalist scruples its security really rested.

End of the Democratic Experiment

While the Right became more determined, the Brizola and Arraes-led Popular Mobilization Front (FMP) shortsightedly assumed a position of total independence in the face of Goulart's not having moved far enough to the Left to satisfy their escalating aspirations. The progressive wing of the Church and UDN moderates were drowned out by radicalizers and reactionaries.[21] Exhilarated by their defeat of the conciliatory policies of Dantas and his moderate allies, radical reformers felt that establishment of a truly "nationalist and popular" government should come immediately, with revolutionary changes to follow closely in its wake.[22]

Even as the crisis deepened, the position of major political leaders was still largely determined by fear that a coup would upset the electoral timetable and introduce changes in the rules of the game that could adversely affect their presidential prospects. Kubitschek, the front-runner, was trying strenuously to hold together the PSD-PTB alliance by pulling Goulart toward moderation and urged his congressional followers to be more receptive to the president's pleas for basic reforms.

IPES under the direction of General Golbery do Couto e Silva was behind the scenes playing an important role in preparing Goulart's downfall. The plotters badly needed a prestigious senior general in the Rio de Janeiro area to assume a leadership role, and Humberto Castelo Branco admirably filled this bill. A hero of the Italian campaign who enjoyed a reputation for scrupulously avoiding involvement in civilian political affairs, he had developed a large following among those who were by now middle-grade officers during his long tenure with the command and general staff school and among more senior officers through his service as ESG commandant. By late 1963 he had conditionally agreed to assume military leadership of the movement—if plans to move against Goulart were contingent upon the president's violation of accepted rules of the game.

At the end of February 1964 Goulart took measures bordering on demagoguery and indicated that he had stopped listening to Kubitschek and was falling more under the influence of Brizola. Relying on staff advice that his military support was sufficient to overwhelm any reaction, Goulart decided to go all out for mobilization of mass pressures for basic structural reforms. Intended to strengthen the president's hand, the move cost him his job and spelled an end to competitive civilian politics for over two decades.[23] On Friday March 13, Goulart announced an agrarian reform by decree and the nationalization of private oil refineries. Brizola's denunciation of Congress and invitation for a popular revolution aroused the most enthusiastic response from the crowd—and the most negative reaction from the middle class, military, and businessmen watching with dismay on television. Instead of an "irreversible" popular movement for drastic reforms, a backlash mobilization was gathering momentum.

As the Easter holidays neared, the close cooperation evolving among the governors of five of the country's six most important states—with many of their colleagues from smaller states falling into line—meant little to the administration. Instead and shortsightedly, the presidential staff feverishly prepared new decrees for radical reform measures to be announced at a series of mass rallies. But for Goulart as the country's chief executive, April would never come. Instead the crisis that would lay him low within a week began on the night of March 25 when 2,000 discontented servicemen gathered at the headquarters of a Communist-controlled union. Egged on by radical labor leaders and nationalist politicians, the mutineers resolved to hold out until all punishments were revoked and a new minister sympathetic to their movement was appointed. Goulart's acquiescence to these demands sent shock waves through the officer corps of all three services and civilian advocates of order. Within a few days Minas Gerais was in open revolt. The regime's scheme of support simply evaporated—for in large part it had only existed in the minds of incompetent aides operating on misfounded assumptions.[24]

Although military action was decisive to the revolution, the support of organized civilian groups—particularly cooperation of state administrations—was of great importance. Within Brazilian society activity on behalf of the revolution was much greater than were the scattered efforts to mobilize in defense of the regime. By afternoon Goulart fled, leaving Brizola the impossible task of trying to mount armed resistance. Although the errors of the Goulart regime stand out, from a technical point of view the uprising was extremely well planned and executed. The greatest contrast between the two sides was in the leadership sphere as the revolution could call upon the army general staff, the ESG, and the command and general staff school. In a general sense, the *tenentes* of the 1920s, with their experience in the 1930 revolution and World War II, were more able when it came down to a military operation than were their opponents. The question was now how capable they would be at running the country.

4

FROM MILITARY RULE
THROUGH DEMOCRATIC
TRANSITION:
BRAZIL 1964–1989

H AVING AGAIN EXERCISED the moderating power, the armed forces had to decide what to do next. Their first decision, to establish a semiconstitutional regime to replace the junta, would be followed by protracted disagreement over whether to remain in control of the government, return to a role of tutor, or retreat to being "just" the arbiter of national political life. Once the die was cast for a second military government, the country would embark upon a much longer period of rule by the armed forces than anyone imagined at the time—with the first decade spent on becoming more deeply entrenched in power as abortive normalization efforts led instead to an increasingly authoritarian political system.[1]

Castelo Branco and the Arbiter-Ruler Dilemma

The forces that easily overthrew the Goulart government were united chiefly by agreement that the radicalization and lack of discipline of the preceding weeks were intolerable. Beyond a shared desire to end "subversion," the various components of the March 31 Movement possessed no consensus as to what should come next. Historical conspirators within the military advocating a prolonged period of purges stood alongside conservative UDN elements wanting the lengthy period of political dominance they had expected after the 1960 elections. Each coexisted uneasily with moderates for whom Goulart had been acceptable as long as they could expect a return of Kubitschek to power by 1966. Relations were equally shaky with legalists who had reluctantly acted only when they were convinced of Goulart-Brizola efforts to subvert military discipline and "unconstitutionally" change the constitution.[2]

Within the military there was a feeling that power could not be allowed to fall back into the hands of the Vargas lineage as in 1951, 1956, and 1961. Forces advocating an arbiter function by the military would carry the day in April 1964 and remain in control of the situation until October 1965. Only with the 1967 presidential succession was it obvious that a long authoritarian night under a military determined to be the nation's ruler would be inevitable.

Avoidance of Dictatorship

The immediate aftermath of the Goulart government's ouster was a short period of intense purges. General Artur da Costa e Silva organized a Revolutionary Supreme Command made up of himself, Admiral Augusto Rademaker Grünewald, and Air Force Chief of Staff Francisco de Assis Correia de Melo. Officers closely tied to Castelo Branco worked effectively behind the scenes to articulate Castelo Branco's successful candidacy to fill the rest of the Quadros-Goulart term, and Congress duly ratified this choice on April 11. By this time the Revolutionary Supreme Command had taken action to ensure that the "subversive" and "corrupt" elements linked to the overthrown regime were removed from political life. An "institutional act" made clear the military's view that rescuing the nation vested the armed forces with authority to decree a new order. This overriding of the existing constitution suspended for six months all legal rights of job tenure for public employees. Moreover, it authorized the executive to suspend political rights for ten years and to cancel the mandates of congressmen, state legislators, and members of municipal councils.[3]

Castelo Branco deprived Kubitschek of his political rights on June 8, acting under heavy pressure from Costa e Silva—who had remained as war minister. Significant for the future was the emergence of the hard-liners, an influential grouping of younger officers of a radical rightist position. When against the advice of this *linha dura* faction the president let his major discretionary powers lapse on June 15, they became increasingly uneasy over the government's stress on moderation and rationality.

The heart of the Castelo Branco administration was the Sorbonne group for whom the necessity of military exercise of the moderating power arose from basic flaws in the country's political structures. Through the long association of its ESG-linked core with politicians, businessmen, industrialists, journalists, and bureaucrats, this faction had manpower adequate to its self-assumed task of overhauling the nation's political and administrative institutions. Whereas for their rightist rivals, subversion and corruption were still the fundamental problems, for them it was essential to put the punitive phase of the revolution behind and come to grips with the underlying structural problems. Planning Minister Roberto Campos's emergency measures at the end of April had been glumly accepted as necessary in light of the country's financial chaos and galloping inflation. When the Program of Government Economic Action (PAEG) was unveiled in August, groans turned to screams of anguish. Campos felt free from the considerations of political feasibility that had constrained previous stabilization efforts and took a strictly technocratic approach to the complex and intractable problems of economic policy. In retrospect, GDP growth of 3.4 percent in 1964, 2.4 percent for 1965, 6.7 percent in 1966, and 4.2 percent the next year appears exceptional for a period of adjustment and austerity.

The 1965 Elections and the Revolution Within the Revolution

As those opposed to reopening political competition so soon issued dire forecasts, Castelo pushed ahead with direct elections of governors in the eleven states where they had been elected in 1960—a test of public reaction to his brand of tutelary democracy and institutional renovation. Although "revolutionary" candidates carried the day in most of the states, public perception was that of repudiation of the administration in major urban centers.[4] Thus a behind-the-scenes military crisis developed; as a result, Costa e Silva consolidated his position as the leading contender to be Castelo's successor. When Congress failed to pass a series of constitutional amendments strengthening the executive's hand, a sweeping second institutional act was decreed on October 27. Under its provisions, presidents would henceforth be chosen by Congress and the existing political parties were dissolved. With this sacrifice of important features of democratic formalism, tutelage moved closer to control in the president's dealings with Congress and political groupings. By November a foundation was laid for a two-party system composed of the government-sponsored National Renovating Alliance (ARENA) and opposition elements banded together in the Brazilian Democratic Movement (MDB). Although the MDB had but 21 senators and 150 deputies, they included such a wide range of interests and ideological positions that it would never achieve a significant degree of unity and coherence.[5]

Costa e Silva formally launched his presidential candidacy in January 1966. Then on February 5, Institutional Act No. 3 implanted indirect selection of governors, scheduled congressional elections for November 15, and eliminated election of mayors of capital cities. Castelo Branco thus yielded to hard-line pressures and established a system under which the government candidates could not lose. As Costa e Silva's election was never in doubt, the MDB decided not to compete. Thus, on October 3 Costa e Silva became Brazil's president-elect but under circumstances closely paralleling those of Floriano's selection nearly three quarters of a century before. Rebuffing congressional desires for a significant voice in the process, the regime shaped a new constitution.

When the results of the voting were in, the government had strengthened its hand, electing two-thirds of the Chamber of Deputies and eighteen of twenty-two senators. ARENA had won 277 seats in the lower house on well over 8.7 million votes; the MDB's nearly 4.9 million votes were good for 132 seats. Yet in Guanabara, Rio de Janeiro, and Rio Grande do Sul, the opposition held decisive edges, and in São Paulo it came close. Even in the states where ARENA won, the MDB did quite well in the larger cities.[6]

Dominance by the Duros

The inauguration of the amiable, quite ordinary Costa e Silva ushered in the first of three periods during which the presidency would be occupied by someone committed to the idea of the armed forces as the country's proper and semipermanent ruler, for Costa e Silva was clearly the choice of the hard-liners. Far from a more humane tutelary democracy, Brazil under Costa e Silva was to slide into the type of unrestricted military dictatorship Castelo Branco had largely been able to avoid.

Costa e Silva and the Failure of Humanization
A line officer in contrast to his predecessor's experience in school and staff positions, Costa e Silva was adept at routine military politics but inadequately prepared for other areas of national policymaking. Since most cabinet members were ordinary figures, the way was open for Antônio Delfim Netto (b. 1928), a Paulista economist, to emerge as the administration's leading light. Presiding over a homogeneous economic team, he would move ahead while the rest of the government was painfully slow to define policies and programs.

Although the opposition's broad front was only an alliance at the top—since mutual distrust reigned within this mélange of Lacerdistas, Juscelinistas, Janistas, and Janguistas—the government viewed it as a potentially dangerous threat to be neutralized at any cost. Meanwhile developments of greater lasting significance had been taking place, especially within the student movement and the Church.[7] These institutions would be critical elements in the radicalization and polarization that this time would result in the implantation of an openly dictatorial regime. Accustomed to the Catholic Church as a bulwark of stability, many in the armed forces confused its newly found social conscience with giving aid and comfort to subversive agitators. The numerically predominant moderate current within the hierarchy wished no confrontation but was unwilling to forgo its right to speak out in the future.

The second half of the 1968 legislative year found Congress in an insubordinate mood and extreme rightist groups carrying out acts of terrorism for which the leftist opposition would be blamed. Hence, although a good part of the responsibility for renewed terrorism rested with the increasingly active leftist revolutionaries, the right-wing extremists were more instrumental in escalating violence. Lack of presidential leadership was another factor contributing to a growing sense of malaise. Moreover, the question of presidential succession aroused civilist attitudes among some ARENA leaders and fed ambitions within the military. Interior Minister General Afonso de Albuquerque Lima advocated a greater say on economic policy for the military.

On September 3 Deputy Márcio Moreira Alves issued an impassioned plea for a "boycott of militarism." Considering this part of a concerted conspiracy to discredit the armed forces in the eyes of the public, the military demanded that the young journalist-politician be punished. To this end heavy pressure was placed on the Chamber of Deputies to strip Moreira Alves of his parliamentary immunity. But on December 12 this was voted down. Since ninety-four government party congressmen balked on a measure considered vital by the executive, in the minds of hard-line officers punitive action was required.

The Fifth Institutional Act
and the Defeat of Normalization

The executive's reaction was devastating. Opposition leaders and militant critics of the regime were arrested, and the draconian Institutional Act No. 5 (AI-5) granted the president authority to recess legislative bodies, intervene in the states without limit, cancel elective mandates, and take away political rights.[8] Congress was closed indefinitely, which ended lingering hopes that the armed forces would soon return to an arbiter role. (Almost 1,400 individuals would be punished under AI-5.) Subsequently all elections scheduled prior to November 1970 were eliminated.

Thus as Brazil entered the third year of Costa e Silva's administration, only the faintest traces of representative processes remained operational. The armed forces were in control of the country but deeply divided over how to exercise the responsibility they had assumed; political parties were virtually nonfunctioning; stringent censorship was strongly resented by media accustomed to substantial freedom; universities were crippled by faculty purges; and even the Catholic Church was torn between a fear of subversion and repugnance for the regime's repressive measures. Indications of turbulent political waters ahead were abundant, but the crisis was nearer at hand than anyone imagined. On August 31 the country awoke to the startling news that, in light of a cardiovascular problem that incapacitated Costa e Silva, the service ministers had formed a junta. As the armed forces had vetoed assumption of the presidential office by the civilian vice president, it was clear that for the fourth time since 1964 progress toward political normalcy had been bulldozed into oblivion by military imposition of an even more arbitrary regime than had previously existed.

The dramatic kidnapping of U.S. Ambassador C. Burke Elbrick did not divert the junta from finding a military replacement for the president and installing him for a full presidential term rather than merely the remainder of Costa e Silva's period. The ranking generals and admirals distilled the preferences of the flag officers serving under each of them, and a seven-man high command ratified on October 7 the army's choice of General Emílio Garrastazu Médici with Admiral

Rademaker as vice president and runner-up Orlando Geisel as army minister. Moreover, the extensive set of constitutional amendments decreed ten days later increased centralization of power in the hands of the federal government, augmented the concentration of authority in the executive, and further extended the scope of the national security law and military courts. After ten months of enforced recess and minus the large number of its most determined members who had fallen afoul of the institutional act, Congress was summoned back to Brasília to ratify the military's decision.

The Médici Years: Institutionalizing
the National Security State

"Project Brazil: Great Power" was the leitmotif of Médici's administration, one in which high rates of economic growth would coexist with effective repression. Feeling strengthened by the capture-killing of guerrilla leader Carlos Marighella, Médici made it clear that in his "revolutionary state," the president retained emergency powers as leader of the revolutionary movement and chief executive. Economic growth had held at 9.5 percent in 1969—after an astounding jump to 9.8 percent in 1968—and was accelerating, and the regime found it easy to keep public attention diverted from politics during 1970. In this respect the World Cup soccer finals in Mexico helped significantly, as Brazil won its third title in the past four tries, making up for a poor showing in 1966.[9] Hence on October 3 all but one state legislature duly confirmed the governors handpicked by Médici.

Congressional elections followed on November 15 with 29 million registered voters, in a population approaching 95 million, giving the government party 220 of 310 lower house seats and victories in 40 of 46 Senate races. On the strength of 10.9 million valid votes racked up by ARENA to but 4.8 million for the MDB in the Chamber of Deputies voting, the balloting was a victory for the regime. Yet the MDB had won once again in Guanabara, come close in Rio Grande do Sul, and run well in São Paulo city—showing that the opposition retained a solid base in the most advanced regions of the country.[10]

Determined to end armed opposition, the Médici government combined improved intelligence, systematic use of torture, and more sophisticated counterinsurgency tactics to destroy the violent Left. These tactics were masked behind a veil of censorship and trumpeting of the regime's economic accomplishments. The early 1970s was the heyday of out-of-control secret repressive organizations within the sprawling security apparatus and of officially condoned "death squads" among the civilian police, especially in São Paulo and Rio de Janeiro. Repression was brutally efficient, although not nearly on the same scale or marked with as great a disregard for human life as was the case in Argentina.

Long viewed as Brazil's only truly national institution aside from the armed forces, the Catholic Church became the chief critic of human rights violations and, to an increasing degree, of social injustice as well. Yet substantial elements of its hierarchy sympathized with the technocratic side of the regime. Many were

Student demonstrations in the 1970s (photo by Sérgio Sade, courtesy of Abril Imagens)

preoccupied with their own problem of inadequate manpower combined with the loss of Catholic rural workers to Pentecostal sects and to *umbanda* (a blend of religions drawing heavily on African roots) as they migrated to the outskirts of Brazil's cities.

A major lesson of the Médici period was how great a degree of acceptance could be engendered by a repressive government through sustained economic growth when gains were loudly proclaimed and costs swept under the censorship rug. The dramatic positive side of the coin was economic growth; fueled by heavy industrial investment, it steamed ahead at 10.4 percent for 1970, 11.3 percent in 1971, 12.1 percent during 1972, and 14.0 percent for 1973. This economic miracle provided the foundation for the national mood of optimism generated by the regime's carefully orchestrated campaigns behind such slogans as "Brazil: love it or leave it."

Critics stressed extremely inequitable income distribution, failure of growth to lead to improvement in the standard of living for the masses, wasteful expenditures on showy infrastructural projects, and neglect of pressing social problems.[11] Often lost in the debate was the fact that inflation—generally the dragon in Brazil's economic garden—averaged under 20 percent a year during this period, and foreign exchange reserves increased almost tenfold. Foreign trade flourished with exports rising sharply to $4 billion in 1972 and $6.2 billion for 1973.

In this environment the government scored resounding victories in the November 1972 municipal elections. These impressive results in both the economic and political realms increased Médici's ability to keep the succession process from slipping out of control as it had for Castelo Branco and Costa e Silva. Médici had delegated authority in the military field to Army Minister Orlando Geisel. Hence his younger and more intellectual brother Ernesto Geisel was announced as the government candidate in June 1973. Ratified by the ARENA convention, Geisel was named to the presidency on January 15, 1974, by an electoral college composed almost exclusively of the incumbent Congress.

The Road Back Under Geisel

Brazil had taken half a decade to slide into a fully authoritarian regime under armed forces inclined to the role of long-term rulers, then spent almost an equal period under a repressive government determined to institutionalize this into a permanent system. By 1974 the midnight of military rule had passed, and the next five years would be a reversal of the late 1960s as champions of the military as arbiter outwitted and outfought the entrenched hard-line advocates of indefinite military rule. The new president—in the face of heavy resistance within the armed forces and with only limited understanding and sporadic cooperation from a distrustful civilian opposition—would steer the country through a phase of decompression of the repressive authoritarian regime and set it on the path to political opening (*abertura*).[12]

End of the Economic Miracle, Beginning of Decompression

In power after a seven-year hiatus, Castelo Branco's heirs faced serious obstacles in their effort to get Brazil back to where it had been before the fifth institutional act and the Médici administration. Although coming to power in the midst of a continuing economic boom, Geisel was clearly not going to be able to outperform his predecessor in the growth realm. The global energy crisis had already begun during the last quarter of 1973, so the boom was due to moderate, if not end. Instead of an all-out pursuit of economic expansion, Geisel assumed office with a flexible timetable for dismantling the repressive apparatus as it had burgeoned under Médici and for turning the country out of the cul de sac of authoritarianism.[13] Knowing that this would be a long and arduous task—one well beyond the scope of a single presidential term—he provisionally selected his successor at the very beginning, to this end moving João Baptista Figueiredo to head the National Intelligence Service (SNI).

Although the core of the new government included individuals who had been associated with Castelo Branco, continuity with the Médici government was provided by Planning Minister João Paulo dos Reis Velloso (b. 1931), with young economist Mário Henrique Simonsen (b. 1935) as finance minister.[14] The administration's "decompression" (*distensão*) project was to a large degree designed in its initial stages to stabilize the regime. In fact, Geisel could not have attempted to do more than this, since he would have to work hard to mobilize support within military ranks for even the first steps in diminishing rampant authoritarianism. Encountering the hard-liners well entrenched in the military establishment, becoming leader of the military institution as well as head of government would have to be his first priority if he was to be able to implement the changes he had in mind for legitimatization without loss of control and direction.

Geisel's plans foresaw a system of safe competition to be dominated by a strong ARENA with the MDB functioning as a loyal opposition and the far Left isolated. But this opposition was not to be allowed to get out of hand; it would be manipulated by playing on fears of hard-line reaction and changing the rules of the electoral game and disciplined if not fully controlled by the continued threat of AI-5. At the center of Geisel's decision to begin decompression was the perception that the effective repression of the violence-oriented opposition during Médici's term had led to a dangerous degree of autonomy on the part of the security apparatus. This had resulted in a widening gap between centrist to moderately reformist forces in Brazilian society and the military, which they held responsible for human rights abuses. Moreover, since continuation of such vigorous repression was unnecessary, as the guerrilla threat no longer existed, the armed forces were becoming deeply divided over the issue. Yet if he wished to do away with extralegal repressive capabilities, it was necessary for Geisel to demonstrate that he would brook no subversive activity.

To this end decompression should go forward sufficiently to justify self-restraint and cooperation with the government on the part of the MDB's responsible elements, but changes should not be allowed to build up their own momentum; the impulse for liberalization must remain channeled, with the initiative firmly in the government's hands. For this strategy to work, major elements of the opposition would have to be willing to accept limited and piecemeal reforms spread out over an extended period of time—as well as tactical detours. Despite repeated setbacks encountered in what he knew from the beginning would be a difficult struggle, Geisel doggedly pushed ahead. This led him at times to behave autocratically to remove obstacles and to resort to authoritarian measures or risk losing military support to the siren songs of the hard-line foes of *distensão*.

His first step in the political realm was to hand-pick governors, who were duly confirmed by state legislatures in October. Then Geisel insisted on holding essentially free congressional elections on November 15. At 35.8 million in a population nearing 105 million, Brazil's electorate had grown sharply since 1970, and the turnout of just under 29 million matched that year's number of registered voters.[15] The balloting resulted in a strong comeback by the MDB, which scored a 16-6 victory in the Senate races and elected 45 percent of the lower house. The government was more sobered than shaken by this poor showing of its party's senatorial candidates, since it retained a decisive 204 to 160 edge in the Chamber of Deputies—compared to its previous 220–90 advantage—and an even more comfortable margin in the upper house, where holdovers gave ARENA 46 seats to the MDB's 20. From the government strategists' point of view, opposition gains were healthy in that they reflected the return to the normal channels of electoral politics of alienated elements who had abstained or nullified their ballots in 1970. To keep this going it was necessary to hold out hope to the MDB that it might eventually win power within the existing system.

The Trials and Tribulations of
Geisel's Second and Third Years

March 1975 saw resumption of full functioning of Congress, but in early May the president invoked the extraordinary powers of AI-5 after years of disuse. By the last quarter of 1975 hard-line elements, particularly in São Paulo, were heating up the issue of subversion in answer to opposition efforts to focus attention upon torture and violations of civil liberties. On October 25 the death of journalist Vladimir Herzog while being interrogated brought matters to a head; in spite of the authorities' verdict of suicide, public opinion overwhelmingly considered him a victim of torture. When a worker accused of distributing Communist propaganda died in custody of a Second Army security unit, Geisel swiftly relieved personal friend General Ednardo D'Avila Mello of his command—turning this incident to his advantage. Temporarily at least, many wavering officers reacted against the hard-liners' excesses and rallied to the president's vigorous leadership initiatives. Yet this also appears to have led to a definite drifting away from the president on the part of Army Minister Sylvio Frota.

In the November 1976 local elections 18 million votes were cast for ARENA's municipal council candidates compared to 13 million for the MDB. Yet the opposition elected mayors or a majority of councilmen in 63 percent of cities over 250,000 population. The most important impact of these elections was to confirm the government's belief that it could retain sufficient control of the system at the national and state levels in 1978 with ARENA as its vehicle—albeit only through further tinkering with the electoral rules.

Indeed, 1977 would prove to be critical for the continuation of Brazil's progress toward less restricted democracy. The problems facing Geisel involved both the succession process and the degree of control over the military institution required to see this through. Frota was moving toward establishing himself as the candidate of the armed forces. Moreover, relaunching of *distensão* was complicated by mediocre performance in the economic realm—exactly the factor that had served so effectively to ease opposition during the Médici years. The Geisel administration had announced ambitious economic goals shortly after coming to office. Its Second National Development Plan: 1975–1979 called for a shift of emphasis to intermediate and capital goods in order to maintain high growth rates. Yet it was to be undermined by the soaring price of crude oil and the heavy investments required by consequent efforts to reduce Brazil's dependence upon petroleum imports.[16] During 1974 problems were most evident in trade; imports more than doubled—resulting in a $4.7 billion trade deficit. Foreign exchange reserves dropped and foreign debt rose. GDP growth, in large part a carryover from the dynamism of the Médici period, was 9 percent, and inflation was edging up to nearly 35 percent. This economic downturn was more noticeable during 1975. GDP growth fell to 6.1 percent, and inflation leveled off. Although in 1976 GDP growth improved to 10.1 percent, inflation jumped to 46 percent. But the last years of the Geisel government would take place in a deteriorating economic environment as growth fell to 5.4 percent for 1977 and 4.8 percent in 1978. Moreover, inflation remained near 40 percent. A harbinger of problems ahead was the rapid rise of Brazil's foreign debt. Brazil achieved a balance between exports and imports in 1977 and 1978, but the time bomb was ticking, as debt service required a large sustained net capital inflow.

Structurally the Brazilian economy of the mid-1970s was substantially changed from that prior to the military's seizure of power. By 1978 agriculture was down to 14 percent of GDP and industry up to 33 percent. Steel production exceeded 9 million tons by 1979, triple that of 1964. The auto industry was up to nearly a million vehicles per year. Electrical generating capacity had doubled between 1964 and 1971 and again by 1978. These changes were reflected in the workforce; by 1978, 20 percent of the economically active population (EAP) were employed in industry, with agriculture down to 36 percent and services up to 40 percent—compared to 14, 60, and 26 percent in 1950. Indeed, during the 1970s industrial employment grew by well over 500,000 a year and jobs in the service area by nearly 900,000 annually.

Winning the Succession Battle

In early 1977 the regime was faced with finding a way to guarantee an ARENA victory in the next year's national elections while heading off Frota's unwanted presidential candidacy. So Geisel flexed his muscles, placing Congress in temporary recess and decreeing changes in the rules of the electoral game—including a six-year term for his successor. With one senator from each state chosen indirectly, the government was assured of retaining control of that body, reinforcing its majority in the electoral college. These decisive moves, by reaffirming Geisel's determination to keep decompression within the confines he had dictated and to control its pace, contributed to the consolidation of military support necessary for dealing with the succession question. Frota was astutely manuevered into overplaying his hand and dismissed in October.[17] This was followed by Figueiredo's nomination by ARENA in April 1978. His candidacy was aided by a series of political reforms put through Congress before the elections. These eliminated the most authoritarian features of the political system by replacing the sweeping arbitrary powers of AI-5 with provisions for a state of siege or a state of emergency. Against this backdrop, on October 15 the electoral college ratified Figueiredo, and the selection of governors went off smoothly with the major exception of São Paulo, where upstart Paulo Salim Maluf had managed to defeat Geisel's choice at the ARENA convention.

With Brazil's electorate up to 46 million in a population of 114 million, nearly 38 million of whom went to the polls on November 15, the government party elected 231 federal deputies to 189 for the opposition. Yet even more than had been the case in 1974, the gross underrepresentation of populous urban states was crucial to ARENA's comfortable margin of seats; in terms of popular vote, the difference was only 250,000 votes—at a bit over 15 million to 14.8 million in favor of ARENA. The government party also won fifteen of the twenty-three Senate seats at stake (despite the fact that the popular vote for these offices was 57 percent to 43 percent in favor of the MDB); twenty-two others had been filled previously by state electoral colleges with ARENA gaining twenty-one of them.[18]

The mixed results were in reality advantageous for the process of political decompression and its transformation into *abertura*. The electoral vitality of the MDB convinced wavering elements associated with the regime of the need for continuing political reforms, and ARENA's firm control of Congress and state legislatures forestalled any reaction by hard-line elements in the armed forces. A moral victory for opposition elements drew them further into the game of liberalization through elections—the slow and conflict-free road.

Thus, following Geisel's year-end revocation of banishment orders against a number of exiles, Figueiredo was inaugurated as constitutional chief executive on March 15, 1979. With AI-5 and its prodigious arbitrary powers now history, *distensão* had become *abertura*—in its first stage still part of a process of liberalization, not yet democratization. By the end of his watershed term Geisel had reduced the regime's reliance upon arbitrary powers by making it far less likely to encounter situations in which their application might seem necessary. The extreme Left—particularly its violence-oriented and maximalist components—was essentially irrelevant from this point on, and the new government would, much as Geisel had done, contain attempts by the radical Right to derail *abertura*.

Figueiredo: Political Opening and Economic Difficulties, 1979–1984

For the first time since 1926 one Brazilian administration was followed by another committed to continuing its policies. Not only did Couto e Silva continue as presidential chief of staff, but Simonsen stayed on though shifted over to planning minister, and former economic czar Delfim Netto took over the Agriculture Ministry. This was an administration reflecting all major currents within both the military establishment and the technocratic stratum. As a result of its heterogeneity, it lacked unity and coherence and would require significant personnel changes after the shakedown period.

Hitting the Ground Running

Attention quickly fixed upon the new government's proposal for a broad amnesty, which became law at the beginning of September. Two months later reformulation of the party system was approved, resulting in not only the Democratic Social Party (PDS) as ARENA's replacement juxtaposed to the Party of the Brazilian Democratic Movement (PMDB), but also the Popular Party (PP), the Brazilian Labor Party (PTB), and the Democratic Workers' Party (PDT). There was only one really new factor on the party scene: the Workers' Party (PT) headed by São Paulo metalworkers leader Luís Inácio Lula da Silva (b. 1946).[19]

The economic legacy Figueiredo received from Geisel was mixed. GDP growth reached 7.2 percent for 1979, but inflation doubled to 77 percent. In light of the global energy crisis and its heavy impact upon a country so dependent on imported crude oil, Simonsen felt that continued stress on growth would lead to problems. Thus he advocated adjustment to the harsher economic realities, even if this meant a corrective recession. Defeated, Simonsen gave way in August 1979 to Delfim Netto and his 30 percent devaluation.

Terrorist bombings, largely the work of the extreme Right although blamed on the Left, escalated into the Riocentro incident in May. The public's refusal to swallow a whitewashing of army intelligence contributed to Couto e Silva's decision to resign in August in the face of the president's waffling on the question of a civilian successor versus the ambitions of SNI chief General Octávio Medeiros. Moreover, the economic situation appeared to him to be worsening. Although Brazil's GDP growth in 1980 had been a high 9.2 percent, inflation had also climbed to the 110 percent level. But the full brunt of recession was being felt in 1981 as GDP shrank by 4.5 percent—6.6 percent in per capita terms—and inflation hovered at 95 percent. The Figueiredo government also saw interest payments on foreign debt zoom toward the stratosphere as U.S. policy unleashed a sharp upward rate thrust. By 1980 debt service exploded to $11.3 billion, depleting foreign exchange reserves. Rather than undertake a major adjustment program with its concomitant economic slowdown and consequent political impopularity, Figueiredo chose to persist in a drastically changed context with the policies that seemed to have worked during the early years of his administration.

Figueiredo's September 1981 heart attack removed him temporarily from the scene, and in sharp contrast to 1969, the regime's inner core decided to let the civilian vice president take over. In reaction to regime fiddling with electoral legislation, the PP under Tancredo Neves decided to merge with the PMDB.

The 1982 Elections and Their Aftermath

The November 15 voting constituted an important triumph for moderation and a step toward sensible political modernization. Brazil emerged strengthened by elections whose results encouraged all major political actors to pursue their objectives through normal channels. The PDS won in a majority of states—guaran-

Lula da Silva addressing striking metal workers, 1979 (photo by Irmo Celso, courtesy of Abril Imagens)

teeing in the process control of the Senate, a near majority in the lower house, and a slim margin in the electoral college that would choose the new president a little over two years later. Yet return to direct elections created a situation in which the central government would at times need to truly compromise. Most notable was the fact that whereas in 1965—the most recent time governors had been directly elected—opposition victories in Rio de Janeiro and Minas Gerais by moderate figures had led to a hard-line coup, this time even Brizola's win in Rio de Janeiro was accepted by the armed forces with more resignation than trauma.

Nationally, 48.5 million of 58.6 million voters turned out, giving the opposition parties—especially the PMDB—victory in ten states with three-fifths of the country's population and nearly 75 percent of its GDP.[20] Continuing secular trends, the government party for the first time failed to get a majority of the valid vote in the balloting for Chamber of Deputies. Yet the PDS enjoyed a very modest edge over the PMDB on this dimension of national voting, as the PDT got only 2.4 million votes (almost all in Rio de Janeiro and Rio Grande do Sul), the PTB 1.8 million, and the PT 1.4 million—more than three-fourths of them in São Paulo. Moreover, the PDS emerged from the elections with a solid majority in the electoral college.

With the elections over, the government admitted that the country was on the verge of insolvency. To add to its woes, not only had 1982 been a bad year economically, but 1983 would prove to be a worse one in almost every respect. In 1982 GDP growth was a meager 0.5 percent, inflation was up marginally to 100 percent, and the accumulated foreign debt took a quantum jump. Moreover, after mid-1982 Mexico's virtual bankruptcy and foreign debt moratorium raised prospects of default and brought home to the international banking community its dangerous overexposure in Latin America. This caused a rapid dropoff in the flow of new credit to Brazil, so that only a hastily assembled emergency package avoided default on interest payments with amortization having quietly been suspended in midyear. Finally the first in a long series of letters of intent—none of which would be fulfilled—was signed with the IMF in January 1983. By dint of a 23 percent devaluation of the cruzeiro, exports were made competitive, as Brazil embarked full force upon a strategy of attaining increased trade surpluses (by reduction in oil imports as well as export expansion) in order to keep up interest payments to convince banks to roll over the principal.

In these spheres Brazil's performance was impressive, and the 1983 trade surplus doubled the following year. Yet the government met with little success in getting the economy under control as the erosion of the previous two years turned into a precipitous drop. GDP shrank by 3.5 percent, and the entailed reduction in standards of living caused a sharp rise in social unrest. Despite recessionary measures, inflation doubled to a record 211 percent, aggravated by a sharp climb in unemployment.

Opening Becomes Transition: 1984—A Crucial Year

As the Figueiredo government limped into its sixth year, transition to civilian, fully competitive politics was far from assured. Although the regime was losing its control over *abertura,* it still appeared likely that Figueiredo's successor would come from within his administration or from the conservative wing of the regime's party. Yet by the beginning of the final quarter of the year, *abertura* had become democratic transition, and the election of a civilian from opposition ranks was all but certain. Indeed, the crucial turnaround from a controlled opening to a situation in which initiative had escaped the government's hands took place in the short span of three months—June through August—largely as a result of weak leadership on Figueiredo's part. His failure to define a preference for successor led by mid-1984 to disaggregation of the government party that was reflected in the cabinet and higher reaches of the bureaucracy. In this context, Paulo Maluf (b. 1932), actively seeking support of PDS delegates and electors since even before the 1982 elections, continued his relentless drive to force the government to accept him as its candidate.

Maluf—determined and intelligent but open to attack as a nonideological demagogue with limitless ambitions—proved capable of winning the PDS nomination. But that this success was achieved largely through lavish expenditures and promises of future benefits sat badly with his rivals.[21] Thus, as the candidate with the lowest national popularity quotient moved closer to gaining the government party's nomination, its most popular figure, Vice President Aureliano Chaves, edged toward destabilizing the controlled process by reaching an agreement with fellow Minas Gerais statesman, Governor Tancredo Neves. Once the excitement and letdown of the unsuccessful campaign for direct elections was over, the battleground shifted to the behind-the-scenes maneuvering that usually proves more effective in changing the course of Brazilian politics. By midyear the dominant pragmatic wing of the PMDB decided that the best course was to do battle within the electoral college in the hope that Neves could gain support from disappointed backers of unsuccessful aspirants for the government party's nomination. This strategy gained substance as Chaves and his followers formalized their dissidence as the Liberal Front. Hence, immediately on the heels of Maluf's convention victory, the marriage of the Liberal Front dissidents and the PMDB was consummated. Faced with the reality that there would be no direct election for the presidency, the progressive wing of the PMDB had no choice but to acquiesce in the nomination of Neves.

In a very short time the new Democratic Alliance bandwagon evolved into a steamroller. Maluf remained confident that electors would ultimately prove as susceptible to his blandishments, but he would be disappointed in this as well as in his hopes to see further manipulation of the rules governing the electoral college. The mass rallies held by Neves served as a constant reminder to the 686 electors of the political perils of going against the surging tide of public opinion with return to competitive democratic politics imminent. Northeastern governors joined the Democratic Alliance. More important, private meetings between Neves and the army minister removed most of the latter's most serious reservations, and the ever cautious opposition candidate went out of his way to reassure the military that the armed forces as an institution would be free from political interference.

By a vote of 480 to 180 on January 15, 1985, the electoral college made Neves the country's new chief executive. Some 271 of the Democratic Alliance's votes came from the PMDB, the PFL delivered 113 more, and PDS dissidents chipped in with 55. Thus, Brazil was about to get a civilian government—and a broad-based centrist one to boot.

The Sarney Government:
Transition Under a Caretaker

As had been the case in 1822, 1889, 1930, and 1946, many elements of Brazilian society expected that this transition would lead almost automatically to a substantially transformed political system. To the extent that they foresaw a sharp break with the past and a regime based on new forms of political organization, they were soon to be disappointed. For this had been a transition without rupture, one in which the adherence to the movement for change of regime by experienced politicians and powerful interests associated with the prior order would guarantee that the bottle might be new, but that the wine would be substantially the same.

Forbidding Challenges

Although twenty-one years of military rule had come to an end, transition to a viable system of competitive civilian politics would prove an arduous chore. The first civilian government in almost a generation needed to work out a viable relationship between the executive and legislative branches of government as well as infuse life into the immense and ponderous state machinery built up since 1964. Then it would have to restructure the political party system and devise a new constitutional framework adequate to the needs of a complex society with enormous social inequalities and vast developmental needs.[22] Moreover, there would be early elections for mayors of state capitals, and then the government would have to conduct nationwide elections in 1986 for all governorships, two senators per state, and the full array of federal and state legislators. All this would have to be accomplished before late 1988 when elections in over 4,000 municipalities were to be held. After that the president would have to steer the country through its first direct presidential election in almost three decades. If this agenda were not formidable enough, there were also the matters of husbanding a still quite fragile economic recovery and dealing with the forbidding social deficit accumulated through twenty years of concentration on economic growth rather than income distribution.

There had been widespread faith that Tancredo Neves, with his experience and political sagacity, would find a way to handle the intimidating mass of challenges awaiting the civilian regime. But Neves could never even assume the presidential office, which would fall instead to Vice President José Sarney (b. 1927)—who was viewed with reserve, suspicion, distrust, or even distaste by much, perhaps most, of the PMDB, the dominant element of the Democratic Alliance. The progressive wing of the PMDB and others who expected that transition to civilian rule would resemble a return to the structural reform orientation of the Goulart years looked askance at Sarney's reliance upon former ARENA politicians grouped in the Liberal Front Party (PFL) and upon cultivation of close relations with the armed forces. For them transition would come only when some authentic opponent of the military governments, not merely a critic of Figueiredo, occupied the presidency.

Permanent harmony between the disparate elements of the Democratic Alliance likely was not possible due to incompatible concepts of what the socioeconomic content of the Nova República should be. As it turned out, the insistence of progressive elements that Sarney himself constituted a major obstacle to change left the president with no feasible option but to follow what was for him the most natural course—governance in collaboration with the Center and Center-Right.

When Sarney was sworn in on March 15, it was as acting president with the country purposely misled into expecting that Neves would eventually recover and assume the presidency. Ministries had been allotted in a manner combining regional balance and equity among the several components of the Democratic Alliance with an eye to the upcoming 1986 elections. São Paulo and Minas Gerais came out particularly well, justifiable since together they had roughly 46 million inhabitants—as well as the lion's share of the country's productive capacity. On the economic and financial side, the government had a pragmatic, nearly orthodox cast. Neves was a fiscal conservative convinced of the need to bring inflation under control. Although Sarney originally accepted Neves's position in this realm, he subsequently sided for a time with the advocates of growth. As there were quite deep political divisions within the political orchestra Neves had constructed, Sarney would need to change the cabinet on a piecemeal basis until he had one congruent with his views, albeit he lacked a firm congressional majority.

Neves's death on April 21 both assured Sarney's continuance as president and allowed Ulysses Guimarães (b. 1916) to emerge as the PMDB's leading figure. Sarney was compelled to move cautiously in seeking support from other parties so as not to alienate the numerically dominant PMDB. Guimarães, a cabinet member as far back as 1961, tended to act as if he were a de facto prime minister. But this was not in keeping with the reality that the PMDB was a heterogeneous holding company of disparate political groupings sharing little more than a long experience of being in opposition and a consequent difficulty in adapting to being the governing party—or even the government's party.[23]

Clearly the party system of the mid-1980s lacked deep roots in the electorate, which had exploded to nearly 70 million from 18.5 million in 1962, and was inadequate for consolidating the democratic transition. One of the major obstacles to any significant reform or reinforcement of the undisciplined party system lay in the incumbent national legislators' unwillingness to discard its most irrational features—for they had managed to get elected through this bizarre system.

Progress Before the 1986 Elections

Legislation in May removed virtually all restrictions on the formation of political parties, extended the right to vote to illiterates, and provided that future presidential elections would be direct. Yet legislation to do away with the national security law bogged down because the fact remained that a majority of Congress had been elected in 1982 on the ticket of the government's party and remained deeply suspicious of anything the PMDB's progressive wing strongly favored. Few clues as to shifts in voter loyalty emerged from the November 1985 elections of capital city mayors—the first such balloting in over two decades. The PMDB could point to 19 wins in state and territory capitals and 110 (of 201 contests) in other localities. Results in Rio de Janeiro, Porto Alegre, and Fortaleza gave the PMDB reason to worry about growth of the PDT and to look over its shoulder at the PT.

The first year of civilian rule brought limited but significant steps toward consolidation and a definite improvement in Sarney's position. In economic matters except inflation, the new government inherited a substantially improved and in many ways still improving situation. Initially dependent upon export expansion, this economic recovery broadened into domestic commerce and agriculture. Internal consumption became the engine of economic growth as real salaries rose and commerce was up in the second semester following a good agricultural harvest—all yielding a dramatic 7.9 percent GDP expansion. On the negative side the fight against the dragon of inflation was a casualty of the administration's pursuit of growth. When the cost of living went up a record 14 percent in August, the president brought in developmentalist businessman Dilson Funaro (b. 1935) as finance minister. Subsequently inflation continued at a high rate pushed by both the financing needs of the public-sector deficit, which led to major expansion of internal debt, and price markups in anticipation of continued high inflation. The impact of this on the foreign debt situation was substantial as the new government was unwilling for political reasons to accept continued close monitoring of the nation's finances by the IMF.

Surging inflation of December 1985 and January 1986 led Sarney to adopt a heterodox shock designed by young economists gathered together by Funaro. The Cruzado Plan was announced with great fanfare on February 28. It combined as its chief features substituting a new unit of currency for the old cruzeiro at a rate of one to 1,000, a one-year freeze on mortgages and rents, an indefinite price freeze, and a new wage system. In the short run this program appeared to be a success. Monthly inflation rates stayed under 2 percent through October, and savings were funneled into productive investment rather than the merry-go-round of financial speculations that had been rampant in recent years. Substantial increases in real income and rising employment led, however, to a consumption boom that often went beyond the bounds of reason. With the upcoming elections choosing a national legislature that would decide the nature of the governmental system and the tenure of the incumbent administration, neither Sarney nor the PMDB could resist the temptation to continue the program that had produced massive public support for the regime. The policy was extended far beyond the point sound economic thinking dictated. It became a case of too much, too long, as what should have been a temporary price and wage freeze was continued several months after it began to distort demand-supply relationships. An artificial atmosphere of prosperity guaranteed an overwhelming electoral victory for the PMDB with the PFL picking up what was left over; it also set the stage for a massive hangover as the public would feel betrayed when the artificial prosperity evaporated soon after the elections and inflation once again threatened to climb back toward new record highs.[24]

The 1986 Elections and a New Constitution

On November 15 with a high proportion of the more than 69 million eligible citizens voting, Brazil elected a Congress that would also function as constituent assembly to write a new constitution. As it would remain the nation's legislative body through 1990, with senators serving until early 1995, this Congress was slated to play a critical role in the consolidation of the still fledgling democratic regime. Governors and state legislatures were also chosen to hold office for four years. Taking place in a climate of rapid economic growth, high employment, and improving well-being, this balloting resulted in sweeping victory for the Democratic Alliance—all governors, three-fourths of the lower house, and 80 percent of the Senate. The government's critics on Left and Right went down to crushing defeats that threatened to derail their presidential aspirations, and two dozen newly established parties failed to find any voter responsiveness, which left leaving the party system essentially where it had been before the campaign.[25]

From the figures, the PMDB had a great deal to celebrate. With 261 federal deputies it had a majority in the 487-member lower house, and its 45 senators gave it a larger one in that body. No fewer_than 22 of 23 governorships went to individuals affiliated with the party—although a number of these were won in coalition with the PFL. The PFL's 119 deputies were just 10 fewer than before, and its 16 senators were more than at the beginning of the Sarney administration. For the PDS it was quite another matter as 33 deputies and 5 senators were less than half its prior representation in Congress, already well down from the 165 and 31 it had at the beginning of the administration.

The PDT could find little solace in its 23 deputies and a senator—one of them a holdover. Since it had begun the Sarney government with 24, this represented stagnation. Similarly, although the PT made much over having doubled its congressional representation, fifteen deputies were in reality a disappointing harvest, as was its roughly 5 percent of the national vote compared to 3.3 percent in 1982. The PTB's 17 seats left it where it had been, but above the 12 held at the beginning of civilian rule; the Liberal Party (PL) elected its 6 deputies exclusively in Rio de Janeiro and São Paulo. Five congressmen were not a good result for those resurrecting the PDC, and as for the two Communist groups, the pro-Soviet PCB and the Chinese-oriented Communist Party of Brazil (PCdoB), three deputies each did not represent improvement over what they had when still hidden within the PMDB.

Corrective economic policies decreed just after the elections were designed to reduce consumption and augment investment while giving the government additional revenues to decrease the public-sector deficit—a poor substitute for directly attacking the deficit by reducing expenditures. Thus, although GDP growth for the year was a robust 7.6 percent, inflation began to climb again, hitting 7.3 percent for December. Moreover, substantial trade surpluses turned into small monthly deficits. Funaro and his PMDB economists convinced Sarney to decree a February 1987 moratorium on payment of interest on the foreign debt to private banks rather than take measures to reduce consumption.

Doubling as the nation's regular Congress, the constituent assembly made excruciatingly slow progress toward producing a new framework for government and public policy. Repeated shifts in government personnel would be closely related to the fluctuating fortunes of the administration in the constituent assembly—much of which depended upon the ebb and flow of a continuing intramural struggle between moderates and progressives for dominance within the PMDB. The national legislature elected in November 1986 reflected the country's political divisions relatively well, tilted slightly toward the Center-Right owing to the underrepresentation of São Paulo. One in eight of its members could be identified as strongly conservative, and 6 to 10 percent were well over on the Left.[26] They were extremely vocal and active, and once action passed from committees to the floor, they would find themselves waging an often unsuccessful battle to preserve initial-stage gains. One-fifth to one-fourth of the legislators were of a Center-Left persuasion, roughly matched by the Center-Right. The remaining third were squarely in the middle. A quarter of the body were rural landowners, and an equal proportion (including some overlapping) had ties to the financial sector.

The most important political event of this period was Funaro's ouster in April 1987 in the face of exploding inflation. His successor as finance minister was economist-businessman Luíz Carlos Bresser Pereira (b. 1934), also from São Paulo. Confident that he understood the nature of Brazil's inflation, in mid-June Bresser launched a plan bearing his name. Centered on a temporary price freeze and formula for holding pay increases in check, the Bresser Plan brought inflation down temporarily but lost momentum as inflation rose rapidly. Inflation hit 14.1 percent for the last month of the year as GDP growth ceased; growth for 1987 dipped to only 3.6 percent—by far the lowest since the dark days of the 1981–1983 recession.

In early December a Center-Right alliance pushed through changes in the constituent assembly's rules and procedures that gave backbenchers more of a voice. As 125 of the PMDB's representatives voted with it against their party's official position, a leader disowned by a large proportion of his party, Mário Covas, began to pack his bags for departure to a new party composed of fellow progressives. Only after the question of the president's term was finally resolved did the government belatedly take meaningful measures to curb inflation from escalating into hyperinflation. In January Mailson Ferreira da Nóbrega, a career civil servant, was confirmed as Bresser Pereira's successor. His orthodox "rice and beans" approach contrasted sharply with the fanciful flights of his predecessors. A five-year term for Sarney was maintained by the full assembly on June 2, and the constitution moved toward completion. The party picture also underwent an important change as Covas and Fernando Henrique Cardoso led an exodus of progressives out of the PMDB into the PSDB (Brazilian Social Democracy Party). Finally on September 22 the protracted and often politically agonizing process of shaping a new constitution came to an end; it was promulgated October 5.[27]

Consolidating the Transition

Now Brazil could turn to choosing a chief executive to carry out changes mandated by the 1988 basic charter. Although the 1987–1988 constituent assembly had taken a long time to produce an unexceptional charter, it did provide for thorough airing of almost every significant issue of governance and public policy.

Fundamental Features and Paving the Way

The basic structure of a federal presidential government was little altered, although Congress saw its powers amplified. The security council was eliminated and replaced by a Council of the Republic and a National Defense Council. On the one hand workers' rights and benefits were augmented, but on the other expropriation of productive land was not permitted. The franchise was extended to sixteen-year-olds, and changes in the distribution of revenues gave states and municipalities fiscal resources for which they had been in the habit of bargaining with the federal executive. Amendment would be by a three-fifths majority of Congress until late 1993, at which time the body elected in 1990 could change it by a majority vote—although bound to follow a national referendum on a parliamentary versus presidential system.

Article 142 defined the armed forces as "permanent and regular national institutions organized on the basis of hierarchy and discipline, under the express authority of the President of the Republic and intended for the defense of the country, guaranteeing the constitutional powers and, by invitation of any one of these, law and order." Although less of a mandate for the military to function as the moderating power than had been the case in previous constitutions, it fell far short of the clear prohibition on this that the Left had advocated.

The 1988 elections for over 4,300 mayors, an equal number of vice mayors, and some 43,600 municipal councilmen did little to clarify the confused presidential succession picture.[28] Since governors failed to elect the mayor of their capitals, their setbacks canceled out. Furthermore, although the two largest metropolitan centers were won by the PT and the PDT, neither of these parties of the Left demonstrated significant strength on more than a regional basis. The artificially high proportion of offices the PMDB had gained in 1986 was not duplicated in the midst of runaway inflation and disenchantment with the conduct of the country's affairs by this numerically hegemonic but internally divided behemoth. Yet it still remained Brazil's largest party by a substantial margin, electing over 1,600 mayors compared to 1,060 for the PFL and 450 for the PDS. Despite shifts in voter support in the larger urban centers, parties of the Left had not attained electoral superiority there; those of the Center and Right still possessed a marked advantage in municipalities of under 50,000 inhabitants where 40 percent of the electorate was to be found.

The new year opened in a climate of malaise and uncertainty similar to that prevailing in early 1986. With inflation for 1988 at over 1,000 percent and GDP growth at zero, the dreaded phenomenon of stagflation had clearly already arrived. The government's response was to launch the Plano Verão on January 15. The new cruzado with three zeros lopped off became the unit of currency, and steps to end monetary correction were paired with a price freeze and abolition of automatic pay raises as the key elements in an effort to bring inflation under control. To avoid the problems caused by the original Cruzado Plan, these were to be of a clearly temporary duration.

The People Choose a President

By February all else would take a back seat to directly electing the nation's president for the first time since Quadros had been chosen in 1960. As the PDT's Brizola (b. 1922) and the PT's Lula da Silva rushed their campaigns to the streets, several political factors became apparent: The unpopularity of the Sarney government would prevent it from playing a decisive role in shaping the succession; neither of the early front-runners managed to ignite the bulk of the electorate; and only a small minority of Brazil's voters identified with the plethora of competing parties. The vast majority still tended to vote for a candidate and not a party, for an imagined savior instead of a program. Finding little appeal in ideologies and relatively uninterested in specific policies, voters were looking for someone they could view as deserving their trust and possibly capable of pulling Brazil out of the morass into which it had slipped.

Brizola and Lula soon ran into a serious challenge from a candidate they had refused to take as a serious threat: Fernando Collor de Mello (b. 1948), the handsome and athletic son of an old-line northeastern politician. At 6' 1" and weighing in at a trim 185 pounds—and with an even younger and quite photogenic wife—this governor of the small northeastern state of Alagoas was the nearly perfect media candidate. While Collor was shooting up from obscurity to status as the leading contender, the country's strongest parties facilitated his task by planting and cultivating the seeds of their own downfall. Indeed, the PMDB's decision to go with seventy-three-year-old Ulysses Guimarães paved the way for Collor's triumph. Guimarães and the PFL's Aureliano Chaves, who had been Sarney's minister of mines and energy, could not get the electorate to swallow the palpably untrue line that they had not really been closely associated with the incumbent government.

Economically conservative but socially centrist, Collor posed effectively as a potential reformer of the widely discredited practices of Brazilian politics. Substituting talk about modernization and blistering attacks upon corruption and abusive bureaucratic privileges for any profound criticism of the existing sociopolitical order, he made moralization and scathing denunciation of politicians the heart of his appeal. By assuming a position of intransigent critic of the Sarney government, Collor effectively preempted the efforts of the Left to benefit from the administration's unpopularity and the public's dissatisfaction with the economic and social situation. By criticizing the São Paulo Federation of Industries as "backwards and reactionary," he avoided being tagged as the darling of the Right—a position left to Maluf. His ability to satisfy centrist constituencies spelled doom for Covas's dream of staking out the middle road in a polarization between Lula and Brizola on the Left and Collor and Maluf on the Right.

At just over 82 million, the electorate was up sharply, largely owing to the inclusion of sixteen- and seventeen-year-olds. The dominance of the center and south remained pronounced: São Paulo led the way with 18.5 million voters, followed by Minas Gerais's more than 9.4 million and Rio de Janeiro's 8.2 million—for a combined 44 percent of the national total. Voters were young; nearly half were under thirty and fewer than 15 percent were above age fifty. Only a sixth of potential voters had graduated from high school, at least a tenth were totally illiterate, and another 30 percent were barely able to read and write. But what most distinguished the Brazilian electorate in 1989 was inexperience in voting to fill national offices and very weak ties to political parties. The overwhelming majority had never voted before the abrupt 1964 regime change; most had been socialized into the either-or choice of ARENA or the MDB between 1966 and 1979 or after the subsequent reemergence of a multiparty system. The greater part of the electorate would disregard party labels and vote not even for the man but for the image.[29] This they did on November 15, confirming Collor as the favorite and making Lula his runoff rival, albeit this by the narrowest of margins over Brizola.

Elimination of a score of candidates left only Collor, professing to be a social democrat while championing a modern market economy, and Lula, articulator of a consistent ideological position for the Left. The contest was essentially a battle to gain the support of the majority of the electorate orphaned by defeat of their preferred candidates. Despite inclement weather in large parts of the country, the vast majority of Brazil's electorate turned out on December 17 to put an end to the almost yearlong campaign. Some 35.1 million, over 53 percent of the valid vote, opted for Collor, whereas 31.1 million favored Lula.[30] The efforts of the pro-Lula forces to build up from the 11.6 million votes for the PT candidate in the first round to the over 33 million that would be needed for election had proved impossible. Mainly middle-class Brazilians who had originally opted for Covas or Guimarães as their first choice drifted in large numbers to Collor. Thus, starting with his 20.6 million votes from November 15, Collor fell heir to most of Maluf's nearly 6 million votes as well as the lion's share of the combined 1.5 million of the PFL's Chaves and PTB nominee Affonso Camargo Neto. To this he added over half the 3.3 million received by the PL's Guilherme Afif Domingos and at least an even split of the minor candidates' support for over another 1.5 million. His substantial slice of the 10.8 million Covas-Guimarães center vote put him comfortably over the top. Collor's support was greater the smaller the town or city. Yet he scored a 700,000-vote victory in São Paulo—South America's largest city. Voters' preference for a new face representing the entrepreneurial stratum of the private sector confirmed that large sectors of the Brazilian masses were little interested in ideological politics.

The country then could settle back, anticipating with generally high hopes the first inauguration of a directly elected president since the beginning of 1961. Inflation, which had pushed 1,800 percent for the year, soared to 68 percent in January and 73 percent the following month with a new record clearly in sight for March. Even carnival could not divert public attention from anxious speculation over what magic formula the new providential man could concoct to save Brazil from the perils of hyperinflation. For most Brazilians the Collor era had already begun. Unfortunately, Collor would prove to be a rocket that took off in a great surge of power, entered into an unstable orbit, then crashed to earth in a great ball of flame—from which the pilot walked out badly burned but alive.

5

POLITICS AND GOVERNMENT POLICIES IN THE 1990S

STRUCTURES, PRACTICES, and attitudes built up over generations are resistant to change. Hence it is not surprising that after two and a half years of Collor's presidency, an equal span under Itamar Franco, and a year of Cardoso, Brazil's political life has not been drastically transformed. Initially a dent was put into some deep-rooted "anti-modern" practices, but 1992 was spent containing damage from corruption and influence-peddling scandals leading to Collor's impeachment. Yet the fact that a very grave crisis was handled strictly within constitutional processes and without involvement of the armed forces is noteworthy.[1] During 1993 Franco operated as a caretaker, paradoxically coming to enjoy greater authority during 1994 when the contest for his successor was already under way. He in turn has concentrated on economic and fiscal problems.

Implantation of a market-oriented liberalism tempered by moderate social democratic precepts—Collor's basic project—would still be far from fully accomplished even if he had survived as president. Throughout at least the past century, the "art of not choosing between conflicting objectives" has been highly developed in Brazil, accompanied in the more recent period by a "proliferation of disguised mechanisms for transferring resources" stemming from a lack of clarity in perceiving the consequences of economic policy upon social groups. This has been fostered by a state acting as distributor of benefits to holders of political power.[2] Moreover, Brazilian elites' liberalism has been chiefly rhetorical as they have historically demonstrated little faith in the market as an allocator.

Over its thirty months in office the Collor administration had a roller coaster ride that began at the top, plunged in the second half year, bottomed out in mid-1991, and entered into a fatal tailspin a year later. Despite the bitter disillusionment of the public to find that the anticorruption champion condoned widespread payoffs and influence peddling, the traumatic experience had the salutary effect of focusing attention on building stronger institutions rather than trusting all to a demagogic savior. His successor followed a different uneven trajectory, beginning with a political honeymoon before falling on harder times and then rising to an exceptionally high level of popularity and accomplishing the rare feat of easily electing his successor. Thus over the 1990–1995 span some necessary reforms were accomplished through the workings of a competitive democratic system in which presidents had to cope with an independent and often opposition-dominated Congress. This chapter is a survey of the obstacle-filled course these developments have followed, the nature of the current government, major public policy issues, and the most important organized interests active in the political arena.

The First Year:
Shakedown Cruise to the Doldrums

Most of the original administrative team early on failed to perform up to Collor's expectations, and this led to repeated personnel changes. In common with Sarney's experience, Collor's approval rating varied directly with public perception of economic performance. Also similar between the two civilian governments was the lack of a firm base of congressional support, as the party system remained fragmented, undisciplined, and motivated by short-range electoral considerations. The sharpest contrast was Collor's determination to push ahead with privatization of state-owned enterprises to which Sarney had paid lip service and to attack inflation at its roots—reversing the protracted upward surge.

Hitting the Ground Running

Portrayed as a "northeasterner" largely on the basis of tours of duty as mayor of Maceió (1979–1982) and governor of Alagoas (1987–1989), Collor was more a product of Brazil's heartland, his home for most of his life. Educated through high school in Rio de Janeiro, he studied at the University of Brasília before graduating from the University of Alagoas. Originally married into a wealthy Rio de Janeiro family after a playboy existence, he remarried into a regionally important family during his stint as mayor.

Collor's priorities included reducing the state's role in Brazil's economic life, curbing government spending, halting the inflationary spiral, attracting new flows of investment and technology, and inserting a rehabilitated and modernized Brazilian economy into the competitive mainstream of international life. São

Paulo economist Zélia Cardoso de Melo (b. 1956) was entrusted with the Economy Ministry—composed of the Finance portfolio plus nearly all of the Planning Ministry and most of Industry and Commerce as well.[3] Responsibility for a substantial portion of the federal bureaucracy fell to retired air force Lieutenant Colonel Ozires Silva (b. 1930), also from São Paulo. His Infrastructure Ministry was composed of the former ministries of Transportation, Communications, and Mines and Energy as well as elements of Industry and Commerce. On the basis of an inflated assessment of his work as rapporteur of the constituent assembly, Bernardo Cabral (b. 1932) was made justice minister. Closest to the president was Secretary General of the Presidency Marcos Coimbra (b. 1927), a career ambassador married to Collor's older sister. On the military side Collor chose competent professionals with reputations for having avoided political involvement.

Exploding off the starting blocks, the economy's liquidity was reduced from over 30 percent of GDP to under 10 percent—with $85 billion frozen in blocked accounts while the cruzeiro became Brazil's currency. Key in this was the $50 billion of the bloated "overnight" capital market that had become an inflation-feeding way of financing the government's domestic debt. Savings accounts, certificates of deposit, and other types of funds were also blocked as liquidity dried up initially from some $140 billion to only $35 billion.[4] Other measures sharply raised fuel and public utility rates and rolled private-sector prices back to the March 12 level, where they would be held for forty-five days. Moves were made to abolish two dozen federal agencies. The objective at the program's heart was to keep inflation down by transforming the huge prospective public-sector operating deficit into a small surplus—a $35 billion turnaround. Privatization, fiscal reforms, and improved tax collection were major pillars of this effort—essential for credibility in renegotiation of the overhanging foreign debt.

In early dealings with Congress, Collor's negotiating ability, his disposition to wheel and deal when essential, and the extent of his public support proved sufficient. Thus, during the initial fortnight of April, the Collor Plan was approved by Congress with little modification in voting that demonstrated once again how little parties mattered. Despite defections before the filing deadline for the October elections, the PMDB still had 28 percent of Congress, the PFL 20 percent of the seats, and the PSDB 13 percent of congressional strength. Together the PDT, PT, PCB, PCdoB, and PSB (Brazilian Socialist Party) (the Left opposition) mustered 13 percent. On the Right, the PDS, PRN (National Renovation Party), PTB, PDC, and PL aggregated 23 percent.

At midyear an industrial policy reducing protectionism and facilitating imports dealt a stiff blow to sectors of the Brazilian economy accustomed to virtually guaranteed profits at no real risk. Tariffs were sharply cut, other import limitations eliminated, and price-fixing practices challenged.[5] Inflation was sharply cut and kept down for a half year. Given the inflationary culture that had become part of Brazil's everyday life, this was no mean accomplishment. From 80 percent in March, the cost of living moderated to a rise of 14.7 percent in April, which was halved in May but bulged again as price controls were relaxed—forcing the executive to prepare more stringent austerity measures.[6]

The 1990 Elections

With the initial euphoria dissipating, some 84 million registered voters went to the polls on October 3 to choose which of roughly 20,000 candidates would fill nearly 1,700 posts as governors, vice governors, senators, alternate senators, federal deputies, and state legislators. In the presidential contest the premium had been on new faces, but for governors Brazil's voters looked for experience and proven performance. Thus, 6 of the 27 governors chosen had occupied statehouses before—some more than once—and a good proportion of the others came from the ranks of big-city mayors (another 6 former governors were eliminated at the runoff stage). On the Senate side, with 31 of 81 seats at stake, experience was also in demand, as the winners were a mix of incumbents, outgoing governors, and former state chief executives. The 503 individuals elected to the lower house included less than half incumbents; most of the rest were veteran state legislators and mayors seeking to move up to the national scene—some of whom had previously served in Congress. Among the victors was only a sprinkling of newcomers to elective politics cashing in on reputations in other fields.[7] Women and Afro-Brazilians were few in the winners' circle—the former totaling but 27 federal deputies (virtually the same as before) and the latter a sparse 11 in the lower house.

Once again the elections underscored the weakness of Brazil's political parties, and with local and regional issues playing an important role there was a strong Center-Right tilt to both the new Congress and lineup of governors. The gross underrepresentation of São Paulo combined with the grotesque overrepresentation of the smaller agrarian states made leftists' efforts to increase their weight in Congress an uphill battle. The PMDB suffered further erosion, electing only 107 to the lower house along with 8 senators and 7 governors. Its 1985–1988 junior partner, the PFL, moved up to near parity on the strength of 86 seats in the Chamber of Deputies and 8 of those at stake in the Senate. On the gubernatorial side, the PFL was the big winner with 9 victors and 5 others from coalitions in which it was a major factor. The PSDB fell far short of its goal of catching the PMDB, electing 37 national congressmen, 1 senator, and 1 governor. At 43 seats in the lower house and 2 in the upper, the PDS gained substantially, although it elected only 1 governor from a small state.

The PDT, despite Brizola's win for governor of Rio de Janeiro, made little national progress, electing 47 federal deputies, 1 senator, and 2 governors. This kept it well ahead of the PT, which also elected 1 senator and no governor and won only 35 seats in the lower house. Its allies fared poorly, the PCB electing 3 federal deputies, the PCdoB 5, and the PSB 11. Conservative flag-of-convenience parties did little better than hold their own. The PTB elected 36 deputies, 1 senator, and 2 governors; the PDC came away with 22 seats in the lower house along with 5 in the upper; the PRN could muster 40 deputies and 2 senators; and the PL lost ground with but 15 Chamber of Deputies seats. Luiz Antônio Fleury Filho's election as São Paulo governor made Orestes Quércia one of the few incumbent executives not to have been electorally embarrassed.

By the time vote counting was over from the governorship runoffs, the year-end holidays were at hand. An apathetic tranquillity was interrupted only by the early February announcement of the Second Collor Plan. Featuring a price and wage freeze, elimination of the overnight financial market, and a formal abolition of monetary correction, this package elicited more yawns than screams of dismay, as such ballyhooed measures had become virtually an annual affair. A month later the reconvened Congress approved most of the plan's key elements.

The Second Year: Stemming the Slide and Regaining Momentum

Round two of the Collor government lacked the dramatic political events to which Brazilians had become accustomed. There were no electoral campaigns to give focus to political life and capture public attention. Hence the political situation came to be viewed largely through the lens of economic performance with refraction through the prism of societal unrest. Although falling far short of the administration's promises for an end to inflation and a new beginning of sustained growth, economic developments also steered clear of demoralizing hyperinflation and profound depression. Inflation in 1991 would be by far the lowest since 1987 and but a fraction of 1989's or 1990's nearly 1,800 percent. Moreover, several important steps were taken in the economic sphere, the most notable being a solid beginning to privatization of state enterprises, fiscal legislation providing a substantial increase in government revenues, opening of the stock-market to foreign institutional investors, and abandonment of emergency programs featuring price freezes as the chief means of attacking inflation. This renunciation of the standard last resort patch-up solution required replacing the economy minister's team of young activists with a more experienced and orthodox crew.

Changing the Team and Driving Ahead

May 10 witnessed the firing of Cardoso de Melo and a wave of personnel changes as banker-diplomat Marcílio Marques Moreira (b. 1931) took her place. Indeed, the Collor government was by now profoundly transformed from the team that had taken office fourteen months earlier. The czarina of the economy was gone, a victim of rising inflation, an agricultural disaster (aided by a drought), alienation of many congressmen, and accentuated tensions with the international banking community, U.S. Treasury, the IMF, and Paris Club. Her replacement had been a career diplomat before being seconded to the Bank of Guanabara and moving into Unibanco. His competent team increased credibility with the political class, business community, and international bankers.

May ended on a positive note as a general strike was a nearly complete fiasco. Then in June Congress approved the phasing out of extreme protectionism in the computer industry, a step needed to smooth relations with the United States and improve Brazil's image as a field for foreign investors. In July Congress finally passed the new social security law required by the 1988 constitution. A quite turbulent and tense October opened with a 15 percent devaluation of the cruzeiro; it closed on a mixed note with the successful privatization of the Usiminas steel company but an explosion of inflation back into the 20-plus percent danger zone. Disappointing many businessmen who were gambling on another price-wage freeze, the administration showed a newfound determination to let the market work its medicine. Price rises declined in velocity in December, the dollar slipped back from its earlier speculative explosion, and interest rates receded from obscene levels they had reached when hyperinflationary panic had run amok. Tax increases were enacted, but none of the constitutional amendments necessary for elimination of the inflation-feeding public-sector deficit neared passage.

Collor: Burning Out, Getting a Second Wind, or Maturing?

By the beginning of 1992, being president had proved to be a much more difficult job than Collor imagined either before taking office or during the initial honeymoon phase of his government. Relations with Congress were frustratingly thorny, and he had become healthily skeptical about economists' promises and magical potions. Yet disaster had been avoided in all realms during 1991 as important steps toward growth, progress, and development were taken. Collor both effectively stymied the bid of former São Paulo Governor Quércia to establish himself as favorite for the 1994 presidential sweepstakes and demonstrated skill in dealing with Rio de Janeiro Governor and PDT leader Brizola. A more difficult relationship was with Antônio Carlos Magalhães (b. 1927), back in Bahia's governorship for the third time. Holder of high executive positions under Figueiredo and Sarney, the PFL powerbroker discomfited the government by assuming the role of paladin of administrative and financial probity and crusader against corruption. Magalhães's influence was magnified by ties to Roberto Marinho, owner of the Globo television network and mass-circulation daily newspaper.

During his second year Collor avoided potentially crippling defeats in the legislative arena. Even though constitutional amendments he requested were not voted, they spurred limited fiscal reform legislation enacted at year's end. The party scene saw a modest amount of realignment within Congress and normal movement by individual politicians and small groups from one party to another. The PT at the end of November took a more moderate line, handing a defeat to radical groupings as Lula da Silva's Articulation faction carried the day. Similarly the PCB dropped the hammer and sickle as its symbol, adopting the name Popular Socialist Party (PPS).

The Economic Front and Shifting Gears

Economic performance, albeit lackluster, was a marked improvement over 1990. Inflation was cut to 480 percent, and GDP grew 0.9 percent rather than shrinking by 4.4 percent. Moreover, the 1991 census demonstrated that the rate of demographic growth was significantly lower than had been estimated; the country had only 147 million inhabitants—5 percent below the expected figure. This meant, of course, that per capita GDP growth in recent years had been measurably higher than officially calculated, enough to reduce the various facets of the country's massive social deficit. A number of necessary steps were taken by early 1992 to increase the prospects for bringing inflation under control. Privatization got under way despite concerted efforts to sidetrack it, Brazil's stock markets were opened to foreign institutional investors with almost immediate boomlike results, and liberalization of imports made significant headway. Moreover, a tentative agreement was reached with the IMF, and foreign exchange reserves were maintained at a minimally adequate level through a trade surplus of $10.6 billion (on exports of $31.6 billion).

Agriculturally 1991 was a bad year. Grain production of 58 million tons was far below 1989's bumper crop or even the 65 million for 1987 and 1988. The silver lining for the administration was sharp recovery at the beginning of 1992 to a near-record 71 million tons of grain. On the negative side, the social security system balanced on the brink of bankruptcy, with public confidence undermined by scandals showing that an enormous range of large-scale frauds had gone on for years. But the problem was more fundamental; the ratio of contributors to recipients was down to a nonviable two to one, compared to eight to one a decade earlier, and elevation of benefits to the level required by law created a shortfall of $4.4 billion in a system that mobilized but $26 billion in 1991.

Collor himself emerged from the second year of his presidency significantly sobered if not seriously shaken and adopted a different stance in dealing with Congress—jawboning rather than finger pointing, preaching, and exhorting. In early 1992 the lower house was divided into an undependable and often rebellious government bloc made up of the PFL and PRN; an officially opposition PMDB, from whose ranks the government compensated for defections from its nominal base; an informal opposition alliance lacking discipline or unity of purpose based on the PDT, PT, PSDB, and PSB calculating their particular interests largely in the context of competition with one another for presumed electoral advantage; and a grouping of centrist conservative parties including the PDS, the PTB, the PDC, and the PL. Their support was generally available in return for pork and patronage. On the Senate side, the government had 38 seats to the opposition's nominal 43 but could usually count on support of several of the PMDB's 27 solons to pass essential measures.

The Third Year: Disaster for Collor,
Opportunity for Franco

March 1992 found an apparently secure Collor battling to get legislation out of Congress before its members became immersed in campaigning for the October 3 municipal elections. But within four months he would be fighting for his political life, and by October he would have been removed from the presidency and be facing impeachment by the Senate. First, however, he kicked off his third year in office with a profound reformulation of his government. Keeping Marcílio Moreira's economic team and the military ministers intact that included some recent replacements, the president brought in highly qualified intellectuals and experienced professionals to complement that reputable nucleus.

Onto the Rocks and a New Helmsman

Hopes that positive reaction to cabinet changes would translate into congressional approval of fiscal reforms were soon dashed. Instead the administration found its survival at stake. Congressional investigation of Paulo César Farias's influence peddling and financial misdeeds escalated by July into a probe of Collor's ties to his longtime chief campaign fund-raiser. Hard pressed to deny Farias's role in his personal finances as well as this unprincipled opportunist's rapacious profiteering from governmental connections, Collor found his credibility seriously undermined with important media urging resignation or impeachment. August was marked by a struggle over putting the formal impeachment process into motion.[8] Having done business as usual after posing as an implacable foe of corruption, Collor saw his presidency end just after its scheduled midpoint, as the Chamber of Deputies decisively voted on September 29 to remove him. Yet the crisis was a landmark, for the armed forces played no discernible role—in stark contrast to the unscheduled ends to presidential tenures in 1969, 1964, 1961, 1954–1955, 1945, and 1930.

Sworn in on October 2 as acting president, Itamar Augusto Cauteiro Franco (b. 1930) became the sixth Mineiro to attain Brazil's highest office—not counting Tancredo Neves, who was never inaugurated. His administrative experience was limited to two stints as Juiz da Fora mayor, the second having ended nearly two decades earlier. Elected to the Senate in the MDB tidal wave of 1974, he lost its gubernatorial nomination in 1982 and was roundly defeated in a 1986 statehouse bid. Recruited by Collor after almost signing on as Brizola's running mate in 1989, Franco was extremely sensitive to his shabby treatment as vice president.

Franco appointed a coterie of Juiz da Fora friends to key offices along with others from his home state before turning to old Senate chums to minimally meet requisites of party and regional balance. Moreover, he undid the administrative reform of his predecessor, re-creating ministries that had been merged or eliminated. To head his staff he selected Henrique Hargreaves (b. 1936), a legislative

Congress voting on Collor's impeachment, September 1992 (photo by Moreira Mariz, courtesy of Abril Imagens*)*

aide from his hometown who had handled congressional liaison for Sarney. His secretary general of the presidency was an aide from Franco's days as mayor, another Juiz da Fora neighbor became solicitor general, and a hometown history professor was education minister. Senator Fernando Henrique Cardoso (b. 1931) as foreign minister helped compensate for the lack of international standing and experience of the economic team. Rio Grande do Sul congressman Antônio Britto (PMDB) became social security minister, with individuals passing rapidly through the Finance Ministry. Career officers were selected to head the military ministries. The president's early pronouncements projected an image of a provincial figure with one foot in the past in terms of an antiquated brand of 1950s nationalism, a statist inclination, and an old-fashioned petty electoral populism—all reflected in a protracted failure to establish a coherent economic policy.

The October 3 municipal elections were remarkably unaffected by the national political crisis, and no party dramatically improved its position over the very mixed results of 1988. On the whole, mayors perceived as having performed reasonably well elected their successors, and those who had promised much more than they managed to deliver saw their candidates go down to defeat. As for the first time runoffs were held in municipalities of over 200,000 registered voters, the dust did not settle until after November 15. The top prize, São Paulo, fell to Paulo Maluf, who thus put an end to a string of electoral setbacks dating to losing the presidency in 1984 and gave new life to the PDS. In Rio de Janeiro, the PMDB's economist Ceśar Maia (b. 1945) foiled the bid of the PT's Benedita da Silva to become the first Afro-Brazilian woman to reach high electoral office. Belo Horizonte and Porto Alegre saw PT victories, and Recife and Fortaleza gave the PMDB something to cheer about. The PDT's most important win was in Curitiba; the PSDB's in Salvador. Nationally, Center and Right parties fared better than their rivals on the Left as the PMDB elected well over 30 percent of the more than 4,900 mayors, followed by the PFL with 20 percent, the PDS at 12 percent, and the PDT with over 10 percent. The PSDB won 325 mayoral races, and the PT emerged on top in but 55. The PTB with over 300 mayors and the PDC with 200-plus came closer to being national parties than did the PT—as did even the PL (170) and an alliance of two splinter parties (175).[9]

1993: Muddling Through

With Collor's resignation and the Senate impeachment vote occurring on December 29, 1992, Franco could concentrate on staying in office through 1994. Meanwhile Maluf merged his PDS with the PDC in a Progressive Renovating Party (PPR); inflation moved toward the dreaded 30 percent monthly mark; and the referendum on system of government on April 21 was anticlimatic as a confused electorate opted overwhelmingly to stay with presidentialism. The president insisted on pursuing his own ideas, and personnel changes continued until the right combination emerged.

The Quest for Political Viability

By the end of May, Franco attempted to gain majority support in Congress through cabinet shifts aimed at satisfying parties that had banded together to remove Collor. His insistence on Cardoso to head the Finance Ministry unleashed a congressional backlash as leaders of other parties realized with good reason that if successful in taming the dragon of inflation, this PSDB stalwart might well become a prohibitive favorite in the presidential sweepstakes. In an effort to reconcile Brazil's development needs with international demands for conservation of the Amazon tropical rain forests, Ambassador Rubens Ricupero was appointed in August to the Ministry of Environmental and Amazon Affairs. Caught between zealous environmentalists and irresponsible exploiters of lands and lumber, and with the security-conscious military looking over his shoulder, this diplomat strove to work out a plan for responsible development of the region's resources combined with conservation of environmentally critical areas. He would be aided in this thankless task by discrediting of some of the most reckless developmentalists by a massive scandal involving widespread corruption in Congress's shaping of the budget as well as revelations concerning misuse of agricultural subsidies. Yet despite the substantial skirmishing that has gone on, the critical battles over saving the rain forests are still to be fought; devastation of the coastal forests, begun in the 1500s, has run its destructive course.[10]

All this was overshadowed by October when it became evident that many in Congress who had so self-righteously impeached Collor—including leading figures—were themselves equally corrupt. As the investigation dragged on into the new year, it was clear that congressional authority to amend the budget had been seriously abused by officials who took bribes and kickbacks to include questionable projects of interest to contractors and pocketed appropriations to supposedly charitable groups.

Renewed Growth with Galloping Inflation

Economic performance in 1993 was mixed. Inflation shot up to a record 2,670 percent, but the stagflation of recent years was broken with a lusty 4.2 percent GDP growth—led by industry—at 7.5 percent compared to 0.8 percent for 1992. Exports were at a high of $39 billion, producing a $13 billion trade surplus and pushing foreign exchange reserves up by more than $8 billion to $32 billion. The inflow of investment, largely through the stock market, exceeded $7 billion, and new foreign loans reached $10 billion. Indeed, net foreign equity investment was $5.6 billion compared to $1.3 billion the previous year as stock market prices rose over 100 percent in real terms. At $46.3 billion, federal tax receipts were up sharply over 1992's $36.9 billion—and improved collection procedures promising further gains in 1994—and interest on internal debt was still nearly 3 percent of GDP. As the much heralded Cardoso Plan, later renamed the Real Plan (incorporating a new currency, the real), would not go into effect until well into the new year, some observers held that the private sector had gone ahead on its own, breaking the ingrained habit of looking to Brasília for direction. Others maintained that businessmen were anticipating approval of Cardoso's plan focusing upon elimination of governmental deficit financing and a partial and indirect economic shift toward a dollar-linked real.[11]

Overhauling the Constitution and Choosing a President

Early months of 1994 saw a divided Congress grapple ineffectively with obstacles to governability and development embedded in the 1988 constitution. Legislators' eyes were already fixed upon the October national elections—in which almost 12,000 candidates would seek the favor of nearly 95 million voters to fill over 1,700 positions. Hence considerations of rationality again took a backseat to political expediency. When the dust settled after months of wheel spinning, the only major change involved cutting the presidential term to four years. By this time campaigning had begun in earnest, with Lula—who had never stopped running since 1989— far out in front while his rivals were still seeking nomination. At the end of March when Cardoso left the Finance Ministry to run, he was replaced by Ricupero, who remained on his team and showed determination to implement the Real Plan.

The 1994 Elections

By mid-June, as attention shifted to soccer's World Cup (in which Brazil prevailed through a month filled with dramatic cliff-hangers culminating on July 17 in an overtime penalty-kick victory to become the first four-time winner), Cardoso had begun to make inroads into Lula's still substantial lead. His alliance of the PSDB, PFL, and PTB benefited from having much stronger coalitions and candidates at the state level than did the PT. Cardoso received a great boost from a dramatic fall in inflation rates following the introduction on July 1 of a new currency as well as from World Cup euphoria. By late July he pulled even, and as television coverage kicked in during August, Lula fell steadily behind. Hopes to block a first-ballot victory by Cardoso were thwarted by weakness of also-ran candidates—Brizola of the PDT, the PMDB's Quércia, and Espiridão Amin for the PPR. As confidence in the real grew with dramatically lower inflation, and replacement of Ricupero by Ceará's Ciro Gomes at the beginning of September had no adverse effect, Cardoso moved ever closer to the goal of avoiding a runoff by polling more votes than the sum of his rivals.

These elections were the most complex and arguably most critical in Latin American, if not Western Hemisphere, experience. Although those in the United States involve a larger electorate, this is sharply reduced in terms of numbers actually voting. Moreover, Brazil's elections were for not only the presidency but also all governors, the entire lower house of Congress, and two senators from each state (as well as all state legislators). Nearly 78 million voters cast ballots on October 3, with Cardoso's popularity carrying over to PSDB, PFL, and PTB hopefuls for other offices. The PMDB and PPR avoided the disaster of their presidential candidates by abandoning their nominees and climbing aboard Cardoso's bandwagon. Key in this regard were former President Sarney and Rio Grande do Sul gubernatorial winner Antônio Britto.[12] Thus Quércia received an embarrassing 4.4 percent of valid votes, and Brizola was a demoralizing fifth—which still put him ahead of Amin by 3.2 to 2.8 percent. Third place at 7.4 percent went to Enéas Ferreira Carneiro of the National Reconstruction of Order Party (PRONA), an authoritarian and archconservative group tying into the urban sectors in which Integralism found roots in the 1930s.

When the protracted vote counting was over, Cardoso was president-elect with 34.4 million votes compared to 17.1 million for Lula; he had carried all states except Rio Grande do Sul and the Federal District. Moreover, candidates linked to him had won all key statehouses: Longtime political associate Mário Covas (b. 1929) (PSDB) was victorious in São Paulo (20.8 million voters), as were political coreligionists Eduardo Azeredo in Minas Gerais (electorate of 10.6 million) and Marcello Alencar in Rio de Janeiro (registration of 9.1 million). Cardoso's solid foundation in major states was broadened by PFL ally Antônio Carlos Magalhães's clean sweep in Bahia (7.0 million eligible voters), where he elected Paulo Souto governor while easily gaining a Senate seat for himself and the other for a close follower. Moreover, the PMDB's Britto in Rio Grande do Sul (6.3 million voters) was a former cabinet colleague, and Jaime Lerner in Paraná (over 5.7 million registered) was a moderate progressive whose PDT affiliation did not prevent him from being backed by Cardoso's coalition.

In the second tier of states, Ceará (4.0 million electorate) saw a big win by the PSDB's Tasso Jereissati, and Maranhão (2.6 million voters) witnessed a close race by PFL's Roseana Sarney (b. 1954) that consolidated her father, the former president, as a vital Cardoso ally within the PMDB. In Goiás (2.6 million eligible voters) senator-elect Iris Resende's PMDB machine, with a loyal follower in the statehouse, showed strong inclination to cooperate with the new president; in Santa Catarina (electorate of 3.2 million) the PMDB's Paulo Afonso Doin Vieira was similarly inclined. Pará (2.8 million voters) experienced a win by the PSDB's Almir Gabriel, another Cardoso Senate colleague, so only Pernambuco (4.5 million registered voters) gave the Left some consolation with the PSB's venerable Miguel Arraes returning to power for the third time since 1962. But at seventy-seven he wished calm political seas and would pose no problems for Cardoso as he would have to compete with progovernment governors of the region for federal projects and investments.

Cardoso also came out well in the medium and small states, with generally friendly PMDB governors elected in Paraíba, Rio Grande do Norte, Alagoas (where Divaldo Suruagy scored the nation's most impressive landslide), Piauí, Mato Grosso do Sul, and Rondônia. The PSDB added victories in Sergipe and Roraima, and the PPR demonstrated the residual strength of conservatism in the north, winning in Amazonas, Tocantins, and Acre. Vitor Buaiz (PT) in Espírito Santo and Dante de Oliveira (PDT) in Mato Grosso won on the strength of impressive performances as capital-city mayors and were supported by Cardoso's party; in the Federal District the winner was a university professor friendly to Cardoso with but a recent and nominal affiliation with the PT. A PSB victory in Amapá was a small consolation prize to the Left.

Over in the Senate, Cardoso's allies won by far the lion's share, with the PSDB's nine victories including José Serra in São Paulo and Arthur da Távola in Rio de Janeiro. The PFL's bumper crop of eleven wins numbered such notables as Antônio Carlos Magalhães in Bahia, Francelino Pereira in Minas Gerais, Vilson Kleinubing in Santa Catarina, and Hugo Napoleão in Piauí. The PMDB compensated for Quércia's abysmal showing in the presidental balloting by winning fourteen Senate races including José Fogaça in Rio Grande do Sul, Roberto Requião from Paraná, Iris Resende in Goiás, and Jader Barbalho in Pará. The PP's four winners featured Bernardo Cabral in Amazonas. The PT salvaged something out of the ashes of their high hopes by electing Benedita da Silva in Rio de Janeiro along with three others, while the PDT got four, the PTB three, and the PPR two. The PPS gained a beachhead with Roberto Freire in Pernambuco, the PL got one, but that in São Paulo, and the PSB a single seat from a minor state. In combination with a majority of the twenty-seven holdovers, this gave Cardoso a reasonably comfortable margin in the upper house. A 60 percent turnover in the seats being contested is deceiving in that ten of the twenty former governors elected were also former senators, and half the "new" winners had previous service in the lower house.

The Chamber of Deputies lineup was the PMDB 107, PFL 89, PSDB 62, PPR 53, PT 49, PP 36, PDT 33, PTB 31, PSB 15, PL 13, PCdoB 10, and minor parties the remaining 15 seats. This held out prospects for a working congressional majority for the new administration not requiring support from the far Right—and only a slight increase for the Left opposition. The magnitude of Cardoso's triumph and its broad geographic and class support would stand him in good stead with a body accustomed to his playing a leadership role. Indeed, the three-fifths majority in each house needed for constitutional amendments appeared realistically attainable.

Brazil's voters apparently learned well from the experience of the previous five years. Essentially they demonstrated maturity and discrimination: Governors who had done well earlier were in many cases returned for another stint, those whose terms were ending were generally rewarded with Senate seats good to 2002, capital-city mayors who had performed well were often promoted to governor, and candidates of governors who had failed to measure up to their 1990 promises paid for their sponsor's shortcomings. In the presidential sweepstakes, performance and credibility took precedence over promises and charisma. Cardoso was generally viewed as representing continuity with conditions that were perceived as significantly improved during 1993 and 1994. Being father of the Real Plan was more than enough in the eyes of most voters, who identified him with all they approved of from the Franco administration combined with a more presidential demeanor. They had leaped without a safety net in 1989; this time they were determined to act prudently by voting for a known quantity who, at the same time, was not at all cut from the mold of traditional Brazilian politicians.

For some voters there was clearly an undercurrent favoring presenting Brazil's best face to the world—choosing a president who commanded international respect and could hold his own with the most sophisticated world leaders. This and his personal integrity and aura of respectability were the frosting on Cardoso's electoral cake. Details of his program were much less important than a pervasive impression that it approached Brazil's problems realistically and responsibly. A majority felt, in sharp contrast to 1989, that the country's priority need was to be kept on the tracks, not be turned sharply around or to strike out on a dramatic new path. Hence a century after Brazil's first popularly elected president got 276,000 votes in a country nearing 16 million inhabitants, Cardoso would begin with 125 times as many out of a population less than ten times larger.

Economic Performance

The elections took place in the context of apparent economic recovery as the growth momentum of 1993 carried through past mid-1994 and actually picked up under the impact of the new economic program. In sharp contrast to 1986 and the Cruzado Plan, this time there was a record agricultural harvest of 75 million tons of grain to absorb increased consumer demand with an even larger bumper harvest of 8 million tons in 1995. Moreover, exports continued at a high level and foreign investment accelerated—attracted by the generally positive economic performance and the prospect of its continuation under the new administration.[13] The real demonstrated great strength relative to the dollar, and foreign exchange reserves pushed up near $40 billion as Brazil ran a $10.4 billion trade surplus on exports of nearly $44 billion despite greatly increased imports. Inflation for the year was over 900 percent, but for the semester of the Real Plan it was only 22 percent—well under half June's monthly rate—and GDP growth was a lusty 5.7 percent.

Composition and Orientation of the Cardoso Administration

On January 1, 1995, Cardoso took office under the most propitious circumstances of any Brazilian president. In addition to polling 54.4 percent of the valid vote, he was probably the second choice of 14 percent more. He was credited with the generally satisfactory economic situation and enjoyed broad congressional support. Yet he also benefited from the public's realistic expectations; no one saw him as a miracle worker but rather used Sarney, Collor, and Franco as the basis for com-

Inauguration of Fernando Henrique Cardoso, January 1, 1995 (photo by Paulo Jares, courtesy of Abril Imagens)

parison. Moreover, the international environment was more promising to Brazil's interests than ever before. Even eventual amendment of the constitution to permit his reelection was far from out of the question.

The New President

Born in Rio de Janeiro to a family with a long tradition of army generals, Cardoso studied and made his academic career in São Paulo. Fourteen at the time of Vargas's 1945 ouster and twenty-three when Vargas took his life, he has followed a long and gradual path from Left toward Center, particularly over the past two decades. A protégé of Florestan Fernandes, a radical Marxist-Leninist in the sociology department of the University of São Paulo, Cardoso abandoned communism by the late 1950s but still found it prudent to go into exile in Chile after the military takeover in 1964. There he played a leading role in developing the underpinnings of dependency theory before accepting a professorship at the working-class suburban branch of the University of Paris where the May–June 1968 uprisings involved many of his students. Cardoso began to modify and moderate his views following his 1968 return to Brazil. Forcibly retired from the university in early 1969, he played the leading role in founding CEBRAP (Brazilian Center of Analysis and Planning) before running for the Senate in 1978 on the MDB ticket.

Polling a sixth the vote of André Franco Montoro, Cardoso became Montoro's alternate and moved up to the Senate after that distinguished politician was elected governor in 1982. Having participated in the discussions that led to formation of the PT, Cardoso decided to stay with the PMDB, working increasingly closely with the late federal deputy Ulysses Guimarẽs, who required a reliable collaborator in the upper house. Following a narrow loss to Jânio Quadros in the 1985 race for São Paulo mayor, he was comfortably returned to the Senate in 1986 and continued to occupy the position of Sarney's government leader in Congress. In 1988 Cardoso played a major role along with Senator Mário Covas in founding the PSDB—largely because of Quércia's stranglehold on the PMDB machinery in São Paulo and designs upon becoming its national leader.

Cardoso stayed out of Collor's cabinet because of pressure from his party, but he became foreign minister and then finance minister under Itamar Franco and came to function as a superminister, if not virtual prime minister, before launching his presidential bid with Franco's full blessing. Although the success of the Real Plan, in large part his handiwork, was crucial to Cardoso's election, during the triumphal come-from-behind campaign he demonstrated ability to accept sound advice from his major coalition allies, especially Bahian strongman Antônio Carlos Magalhães and former president Sarney, when electioneering outside of Brazil's developed heartland. Competence and reliability were key facets of the image he projected through the electronic media. By winning a clear majority in the first round, he avoided a runoff against Lula that would have been much more polarizing than the statesmanlike stance he assumed while candidates to his Right flayed the PT standard-bearer. Hence he could maintain credibility as a pragmatic social democrat rather than as a stalking horse for neoliberalism.

The New Government and Its Policies

Cardoso took over a country coming off two years of substantial economic growth coupled with six months of low inflation. Moreover, he represented a continuation of the previous administration's policies with a much strengthened popular mandate and enhanced congressional support. He pushed ahead determined to consolidate the measures that had contributed greatly to the country's economic resurgence. Relatively free from need to trade cabinet positions for congressional support, Cardoso put together an upper echelon ranging from competent to distinguished, drawing upon highly qualified and experienced cadres of his PSDB, the PFL, the PTB, and the PMDB as well as several nonpartisan technicians.[14] In keeping with their contributions to the victorious campaign, Magalhães and Sarney remained influential brain trusters from their seats in the Senate, with the former's son, Luiz Eduardo (b. 1955), presiding over the lower house and Sarney elected Senate president, as the elder Magalhães contented himself for the time being with the chairmanship of the Foreign Relations Committee. In testimony to how far Brazil had come, Cardoso's choice of military ministers was almost routine, falling upon ranking active-duty officers. Moreover, civilianization of the Special Affairs Secretariat was continued under Ambassador Ronaldo Mota Sardenberg.

Influential advisers included Vice President Marco Maciel (b. 1940), Sérgio Vieira de Motta (b. 1941), PSDB general secretary, as communications minister; former University of Campinas rector Paulo Renato de Souza (b. 1944) heading the Education Ministry; Eduardo Jorge Caldas (b. 1942) as secretary general of the presidency; and Clóvis Carvalho (b. 1938), former deputy finance minister, directing the presidential staff. Continuity of economic policy was further guaranteed as Pedro Sampaio Malan (b. 1944) moved over from the Central Bank to the Finance Ministry, being replaced there by Pérsio Arida as Edmar Bacha took his place at the helm of the National Economic and Social Development Bank (BNDES).

Colleagues from the São Paulo PSDB were heavily represented with Motta, Souza, newly elected senator José Serra (b. 1942) as planning secretary, and Adib Jatene (b. 1929) back as health minister. The PFL placed former Recife mayor Gustavo Krause (b. 1946) and Santa Catarina's Reinhold Stephanes (b. 1939), both with previous cabinet experience, in Environment and Social Security; the Agriculture Ministry went to Paraná senator José Eduardo Andrade Vieira (b. 1939), PTB president, owner of Bamerindus bank, and a former industry and commerce minister. The PMDB joined in with Nelson Jobim (b. 1946) and Odacir Klein (b. 1943) of Rio Grande do Sul as justice and transportation ministers and a northeasterner as secretary of regional integration. Tucano Dorothéa Werneck (b. 1948) from Minas Gerais got the Industry and Commerce Ministry, colleague Paulo Paiva (b. 1940) became labor minister, and the Science and Technology Ministry stayed with a carryover compatriot.

Former finance minister Luiz Carlos Bresser Pereira (b. 1934) agreed to serve as secretary of administration, and Ambassador Luiz Felipe Lampréia (b. 1941) became foreign minister. By incorporating as culture minister a leading PT moderate, Francisco Weffort (b. 1938), with whom he had long been associated, Cardoso helped draw that party's teeth. Coupled with a policy of extending subcabinet positions to PPR moderates, this put the administration at a decided advantage in dealing with Congress.

A first priority was to push through constitutional amendments to provide better balance between revenue and expenditures to undergird economic stability. Constitutional amendments eliminating state monopoly in the petroleum and telecommunications fields were passed with surprising ease, but overhauling the tax system and administrative reform occupied the entire second semester. The politically explosive issue of social security reform was left for 1996. Since new taxes would be effective only in 1996, Cardoso broadened privatization to include significant interests in the Vale do Rio Doce mining empire and government telecommunications companies. Legislation was passed to facilitate foreign as well as Brazilian private-sector investment in energy, transportation, and telecommunications—which made up a major portion of Cardoso's proposed $100 billion infrastructure plan. A firmer hand was shown than by his politically less strongly based predecessors in forcing state and local governments to assume service on their $26 billion of public-sector debt burdening the financial markets. In the social field, Mexico's Solidarity Program was adapted to Brazil's less centralized governmental system and lack of a ruling party, and Brazil's program was placed under the watchful eye of First Lady Ruth Cardoso, herself a respected social scientist. Yet the president encountered resistance from entrenched interests and was repeatedly frustrated by the lack of discipline in Brazil's parties and by legislators' voracious appetites for patronage. This created tension between the PFL and PSDB and made relations with Antônio Carlos Magalhâes and Sarney less harmonious. Inflation around 2.5 percent for the year and GDP growth near 5 percent kept Cardoso's popularity relatively high.

Political Organizations and Machinery of Government

Continuities have overshadowed change as Brazil's political system has proved resistant to basic change. Historically, Brazilians have combined excessive faith in the transforming power of constitutional engineering with disregard for the need to develop adequate political parties of a national scope.[15] Also contributing to failure to develop institutionalized democracy is the fact that co-optation (participation manipulated from above) has prevailed over effective mobilized participation of the populace in response to social modernization and economic development.

A Flawed Party System

In the aftermath of the 1994 elections, Brazil's party system remained fragmented to the degree of chaotic. The combination of excessively permissive requirements for recognition as a national party and failure to institute a less irrational electoral system encouraged the persistence of parties that aggravate divisions within the body politic rather than aggregate interests. Brazil's parties have "alternated between being instruments of domination and of political representation," since they have been cadre parties born on the issue of opposition versus support for the regime and built from above with an almost exclusively electoral function.[16] Generally both artificial and fragile as vehicles for expressing society's interests and demands, parties in Brazil have never found significant space in decisionmaking, where the executive bureaucracy has played a dominant role. Although after a long period of narrowly circumscribed powers Congress has come to reassert itself in many areas of policymaking, it has not been able to do so consistently. Its antiquated internal procedures render it unable to keep up with a legislative agenda largely defined by the president even when he may be politically weak.[17]

A major obstacle to drastic restructuring of the party system resides in Brazil's peculiar electoral system; it minimizes both responsibility of representatives to constituencies or meaningful party discipline while encouraging alliances of transitory electoral convenience at the state and local levels. These alliances are often contrary to the parties' alignments on the national scene. This critically dysfunctional feature remains impervious to reform for the powerful reason that those with the authority to change it—the sitting Congress—are its chief beneficiaries. National legislators repeatedly have backed away from significant change because their individual prospects for reelection might be lessened by rationalization of the electoral system.

The flaws of the electoral and party system are intimately related to grotesquely unrepresentative apportionment of Congress. Chamber of Deputies seats for the three big states—70, 53, and 46 (an increase of 10 from 1990 for the premier state)—are disproportionate to population ratio—34 million, 16.7 million, and 13.2 million. In short, each São Paulo congressman represents 486,000 persons compared to 315,000 for a Minas Gerais representative and 287,000 for each deputy from Rio de Janeiro. At the other extreme, each of Roraima's eight congressmen represents but 36,000 inhabitants, their Amapá counterparts 42,000 citizens, and those from Acre 58,000 persons. Put another way, the fewer than 6.5 percent of the electorate in Brazil's nine smallest states elect 72 deputies compared to the 70 chosen by São Paulo's 22 percent of the national electorate. The distortion is so profound and extensive that a majority of the lower house represents only two-fifths of Brazil's population, and half the Senate speaks for an inexpressive one-seventh of all Brazilians. There is a political triple standard of one per 486,000 for São Paulo, one per 89,000 for the five smallest states, and one per 297,000 for the rest of the country. It takes the fifteen least populous states plus the Federal District to equal São Paulo's population, but they have 146 congressmen to the leading state's 70. Moreover, for the Senate the corresponding figures are one per 11 million for São Paulo, one for each 235,000 in the five smallest states, and one per 1.9 million in the other twenty-one states. Certainly, it is difficult to consider this to be "representative democracy" in any but the most elemental and general sense of the term. Yet Brazilians seem as little concerned with these gross inequities as they do with the absurdity of their electoral system.[18]

A System Resistant to Reform

Obstacles to modernizing and democratizing Brazil's political system are not limited to the party-electoral-legislative sphere. The bureaucratic apparatus inherited from past regimes manifests strong continuities with undemocratic traditions. In keeping with the elites' dominant political mentality of preventing conflicts from leading to sharp change, over generations they have maintained the state's stability in the face of great social inequalities by bolstering patrimonialism. Thus, a state relatively autonomous from society and oriented more toward order than progress intervenes preventively in social conflicts to avoid emergence of new organized forces that could threaten its role. This is done less through outright repression than by bringing conflict into the public arena—which in turn further blurs the fuzzy distinction between public and private. In this way certain "rent-seeking" groups are able to survive within a fragmented pattern of modernization, with society in general paying the bill.[19]

The state apparatus is still marked by a closed style, low transparency, very limited accountability, strong clientelistic ties, and a low capacity for implementation and enforcement.[20] What Camargo and Diniz have termed "the overload of expectations about the state's performance" persists, for nothing has yet happened to change the paradox of a state "strong in terms of the prerogatives accumulated, but weak in its capacity for implementation."[21] Congruently, O'Donnell stresses the "predominance of personal relations, clientelism, strong regionalism, scarce or nonexistent party discipline, and highly diffuse ideologies" as obstacles to consolidating Brazilian democracy.[22]

Jaguaribe's analysis holds that *cartorial* groups acquire parcels of public power that give them control of strategic sectors and influence the regulatory action of the state in detriment to collective interests, creating niches of immunities and privileges.[23] The situation is aggravated by incompatibility between a comparatively modern state and a primitive party system as well as by broad powers for Congress that leave the president with insufficient power for conducting the government. Acutely aware of these analyses, Cardoso has undertaken to remove the structural bases of such progress-hindering behavior in order that the attitudes undergirding them may weaken over time.

Soldiers, Property Owners, and Workers

Brazil's armed forces remain more than just a potent veto group, if far less than the regime's tutor. The country's 1964–1984 ruling institution still retains a capacity to be arbiter of national life—should it again develop the will to do so. Recent years, from the 1986 elections and constituent assembly through presidential succession and the 1990 and even the 1994 elections, have demonstrated growth, not deterioration, in the power and influence of the propertied strata. With the military having vacated the center of the political arena, these elements have come increasingly to the forefront. Indeed, nearly half the 1987–1990 Congress—whose role expanded greatly with democratization—were linked to business and capital; the body elected in 1990 had perhaps the highest concentration of landowners in the republic's history. In contrast, labor has gained attention but not policymaking influence and remains the short leg of this tripod—still involved in emancipating itself from government controls.

The Armed Forces: Watchfully Waiting in the Wings

Participation by the Brazilian military in governmental affairs is near a historical low, and activity in the political realm is at ebb tide. Yet military disengagement from responsibility for conduct of the nation's affairs came only at the beginning of 1985, and this after more than two decades in the saddle. Moreover, since the traditional role of the armed forces has been that of arbiter rather than ruler, and as they exerted great influence during the Sarney years, their period of abstinence from overt political involvement dates only to 1990. In striking contrast, their tradition of exercising "moderating power" dates to before the founding of the republic more than a century ago.[24]

Brazil's armed forces are seeking to define their role in a drastically changed international environment before succeeding in redefining their domestic mission. The end of the Cold War removed a long-presumed foreign threat and all but eliminated the internal enemy, as the domestic Communists both lost their external sponsor and abandoned revolution as a goal and violence as a tactic. Moreover, the military has had to absorb significant budgetary cutbacks as well as see pay and perquisites sharply eroded.[25] A key point to bear in mind is that the Brazilian armed forces have not "gone back to the barracks," because they have never been fully subject to civilian control as that image implies. They have always at least done a significant degree of coaching from the sidelines and have been ready to step in if the game of politics got out of hand—they being the judges of whether this has occurred. In their preponderant self-image, subject to exceptions and variations in intensity, the armed forces have saved the nation, constitutional order, republic, or the country's Christian, Western, and democratic values on at least twenty-seven occasions dating back to independence 173 years ago. Although manifesting little disposition as of 1995 to again become directly responsible for the conduct of government, they were showing even less inclination to forgo the capacity to do so should conditions sharply deteriorate. Thus the military's political behavior is heavily mortgaged to the success or failure of democratic politics.

Potential danger resides in the fact that the middle ranks of the officer corps are composed of individuals who opted for a military career when this was the main channel to political influence and even high governmental office. Although there is no strong evidence that significant numbers chose to enter the academies primarily for this reason, this possibility cannot be disregarded. Moreover, as junior officers they saw their hierarchical superiors run the country for two decades and may harbor latent ambitions to do the same. For anyone assessing trends within the armed forces, the formative experiences of the various cohorts of the officer corps must be borne in mind. Lieutenants and captains have been socialized since decompression if not after the transition to civilian rule. But majors on average have eighteen years' service since becoming cadets, and this rises to twenty-five years for lieutenant colonels and thirty-two for colonels. For the brigadier generals, thirty-nine years in the service is the average; this increases to forty-four for the divisional generals. The dozen and a half top-ranking generals average forty-seven years since matriculation; they were schoolboys during the Estado Novo and at the academy between the end of World War II and the Korean conflict. Direct memories of Vargas will persist in the upper reaches of the military well beyond the turn of the century.

Property Owners: Still on Top

Democratic politics has not put a crimp in the dominance of the propertied elements of Brazilian society. Indeed, with the withdrawal of the military from direct exercise of power and the at least temporary neutralization of the progressive wing of the Catholic Church, they increased the scope of their political activity and range of influence after 1985. Furthermore, the outcomes of the most recent elections were highly advantageous to their continued leading role in national political life. Hence predictions that the balance of power would shift drastically to the left through the installation of fully competitive electoral politics have proved unfounded—as reaffirmed by the 1994 elections.

Brazilian social scientists who have closely studied this topic, concentrating on the industrial sector, have pointed out a strengthening of this sector's organizational capabilities that extended to gaining electoral offices and occupying appointive positions in the economic side of the federal executive.[26] Landowners were especially effective in defending their interests within the 1987–1988 constituent assembly. The impact of this expanded role of entrepreneurial elites on Brazil's political development, retarding modernization and enhanced governmental rationality, stems from the fact that

> the strengthening of their capacity for organization was done without breaking the
> historical pattern of representation of business interests in the state apparatus. The
> direct access of groups, associations and individual companies to segments of the
> state bureaucratic apparatus persisted as the dominant trait in articulation between
> the public and private sectors.[27]

In addition to sectoral organizations like the National Confederation of Industries (CNI) and state affiliates—especially the São Paulo branch (FIESP)—urban propertied groups operate through a variety of associations and institutions.

The Working Class and Trade Unions

The political clout of labor in Brazil is still well below its potential. Although greater than in the past, it falls far short of that in Argentina or Mexico. A major limitation on labor's influence is the fact that as the union movement slowly and belatedly escaped from government control and co-optation, it was beset by deep doctrinal and organizational divisions. This still prevailing lack of unity, along with serious leadership deficiencies, undercuts its effectiveness in the political arena.[28] As numerous as working-class voters have become, they have not yet been mobilized overwhelmingly in support of any one party—including the PT. From a comparative perspective the inability of the Brazilian trade union movement to develop a capability for delivering a large vote to one party or candidate—rather than some support to several (by definition offsetting and often countervailing)—is striking. Equally dramatic is its inability to mobilize and conduct a successful general strike, even in periods of severe losses in real purchasing power and strong antigovernment sentiment.

The key political actors with respect to the pre-1964 labor movement are gone from the scene. Goulart is a distant memory, the present PTB is not a working-class party, the CGT (General Workers Command) of the early 1960s has no connection to the organization bearing these initials in the 1980s and 1990s, and the PCB, important in the labor movement before the military regime, is no longer a significant factor. A thin thread of continuity was maintained into the early 1980s through the docile and co-optable Ary Campista, who was finally forced to yield the presidency of the National Confederation of Industrial Workers (CNTI) in 1983 after two decades in control of the country's largest union organization. His successor, Joaquim dos Santos Andrade (b. 1926), was socialized into the labor movement before 1964, but those who pushed him aside by the late 1980s began their careers well into the military regime.

Santos Andrade played a leading role in convoking the National Conference of the Working Class (CONCLAT) in 1981 out of which came the National Pro-CUT (Single Workers Center) Commission. In this group he was in conflict with PT-oriented elements led by São Paulo metalworker Lula da Silva and their allies—products of union activism at the plant level and the waves of strikes that had accompanied *abertura* at the end of the 1970s. This division was deepened by alignment on opposite sides in the 1982 São Paulo elections, as Santos Andrade's group undercut the PT's dreams of major electoral impact. Mid-1983 saw a general strike attempt that enjoyed some success only in São Paulo and Rio Grande do Sul. In its aftermath Lula and the PT group founded the Single Workers Center (CUT).[29]

With central national labor organizations legalized in 1985 and CUT winning the competition for union affiliation, CONCLAT was transformed in 1986 into the General Workers Center (CGT). Santos Andrade stayed close to the PMDB and attempted to maintain his position through clientelistic and manipulative tactics and government favor. As Lula moved further into the political arena as party leader and frequent candidate, fellow metalworker Jair Meneguelli (b. 1947) assumed leadership of CUT. In April and May 1985 they led a prolonged strike of autoworkers and related São Paulo unions that resulted in a settlement very close to that the employers had offered almost two months earlier.[30]

Hoping to capitalize on dissatisfaction with the collapse of the Cruzado Plan house of cards, they catalyzed a general strike effort in December 1986 that fell far short of making a dramatic impression of strength upon the soon-to-be-convened constituent assembly. With an eye to erasing this embarrassment, CUT tried again in August 1987, but this effort resulted in a full-blown fiasco; fewer than 10 million refrained from working compared to perhaps twice that number eight months earlier. In its aftermath Santos Andrade lost ground to younger leaders advocating "results-oriented unionism" against priority for ideological considerations and PT aims in the labor movement.

Luíz Antônio Medeiros, a São Paulo metalworker the same age as Meneguelli, and that state's electricians leader, Anônio Rogério Magri (forty-six at the time) undertook to build support for a labor movement concentrating on material gains rather than political causes but free from the opportunism represented by Santos Andrade. CUT and CGT needed to establish credibility and hoped to influence the presidential race, and in March 1989 they held a two-day general strike against the government's economic program. Roughly 40 percent effective compared to 20 percent in 1987, it set the stage for Magri to lead the General Workers Confederation (CGT) against Santos Andrade's rump CGT.

These organizations, like their member unions and federations, remained bureaucratic, unrepresentative, and unable to effectively channel the aspirations of the rank and file—hence incapable of directing their political behavior. After Magri was elevated to Collor's cabinet, the way was clear for Medeiros in 1991 to found the Força Sindical (FS) as a frontal challenge to CUT. His ability to garner affiliation of important unions as well as secure international funding to supplement his pipeline to the government enabled Medeiros, ably assisted by secretary general Emílson Simões de Moura ("Alemão"), to build the FS into a powerful and effective movement—although well behind CUT's 1,800 unions with 17 million affiliated workers.[31] For his part, Meneguelli found himself losing ground, and in May 1994 he was replaced by Vicente Paulo da Silva (b. 1959), known popularly as "Vicentinho," leader of the São Bernardo do Campo–Diadema metalworkers—Lula's and Meneguelli's springboard. Yet representatives of public employee unions predominate in the CUT's national directorate.

Organization of rural workers in Brazil trails far behind the modest progress in urban areas. Indeed, the situation may even lag behind that temporarily achieved in the early 1960s through the peasant leagues movements of Francisco Julião and progressive Catholic Church elements.[32] If one takes into account the currently far greater organization of landowners, rural workers' political influence has declined in relative terms rather than just stagnated in an absolute sense. Yet there is little doubt that in the years ahead as agrarian reform returns to the center of the political arena, the rural union movement will become a more important factor in a number of states, if not necessarily on the national scene. Such an assessment rests upon an analysis of economic and social developments that are explored in subsequent chapters.

6

THE ECONOMY AND FINANCES

PRECEDING CHAPTERS INCLUDED much information concerning Brazil's economy as an aid to explanation of the complex course of political development and societal change. Yet several economic problems crucial to Brazil's future remain to be be considered: growth, industrialization, modernization of agriculture, infrastructure development, inflation, fiscal policies, debt, trade, the pervasive presence of the state, and recent efforts to liberalize the economy.

Brazilian Growth: Demographic and Economic

Population growth has been heavy and sustained in twentieth-century Brazil, particularly since World War II. Yet economic expansion has moved at a considerably faster pace, allowing for progress from a very poor country to one that can reasonably set its sights on gains made by southern Europe during the postwar period. Along the way Brazil has become highly urban, and changes in sectoral composition of the economy, mirrored in the workforce, have led to predominance of industry over agriculture. Rather than the latter stagnating, industrial development has surged ahead even faster than its sustained growth. Thus, as late as 1952 coffee was responsible for 73 percent of export earnings; larger exports in the early 1990s contributed under 5 percent of foreign sales—behind automobiles, steel, soy, and iron ore. As a result of this industrialization, disparities between the urban-industrial and rural-agrarian sectors have widened, leading to perpetuation of grave regional variations in levels of well-being and opportunity.[1]

These inequalities cannot fully conceal the fact that although absolute economic growth has far outrun per capita gains, the latter have also been substantial. Though not as fast as might be desired, this progress is impressive by comparative standards. Its critics rely upon unprovable assertions as to what might have been accomplished by other policies or what gains could be made in the future if their panaceas were adopted. Meanwhile, Brazil's policymakers strive to resolve the dilemma between more equal distribution of what wealth has been created and a return to levels of investment that led to high growth rates through 1980. In this endeavor they are aided by the fact that Brazil is clearly off the population treadmill; demographic expansion dropped to 1.9 percent a year during the 1980s from 3.2 percent for the 1950s, 2.8 percent in the 1960s, and 2.5 percent during the 1970s. By 1995 it was down to an annual rate of 1.5 percent.

Population and Demographic Trends

By 1995 Brazil's population passed the 157 million mark, increasing by 2.6 million a year. This was up from 119 million in 1980, about 93 million a decade earlier, and 70 million in 1960. Live births total 3 million a year and infant mortality is still around 55 per 1,000. Demographic growth is lowest at the bottom of the age pyramid, reflecting sharply declining fecundity rates.[2] From 5.7 children in 1970, the average number of children a Brazilian woman bore fell to 2.6 by 1991. Yet Brazil still has a young population with 63 percent below age thirty and 78 percent under forty. Indeed, there is a nearly straight-line decline in the proportion in each age bracket: 23.2 percent from zero to nine years; 21.9 percent between ten and nineteen; 17.9 percent from twenty through twenty-nine; 13.9 percent between thirty and thirty-nine; 9.5 percent for forty to forty-nine; and 6.4 percent for fifty and fifty-nine. Thus, 71.0 million under twenty and 11.3 million over sixty must be supported by 75.1 million persons of productive age.

Throughout Brazil's history, elevated rates of infant mortality and low life expectancy offset high birthrates to keep population growth short of threatening overpopulation. Now a sharp fall in birthrates is counterbalancing decline in infant mortality and a steady rise in life expectancy—trends that have not yet reached levels considered normal for modern nations. Life expectancy was still below thirty-nine years in 1940 and rose to fifty-one over the next three decades. By 1980 it reached sixty-three, and for those born in 1994 it is estimated at over sixty-eight. From 160 per 1,000 during the 1930s infant mortality dropped to 88 per thousand by the 1970s and is now around 50 per thousand. Great disparities continue between urban and rural areas, which leads to regional variations, as much as five years in life expectancy between the south and the northeast.

Such dramatic differences help explain the sustained flow of people from the less developed regions and rural areas into the cities—especially those of the south and southeast. Between 1950 and 1980 some 39 million Brazilians left rural areas, and this was accelerating: 8 million in the 1950s; nearly 14 million during the 1960s; and 17 million in the 1970s.[3] Over 15 million more have done so since 1980. This internal migration helped push the urban proportion of Brazil's population from 36 to 68 percent over the 1950–1980 span, and by 1994 the continuation of this flow had made Brazil more than 75 percent urban—with 117 million town and city residents to 38 million country folk. During the 1950s rural population grew almost 17 percent (compared to 67 percent for the urban sector), whereas for the decade after 1970 there was a 6 percent rural population loss accompanied by a 55 percent rise in urban areas. Moreover, the 1980s showed a 2 percent drop in rural population compared to a 26 percent expansion of urban dwellers.[4] In 1950 some 31 percent of Brazilians lived in places of over 2,000 inhabitants, two-thirds of these in cities of over 20,000. By 1995 the proportion in towns of over 2,000 had exploded to over 80 percent, with fully four-fifths of them in centers of 50,000 or more.

Even with a slowing rate of population growth, by mid-1995 São Paulo state reached 34.0 million inhabitants, Minas Gerais 16.7 million, Rio de Janeiro 13.2 million, and Bahia 12.8 million, Rio Grande do Sul 9.6 million, and Paraná 8.7 million. Hence these six states exceeded the country's 1970 total, and the addition of Pernambuco (7.5 million in 1995), Ceará (6.8 million), Pará (5.8 million), and Maranhão (5.3 million) brought this figure up over the national total for 1980. Proportional to this growth, Brazil's economically active population reached 75 million by 1995.

Economic Growth Patterns

Brazil is an urban country with a large population, not the sparsely inhabited and predominantly rural one it was a generation ago. This demographic explosion has been accompanied by rapid, relatively sustained, and industry-led expansion of the economy. In comparative terms growth has been impressive, as between 1870 and 1987 real GDP multiplied 157 times.[5] Average 2.3 percent annual growth between 1870 and 1912 jumped to 4.9 percent for 1913–1949 and on to 7.5 percent for 1950–1973 before falling to 4.9 percent a year through 1987. Analysis of these figures shows that expansion from 1900 through 1913 reached 77 percent as industry began to kick in; its growth was limited by the export sector's performance until the mid-1920s. World War I demonstrated the capacity of Brazil's economy to withstand external shocks and even use them as a stimulus to growth and diversification. Cut off from sources of imports, subjected to interruption of foreign investment, and deprived of traditional markets, Brazil still grew economically. From zero for 1914–1915, the rate of GDP expansion averaged 4 percent for the next three years before climbing to 5.9 percent in 1919 and 10.1 percent in 1920.[6] Similar ability to weather international economic blows was manifested during the Great Depression, as by 1933 industrial production returned to the predepression level, rising 50 percent by 1937. Cushioned by industry's performance, Brazil's economy recovered quickly from the initial traumatic impact of the global depression. GDP rose 4.3 percent annually during the 1930s and over 3.3 percent from 1940 through 1945.

Compared to the 1913–1946 norm of under 5 percent a year, from 1947 to 1980 annual GDP growth averaged 7.1 percent, ranging from a high 8.3 percent average for the Kubitschek years (1956–1960) down to near stagnation during the crisis of the early 1960s. Rapid expansion that more than doubled the economy between 1967 and 1973 could not be sustained after the international situation turned unfavorable with the oil crisis, yet the rest of the 1970s still saw growth at an average of just over 7 percent yearly—enough to increase Brazil's economy by three-fifths. The 1981–1983 recession largely offset the 9.2 percent expansion of 1980, and recovery from 1984 through 1986 produced a 22 percent gain, so that even with a slump to 3.6 percent in 1987, the first eight years of the 1980s resulted in average annual growth of over 3.2 percent—which with population expansion down to under 1.9 percent a year led to an 11 percent per capita gain.

In the 1988–1992 period Brazil experienced a severe recession as marginally negative growth in 1988 before 1989's modest 3.3 percent was negated by 4.4 percent shrinkage in 1990 and near stagnation in 1991–1992 before climbing to 4.2 percent in 1993 and 5.7 percent for 1994. This gloomy picture is brightened by the fact that in recent years Brazil's economy has grown more than official figures indicate since the informal sector expanded substantially during this time. To avoid social security taxes as well as escape the turnover tax on merchandise transactions and evade income taxes, small businessmen in Brazil operate largely "off the books." Recent studies reported in *Veja* (September 6, 1995) place the portion not captured through conventional means of calculating GDP at well upwards of $200 billion.

Viewed in these terms, the 1980s were more a decade of lost opportunities than a lost decade, especially when compared to other Latin American countries. With Brazil's GDP stagnating from 1988 through 1992 and declining in per capita terms, new policies would be needed to sustain the 1993–1995 recovery. Yet despite recent stuttering growth, the basic fact remains that although Brazil still lags far behind the industrial nations of the world, it has broken out of the treadmill syndrome of a small GDP combined with rapid population growth. The 1968–1974 economic miracle more than doubled GDP, and even the lower growth rates through 1980 saw it expand by 50 percent—exceeding absolute expansion during the superboom period. Following the brief recession of 1981–1983, accumulated economic growth for 1984–1986 meant $70 billion added to GDP. Hence, per capita income by 1993 was a bit over $3,000, but in real terms this was more than five times what it had been in 1940, having doubled between that year and 1961 and again from 1962 through 1976 before rising by another 26 percent 1977–1987. Yet this seriously understates the true size of the economy, as to the $531 billion GDP at the end of 1994 must be added the substantial invisible component. Also, a shift to purchasing parity rather than foreign exchange rates as the basis for converting GDP into dollars put Brazil at over $800 billion or $5,300 per capita. Hence at the end of 1995 Brazil's real economy was almost certainly nearing $800 billion through the traditional means of converting into dollar terms and well over $1 billion in the more meaningful perspective of comparative costs and prices. This would be $7,000 per capita.

Industrialization, Modernization of Agriculture, and Natural Resources

Sustained growth has brought in its wake deep changes in the relative importance of agriculture, industry, and services—with the latter two coming to overshadow the long-dominant agrarian sector. This has also involved qualitative changes within industry and agriculture along with a drastic transformation of mining—in which Brazil has become one of the world's leaders. Whereas in 1900 agriculture accounted for 45 percent of GDP and industry 10 percent, by 1947 the figures were 28 and 20 percent, reversing to 19 and 27 by 1966. In the 1990s agriculture was down to 10 percent and industry up to 36 percent. Yet the service sector at 54 percent of GDP is extremely important.

Industry: Motor of Modernization

The long-run growth of Brazilian industry demonstrates dynamism and staying power. If 1949 is indexed as 100, industrial production had been 80 in 1947—a level doubled by 1955, trebled by 1959, and quadrupled by 1962. After stagnating for three years, industrial growth took off in 1966, rising over 60 percent in a five-year period and doubling again between 1971 and 1980. Following a 1981–1983 drop of nearly 15 percent, industry almost recovered to the record 1980 high by 1985, then grew by 11 percent in 1986. Stagnant in 1987–1989, industry took a sharp drop of 9 percent in 1990 before dipping in 1991 and 1992, and coming back by 7.5 percent in 1993 and 7.6 percent in 1994.[7] In 1949 Brazil's leading industries were food processing (at 32 percent of output by value), followed by textiles (with 18.5 percent). Metallurgy was a distant third at 7.5 percent, and the chemical industry lagged at but 5 percent. By 1980 chemicals had vaulted into the lead at 19 percent, metallurgy at 13.5 percent was challenging food processing, and textiles had been overtaken by both transportation equipment and mechanical industry (at 7.7 and 7.5 percent respectively). Between 1959 and 1980, metalworkers tripled, those in mechanical industry multiplied 8.6 times over, clothing industry employment rose 4.7 times, and food processing half that fast; the textile industry increased employment only marginally.

The foundation of Brazil's heavy industry is metallurgical, especially steel. Extremely well endowed with iron ore, both in Minas Gerais and the south of Pará (Carajás), Brazil has created the world's seventh largest steel industry—ahead of France or the United Kingdom—and gone from importer to major exporter of this basic material in a short time. With production at 9.1 million tons in 1976 (triple that for 1964), imports were still significant. As output rose to 24.2 million tons for 1987, Brazil could export 8.2 million tons despite rising domestic consumption. By 1991 Brazil accounted for 57 percent of all Latin America's steel with capacity of 28 million tons and exports of 10.4 million tons worth $3.2 billion.[8] Moreover, steel mills are now found from Rio Grande do Sul to Maranhão.

The most noteworthy user of steel in Brazil has been the automobile industry. A luxury item through the 1950s, 28 million cars and trucks have been manufactured since that time, and there are now over 20 million vehicles on the country's roads. By 1974 production started from scratch in 1959 was up to 861,000 units, and the next year exports reached $350 million. This was only the harbinger of things to come as in 1987 the automotive industry consolidated its lead as Brazil's number-one exporter, selling 345,000 vehicles abroad for $2.8 billion plus auto parts valued at $1.7 billion; the total rose to $4.9 billion in 1993. Lagging domestic sales picked up dramatically in 1988, lifting production to over 1 million vehicles for the second time since the recession of 1981, and in 1993 this passed 1.3 million and reached 1.6 million in 1994 and 1995. Brazil's automakers, led by Volkswagen, Fiat, General Motors, and Ford, moved ahead with major new investments. The auto industry has not only given rise to a full array of parts and material suppliers but also made possible an armaments industry—whose backbone was foreign sales of a wide variety of armored vehicles—and given birth to an aviation industry that placed hundreds of Bandeirante and Brasília sixteen- and thirty-two-passenger planes on U.S. regional lines and sold military aircraft to many countries.[9]

Fiats (automobiles) awaiting export (photo by Antônio Augusto Fontes, courtesy of Abril Imagens)

Diversification and Technology

Through the 1960s Brazil had no significant beginnings of a petrochemical industry, a situation requiring expensive imports. A private company began operating in São Paulo in the late 1960s, but major growth did not come until creation in the 1970s of the Camaçari Petrochemical Pole in Bahia. Recipient of investments of $6 billion, this complex with its sixty-six companies and 25,000 direct employees produces well over $4 billion a year. It has given major impetus to development of the Salvador metropolitan region, especially since more than half its employees earn above ten times the country's minimum salary. Moreover, it has made possible a Chlorochemical Pole in Alagoas, the Sergipe Fertilizer Pole, and the Pernambuco Alcohol-Chemical Pole. Just as the Vargas government gave rise to a steel industry through the National Steel Company, the petrochemical industry has been fostered by Petroquisa—a subsidiary of Petrobrás and major stockholder in many of Brazil's petrochemical ventures. With assets of $8 billion, in 1992 it was still the dominant force in the petrochemical industry—whose total production reached $11 billion. But as the state's capacity to invest diminished, it could no longer play the role of a vital catalyst, and petrochemicals were included in the privatization program.

The most dramatic growth industry in recent years has been electronics and computers. The former sector is heavily concentrated in the Manaus Free Zone—established in 1968—and nearly meets the country's needs for radios, cassette players, television sets and, in recent years, VCRs. It peaked in 1989 at production worth $8.8 billion and employment of 73,000 individuals. The computer industry, located chiefly in the northeastern part of São Paulo, with an output of only $200 million as recently as 1977, jumped from $1.75 billion to $2.5 billion between 1984 and 1985 and was producing $9.8 billion annually by 1989; then it slumped before full recovery in 1993–1994.[10] If it were to follow the lead of the steel, automotive, and petrochemical industries in exporting a significant share of its output, an end to excessive protectionism would be required—and has taken place. Only in 1991 did legislation to this effect clear Congress. This entailed the demise of a number of companies dependent on copying and selling an overpriced outdated product behind the shield of protectionism. But it also led to strengthening of companies able to compete internationally.

Although figures on factories, industrial employment, and sectoral output tell an important part of the story, Brazil's growth as an industrial power also involves important qualitative changes, such as the high-technology industries emerging alongside more traditional and labor-intensive ones. The last decade of the military rule witnessed import-substitution industrialization involving capital goods and basic inputs; then the jump to high-technology industries was slowed by the economic slump of the late 1980s, the explosion of inflation, and the deadening impact of the burgeoning foreign debt.

Brazil's industrialization has not only made possible a manyfold increase in exports—surpassing $45 billion a year—but has also greatly reduced the country's import needs. Steel, automotive, petrochemical, electrical-electronic, aviation, and computer industries are good examples of this and demonstrate the success of import-substitution industrialization—in its appropriate time and place. In addition, some traditional industries have greatly expanded production with exportation providing the impetus. The shoe industry in 1986 produced 270 million pairs, exporting 144 million of them for just over $1 billion. By 1993 earnings were over $2 billion on 180 million pairs. The clothing industry in 1986 produced 4.8 billion pieces worth $25 billion and employed 1.8 million persons. Even in postrecession 1993 some 1.1 million registered workers produced over 3 billion pieces valued at $17 billion (and much more was produced in backyard factories).

Paper and cellulose exemplify a rapid-growth industry based on use of Brazil's abundant natural resources. Responsible for production worth $5 billion in 1991, it received substantial investments to increase annual production of paper and cellulose to 5.6 and 5.7 million tons respectively in 1994. Exports of each exceeded 1 million tons in 1988 for a total of $1.24 million, and cellulose earned $1.4 billion in 1991 on foreign sales of 1.4 million tons. Aracruz is Espírito Santo's leading industry; Riocell holds this distinction in Rio Grande do Sul.

Then there is Brazil's shipbuilding industry, which from a production of 268,000 deadweight tons in 1974 rose to 1 million in 1976 and stayed high until hit by the recession of the early 1980s. It built a number of ships of over 277,000 tons displacement and diversified into construction of warships. After middecade, contracts from Petrobrás and the Rio Doce Valley Company for their large fleets (Fronape and Docevave) helped the industry get back on its feet, as did resumption of substantial construction for export—it had provided two ships of 400,000 deadweight tons to a Norwegian shipper. Installed capacity of 2 million tons a year is far from fully employed, but Brazil has recaptured fifth place in a field led by Japan and Korea. Through 1991 the industry had built nearly 15 million tons, 30 percent for export, as Brazil's own merchant marine grew to nearly 10 million tons.

Agriculture: High Production, Low Productivity, Limitless Potential

Industry has come to overshadow but not eclipse agriculture. The latter's contribution to GDP has dropped to 10 percent, but agriculture employs 30 percent of the workforce. Indeed, from 1950 to 1985 the number of farms rose from 2.1 million to 5.8 million, with cultivated area increasing from 19 million hectares (47 million acres) to 52.4 million hectares (130 million acres). Persons involved in farming doubled over the span from below 11 million to nearly 23.3 million. Pigs and hogs grew from 22.9 million to 30.1 million, chickens reached 510 million in 1988, Brazil's cattle now exceed 150 million head, and sheep exceed 21 million.

Landholding continues to be concentrated, as 4 million rural producers average only a hectare each, whereas 50,000 individuals having 1,000 hectares or more combine to control 165 million hectares. Indeed, forty-six large agroindustrial groups hold 22 million hectares. In between are 2.5 million family farms averaging 36 hectares and 450,000 larger farmers with holdings averaging 600 hectares.[11] Put another way, the largest 5 percent of landholdings in Brazil cover 69 percent of arable land; 13 million rural dwellers lack land of their own. The latter group includes 6 million *sem terras* (renters, squatters, and sharecroppers) and 7 million, including minors, who work as migrant day-laborers (called *boias frias* for their brownbag lunches) or low-paid workers. At least 5.2 million rural workers earn less than the minimum salary, and 1.3 million declare no cash income.

Roughly 4.2 million hectares (10.5 million acres) are planted to sugarcane. The yield of 269 million metric tons results in 30 million tons of raw sugar converted into as much as 12 million tons of refined sugar and 12 billion liters of alcohol.[12] Rice is grown on 4 million hectares (10 million acres) with a production of 11 million long tons. The champion in area planted is corn with a harvest of 31 million metric tons on 11.2 million hectares. Coffee occupies about 3 million hectares, averaging 26 million 132-pound sacks annually during the 1980s (the equivalent of 1.7 million tons); exports in 1991 hit 21.1 million sacks. Soy is planted on 11.5 million hectares throughout the south and center-west and up into interior regions of the northeast; the 1993–1994 crop yielded nearly 25 million tons. With foreign sales bringing in $3.7 billion, the value of Brazil's soy production—beans, oil, and cake—exceeded $7 billion, surpassing the sugar-alcohol complex. Black beans, a staple of the Brazilian diet, come annually to 6 million tons on 6.1 million hectares. Mandioca, a basic foodstuff in rural Brazil, occupies 2 million hectares with a yield of 22–26 million tons. Wheat, long a major import, runs around 2.4 million tons a year on 1.6 million hectares. Cotton, cocoa, oranges (300 million crates of them), cashews, peanuts, bananas, tobacco, sisal, and grapes are also grown on a large scale as, of course, are common vegetables. Woods, waxes, oils, and fibers are produced on an important commercial scale. Fish and other seafoods (especially lobsters) come to 1 million tons a year. Beef production is 4.7 million tons annually, along with 1.3 million tons of pork and 3.3 million tons of chicken. Milk production runs at over 15 billion liters a year, with eggs totaling 2.2 billion dozen.

Expansion of production has resulted more from significant increases in productivity than from putting more land to the plow. Since over the last fifteen years the total grain harvest has risen from 38 million tons to the 1994–1995 record of 81 million, there is a substantial surplus to export—albeit in large part owing to low levels of domestic consumption—with soy, coffee, and orange juice together coming to well over $6 billion annually. Cocoa normally brings in $600–$850 million and meat $500–$600 million. Oils, fats, and waxes are good for about $850 million a year, sugar fluctuates but reached $1.8 billion in 1995, and tobacco generally runs close to $500 million. Indeed, with production of 440,000 tons of leaf

Soybean fields (photo by Joel Roch, courtesy of Abril Imagens)

tobacco (mostly from the three southernmost states), Brazil is the world's third producer and second exporter. Thus, although trailing manufactures, agricultural exports are still important to Brazil, and they are already of increasing importance to the world. Yet Brazil could at least double grain production by better land utilization and increased use of fertilizers, and through future substantial investments in irrigation, this expansion could be duplicated.

Mining: Tapping Untold Mineral Wealth

The minerals and mining sector of the Brazilian economy merits attention for its significance to the world even more than its importance to Brazil. The country has reserves of at least 18 billion tons of high-grade ore and is a leading source of the globe's iron with annual production of over 130 million tons of metal from over 200 million tons of ore. Bauxite output exceeds 11 million tons a year from reserves of 2.5 billion tons, and Brazil ranks fifth in aluminum production at 7.5 million tons. Annual manganese production runs at 2.6 million tons, with tin-bearing ores (in which it is third in production and reserves) mined at a rate of over 35 million cubic meters. Brazil also has 90 percent of the world's niobium. Chromium, copper, zinc, lead, nickel, cobalt, molybdenum, and titanium are also mined on a large scale, along with silver, quartz, and a wide variety of gemstones. Gold reserves of 35,000 tons place it fifth in the world. Brazil also ranks fifth in uranium and is the eighth nation to master the technology for enriching it to the degree needed for fuel—if not that for weapons. In such a mundane but essential product as cement, Brazil's production passed 26 million tons by 1989.

Infrastructure: Energy, Transportation, Communications, and Financial Institutions

Profound economic changes would not have been possible without accompanying transformation of sectors responsible for providing energy, roads, railroads, means of communications, and financial resources absent which a complex and diversified modern economy could not come into being, much less flourish. Cognizant of the contribution of infrastructural development to growth of productive capacity, the government has taken a very active part in channeling investment into these essential but not directly profitable areas.

Energy: Engine of Industrialization

Expansion of industry has, of course, required a vast increase in energy production and resulted in major shifts in sources and use. Primary energy consumption in Brazil in 1992 was equivalent to 185 million tons of petroleum, with hydroelectric power leading the way at 35.0 percent, followed by oil at 30.0 percent and firewood at 13.8 percent—very largely in rural areas. Fuel produced from sugarcane, chiefly the residue after milling but also alcohol, came next at 10.0 percent; coal accounted for 5.5 percent trailed by natural gas at just 2.4 percent. These were significant changes in proportions from even thirteen years earlier, although not as striking as the rise in total consumption of over 67 percent. The biggest jump was in hydroelectric power, which had provided only 21.9 percent of energy needs in 1976, when petroleum had weighed in at a high 42.7 percent.[13] During the 1980s Brazil invested $8 billion annually in the energy field, but by 1994 this was down to an inadequate $2.3 billion.

Installed electrical generating capacity in Brazil is now twelve times what it was in 1960 and more than two and a half times the 1977 figure of 22,500 megawatts. Growth was gradual until the mid-1950s, then doubled from 1956 through 1963 and again in the periods 1964–1971 and 1972–1978. From 1979 through 1986 the rise was a remarkable 2,500 megawatts per year, and the 50,000 megawatt level was reached. Despite a slowdown caused by financial constraints, capacity by 1995 had passed 57,000 megawatts. Production of over 200 billion kilowatt-hours in 1986 was twice the figure for 1977, which in turn was double that of 1971, itself two times that of 1961. Much of remaining hydroelectric potential is located on tributaries of the Amazon and has become a focus of attack by environmental groups. Since demand is projected to exceed supply by 1996, Brazil's development urgently requires completion of many unfinished projects—feasible at present only with private investment, which began to enter this field in 1995.

As it is, Brazil possesses a major share of the world's largest hydroelectric facilities, beginning with Itaipu on the Paraguayan border with its eighteen 700,000-kilowatt generators. This giant is followed by Tucuruí in lower Pará, which has a capacity to grow to nearly 9 million kilowatts by the turn of the century. The hydroelectric potential of the São Francisco has been heavily tapped but not exhausted. First came the several stages of Paulo Affonso, followed by Sobradinho and Itaparica. Yet the newly inaugurated Xingô dam will jump this by 5 million kilowatts. Compared to these massive works, the hydroelectric complexes of the center-south seem small, but those in São Paulo and Paraná have a generating capacity of over 16 million kilowatts.

Nuclear power is still in an infant stage in Brazil. The Angra I plant, designed by Westinghouse, encountered major cost overruns and has been subject to frequent breakdowns. Construction on Angra II has fallen far behind schedule—with $4.6 billion spent and $2 billion more needed. Angra III is to be abandoned, and other nuclear facilities envisaged in the 1974 agreement with the German Federal Republic will not be built. Indeed, by the mid-1980s, the Brazilian nuclear program had become essentially a military concern.

Until acceleration of industrialization and the widespread use of the automobile, Brazil's consumption of crude oil was negligible. In 1955 it jumped to 4.4 million cubic meters, a figure that quadrupled by 1963. Although domestic production was up to 5.7 million cubic meters, imports were twice as large. Consumption doubled from 1964 through 1972—reaching 35 million cubic meters—but domestic production expanded far less. By 1979 consumption had leaped to 67 million cubic meters as Brazil's production stagnated. The need to

Itaipú Dam (photo courtesy of the Brazilian Foreign Ministry)

import 58 million cubic meters—with the price of oil having shot up by mid-1973 from $2 dollars a barrel to peak at $40—placed an extreme strain on Brazil's finances and threatened to destabilize the country's shaky international financial position.

With the country's international financial stability in grave jeopardy, the government undertook a crash program to increase production, chiefly from new deepwater offshore fields. Between 1976 and 1987 Petrobrás invested $26 billion, supplemented by development of alcohol, first as additive, then as substitute for gasoline. Although this required investment totaling $10 billion between 1979 and 1987, positive results were apparent by the early 1980s in terms of a drop in crude oil consumption and a sharper decline in imports. As Brazil tripled output—from 187,000 to 561,000 barrels a day—and halved imports to 466,000 barrels per day between 1980 and 1985, domestic production finally came to fill more than 50 percent of Brazil's needs. Use of alcohol as fuel exploded from 172,000 cubic meters in 1976 to over 8 million in 1985, as natural gas production also rose from 1.9 billion cubic meters in 1979 to three times that figure by 1985—compared to crude oil production of 35 billion cubic meters by 1989. Coal production quadrupled between 1975 and 1985—to 24.6 million tons—with consumption leaping from 7 million to 33 million tons a year. Moreover, the alcohol program came to provide 700,000 direct jobs and another 700,000 indirect ones. From 2.5 billion liters in 1978–1979, production of alcohol jumped to 7.9 billion in

1983–1984 and 9 billion the following year. Its value in 1988 reached $3.4 billion, yet the financial costs, including easy credit and subsidized prices, were substantial if not excessive.

Petrobrás has been pursuing the goal of achieving energy self-sufficiency by the end of the century. With proven reserves of crude oil at over 3 billion barrels and natural gas supplies of 124 billion cubic meters being augmented by new discoveries (for 1994 totals of 11 billion barrels of crude and nearly 300 billion cubic meters of gas), this is now possible—pending adequate investments. Production in 1995 passed 740,000 barrels of crude a day (compared to 647,000 in 1991) with 1.8 million the 1996 target for refining capacity (1.4 million in 1991). (Brazil holds the record for the deepest offshore oil wells and is developing robot minisubmarines to drill producing wells in ocean depths of over a thousand meters.) Moreover, large reserves of oil-bearing schist in Paraná have only recently begun to be exploited on a commercial scale. Hence crude imports are down to 470,000 barrels a day, with domestic production of natural gas up to 23 million m^3 per day.

Transportation and Communications

Brazil's industrialization has required major transformations in transportation and communications. From 300,000 kilometers of roads in 1952—extremely low for Brazil's vast expanse—the total reached 1.2 million by 1971 and 1.6 million by 1988. Moreover, paved roads rose from 56,000 kilometers to 130,000 by 1987 and to 158,000 in 1992. On the use side, the 410,000 vehicles on the country's roads in 1950 rose sixfold by 1967 and by 1980 soared to nearly 11 million. By 1988 this total had passed 15 million—8.5 million in São Paulo alone—with 18 million licensed drivers. Included by 1994 were 1.2 million trucks, two-thirds of them operating on the highways. During the period of intensive industrialization, roads gained greatly in importance. Not only did their share of passengers go from two-thirds in 1955 to 95 percent by 1974—a level at which it stabilized—but their proportion of freight rose from 56 percent in 1955 to a peak of 72 percent in 1972. Subsequently the oil crisis led to a resurgence of railroads, which from 16 percent of bulk in 1972 climbed to 24 percent by 1980. In terms of freight carried, roads reached their high in 1976 at 226 billion metric tons. Although the proportion of freight carried on waterways declined from 25 percent in the mid-1950s to 13.4 percent in 1980, the total transported in this manner rose from 13 billion to 48 billion tons over the same period. The railroad network, totaling only 1,130 kilometers in 1874, expanded to 6,130 kilometers during the next ten years before growing steadily to 27,000 kilometers at the time of World War I; it added only 11,000 kilometers during the next forty-five years and decreased from 1960 into the 1980s—when trackage in use had fallen to under 30,000 kilometers. Since the 1970s several major projects have been carried through to completion, including one connecting the Carajás mineral region to São Luís and another to carry the harvests of the western frontier to the port of Santos. Most railroads are government-operated, and the Federal Railroad System (RFFSA) has 49,000 employees, 1,200 engines, and 42,000 cars.

Although Brazil's ports, led by Santos Tuberão and Rio de Janeiro, handle nearly 400 million tons of freight each year, they are highly inefficient and costly, factors that seriously reduce the competitiveness of Brazilian exports. The political clout of the port workers and longshoremen unions held up reform for years until significant modifications were pushed through Congress in early 1993.

Deficiencies persist, but great progress has been realized in the communications field. Letters handled exploded from 2 billion in 1950 to 4.4 billion by 1989—along with 69,000 tons of packages. By 1993 the postal service was one of the world's most efficient, processing 15 million items a day for annual revenue of over $1.4 billion. By 1992 telegrams shrank to 20 million, largely owing to expansion of the telephone system from 521,000 phones in 1950 to 7.4 million in 1980 on the way to 13 million in 1994. From an average of under 500,000 new lines a year from 1985 through 1991, installation doubled in 1992, yet a deficit of 10 million lines remained.

Banking and Finance: Irrigating the Economy

The Brazilian financial system has evolved greatly in size and complexity during the post–World War II period. The first important step was the creation of the Superintendency of Money and Credit (SUMOC) in 1945 to bring together components of a rudimentary central bank function.[14] This still left the Bank of Brazil—an enterprise with thousands of shareholders but with a majority of voting stock in the hands of the federal government—in the anomalous position of being both the government's chief financial agent and the country's largest commercial bank. Establishment of the Central Bank in 1965 further rationalized the system, but not until February 1986 did the Bank of Brazil lose its role as fiscal agent of the monetary authorities. In 1992 it was responsible for 26.6 percent of all loans.

During the last three decades many important private banks have expanded their activities. Moreover, Brazilian states established their own banks, in many cases setting up development banks as well. Overall the financial sector accounted for 9 percent of GDP in 1991. At the end of 1992 some 216 banks operated 17,000 branches around the country with the Bank of Brazil having 2,500 and the Federal Savings Bank (Caixa Econômico Federal) another 1,800. Also part of the financial system were over 1,700 offices of insurance companies and roughly 2,300 firms and branches linked to stock and securities trading. In 1994 the Bank of Brazil had over $29.0 billion in deposits; the National Economic and Social Development Bank (BNDES) had approximately $8.8 billion available for new loans during 1995. The financial sector's profitability was a healthy 14.2 percent in 1990 and even higher by 1993.

Shadows on Development: Inflation,
the Public Sector, and Paying the Bills

Brazil's road to becoming at least the world's ninth largest economy and biggest newly industrialized country (NIC) was marked by a high rate of growth and its undesirable companions: chronic inflation, expansion of the public sector to a prominence without precedence in a capitalist system, and erosion of traditional sources for financing growth. Recent years witnessed rates of inflation unheard of in Brazil's long experience of coexisting with rapid price rises—roughly 1,038 percent in 1988, then surging to 1,783 percent in 1989, moderating slightly in 1990, declining to "only" 480 percent in 1991, climbing to 1,158 percent in 1992, and exploding to 2,670 percent in 1993. Internal national debt belatedly came to be recognized as a major obstacle to bringing inflation under control.

Through the 1980s the state not only was chief mobilizer of and channel for infrastructural development and new industries but also continued to control or administer the enterprises brought into existence for this end. The government's effectiveness as operator rather than builder of industries had become highly suspect, and its ability to mobilize new investment declined to near exhaustion. During its short tenure the Collor government initiated a program of privatization, carried on by his successor and expanded by Cardoso.

What the government spends, how it finances its expenditures, and the growth and management of its debt are intricately interrelated matters. They are important determinants of monetary and fiscal policy and crucial elements in Brazil's chronic inflation problem. Traditionally viewed as domestic matters, they came in recent years to interact with international financial issues, as a sharp reduction in the public-sector deficit became a precondition to IMF approval that foreign banks and governments demanded as a requisite for renegotiation of the overhanging external debt.

The Chronic Problem of Acute Inflation
and Deficit Financing

A major price paid for Brazil's development has been persistent rapid rises in the cost of living. Prior to 1964 inflation was not considered a major problem, particularly since during the 1950s and early 1960s it served as a cushion to the state's inability to solve distribution conflicts in a political system laboring to adapt to fundamental societal changes. This carried over after 1964 into a quest for ways to tame inflation rather than eliminate it. Brazil tried to coexist with high rates of constantly rising prices through a comprehensive system of tying everything from wages to debts to the cost-of-living index. This worked for a number of years, with the average inflation rate in the 1967–1974 period under 20 percent and even at 40.8 percent in 1978, but it gave inflation a strong inertial component, making it all but impossible to reduce it sharply short of a complete freeze. Hence inflation of 77 percent in 1979 rose to 110 percent the next year and, after leveling off, jumped to 224 percent in 1984 and 235 percent for 1985. At this point many actors in the policy arena were willing to admit that gradualist means of combating inflation might be insufficient. Yet few were ready to accept the costs of an orthodox recessionary solution.[15]

Although a sharp cut in inflation was achieved in 1986 through the heterodox Cruzado Plan—to about 65 percent—the 1987 total of 416 percent wiped out the gains of the preceding year. In 1988 it threatened to escalate into hyperinflation as monthly rates neared 30 percent by year's end. Needing to show Brazil's creditors headway in attacking the roots of the inflation problem, the Sarney government held the 1988 deficit to 3.8 percent of GDP, yet inflation for the year passed the 1,000 percent mark. The New Cruzado Plan of mid-January 1989 was doomed to failure by the lame-duck status of the administration. Quite relative progress on the inflation front by the Collor government—cutting it by 1991 back to near the 1987 level but then seeing it stabilize at a monthly rate above 20 percent—was followed by a new surge under Franco's loose reins to twice that rate by early 1994 before the Real Plan slashed it drastically. From 760 percent for the first half of the year it fell to 22 percent the second half and 11 percent for the first six months of 1995 (on its way to less than 25 percent for the year).

Failure to undertake stringent measures until faced with rampant hyperinflation vividly demonstrated the strength and resiliency of Brazil's inflation psychology. Producer, middle-man, consumer, and worker have all been addicted to the illusion of great nominal gains, even when in real terms these may be losses. Convinced that other actors on the economic scene are working to better their relative position, each strives to keep from being left behind. Furthermore, over the span of recent decades many Brazilian businessmen lost the habit of seeking profits through increased productivity and administrative efficiency. It was easier just to increase their prices regularly—especially when substantial profits were to be made from investing their receipts in the highly rewarding overnight financial market, which in early 1990 tied up $60 billion. Repeatedly, industry and commerce were on a quest to make up for past inflation and get a jump on that to be expected in the near future, plus a bit more as insurance against a possible price freeze. Automatic pay raises tied to the cost of living guaranteed that these hikes would be passed on into the next round of price rises and feed inflation once again.

Domestic Debt Explosion

Through the 1980s the soaring cost of servicing a snowballing internal debt fueled inflation and destabilized government finances. Heavy foreign and domestic borrowing pushed Brazil's consolidated public-sector debt by 1988 to $140 billion, half domestic, raising the federal share of outstanding government paper to 24 percent of GDP in 1989. Interest on internal public debt shot up from 0.5 percent of GDP in 1975 to 5 percent in 1989. Servicing it had become as serious a burden as the foreign debt. Indeed, only in the 1986–1988 period did interest on foreign debt exceed that on the government's internal indebtedness. Public-sector savings, 2 percent of GDP annually before the 1982–1983 crisis, averaged less than

0.6 percent in the mid-1980s. This led into a protracted period in which the government was unable to sustain the heavy investments required by the country's statist developmental model.

Undisciplined expansion of internal debt was rooted in public-sector deficits escalating from manageable to destabilizing over the course of the 1980s. The operational public-sector deficit (excluding monetary correction of debt service) climbed to 6.6 percent of GDP in 1982 before dropping to 3.0, 3.1, and 4.4 percent during the 1983–1985 period.[16] Held to 3.6 percent in 1986, this gap between receipts and expenditures rose to 5.7 percent in 1987. Success in reducing the deficit to 4.8 percent of GDP in 1988 still pushed the consolidated public-sector debt up, and in 1989 the deficit escaped control, zooming to 6.9 percent of GDP.

Collor encountered a greater prospective deficit that he turned into a modest surplus in 1990 and 1991. By temporarily freezing $85 billion of the economy's $120 billion liquidity (M4, the most comprehensive concept of monetary supply, was 37 percent of GDP on the eve of the Collor Plan), the Collor Plan reduced national debt from $160 billion to $40 billion, cutting its service to under 2 percent of GDP. Yet in subsequent years high interest rates and the need for the Central Bank to buy up dollars flooding into the country increased expenditures on interest on treasury and central bank financial paper. Privatization after 1992 retired a portion of this heavy debt burden. Yet the basic problem remains as long as government spends beyond its revenues, something likely to continue as long as interest on the national debt remains a major expenditure. Even in 1995 high interest rates meant that interest on a federal government debt of over $80 billion might be $44 billion for the year, with that on the $28 billion debt of states and municipalities an additional $12 billion—averted only by some success in lengthening the duration of some government securities and reducing interest rates as the economy cooled off.

Issuance of securities has been basic for covering deficits. Most of its paper is short-term, and the Brazilian government has been forced to refinance a major proportion at frequent intervals and high interest. As a result the public sector absorbs a large proportion of savings, up to 70 percent in 1987 from 50 percent in 1980. As inflation rose, debt became short-term, creating an overnight market that by 1989 involved 80 percent of federal internal debt—at skyrocketing rates. Although carrying internal debt through securities is highly inflationary, alternative methods of financing public-sector deficits are also inflationary, as with emission of currency or borrowing abroad.

The gross tax burden dropped only from 25.7 percent of GDP in 1978 to 21–22 percent in the 1984–1987 period, but net tax receipts for the federal government declined at a significantly faster rate. With a wide array of fiscal incentives and tax exemptions keeping these well below current expenditures, government capacity to invest underwent a sharp drop. Indeed, total government expenditures fell far below the 27 percent of GDP achieved in 1970. This decline was aggravated by the fact that federal tax revenues by 1988 were only 9.6 percent of GDP. Then between 1988 and 1991 the federal government's share of these revenues fell to 51.4 percent; that going directly to states rose to 30.4 percent and that of localities to 18.2 percent. Moreover, under the 1988 constitution the federal government's share should drop to 36 percent of the tax pie. Because of the great difficulty in getting state and local governments to pay for functions for which the federal till has customarily been tapped and to assume responsibility for their debts, a major overhaul of the tax system was put before Congress by the Cardoso government in mid-1995.

Brazilian Statism: "Let the Government Do It"

Given the leading role of the state in Brazil's economic life, investment cutbacks to reduce public-sector deficits have jeopardized profitability of major firms. The government's mixed capital enterprises have been the chief customers of many sectors of Brazilian industry. Yet government deficits fed inflation and soaked up credit needed by the private sector. The state sector's share of GDP rose to 44.9 percent during the 1976–1980 period, climbing even further before declining after the mid-1980s. From 1988 through 1993 the federal government put $27 billion into state enterprises but received only $1.1 billion in dividends.

Facts presented in earlier chapters bear out Werner Baer's assertion that the Brazilian state's dominant role in the economy was a result of circumstances repeatedly forcing the government's hand rather than a consciously formulated scheme.[17] The drive for rapid catch-up industrialization was the most important factor in expansion of the state's role; next in importance were reaction to international economic crises and the perceived desirability of curbing foreign capital's control over sensitive and strategic sectors of the economy. The result was to make the state the long, thick, and strong leg of a tripod including multinational companies and the Brazilian private sector. Beginning with railroads, banks, and support of coffee producers, governmental involvement spread into other commodities and public utilities. This occurred especially during the Vargas regime, in large part because this coincided with the 1930s depression and wartime exigencies.

By the time the war was over and Vargas left office, the government was entrenched in iron-ore production through the Vale do Rio Doce Company (CVRD) and owned the National Steel Company (CSN). Created in 1952 to foster industrialization, the National Economic Development Bank (BNDE) soon came to be a major stockholder in many of the ventures it financed. Moreover, private capital was often unwilling to assume risks or enter areas of priority to the country's development but not necessarily promising a quick return. Foreign oil companies' failure to make significant investments in the late 1940s and early 1950s made Petrobrás's founding all but inevitable, and the pressing need for power brought the federal government to the fore with respect to hydroelectric projects. Electrobrás was an outcome of this process, as was Siderbrás's domination of the steel industry.

The balance-of-payments crunch in the mid-1970s resulting from an abrupt upward surge in oil prices led to more pervasive involvement of the Brazilian government in the nation's economic life. Between 1966 and 1977 over 200 state enterprises were created at the federal level, often emulated by the states. With imports of equipment, steel, and nonferrous metals costing Brazil $6 billion in 1974—twice its bill for foreign oil supplies—the Brazilian government opted for a drastic deepening of import-substitution industrialization. As the very legitimacy of the regime was subject to serious erosion by a protracted economic recession, the government came to the conclusion that the massive foreign credits and investments required would be obtained speedily only through direct action by the state. Since the international credit of Brazil's major state enterprises was much higher than that of the private sector, and these firms also had substantial funds of their own to invest, the imperatives of the situation all but dictated increased employment of the state as the vehicle for achieving expanded investment during the middle and late 1970s.

After several years of privatization, the state still has a monopoly in all aspects of petroleum except distribution and owns and operates the lion's share of iron mining. It is hegemonic in generation and distribution of electricity and monopolizes telecommunications as well as mail delivery. Nuclear power, most ports, and much of the petrochemical industry are also in its hands—along with almost all the country's railroads. Private savings and loan operations are dwarfed by those of the state. On the personnel side, government employees are numerous enough to serve as backbone of the Brazilian middle class. Numbering well over 7 million at all levels, they exceed 11 percent of the workforce. At the federal level they include 600,000 in direct administration and some 125 autonomous agencies and foundations, 750,000 in the parastatal enterprises, and 300,000 in the armed forces.[18] At the state level there are more than 4.0 million public employees—1.2 million in São Paulo alone. Smaller states are often even less restrained in providing public employment, which takes quantum leaps in election years. Then, too, federal employment is spread throughout the country, with 370,000 civilian federal employees in Rio de Janeiro compared to 145,000 in Brasília. The most prodigious patronage machine is the social security system involved in distribution of $35.0 billion a year in medical treatment, welfare, and pensions—not counting $10.5 billion to retired federal employees.

Although many of the state's problems result from corruption in the monetary sense, others are a manifestation of how co-optative clientelism works in Brazil. In a situation where available benefits (housing units, hospital beds, places in school, or retirement payments) fall far short of societal demand, allocation is essentially on the basis of political criteria—which involves exchange of electoral support by the applicant for intercession with the bureaucracy on his behalf by some broker, usually an elected figure, candidate, or one of their agents. The government functionary is responsive to these interferences because, if not owing his employment to a politician's sponsorship, response will be important for survival and advancement. Political considerations are also key for a majority of the 2 million municipal employees in Brazil, especially as there are no local school boards to insulate the hiring of teachers from political patronage. Moreover, these numbers would be much larger were not most police and many teachers state employees.

It is common to find city councils with forty staffers per member, with the largest proportion appearing only on payday.

Although most public employees are poorly paid, the cumulative burden on government finances is great, with central government salaries climbing from 2.4 percent of GDP in 1985 to 4.1 percent in 1990 and exceeding the budgeted $38 billion in 1995. Indeed, much of the government's loss of capacity to invest stems from this drain. Whereas the federal government strives to bring this under control, state and local governments, which increased their payrolls from 3.2 to 6.9 percent of GDP during the second half of the 1980s, have not followed suit. Hence public-sector salaries doubled from 5.6 percent of GDP in 1985 to 11 percent by 1990 and were on the way toward 16 percent by 1994.

A lasting retrenchment of the government in the economic realm is not yet in place, despite significant beginnings. Only since the the early 1990s has privatization entailed more than turning back to private control those companies that accidentally came under government domain by defaulting on loans or selling nonvoting stock in productive mixed-capital companies. Starting in October 1991 with Usiminas, which exports $570 million a year, the privatization program made strides toward wiping out a significant proportion of government debt while putting these enterprises in the hands of owners capable of making the large-scale investments needed to expand their production and hence help fuel a resumption of economic growth. By late 1995 some thirty-six enterprises had been privatized at a price of $9.24 billion. But Petrobrás—the queen of state enterprises with annual sales of over $18 billion—has so far been untouchable; so have energy and communications utilities, which have been at the heart of the Mexican, Argentine, and Chilean privatizations. Petrobrás, Telebrás, the Bank of Brazil, and CVRD are still the top blue chips on the stock markets, so further shares will be sold—within limits fixed by law to maintain majority control in government hands. CVRD—producer of over 100 million tons of iron ore in 1994 with 69 million tons exported and sales of $4.1 billion yielding gross profit of $1.24 billion—has drawn great interest throughout the industrialized world.

External Factors: Debt, Balance of Payments, Investment, and Trade

Brazil's development has required high rates of investment, a significant share coming from abroad. Since foreign portfolio investment through the stock markets was small-scale before 1992, this involved direct investment and borrowing—with the latter overshadowing the former. So Brazil entered the 1990s with a massive overhanging debt, as overdue interest payments pushed accumulated debt up again. This required the country to continue running large trade surpluses to cover foreign debt service. Yet the massive influx of risk capital since 1993 has rendered a continuation of such unbalanced trade unneccessary as the mounting capital surpluses guarantee a payments balance. Hence in 1995 Brazil failed to run a substantial trade surplus for the first time since 1983 although exports were at a record high. A significant component of the expansion of imports to double the 1992 level were capital goods for the modernization and growth of Brazil's industrial plant.

No Easy Way Out: Every Means of Financing Development Has Its Price

The interrelated nature of deficits, internal debt, and their financing has been sketched. Bringing external factors and constraints into the picture further complicates a complex public policy equation. Although direct investment sets up an outflow of financial resources in terms of profits and royalties, this has been relatively modest in Brazil, as a substantial proportion of profits have been reinvested. More negatively, loans require both interest and either amortization of principal or rollover of it in the form of additional borrowing to cover payments due on old loans. This creates a heavy burden of debt service, depleting foreign exchange reserves and requiring massive trade surpluses, or leads to an even larger accumulated debt with increased interest payments and need for continued—often augmented—borrowing. Since debt service is in hard currencies, these must be earned by expanding foreign sales and reducing imports. This in turn restricts internal consumption and retards growth.

Like most developing countries, Brazil historically has run trade deficits, a tendency accentuated by capital goods imports needed to carry out import-substitution industrialization. This led to additional foreign borrowing to cover the strains trade deficits placed upon the balance of payments. The need to close the balance-of-payments gap forced Brazil from the late 1950s through the 1980s to resort to assistance from the IMF—requiring adoption of a fiscal and financial "adjustment" (austerity) program acceptable to that body. Since such policies have a strong recessive effect, aimed as they are at reducing government deficit spending and curbing inflation, they are politically unpopular. Moreover, they clash with the ingrained belief that Brazil's social ills can only be dealt with effectively through continued economic growth. Hence Brazil attempted during the 1980s and early 1990s to cover foreign exchange needs through giant trade surpluses generated by increasing exports and decreasing imports. Although the best option under the circumstances, this path toward maintaining international solvency had significant negative impact upon development and domestic well-being. After tortuous negotiations, Brazil finally achieved a comprehensive agreement on rescheduling payment of foreign debt and renegotiating its terms with the international banking community, the IMF, and creditor governments, though implementation was delayed into 1994.

Putting Foreign Debt in Perspective

Through the road previously sketched, debt-related questions came to be the crux of economic policymaking until very recently. An overhanging foreign debt of $110–$136 billion worked through the 1980s and into the 1990s as a major restraint upon economic policy. It also became a central consideration in foreign policy, intruding into bilateral relations with creditor countries and Brazil's policy in the multilateral arena.

The impact of foreign debt upon the economy, its societal ramifications, and role as a political issue need to be considered jointly.[19] Whatever the contribution of past borrowing to Brazil's development may have been, the need to pay up to $10 billion a year in interest and to incur more debt to cover its amortization came in the 1980s to be a key limitation upon further development. Yet notwithstanding the magnitude of Brazil's debt and its serious effect upon the economy and implications for the quality of life of the Brazilian people, its burden has often been exaggerated. Contrary to sensationalist interpretations, it was not the root of all of Brazil's economic problems, much less its societal woes. Indeed, by comparative standards, Brazil is not one of the region's most indebted countries. The sheer bulk of foreign debt at its peak was matched only by Mexico but was below the region's norms in relative terms. At 30 percent during the initial stages of the Collor government, the proportion of external debt to GDP was low for Latin America, as was a debt-to-export earnings ratio of approximately 3.3 to 1. A case can be made that a much smaller debt combined with an even more reduced capacity to pay created a more serious balance-of-payments problem and restraint upon development not only at the beginning of the 1960s but also back in the Old Republic and even under the empire. Unlike in those times, Brazil has recently proved capable of producing huge trade surpluses to provide resources for debt service; surpluses totaled $150 billion during the 1983–1994 period.

The pattern of foreign borrowing followed by additional loans to cover debt service is not a recent feature of Brazilian national life. As early as 1825 Brazil's foreign debt exceeded £5 million sterling but climbed only gradually for the next four decades.[20] Then the Paraguayan War led to a quantum jump in 1865, from £7.95 million to £14.74 million. At this juncture, with Brazil's export earnings extremely low and government revenues very limited, expenditures were double receipts. Resort to loans was repeated in 1871, 1875, 1883, and 1886—raising debt to £23.6 million. After this shot up to £30.4 million in 1888, it was refinanced by borrowing the then-staggering sum of £19.8 million.

The republic began its life with a major foreign debt, which necessitated a negotiated moratorium in 1898. Exceeding $204 million at the dawn of the new century, debt more than tripled by 1910.[21] New loans were used largely to pay old ones, and between 1915 and 1921 Brazil paid out £70.2 million to service its debt while receiving under £40 million in new loans. Unable to continue this drain on the nation's finances, the government resorted to massive borrowing in the 1926–1931 period, raising overhanging debt to $1.3 billion. Subsequently, Brazil paid almost all this out of its modest export earnings and reduced it to $301 million by 1950. Then Brazil again borrowed abroad; foreign debt reached $1.16 billion by 1953 and took a jump of $527 million during 1958. Ballooning debt service led to negotiation of a stabilization program with the IMF that Kubitschek dramatically repudiated in 1959. Foreign debt rose to $2.84 billion in 1961, but export earnings stagnated below $1.4 billion. Quadros's mid-1961 renegotiation fell victim to his abrupt departure from office, and Goulart found himself saddled with a program the domestic political effects of which he was unwilling to confront.

Castelo Through Geisel: Debt Growing but Manageable

The low expansion rate of Brazil's foreign debt in the early 1960s was more a result of limited ability to attract lending than lack of inclination to borrow. The military regime increased debt by $1.4 billion in 1965–1966, again borrowing to repay old loans.[22] Augmented exports led to the first current accounts surplus in a decade and a half with 1966 foreign sales of $1.7 billion and imports of $1.3 billion. During the Costa e Silva government external debt rose at a slightly lower rate; exports began to show significant growth, reaching $2.3 billion in 1969. Major changes occurred under Médici, as $8.2 billion was added to foreign debt—almost tripling it to $12.6 billion. Whereas borrowing through 1967 had been chiefly from the IMF, World Bank (IBRD), and Inter-American Development Bank (IADB), Brazil was now attracting Eurodollars at highly advantageous interest rates of 5 or 6 percent. During these years of breakneck growth, annual exports rose from $2.3 to $6.2 billion, but with imports also shooting up, Brazil depended upon heavy inflows of foreign funds. As debt service rose from $692 million in 1967 to $2.2 billion by 1973, loans were obtained not only to finance costly development projects and capital goods imports but also to cover these growing financial costs.[23] Indeed, by 1971 the current accounts deficit had hit $1.0 billion, and by 1973 this shortfall reached $1.7 billion—despite sales and purchases abroad being in balance at $6.2 billion each. Yet with exchange reserves at over $6.4 billion (compared to but $1.2 billion in 1970), and with interest rates low, seeking maximum foreign financing seemed to make sense even at the end of the Médici period. Thus, on the eve of the global oil crisis Brazil's position in balance of payments and debt was reasonably sound, albeit there were potential vulnerabilities in the areas of petroleum-related and industrial raw material imports.

During the Geisel administration, foreign debt grew from $12.6 billion in 1973 to $43.5 billion at the end of 1978—equal to 23 percent of GDP. The time bomb built into this augmented borrowing was that these petrodollars loans were pegged to floating interest rates, low at the time but destined to rise rapidly once the Reagan government took office in the United States. However, the main villain in the picture during the middle and late 1970s was rising oil prices. Net oil imports, which had been $739 million in 1973, quadrupled in 1974, totaling $16.3 billion through 1978—by which year they reached $4.1 billion. As shown in Table 6.1, this sharp rise in imports led to a $4.7 billion trade deficit in 1974 followed by one of $3.5 billion in 1975. The result was a massive $7.1 billion current accounts deficit in 1974 with a $6.7 billion encore in 1975. Holding the line on imports at $12.4 billion while exports rose to $10.1 billion allowed for reduction of the trade deficit in 1976, but the current accounts deficit was still a hefty $6 billion, chiefly because interest had risen to $1.8 billion—from only $652 million in 1974. With the trade deficit eliminated in 1977, the current accounts deficit dropped to $4 billion.

Fearing to jeopardize political decompression, Geisel rejected adjustment via the recessionary route, preferring a massive investment program to keep up development while reducing external vulnerability in the longer run. The downside of this delayed adjustment was emergence of a new complication in the form of sharply rising amortization payments. From $456 million in 1970 and $1.7 billion by 1973, these climbed to $3 billion by 1976 and exceeded $5.3 billion in 1978. This pushed the current accounts deficit again up to $5.9 billion. Albeit foreign exchange reserves were at a record $11.9 billion, this feat had required a net capital inflow of that same magnitude including $13.8 billion in medium- and long-term loans. Hence a sharp increase in any outflow category in the years ahead would mean real trouble. Through this borrowing the Geisel government managed to keep gross investment marginally higher than the 1971–1973 rate of 21.5 percent of GDP. But Brazil paid for the oil shock with an additional financial outflow of 2.7 percent of GDP yearly and a 1978 jump in foreign debt of $11.5 billion.

Figueiredo: Debt Escalation and Explosion

The Figueiredo government reaped the debt whirlwind as it encountered the second oil shock of 1979 and interest payments zooming toward the stratosphere. Interest tied to the New York prime rate rose at a dizzying pace to levels often three times that in effect when the loans had been contracted, with those linked to the LIBOR (London interbank offered rate) following closely behind. From a 7.8 percent average in 1977, the prime rate peaked at an unprecedented 19.4 percent in 1981—a year in which the LIBOR was still a high 14.1 percent after a bloated 18.0 percent the preceding year. As Brazil's loans were at a spread of 2 percent or more above these benchmarks, interest payments erupted from $2.7 billion in 1978 to $7.5 billion in 1980. Combined with amortization, this led to dramatically higher debt service totals, at $8 billion in 1978 and passing $11.3 billion in 1980. Hence by the 1980s Brazil's debt was feeding on itself. With economic growth depending on production for the internal market as well as export expansion, this hamstrung efforts to regain and maintain development.

Such huge outflows could only be partially covered by using up foreign exchange reserves, which dropped to $5.9 billion in 1980. Moreover, rapid growth in exports was more than offset by resurgent oil prices. Although the former grew from $12.7 billion in 1978 to $20.1 billion for 1980, imports exploded from $13.7 billion to $23.0 billion. Trade deficits spurred current accounts deficits to record highs of $10.7 billion in 1979 and $12.8 billion for 1980. Principal had to be rolled, which led to a debt of $53.8 billion at the end of 1980—with economic recession looming.[24]

There was yet another dark cloud on the horizon. New loans minus debt service had to this point been positive, but 1980 witnessed net transfer abroad of $1.8 billion. From 1982 on the drain would grow—totaling $39 billion for the 1982–1988 period, exceeding the growth of Brazil's foreign debt. As interest and amortization

TABLE 6.1   Economic Performance 1971–1994

Year	Inflation[a]	GDP Growth	Gross Internal Investment	Federal Internal Debt[b]	Exports[c]	Imports[c]
1971	20%	11.3%	21.3%	5.9%	2.9	3.2
1972	16%	12.1%	21.1%	7.5%	4.0	4.2
1973	16%	14.0%	22.1%	4.3%	6.2	6.2
1974	35%	9.0%	24.3%	4.6%	8.0	12.6
1975	29%	6.1%	25.7%	6.0%	8.7	12.2
1976	46%	10.1%	23.0%	9.4%	10.1	12.4
1977	39%	5.4%	22.1%	9.7%	12.1	12.0
1978	41%	4.8%	23.0%	9.9%	12.7	13.7
1979	77%	7.2%	23.1%	8.6%	15.2	18.1
1980	110%	9.2%	23.1%	6.7%	20.1	23.0
1981	95%	-4.5%	23.6%	12.6%	23.3	22.1
1982	100%	0.5%	21.9%	16.1%	20.2	19.4
1983	211%	-3.5%	17.9%	21.4%	21.9	15.4
1984	224%	5.3%	17.5%	25.3%	27.0	13.9
1985	235%	7.9%	20.3%	30.8%	25.6	13.2
1986	65%	7.6%	20.0%	23.7%	22.3	14.0
1987	416%	3.6%	23.2%	31.2%	26.2	15.1
1988	1038%	-0.1%	24.3%	33.7%	33.8	14.6
1989	1783%	3.3%	26.9%	47.6%	34.4	18.3
1990	1477%	-4.4%	23.5%	21.1%	31.5	20.7
1991	480%	0.9%	19.9%	21.7%	31.6	21.0
1992	1158%	-0.9%	20.7%		35.9	20.6
1993	2670%	4.2%	23.6%		38.7	25.7
1994	930%	5.7%	21.6%		43.6	33.1

(continues)

[a]IGP
[b]Percent of GDP
[c]Billions of US$

TABLE 6.1   *(continued)*

Trade Balance[c]	Current Accounts Balance[c]	Balance of Payments[c]	Registered Foreign Debt[c]	Foreign Debt Service[c]	Foreign Exchange Reserves[c]
-0.3	-1.0	0.5	6.6	1.1	1.7
-0.2	-1.5	2.4	9.5	1.6	4.2
0.0	-1.7	2.2	12.6	2.2	6.4
-4.7	-7.1	-1.0	17.2	2.6	5.5
-3.5	-6.7	-1.0	21.2	3.7	4.8
-2.3	-6.0	1.2	26.0	4.8	6.4
0.1	-4.0	0.6	32.0	6.3	7.3
-1.0	-5.9	3.9	43.5	8.0	11.9
-2.8	-10.7	-3.2	49.9	10.6	9.7
-2.8	-12.8	-3.5	53.8	11.3	5.9
1.2	-11.7	0.6	61.4	15.4	6.7
0.8	-16.3	-8.8	69.7	18.3	4.0
6.5	-6.8	-5.4	81.3	16.4	4.0
13.1	0.0	0.7	91.1	16.7	12.0
12.5	-0.2	-3.2	95.9	18.2	11.6
8.3	-5.3	-12.4	101.8	20.9	6.8
11.2	-1.4	-3.0	107.6	22.3	7.5
19.2	-4.2	7.0	102.6	26.1	9.1
16.1	1.0	-3.4	99.3	43.6	9.7
10.9	-3.8	-8.8	96.6	18.4	10.0
10.6	-1.4	-4.7	93.0	16.5	9.4
15.2	6.3	30.0	94.3	15.9	23.8
13.0	-0.6	8.4	101.7	18.1	32.2
10.5	-1.1	12.9		18.8	38.8

for these years reached $140 billion, this would lead to a nonviable situation. Indeed, over the span of the 1980s Brazil would pay out more than twice as much in interest—approximately $105 billion—as its debt had totaled when the decade began.

Rather than respond to the oil shock and zooming interest rates through an adjustment program that would entail concomitant economic slowdown and consequent political unpopularity, Figueiredo pushed ahead in 1981 along lines that had resulted in growth during the initial years of his term. Exports increased during 1981, and imports were slightly reduced; this trimmed the current accounts deficit to a still unmanageable $11.7 billion. Rising interest payments brought debt service to $15.4 billion, resulting in a jump in long- and medium-term indebtedness to $61.4 billion. In 1982 imports were again brought down, but exports declined even more sharply, and the trade surplus shriveled. With surging interest payments raising debt service to $18.3 billion, reserves plummeted to an effective level approaching zero. As $12.5 billion was borrowed during the year, much of it short-term, accumulated principal leaped to $70.0 billion and with more inclusive criteria reached $79.6 billion. After midyear the Mexican debt moratorium brought home to international bankers their dangerous exposure in Latin America. This not only caused a rapid dropoff in the flow of new loans and credits to Brazil but also led to a sharp decline in interbank deposits and commercial credit lines. Realizing the need for IMF funds as well as help from the United States and friendly European governments if even a semblance of solvency was to be maintained, Brazil's government began behind-the-scenes negotiations.

Bridge loans from the U.S. Treasury and International Bank for Settlements carried Brazil until installments of a $4.9 billion standby credit and a $1.1 billion compensatory financing facility from the IMF came through. Private banks reluctantly agreed to provide $4.4 billion in new money and roll over $4 billion of the 1983 debt service for eight years. Although this brought immediate relief, it provided no solution to the problem of administering a suffocating debt. By dint of a 23 percent currency devaluation, exports were made competitive but at a high cost in inflation, and Brazil embarked upon a strategy of greatly increased trade surpluses and sharp reduction in oil imports in order to keep up interest payments. As shown in Table 6.1, the $6.5 billion trade surplus of 1983 cut the towering current accounts deficit, $16.3 billion in 1982, to $6.8 billion. Then the doubling in 1984 of the trade surplus to $13.1 billion kept current accounts balanced.[25] Yet capital inflow, $34.7 billion in 1982 that produced a net of $7.9 billion, was halved in 1983 and recovered only partially in 1984.

This feat of eliminating a $16 billion deficit in current transactions in only two years was made possible by halving net oil imports to $4.8 billion in 1984 and posting a $5 billion rise in exports. The third element was return to normalcy in interest rates as the prime rate declined to 11 percent by 1984. Thus interest payments dropped from $12.6 billion in 1982 to $11.2 billion for 1984—although total debt shot up to $97.8 billion. Amortization payments leveled off after reaching $7 billion in 1982, weighing in at $6.5 billion for 1984. The total burden of debt service plus net oil imports was down to a still brutal $21.5 billion in 1984, after having crested at $26.9 billion during the 1982 crisis.

Unwilling to accept a long-term recession as the price of international solvency, the Figueiredo government—as had been the case with civilian administrations in the late 1950s and early 1960s—failed to implement antiinflationary measures agreed upon with the IMF and eventually fell out of compliance. Because this coincided with substantial economic recovery in late 1984 and inflation "stabilized" at 235 percent, it appeared to regime-linked figures that a competent job of damage control had been achieved.

Sarney: Keeping the Debt from Suffocating Democracy

The debt problem changed little during the first two years of restored civilian government. Continued reduction of imports during 1985 produced a healthy trade surplus of $12.5 billion, which left the country capable of coping reasonably well with debt service of $18.2 billion. Still, borrowing to pay old loans pushed debt to $103.6 billion ($95.9 billion by narrower Central Bank calculations). A reduction in net oil imports to $3.9 billion was a major help in holding the line on foreign purchases. Yet there was no net capital inflow. In 1986 explosion in internal consumption engendered by the Cruzado Plan limited exports to $22.4 billion— yielding a trade surplus of $8.3 billion. Fortunately, interest payments had declined, but even so total external debt rose and foreign exchange reserves slipped sharply as net capital inflow was a meager $1.2 billion.

Unable to keep up with scheduled disbursements—interest charges for the 1980–1986 period had exceeded $72 billion (plus $7 billion in 1978–1979)—the government decreed a partial moratorium on interest payments at the end of February 1987. This desperation move was intended to stem the rising net outflow of financial resources—$1.4 billion in 1987 as legal repatriation of capital pushed up toward the $1 billion mark. It was also aimed at strengthening Brazil's position in debt negotiations that had been dragging on. Although a trade surplus of $11.2 billion was achieved, interest payments—chiefly to the Paris Club, the IBRD, and the IADB—still amounted to $8.8 billion. Moreover, interest not paid to the private banks was added to principal to push it over the $115 billion mark.

More disturbingly, disinvestment and capital flight were on the rise, reaching $14.6 billion for the 1983–1987 period, up sharply from $5.8 billion for 1976–1982. During 1987 investment was down, remission of profits and dividends up, and capital flight increasing. As these trends continued, a $2.9 billion net capital inflow in 1988 was wiped out by a negative $4.2 billion in 1989 and a $4.8 billion loss in 1990. Yet with 1988 exports up sharply to $33.8 billion, Brazil still showed a balance-of-payments surplus of $7.0 billion despite foreign debt service up to $26.0 billion. A record trade surplus of $19.2 billion fed recovery of Brazil's exchange reserves, but this had little direct influence upon investment and growth, which was marginally negative.

Brazil's entrepreneurial class was capable of mobilizing only a fraction of funds needed to sustain growth in the face of public-sector retrenchment. For development to regain normal levels, much of the impetus would have to come from abroad. In the election year of 1989 the balance-of-payments deficit hit $3.4 billion owing to a sharp surge in debt service. The capital account deficit was $4.1 billion, and the services deficit pushed $15 billion. Foreign debt stood at $99 billion plus $6 billion in overdue interest, with short-term debt of $14.6 billion compared to foreign exchange reserves of $9.7 billion. A slight rise in overseas sales produced a trade surplus of $16.1 billion.

Collor: Climbing Out of the Hole

Collor encountered a situation in which he was required to straighten out an accumulated fiscal mess. Trade surpluses of $10.9 billion in 1990, $10.6 billion in 1991, and $15.2 billion for 1992 (on record exports of $36 billion) brought the total for the 1984–1992 period to $117 billion—still far below service on the foreign debt over this span. The transfer abroad of a share of GDP often equaling or exceeding the country's annual economic growth seriously undercut development—with Brazilians footing the bill in terms of forgoing a higher standard of living. In 1991 Brazil paid $16.4 billion in debt service, most of which came from the public sector. An agreement in 1992 with the IMF opened the way for resumption of IBRD and IADB loans, important since Brazil was repaying more to these institutions than it was receiving in new credits. Accord with the Paris Club rescheduled $11 billion in return for paying overdue interest and arrears and keeping current on the rest of the $21 billion debt. Although long- and medium-term foreign debt had continued to decline from their 1987 peak, total foreign debt rose as private sector borrowing abroad became common. Reflecting economic recovery, this went from $17 billion outstanding in 1989 to over $41 billion by 1994, so that including short-run credits the gross foreign debt rose from $116 billion to $148 billion.

The Role of Foreign Investment

Direct foreign investment has played a major role in Brazil's industrialization, especially during the 1970s when the inflow of foreign funds averaged 5 percent of GDP yearly. The sum formally registered with the Central Bank grew from $7.5 billion in 1975 to $20.2 billion by 1982, with the total at the beginning of 1989 exceeding $30 billion. Until the 1982 debt crisis, the flow of direct investment into Brazil was steady. In 1980 there was a $1.5 billion net plus $400 million in reinvestment. This peaked in 1982 at $2.9 billion. Direct investment dropped sharply in 1983 as new inflow netted out at but $400 million, which, with $695 million in reinvestment and $452 million of conversion, totaled $1.6 billion—a performance equaled the next year.

The first year of civilian rule saw a further slide to $1.3 billion—only $223 million of it coming in fresh. The picture brightened in 1986, the year of the Cruzado Plan, but the roof fell in immediately thereafter. This abrupt decline was critical to Brazilian development, since between 1975 and 1980 foreign investment had been responsible for over 16 percent of Brazilian capital formation. Deterioration on the foreign capital front was aggravated by the fact that whereas between 1972 and 1981 direct investment had run at two to four times the sum of royalties and repatriation of profits, by 1985 this relationship had reversed, which led toward disinvestment. With shrinking of the public sector's ability to invest from 6 percent of GDP in 1970 to only 2.4 percent by 1980 and down to −0.8 percent by mid-decade, this further weakened the prospects for returning to levels of investment adequate for sustained high growth. Conversion of debt into equity by purchasing loans at a discount became a factor in 1987, with $17 billion involved by mid-1990. Belatedly the government decided in 1991 to use stock markets as vehicles for attracting foreign capital, with an accumulation of $11 billion by 1994. This was accompanied by increased direct investment as the net rose to $561 million in 1991 and $1.16 billion in 1992. Moreover, significant amounts of flight capital returned, some $1.9 billion in 1993 and $2.4 billion in 1994. Under Cardoso the influx of direct investments picked up steam rapidly, with the automotive industry in the van. As established firms announced expansion plans of $1 to $2 billion each, additional multinationals entered the fray.

The Challenge of the Mid-1990s: Finding the Engine(s) for Growth

Investment above 20 percent of GDP is considered necessary in Brazil to generate sustained annual GDP growth of 6 percent. From this level for the 1971–1980 period, gross fixed capital formation dropped off to 18.3 percent of GDP from 1981 through 1987 and fell to under 16 percent for the 1988–1993 period. Import-substitution industrialization had run out of steam. How much emphasis will be given in the second half of the 1990s to trade versus a model centered on rapid expansion of the domestic market will depend not only upon political choices by the Cardoso government but also upon external factors such as the degree of protectionism practiced by Brazil's leading trade partners. In this respect commerce with Western Europe is of vital importance to Brazil, for it is this increasingly integrated region that accounted for the largest share of Brazil's recent trade surpluses.[26] After 1977 surpluses with the United Kingdom, France, and Italy became common, and sales to the Federal Republic of Germany passed the billion-dollar mark. By 1985 exports to the West European countries of $7 billion combined with limited imports provided a positive balance of over $5 billion. In 1986 exports rose to $9.2 billion, producing a surplus of $4.9 billion. Then in 1987 Brazil's sales to this market shot up to $11.1 billion while imports grew modestly to $4.9 billion, yielding a record surplus of $6.2 billion. This three-year favorable balance of $16 billion was half Brazil's global surplus for the period. From 1991 through 1993 Brazil's trade surplus with the fifteen European Union (EU) countries totaled $15.8 billion (on sales of $32.5 billion and purchases of $16.8 billion).

Next in importance as a trading partner for Brazil is the once-paramount United States. From a third of Brazil's exports in 1967–1968, the U.S. share dropped to one-fourth for 1969 through 1972 and then to merely a fifth. In the 1973–1975 period Brazil ran a deficit of $4 billion; it rose sharply during 1976, accounting for roughly half of Brazil's total shortfall. A $600 million deficit in 1980 was turned into a surplus of the same modest magnitude the next year (as $3.5 billion in sales and $4.1 billion in purchases were reversed). Doubling this positive balance in 1982 resulted from a sharp reduction in Brazil's imports compared to a marginal drop in exports. The next year a further reduction of purchases to $2.5 billion combined with a jump in sales to $5 billion produced a surplus of $2.5 billion. Through determined efforts, by 1984–1985 this ratio evolved to $14.7 billion to $5.1 billion in Brazil's favor—for a two-year surplus of $9.6 billion. Decreased exports and increased imports brought this down in 1986–1987 to $6.7 billion (on $13.6 billion in sales)—making the four-year bilateral surplus 36 percent of Brazil's total. In 1988 Brazil-U.S. trade grew to nearly $9 billion in exports versus $4.3 billion in imports, but this was a smaller proportion of Brazil's record surplus, and sales to the United States then diminished to $8.3 billion in 1989, $7.6 billion in 1990, $6.4 billion in 1991, $7.1 billion in 1992, and $8.0 billion in 1993 before rising to $9.0 billion in 1994. Hence the bilateral surplus was down to a thin $570 million by 1991, recovered in 1992 to $1.8 billion as exports climbed to $7.5 billion, and held even in 1993 as both sales and purchases grew for a record total of $14.1 billion—22.4 percent of Brazil's international commerce. Part of the slack in Brazil's trade surplus with the United States was taken up in the early 1990s by Japan, with which Brazil ran a 1991–1993 surplus of $3.2 billion on sales of $7.2 billion.[27]

Aware of the risks of counting so heavily upon trade with the industrialized nations, the Collor government built a foundation for greater commerce with other Latin American nations through development of a free-trade area embracing Argentina, Uruguay, and Paraguay. Brazil's trade with Argentina was balanced at the $1.6 billion level each way in 1991. Exports to Argentina topped $3 billion in 1992 for a surplus of $1.4 billion, which fell to just over $1 billion in 1993 as Brazil bought more, but two-way volume rose to over $6 billion, reaching $7.7 billion in 1994 on Brazilian exports of $4.1 billion. At 22.6 percent in 1993, Brazil's trade with Latin American countries exceeded that with the United States and was close behind commerce with the EU.

Brazil in 1993, 1994, and 1995 achieved renewed growth, debt relief, and increased foreign investment, but the latter must be sustained over the rest of the decade—as must the progress in curbing inflation made since the second half of 1994—if Brazil is to resume the kind of economic progress that marked the years to 1986 and is to mount a concerted attack upon the country's forbidding social problems. Their thorny nature and formidable magnitude are analyzed in the next chapter—along with the societal changes that have accompanied the economic transformation discussed in this chapter.

7

SOCIETY AND
SOCIAL PROBLEMS

E CONOMIC DEVELOPMENTS discussed in the preceding chapter have resulted in social change that has been substantial, even dramatic if viewed over the span of decades. A generation ago Brazil was socially as well as economically an underdeveloped country, and within another it may well be an industrialized nation. Now it is at midstream, with the full array of tensions and problems involved in rapid, uneven, ongoing modernization. Brazil is a middle-income country with a fast expanding workforce reflecting a sustained surge of industry and the service sector as well as a high degree of urbanization. Social changes unleashed by these processes have yet to run their course; some—including the role and position of women and blacks—have still to reach maximum momentum.

Treatment of Brazil's social dynamics centers on the relationship of social structure to economic and racial considerations—for benefits of growth have been very unevenly distributed in terms of social classes as well as by regions and gender. The broad base of the social pyramid is made up of Afro-Brazilians, a large proportion living in the most backward regions and over half of them women. Their fecundity rates have not dropped as dramatically as those of European extraction, giving lie to the hoary myth that racial problems in Brazil would disappear with time and "whitening" of the population. Indeed, race relations are almost certain in the years ahead to become a much more salient issue in Brazilian national and public life than they have been at any time since the abolition controversy in the 1880s.

Education is Brazil's primary channel of social mobility. Substantial upward movement exists, but the key to opportunity is sufficient education to be able to take advantage of expansion of technical, financial, and administrative occupations. Despite tremendous quantitative progress in education since the 1950s, access to schooling is still dramatically less available to rural populations and segments of the urban lower classes than to other sectors of society. Brazil's blacks

169

and mulattoes are a disproportionate share among these heavily disadvantaged groups. Hence it begs the question to say—as Brazilians often do—that this is essentially a socioeconomic phenomenon. Rather the high correlation between dark skin and poverty should be cause for soul-searching. As discussed in this chapter, other groups have arrived later in Brazil, begun near the bottom, and moved up quickly. In religion the Roman Catholic Church is predominant with protestantism, Afro-Brazilian movements, and spiritism also important. These are rival but not mutually exclusive, as a significant number of Brazilians mix religious practices.

Workforce, Income Distribution, and Social Mobility

Education and income are highly correlated in Brazil, but the relationship is more complex than either the interpretation that only those better off to begin with have access to education or the assertion that education leads directly to higher income. Education is the main vehicle for upward social mobility, yet the channel is far from unobstructed, and getting higher-paying jobs on the strength of schooling alone is far from automatic. When the economy is at the high tide of rapid sustained growth, obstacles in the stream of social mobility are submerged, and the opportunity ferry may pass safely over them. But when growth slows to where the economy is producing fewer new jobs than the number of persons entering the labor market, the sandbar of inadequate employment opportunities and shoals of unemployment imperil passage across class barriers. In these situations "who you know, not what you know" comes into play, and the high hopes of many who have struggled and sacrificed for educational attainment founder on the treacherous rocks of color, sex, and even region of origin. As a result, although tens of millions of Brazilians manage to improve their status and level of living, other millions miss the opportunity boat, and millions more become relatively—if not absolutely—worse off.[1]

Employment and Labor

Brazil's economic transformation is dramatically mirrored in changes that have occurred in the workforce. As late as 1950 only 14 percent of the economically active population (EAP)—then numbering 17.1 million—were found in industry, with 60 percent in agriculture and 26 percent in the service sector. By 1990 those employed in industry had risen to 22 percent, agriculture had declined sharply to 23 percent, and the tertiary sector had exploded to 55 percent. Quantitative changes were dramatic as the EAP climbed to 64.5 million individuals over age ten by 1990.[2] Whereas in 1940 agricultural laborers outnumbered those in industry by five to one, by 1990 industrial employment equaled that in agriculture. This remarkable shift resulted from the increasing proportion of new jobs related to industrialization. Although over the 1940–1980 span the number of individuals employed in agriculture rose by 3 million, those in industry multiplied 5.3 times—an increase of 8.2 million—and employment in the tertiary sector was up 6.6 times for a much larger increment of 17.8 million.[3] Since 1980 four-fifths of the increase in the EAP has been in the service sector.

This fundamental change in employment was accompanied by a dramatic rise in the proportion of women in the labor force. Between 1970 and 1985 women gainfully employed trebled from 6.1 million to 18.5 million—compared to but 2.5 million in 1950.[4] By 1993 women composed 38 percent of the EAP compared to one-seventh in 1950. The most dramatic development in the labor market is an increasing proportion of married women working outside the home, which helped raise the workforce ratio in São Paulo and Rio de Janeiro to under three men to two women by 1989. Although uneducated women from the lower classes are still concentrated in low-paying jobs, educated women have moved quite rapidly into the more desirable careers opened up by modernization and development. Long well-represented among doctors and lawyers, they are increasingly found in the ranks of economists, administrators, security analysts, and brokers—as well as finally in the ranks of uniformed police. Yet women still earn considerably less than do men; in 1987 a high 46.5 percent of women in the workforce earned minimum salary or less in contrast to 27.7 percent of their male counterparts. Indeed, in 1988 women outnumbered men below the minimum salary, and the ratio above ten minimums was four men per woman. Black women are especially poorly paid.[5]

Job figures are distorted by the extremely large informal sector. Thus, during the 1981–1984 recession demand for work in urban areas rose by 4 million, but employment in the formal sector—with the employer signing the employee's working book and hence paying social security and other wage taxes—fell by 1 million. Yet this labor surplus was largely absorbed by an increase of 4 million jobs in the informal sector.[6] This resulted in 71.5 percent of the total labor force (including farmworkers) working off the books. Under the subsequent recovery, many jobs moved from the informal to the formal sector, with a sizable proportion reverting back as microbusinesses encountered hard times from 1987 to 1992. In Brazil small businesses in financial trouble go off the books to reduce costs; hence official statistics are often quite misleading.

The *jogo de bicho*, or numbers game, provides an important case in point. Technically outside the law although generally tolerated by the authorities in major urban centers, it involves over $2 billion a year, furnishes stable employment to 50,000 individuals in Rio de Janeiro, and provides income to 400,000 persons in the country as a whole.[7] The largest "bankers" pay their employees comparatively well, provide medical coverage, and even have retirement benefits. These individuals, as well as the growing legions linked to distribution of drugs, are not unemployed, no matter what they may answer to a census taker. Thus income data based on information from respondents wary of running afoul of authorities is rarely reliable. Moreover, anyone familiar with Brazilian realities knows that many *camelôs* (street vendors) are not living on the edge of poverty but possibly are doing better than some of the small shopkeepers whose overhead expenses they avoid. But even *camelôs* who have hired several others to sell for them will not admit to being fairly prosperous, albeit they have frequently acquired substantial properties in low-rent areas from which they derive additional income. When pressed they will explain their possessions by saying they won the lottery or the *jogo*. Yet they enter the official statistics as having no monetary income. Hence, although official statistics speak of 32 million below the poverty line, scholars have estimated the real figure at below 20 million, perhaps closer to 15 million.

Uneven Distribution of Wealth

Distribution of wealth in Brazil is extremely unequal, but this does not mean that while the rich have indeed gotten richer, the poor have become poorer in absolute terms—particularly when family rather than individual is taken as the unit of analysis. There has been a trend toward an increased number of wage earners in the Brazilian family, chiefly as a result of the sharp rise in the proportion of working wives. Still, Brazil's industrialization has been accompanied by increased income concentration. In 1960 the top 10 percent of earners received 39.6 percent of total income, and the bottom decile got but 1.9 percent. This gap grew to 48.7 and 0.8 percent at the trough of recession in 1991 as the richest 1 percent of Brazilians received 14 percent of income compared to 12 percent for the poorest half.[8]

Income distribution in Brazil is couched in terms of proportions of population earning below, at, or above the minimum salary (expressed in monthly terms). This presents a problem of comparability over time, since the value of the minimum salary is far from constant. Nevertheless, such data do help portray the class structure of Brazilian society. As of 1984 some 1.6 percent of Brazil's economically active population could be considered well-off by Brazilian standards, earning over twenty times the legal minimum and sharing 18 percent of total income. An upper-middle class composed of 3.5 percent of the EAP earning ten to twenty minimum salaries received 16 percent of total income. Also middle class were the 8.5 percent of the workforce earning five to ten times the minimum and getting 20 percent of income. Transitional between this lower-middle class and the upper stratum of the working class were the 11.3 percent of the EAP earning three to five minimums and pulling down 15 percent of the income total. By way of stark contrast, the working-class component earning two to three minimum wages numbered 12.3 percent of the workforce and received 10 percent of income. At the margin of the poor were the nearly 24 percent of the EAP earning one to two minimums for approximately 12 percent of total income. The 38.2 percent of the workforce paid below the minimum wage totaled 8 percent of Brazil's income—a chilling contrast to the more fortunate strata. Yet quality of living involves factors beyond income levels, and progress has been made with respect to material conveniences and social services.

Social Conditions and Problems

Material aspects of life have been improving for many Brazilians, particularly in urban areas. Households with running water increased from 16 percent in 1950 to 71 percent by 1988. This was paralleled with respect to electricity, as the 1950 proportion of 25 percent rose to 86 percent by 1988. As late as 1970 only 26 percent of homes had refrigerators, a share that climbed to 70 percent by 1991. Only 24 percent of families had a television set in 1970; this had exploded to 74 percent by 1991 (over 85 percent in urban areas). Automobiles were owned by only 9 percent of Brazilian families in 1970 but by 1988 were found in over a third of homes.[9] As sales rose to record highs in 1993 and 1994, this figure is by now at least 40 percent—with new television sets reaching 7.5 million a year compared to 3.6 million stoves and ovens and over 2 million refrigerators and freezers.

Brazilians have a marked propensity to own their residences. In 1987 some 20.6 million families were owners, and only 6.7 million rented. One in seven of Brazil's families lived in dwellings provided by employers or loaned to them by relatives. A great number of lower-income Brazilian families live in substandard homes but at least own them. Still, there are several million families in more dire housing straits, with urban administrations varying greatly in the efforts and resources devoted to their plight. Nationally there is a need for 7.3 million new urban housing units and 2.7 million in rural areas if 60 million Brazilians are not to live in substandard accommodations. Yet far from all these inadequate residences are helplessly so; many are being gradually improved by their inhabitants. Indeed, some experts have revised the figure for clearly substandard units to only 5 million if some doubling up of relatives is taken as normal.

Cities: Generations Ahead of the Countryside

In every category of well-being and material conveniences there is a sharp urban-rural disparity, with figures for laggard rural areas in most cases past the 1960 national proportions and closing in on those for 1970. Continuance of trends of the past quarter century will soon sharply reduce the material gap between the vast urban and shrinking rural sectors of society. In regional terms, metropolitan centers in the southern quadrant of the country are well ahead, for there the average

Children playing in the interior of Brazil (photo by Ricardo P. Schneider, reproduced by permission)

income is three to five times the minimum. In brutal contrast, over 60 percent of rural families remain below the minimum salary.[10] Indeed, the states of the southeast and south, with 65 percent of the workforce, have 77 percent of the income earners in the over five minimums bracket. For its part the northeast, with 27 percent of the EAP, has less than 12 percent of the relatively well-off; at the bottom of the income pyramid, this retarded region has 54 percent of families in this distressed situation. Thus, under any analysis, the northeast has far more than its fair share of Brazil's poor and disadvantaged. This is rooted in the fact that in this region there are over three relatively low-paying jobs in agriculture for each one in industry. Even in the northeast 55 percent of industrial workers get more than the legal minimum, compared to only 20 percent of agricultural workers.

Social Problems and Policy

Certainly, social conditions leave a great deal to be desired in Brazil, but they are changing for the better, and the problem is more one of some elements of society being left behind rather than the lot of the vast majority showing little improvement. Poverty is the fate of several million children neglected if not abandoned by their families. Many are cared for in orphanages and juvenile facilities; hundreds of thousands are street urchins for whom life is perilous and degrading. There are millions of *favelados* (urban squatters and slum dwellers) in Brazil's cities with a

Locals fish on a northeastern river (photo by Ricardo P. Schneider, reproduced by permission)

Street children huddle together for warmth in São Paulo (photo by Nani Gois, courtesy of Abril Imagens)

substantial proportion indigent. The largest concentrations are in São Paulo and Rio de Janeiro cities, but swollen northeastern cities like Recife have a disproportionate share.

Misinformation abounds concerning birth control in Brazil, where 13 million women of childbearing age have had tubal ligation, and are not candidates for pregnancy. There are estimates of 1.4 million abortions yearly; the most alarming statistic is that one-fifth of deaths of fifteen- to nineteen-year-old women are probably from badly done abortions. Health care still leaves much to be desired, although there has been steady improvement from a low baseline. By 1984 some 27,552 hospitals, clinics, and other medical facilities provided 540,000 beds and employed 932,000 persons.[11] From 1 percent of GDP in 1950, expenditures on health care reached 3.6 percent in 1974 and 5.6 percent by 1982. Yet in 1993 the Ministry of Health was limited to $9 billion in expenditures. The six southernmost states have 70 percent of hospital beds and 68 percent of health-care personnel. Urban residents accounted for 83 percent of hospital internments and 93 percent of specialized treatment. Brazilians are highly subject to internal parasites and poor nutrition, and 11 million Brazilians are estimated to be affected by some infectious disease. Unfortunately, AIDS has become a major health problem just as headway was being made with respect to other infectious diseases. Only a small proportion of cases are reported, but informed estimates of HIV-infected persons run from 400,000 to over 1 million.[12]

The Brazilian social security system, although lagging far behind standards of Western industrial nations, has become much more inclusive during the past generation and extends to medical and hospital treatment. As recently as 1950 it covered only 2.9 million individuals but leaped to 30 million by 1988. Individuals receiving benefits rose from 2.3 million in 1971 to 15.0 million by 1994. The government's expenditures in this field were $28 billion in 1994, chiefly for pensions with much of the remainder eaten up by administrative costs. The system urgently needs a thorough overhaul as its 1994 deficit of nearly $2 billion threatens to explode if the comprehensive reform bill before Congress in 1995 is not passed.[13]

Education and Increased Income

The relationship between income and education in Brazil is nearly linear. Nearly half the 4.9 million persons earning more than ten times minimum salary in 1990 had completed high school, and another 26 percent had attended one to three years of secondary school. In contrast, just 1.2 percent of this top earnings bracket had less than three years of schooling. For 7.0 million Brazilians earning five to ten times the minimum, these proportions were 20 percent high school graduates, 28 percent with incomplete secondary education, and only 8 percent with less than three years of formal schooling. At the other pole, a minuscule 0.6 percent of 15.4 million persons earning less than the legal minimum were high school graduates, whereas almost 46 percent had no more than two years of primary school.[14] Even between the extremes—where those with a secondary school education predominate in the upper brackets and are all but absent at the wide bottom of the earnings pyramid—the correlation between education and income is striking: Of the 9.5 million individuals earning three to five times the minimum standard, 31 percent had more than eight years of schooling, compared to 14.0 percent of the 12.7 million earning one to two times the minimum. Put another way, nearly seven-eighths of all Brazilian high school graduates earn more than three times the minimum salary; this drops to 53 percent for those with incomplete high school, declines to 36 percent for those with five to eight years of schooling, and slides to 9 percent at less than a year of school. A staggering one-half of the latter group had to make do with less than the minimum salary.

In sum, one is not likely to earn well in Brazil without at least a high school education—or to escape poverty without having over three years of schooling. The relationship between lack of education and abject poverty on one hand and a full education and high standard of living on the other is clear and intimate. Any group without unhindered access to educational opportunity has little chance of significant upward social mobility. A look at the school system shows that there are still structural obstacles to anything approaching equal educational opportunity in Brazil, albeit less so in urban centers than in rural areas. Hence the rural poor are much more likely to stay poor from one generation to the next than are their urban counterparts, and the latter have greater chances of upward mobility in the cities of the southern third of the country than elsewhere—especially in the northeast.

Education

Despite progress in recent years, Brazil's educational system has serious deficiencies. The quality of teaching is often poor, especially at the primary level, where the vast majority attend public schools. Yet this is a price paid for increased access, and space available is catching up to demand in more developed urban centers. Secondary schools have not fully adjusted to the task of educating millions for functioning in an increasingly complex society rather than preparing a few hundred thousand for university entrance. Over the past generation Brazil has managed to build Latin America's largest system of higher education, albeit one of uneven quality between such internationally recognized institutions as the Universities of São Paulo or Campinas and an array of profit-oriented degree factories. Most educators agree that entrance examinations are deeply flawed. Finally there is the absurdity of a system that allows children of the upper and upper-middle classes to fill free public institutions, whereas those who can least afford to pay have to attend private facilities, often working full-time to pay for their studies.

The most serious educational problem is a dual one at the very beginning of the elementary level, which by law begins at age seven. Although there are 31 million seven- to fourteen-year-olds enrolled, this leaves 3 million out of school.[15] One reason for this is the extremely high rate of failure in the first grade, caused in part by the fact that only a small proportion of these children have had a chance to attend kindergarten. The problem is aggravated by large classes and short school day, and teaching rarely approaches standards set by a ministry preoccupied with higher education. The two-fifths repeating the initial year take up space sorely needed for the new crop of seven-year-olds. Only a third make it through eighth grade—averaging twelve years to do so (For the southeast, this is nearly half, but only 16 percent in the northeast.). Just 60 percent of fifteen- to seventeen-year-olds are in school compared to 90 percent in the seven- to fourteen-year-old bracket.

Expansion, Yes! Improvement, Perhaps?

Unsatisfactory as is the present situation, it marks great progress over the extremely restricted access and highly elitist nature of the educational system in the past. In 1857 only one in fourteen seven- to eleven-year-olds in Brazil was in school; this reached one in seven by 1889, one in five by 1907, and more than one in two in 1950.[16] Within a decade the number of students had burgeoned to 8.7 million with 267,000 in high school and 93,000 receiving higher education. By 1970 elementary student population had exploded to 15.9 million; there were 1 million in high schools and 456,000 attending colleges and universities. By 1980 elementary school enrollment passed 22.5 million, that in secondary schools surpassed 2.8 million, and higher education trebled to 1.4 million. In 1985 Brazil had a total of 31.5 million students—over six times the 1950 figure—and the number rose to 42 million by 1994.

Many students repeatedly drop out of school to work, and thus there are several million primary school students in their late teens or even their twenties. In addition, 30 percent of junior high students, 40 percent of high schoolers, and 60 percent of college students in Brazil work at full-time jobs.[17] The lower a family's income, the higher the probability that a teenage member does not attend school at all; in the middle range of family wealth the propensity is both to study and work.

Although the 1988 constitution mandated a sharp increase in educational spending—to 18 percent of the federal budget and 25 percent of state and local expenditures—actual expenditures on education in 1993 were a low 3.4 percent of GDP. Yet there is a strong trend toward a dominant role for over 300,000 public schools, as private education, particularly parochial, continues to encounter grave financial problems. Long hegemonic at the primary level, public schools now enroll 88 percent of these students as well as 65 percent of secondary students and 39 percent in higher education, where private institutions outnumber public ones 652 to 241.

Regional Imbalances

Education still varies dramatically in Brazil from region to region. Thus, the whole northeast had only 719,000 high school students in 1985 with just a tenth of them in rural areas. (Indeed, in all Brazil there were but 200,000 rural secondary students.) Over 61 percent of high schools in 1991 were located in the seven states of the south and southeast. The over 1 million university students in the south and southeast are more than four times the northeast's meager total. Of those graduating from universities, 64 percent came from the three large states and 84 percent from the southeast and south combined. This disparity is perpetuated by the fact that 61 percent of the country's institutions of higher education are in the tri-state area and 82 percent in the seven-state region. With more than 78 percent of new admissions concentrated in this region, little change is likely. Congruently, 95 percent of Ph.D. candidates are concentrated in the three leading states with 70 percent in São Paulo alone, a clear indication of where the country's research-oriented universities are.[18]

Additionally, the distribution of students by field of study is out of line with the job market. The imbalance produces large numbers of doctors who will probably never practice medicine and a great excess of lawyers—the traditional prestige professions for the middle class. Yet in marked contrast with even the 1960s, there are few fields in which it is not possible to get a first-rate education in Brazil, provided one is fortunate enough to get into one of the small number of quality universities and professional schools. Unfortunately, chances of admission are much greater for someone already from the upper class.

Still a Long Way to Go

Given that expansion of educational opportunity is recent, schooling levels remain low. Thus, of those ten years of age or more in 1988, some 19.1 percent had less than a year of formal schooling. At the opposite extreme only 5.5 percent had a year of college or more. In between were 11.5 percent who had attended high school, often not graduating, and 6.8 percent who had completed the eighth grade. Also above the median in educational attainment were the 15.6 percent who had reached the upper primary grades. The large contingent who had gone only through the four elementary grades totaled 17.6 percent, and 23.7 percent had finished but one to three years of basic schooling.

Literacy figures tell essentially the same story. The 1991 figure of 82 percent literacy among those ten and older marked substantial progress over the 1970 figure of 64 percent. Moreover, most of the residual illiteracy was concentrated in rural areas, particularly in the northeast, where over half the nation's total is to be found; the 1992 estimate was a striking 9.4 million over age ten. The illiteracy rate in São Paulo and Rio de Janeiro is down to 9 percent. For urban areas in general it is 12 percent compared to 35 percent in rural ones.

In light of these considerations the basic challenges in the field of education are clear. First is the need to make schooling available in the rural areas. This involves the difficult task of convincing poor and often illiterate parents to send their children to school and keep them there instead of relying on their efforts to supplement family income. Of equal importance is the need to improve the often woefully inadequate quality of elementary school instruction that, particularly in small towns and rural schools, involves an unacceptably high proportion of uncertified teachers and long-term temporaries. This is aggravated by the tendency of experienced teachers to seek transfers to schools in the large towns or to the bloated rolls of supervisors and administrators. Since this often involves political sponsorship in return for electoral support, it is a phenomenon that has proved very resistant to efforts at reform.

As it is primarily the bottom of the socioeconomic ladder—the sector with the least political influence—that still lacks access to the educational system, progress in making elementary education more universal will be slow unless there is a concerted effort in this direction by socially responsible elements of the more favored classes. These groups have been effective in pressuring for expansion of secondary and higher education that has characterized the past four decades. Also of priority importance is extending the school day—which in most areas is under four hours, as schools function with one group of students in the morning, another in the afternoon, and a third at night. Yet marked progress has been made toward fuller school days in such places as São Paulo and Rio de Janeiro.

As with so many of Brazil's needs, the answer lies in a broad-based effort aimed at the roots of the problem, not a narrower quick-fix approach near its highly visible peak. The chief factor inhibiting such root change is that those who most need increased access to education have the weakest voice in setting policy priorities. They are the poor, especially in rural areas, among whom nonwhites are particularly numerous. To a significant degree they are victims of Brazil's peculiar

Family from a typical small town in the Brazilian interior (photo by Ricardo P. Schneider, reproduced by permission)

electoral system, since the statewide constituency method for electing legislators means that these individuals who influence distribution of resources are primarily concerned with the urban centers rather than representation of rural constituents.

Racial Factors and Race Relations

Education is the primary answer to the crucial question of whether sectors of society that have so far been left out of the benefits of industrialization-led development will have a chance at a better life during the next generation. The crux of the matter is that unless educational opportunities for blacks and mulattoes increase significantly, this large segment of Brazilians will remain at the bottom of the social pyramid no matter how much economic growth takes place. It may possibly be, as many Brazilians continue to assert, that the problem is not essentially one of ingrained, much less institutionalized, discrimination on the basis of color, but rather one deeply rooted in limited access to education for the lower classes—be they black, brown, or white. But since the darker-skinned are heavily concentrated in the lower class, this situation perpetuates their disadvantaged position—a condition that becomes less tolerable as other elements of society move forward and upward with Brazil's economic transformation.

Although the country has passed the centennial of abolition, there remains a dramatic racial factor in distribution of income and educational opportunities, one that over time may well have serious political ramifications. In 1984 only 28 percent of white workers earned below the minimum salary, but this rose to 48 percent for brown-skinned and exceeded 52 percent for blacks. Nearly half of whites took home one to five times the minimum; for browns and blacks this proportion was 37 percent—largely concentrated in the one to two times minimum bracket. At the other end of the scale, 13 percent of whites earned above five times the minimum, whereas for brown-skinned this was below 4 percent and for blacks a meager 2 percent. Indeed, in 1980 there were only 2,300 blacks and 46,000 brown-skinned among the elite earning over twenty times the minimum—compared to 579,000 whites.[19] In 1990 blacks earned 41 percent as much as whites; browns were slightly better off at 47 percent.

With respect to education, as of 1976 a staggering 46 percent of nonwhites had less than a year of schooling, compared to 27 percent of whites. Nine or more years of schooling was attained by 11 percent of whites but fewer than 4 percent of nonwhites. Three-fifths of those with less than one year of school were mulattoes or blacks, but nine-tenths of college graduates were white.[20] Whereas 8 percent of white Brazilians were university-educated professionals, businessmen, and administrators, this privileged category included but 3 percent of the country's brown-skinned citizens and but 1 percent of blacks. The poorest 10 percent of Brazilians were 60 percent black or brown; the richest decile was 83 percent white.

This color gap is likely to continue since 1990 figures show fewer than 75 percent of blacks and 79 percent of browns between seven and nine years of age are in school compared to over 91 percent of whites.

Even more serious is that Afro-Brazilians have a life expectancy fourteen years shorter than for whites; an infant mortality rate 30 percent higher; and more than double the proportion of illiterates. This marks a change from when illiteracy was a general phenomenon more pronounced among nonwhites; it is becoming essentially a brown-black phenomenon involving a small number of rural whites. Although Afro-Brazilian illiteracy is still 17 percent in the southeast and 21 percent in the south, it is 43 percent in the northeast. Educational and economic opportunities are very limited in rural areas, especially in the northeast—precisely where a disproportionate number of blacks and mulattoes live. Geographic distribution of Afro-Brazilians may be a carryover from preabolition days, but other aspects of their inferior social position cannot be written off in this manner; involved is some process of perpetuation.[21]

How Black Is Brazil?

The importance of Brazilians of African descent is underscored by the fact that they are as numerous as all others of African extraction in the Western Hemisphere. Even by the flawed procedures of the 1991 census, those with a significant degree of African ancestry would now be 69.6 million—7.8 million *preto* (black) and 61.8 million *pardo* (lumping together mulattoes and mestizos). Indeed, they outnumber the inhabitants of any black African country except Nigeria. From the beginning they have gotten the short and dirty end of the stick in almost every respect. Freedom for slaves coincided with massive European immigration that filled the new jobs opened up by agriculture in the southeast and by incipient industrialization.[22]

Brazilian elites have assuaged their consciences by accepting the myth of Brazil as a racial democracy.[23] For roughly seventy-five years after abolition of slavery, the dominant elements in Brazilian society almost unanimously looked to "whitening"—the lightening of color through miscegenation and European immigration—as the key to elimination of racial problems in Brazil. The influential writings of social historian Gilberto Freyre, especially the classic *Casa-Grande e Senzala* (1933) and his concept of the "Luso-tropical" man gifted in creating harmonious multiracial societies, were of great importance in buttressing the concept of Brazil as a unique racial democracy. The exaggerated application of Freyre's concepts was reinforced by the early works of outside scholars, who emphasized class rather than race as the primary determinant of Afro-Brazilians' inferior position. Although sound empirical scholarship came by the 1960s to undermine this idealized image of race relations, Brazil's dominant elites rejected the new findings, a task made easier by the fact that most of the scholars involved were identified with the radical Left, and this provided a basis for rejecting their work as "ideological."[24] Dominant public opinion was more comfortable with the assertion that mulattoes experienced less discrimination than blacks, and hence the latter could use this as an "escape hatch" by marrying lighter-skinned Afro-Brazilians.[25]

Great Inequalities, Some Discrimination

Careful empirical research of a new wave of social scientists revealed the working of a cycle of cumulative disadvantage that resulted in Afro-Brazilians not only having significantly less access to education and upward social mobility but also at each educational level earning substantially less than whites. There is less inter-generational social mobility for Afro-Brazilians, and in terms of obtaining employment appropriate to educational achievement, at least through the high school level, occupational discrimination increases with their degree of schooling. With four to seven years of education whites earn double what Afro-Brazilians of the same level of schooling do.[26]

Despite abundant evidence of the unfairly disadvantaged position of "Brazilians of color," concerted efforts at promoting racial consciousness among them have met with limited success—even after transition to a competitive political regime. The centennial of abolition in 1988 did not spur gains for black pride and power movements. Many Afro-Brazilians have instead internalized unfavorable self-images and limited their aspirations accordingly. Furthermore, although skin color is important, it alone is not used to categorize people, and classifications based on it are in everyday life subject to modification on the basis of subsequent information about education, employment, and so forth.

Passivity of the underprivileged, except for occasional and isolated outbursts, is a striking aspect of contemporary as well as historical Brazilian reality. Its roots are comprehensible, but reasons for its persistence at the end of the twentieth century are more perplexing. An important part of the explanation lies in the fact that this social stratum is predominantly made up of blacks and mulattoes who, given their large numbers and majority status in many regions, do not perceive of themselves as a collective minority. To a high degree they accept the myth that their plight is a result of the country's underdevelopment. They are also held back from assuming a less passive stance by serious reservations as to whether there is any viable alternative to acquiescing in the hand fate has dealt them. For many of them the relative ease of survival in tropical and semitropical Brazil—the regions in which the vast majority of them live—is an additional incentive to accommodation. (The northeast is 71 percent Afro-Brazilian in sharp contrast to under 16 percent in the three southernmost states.) Yet to a large extent they merely share with other components of the disadvantaged Brazilian masses a submissiveness also deeply rooted in their lack of access to organized political resources. This leads those wishing to escape poverty to pursue their goal through individual efforts at social mobility rather than collective action. The result has been apathy and submission for the great majority and co-optation of a very large share of the more dynamic individuals—which leaves too few for an effective job of organizing and mobilizing the masses.[27] Great inequalities are hence maintained with a minimum of violence and conflict.

The 1986 balloting saw election of just 7 Afro-Brazilians among 559 members of Congress, which improved slowly in 1990 and 1994. Moreover, 1988 and 1992 municipal elections also demonstrated that color is not yet an effective rallying point in Brazilian politics. Indeed, the situation appears closer to Fontaine's 1975 concept of the "powerlessness" of blacks in Brazilian society than to his subsequent efforts to show that their "interstitial," "residual," and "incremental" power was significant.[28]

Whitening, acculturation, and assimilation are considered by the most militant Afro-Brazilians as the functional equivalent of genocide. These vocal but numerically inexpressive elements also denounce Brazilian racism as being more insidious and hypocritical for being disguised and denied, compared to the allegedly open and admitted racism of North Americans.[29] If these Afro-Brazilians exaggerate in one direction, they are in many ways less far off the mark than those white Brazilians who continue to insist that racial prejudice is all but nonexistent in their country. Three and a half decades of personal observation leads me to the inescapable conclusion that other things being equal, a black or even a mulatto may need at least twice the talent, three times the hard work, and four times the luck to make it to near the top in any profession not closely linked to professional sports or some fields of show business—clearly excluding television.

Even worse, there are many areas in which there is almost no chance of substantially equal accomplishment no matter what the combination of talent, determination, and luck. Thus, the Brazilian Catholic Church, with roughly 14,000 priests, 378 bishops and archbishops, and 7 cardinals, has only 200 nonwhite priests and 5 dark-skinned bishops even as thousands of Europeans—at least 45 percent of the total clergy—are imported to fill vacancies, and thousands of other slots go unfilled. The foreign service is still almost entirely white, and the upper reaches of the officer corps in all three services are reminiscent of those in the United States prior to World War II—if not World War I.[30]

The Plight of Brazil's Indians

Although Brazil's indigenous population is down below a quarter million, these groups continue to receive much attention outside of Brazil. Their location, chiefly in highly peripheral regions (see Chapter 1), puts them at the margin of attention for a vast majority of Brazilians, and lack of districts in the Brazilian electoral system denies them political weight. Government policy concern focuses upon a slow process of demarcation of reserves complicated by tribal fragmentation and extreme territorial dispersion. Despite sincere and farsighted exceptions, too often their tribal leadership is occupied selling mineral and lumbering rights and acquiring the white man's artifacts, including not just motors for their boats but expensive utility vehicles and even airplanes. Troops have been used to clear reservations of prospectors (often far outnumbering the Indians), but the lure of mineral wealth brings them back in droves—at times with the support of state politicians and agroindustrial concerns. Brazil's greatly improved international economic position since 1993 has rendered the government far less attentive to international opinion and external pressures. Meanwhile, Indian ranks continue to be thinned by disease and acculturation.

Fast-Rising Latecomers

In marked contrast to Afro-Brazilians, other immigrant groups have done very well in Brazil. Most noteworthy are Japanese; their population has grown to 1.2 million since Japanese were first brought over in 1908 to work in São Paulo coffee fields. They emphasize education for their children and by the 1970s had a frequency of college graduates disproportionate to their numbers. In contrast with Afro-Brazilians, concentrated in backward regions, Japanese were able in São Paulo to take advantage of the availability of schooling and the occupational opportunities opened up by industrialization.[31] Not only were 15.5 percent of 1977 University of São Paulo graduates from this sector (it represents 2.5 percent of the state's population), but Japanese-Brazilians were influential in Paulista politics and beginning to have impact on the national scene.

Brazilian society has Europeans—Italians, Germans, Poles, and Spaniards as well as Portuguese—heavily represented in the upper and middle classes, and their values, lifestyle, and religion, are dominant in Brazilian culture. Thus the marked contrast between how they have fared and the lot of Afro-Brazilians need not be elaborated.[32] But immigrants from the Middle East have also made rapid progress, in some ways more striking than that of the Japanese and starkly different from the low position of the many times larger Afro-Brazilian component.[33] Syrians and Lebanese came first as peddlers shortly before the turn of the century, and the flow picked up before the outbreak of World War I, amounting to ten times the 5,500 of the earlier period. Another 50,000 came in the interwar years, and 20,000 more arrived after 1940. They carved out an important place in trade and business, subsequently entering industry and banking as well as the hotel and communications fields. By the 1970s the Maksouds built São Paulo's ranking five-star hotel, and the Lutfalla-Maluf family controlled industry capable of sustaining the massive expenses of Paulo Maluf's 1984 presidential bid and succession of subsequent electoral campaigns. Lebanese-Brazilians make up 5 percent of the Congress and are prominent in top administrative posts of the soccer clubs and state federations that have served others as a political springboard. In the 1980s Lebanese-Brazilians became major players on the Brazilian stock market scene, and others attained important banking posts—areas in which Afro-Brazilians are strikingly absent. Non-Lebanese Middle Easterners are far less influential, albeit more numerous. The Moslem element is a small minority at around 100,000 out of over 3 million.

Brazil's Jewish community, numbering 220,000 and found chiefly in major cities, is conspicuously present in the business and banking arenas as well as in the communications field—especially print media.[34] Concentrated heavily in São

Paulo (90,000) and Rio de Janeiro (60,000), they are also important in Porto Alegre (15,000), with the remainder highly scattered.

Religion

Although Brazil is overwhelmingly Catholic, many Brazilians are only nominally so or not exclusive in their faith. Afro-Brazilian religions have demonstrated staying power, and Protestant sects—especially those of an evangelical nature—have made dramatic headway in urban areas. Dissident strains of Catholicism have also benefited from the Church's shortage of priests. There are over 10,000 Brazilians per priest, and many rural Catholics consider themselves fortunate to have a circuit-rider priest come by a few times a year.[35] Under such circumstances forms of popular Catholicism have often prevailed over the Vatican-approved version in large parts of the country. Indeed, from 95 percent nominal Catholics in 1940, the proportion declined to 76 percent by 1990—only a third of whom claim to attend mass with any frequency.

Catholicism: Dominant but Divided

As one of Brazil's few national institutions, the Catholic Church continues to be an important factor in the country's social and political life. Yet its influence is limited by deep internal divisions. Members of the mainstream hierarchy exercise a residual hold over much of public opinion, but this is offset by the progressive wing working at cross-purposes to their more conservative brethren. Under the empire the Church depended heavily upon the state, with increased vitality ensuing following disestablishment in 1890—centered in the urban middle class—and important modernizing trends apparent after 1916.[36] Concerned over inroads made by Protestantism and spiritualism in rapidly growing urban areas and increasingly aware of social problems vital to the gradually awakening masses, the Church finally began to undergo significant changes during the 1950s, but polarizing events of the early 1960s contributed to its internal divisions. Emergence of conservative, defensive modernizer, and reformer currents was both a response to societal change within Brazil and developments within the international Church. Pope John XXIII and the Second Vatican Council (1962–1965) encouraged progressive elements within the Brazilian clergy. Conservative modernizers remained in control of the Church's upper echelons, although reformers came to dominate the National Conference of Brazilian Bishops (CNBB). Advocates of liberation theology and a radical preferential option for the poor found a highly placed champion in Dom Aloísio Lorscheider, the leading figure of the CNBB in the 1970s, and Dom Paulo Evaristo Arns (b. 1920), after 1973 the influential cardinal of São Paulo.

During the late 1960s and early 1970s—the peak of military repression—many moderates became alienated from the regime. They came to hold that the Church needed to speak out for the powerless under an authoritarian regime that had shut off most channels of opposition and protest. This was reflected in Lorscheider's 1968 election as secretary general of the CNBB; he subsequently became its president with his cousin, Dom Ivo Lorscheiter, as secretary general and eventual successor. Under the leadership of these progressive prelates, efforts among workers and landless peasants gained momentum, and ecclesial base communities (CEBs) multiplied in low-income areas of major urban centers.[37]

Doctrinal cleavages continued to be aggravated in the context of Brazil's democratic transition, as Pope John Paul II worked persistently to redress the balance in the favor of moderates and conservatives. At the end of 1980 he warned the Brazilian clergy against neglecting its primary religious responsibilities through excessive involvement in social questions. Subsequently the Vatican used powers of appointment and assignment to strengthen elements in line with papal views, including the Church's hierarchical nature. Conservative Dom Lucas Moreira Neves returned from Rome to be cardinal of Salvador and the country's primate. The express preferences of the CNBB were ignored as the Vatican forcefully demonstrated that such decisions remained its exclusive purview. The conservative reaction was under way.[38]

During the Sarney years the Church failed to maintain the substantial unity it had demonstrated during the early 1980s, and it proved unable to support campaigns for social justice as effectively as it had those for an end of repression and return to democratic politics. Insistence by leftists in viewing the progressive São Paulo Church as the wave of the future was as unrealistic as their belief that the PT would shortly come to exert dominant influence in the nation's political life and that the CUT would soon develop into a force capable of confronting the government and entrepreneurial elites. The PT and CUT were contained by the renewed strength of propertied interests through the workings of co-optative clientelism and patronage populism; the Church's progressives were undercut by the concerted efforts of the conservative wing backed by the Vatican.

Elevated to the CNBB presidency in 1987, Dom Luciano Mendes de Almeida acted chiefly as an ally of the progressives. Tension between that wing of the clergy and Rome escalated during 1988 as the latter stepped up its counterattack on several fronts. The most highly placed advocates of this extremely vocal wing received cautionary letters, and Dom Luciano was sent to an out-of-the-way bishopric in Minas Gerais. The huge São Paulo archdiocese was dismembered in order to reduce the power of Cardinal Arns, and the resulting new dioceses were headed by three moderates and a conservative.[39] The third line of attack saw nonprogressives named to key posts around the country. Indeed, over three-fifths of bishops appointed since 1978 have been conservatives or moderates. Most of the progressives are heavily involved in politics, but conservatives and many of the moderates believe the Church should stay out of partisan political activities.[40] The progressives' hold on the CNBB was broken in mid-1995 with Dom Lucas Moreira Neves's election to its presidency.

One of the major problems of the Catholic Church is its serious understaffing. Nearly 7,000 parishes may appear adequate on paper, but with only 15,000 priests—many engaged in education and administration—staffing is often skeletal. This religious army has enough generals with bishops totaling 378, but there is a critical and worsening lack of vocations—aggravated by the fact that in recent decades 4,000 priests have left to get married. Over the years priests have been imported from Europe and the United States for a total of over 3,900. The need for foreign priests stems from the fact that very few Afro-Brazilians have been able to enter the priesthood. At around 200, they amount to a token 1.5 percent of the country's priests. Although Dom José Maria Pires, archbishop of Paraíba, plays a quite visible role in church affairs, there are only four other black bishops. The explanation often given is lack of adequate education, but this is a lame excuse when the Church controls many schools from the elementary level on up. Moreover, there is little desire on the part of much of the Catholic clergy to attract blacks and mulattoes as parishioners, much less recruit them as future colleagues. And although women are much more intensely Catholic than men in Brazil, their requests to play a less frustratingly secondary role have been consistently rebuffed.

Under the conditions sketched here, it is quite natural that in much of the country a kind of folk Catholicism, unfettered and undisciplined by clergy, not only flourishes but often prevails over the pure variety. This is most apparent in small interior towns, though the greater one's firsthand experience in the country, the more widespread it appears. One of its most visible manifestations is in the pilgrimages to such popular shrines as Bom Jesús de Lapa in the interior of Bahia and Nossa Senhora da Aparicida in the upper corner of São Paulo. At certain times of the year the highways are full of trucks carrying pious pilgrims great distances in acute discomfort to such holy places. Cardinals in Salvador are plagued over whether to permit or attempt to block ceremonies at the Nosso Senhor do Bonfím church that strike North American or European Catholics as outlandish if not outright heathenish.[41]

The Challenge of Other Religions

Protestant sects have been growing rapidly in Brazil, especially since the 1970s; estimates of membership run as high as 35 million persons. Leading the surge are the fast-growing Pentecostal sects that appeal to a significant number of Afro-Brazilians and erstwhile spiritualists. Much of their expansion stems from success of religious television ministries with ownership of a channel in Rio de Janeiro and programs in other major cities.[42] Yet they also enjoy an advantage at the neighborhood, street, and street-corner level in having many more ministers than there are Catholic priests and convenient store-front churches. Their gains have often been by default; they seize upon the manifold opportunities afforded by the failure of the Catholic Church to have an active presence in many large neighborhoods or new centers of population. In these situations any church that opens up shop will almost immediately attract a substantial following among those hungering for an opportunity for organized religious activity and some degree of pastoral concern.

Afro-Brazilian religions are categorized into *candomblé, macumba,* and *um-banda.* Most characteristic of the northeast and most readily observed in Bahia, the former takes Yoruban and Dahomeyan deities—called *orixás*—and identifies each of them with a Catholic saint. Each well-structured and permanent cult is led by a *pai* or *mãe de santo* (father or mother of the saint) and possesses its own meeting place, or *terreiro. Candomblé* ceremonies are more elaborate and orderly than those of Bantu-inspired *macumbas,* a term popularly and without justification identified with witchcraft and black magic. *Umbanda,* which is widespread in such population centers as Rio de Janeiro, involves a mixture of African practices with spiritism and elements of Christianity.[43]

Spiritism has a great hold over middle-class individuals and some from the upper classes. Indeed, nonexclusive spiritists may well number close to 20 million. At the core are 7 million followers of Alan Kardac, but there are also intellectuals fascinated with extrasensory perception and other paranormal phenomena and popular centers where African and Brazilian Indian elements become important parts of the mysticism.[44] This aspect of Brazilian character is closely interrelated with other cultural factors treated in the next chapter.

8

CULTURE AND BRAZILIAN WAYS

A NATION IS NOT MADE up merely of geography, history, politics, economics, and society. These help shape its soul—its culture—but they are also shaped by it. Understanding a country's culture becomes even more important when it is little known to the outside world, as is the case with Brazil. Within broad limits a general Hispanic American culture exists into which Brazil only partially fits. Yet it contributes heavily to an emerging more diverse Latin American culture also containing important Caribbean elements.[1]

Brazil's continuing progress toward achieving a national identity consonant with its increasing integration into the broader international system is profoundly reflected in the cultural realm. Distinctly Brazilian qualities combined with fuller awareness of global trends are evident in literature, music, architecture, and television; they are significantly present in painting and cinema and slowly emerging in theater. Machado de Assis, Jorge Amado, Villa-Lobos, Oscar Niemeyer, Portinari, di Cavalcanti, and Glauber Rocha are thoroughly Brazilian in themes and styles, in concerns and their expression, at the same time as they are part of the developing great global culture—particularly its Atlantic basin core. Brazil's culture continues to interact with the outside world as it feeds upon internal sources and inspirations.

Although a considerable gap still exists in Brazil between popular culture and fine arts, there is an approximation of folk art and music with the European-influenced sophisticated tendencies in these fields. Meanwhile literature is reaching the masses through the electronic media and films as well as by means of increased dissemination of books and magazines. As with so many aspects of Brazilian reality, elite culture and that of the masses meet and mingle at the level of the middle classes.[2] Within the realm of communications the electronic media—especially television—have come within a single generation to have an enormous impact, even greater upon the largely unschooled broad bottom of the social pyramid than upon those whose literacy and access to print media expose them to other sources of information and opinion. Prime-time *novelas* have a hold on the public far beyond that exerted by soaps or prime-time series in the United States. Moreover, political campaigning in Brazil has come to rely more upon television than face-to-face contact with the voters. Despite the blurring caused by the homogenizing media and internal migration, distinctive regional types and cultural variations survive in Brazil. Along with other customs and practices heavily affecting economic and political life as well as social relations, these require consideration—as do their reflections in the arts.

Cultural Traits and the Media

Racial and religious tendencies discussed in the previous chapter are important aspects of what makes Brazil, Brazil. The essence of *Brasilianidade* is elusive, in large part because of the multiple non-Brazilian influences upon Brazilian society and culture. Likely to be cordial, adaptable, and conciliatory (often more in form than in substance), Brazilians are apt to manifest other traits depending upon the socialization process to which they have been subjected. This varies by individual with social origin, as the family is prime agent of socialization for large numbers little affected by the educational system or by organized religion. Television exercises a fundamentally homogenizing effect in spreading a more national culture to the detriment of once very distinct regional variations.

Types of Brazilians and "Universal" Characteristics

Regional types, blurred by internal migration and the effects of the mass media, are still important in Brazil. Indeed, given the lesser impact of formal education and the absence of immigration in comparison to the United States, they are probably more distinctive than the analogous variations (New Yorker, New Englander, Southerner, Texan, Midwesterner, etc.). Thus the prototype Paulista (resident of São Paulo) is the country's most pragmatic, materialistic, and hard-working strain—mated to a strong sense of superiority—whereas the Carioca (Rio de Janeiro resident) is more pleasure-seeking, laid back, and perhaps a bit devious (if not a real *malandro,* or mischievous rascal) behind a facade of open-ness. Yet there are millions of internal immigrants in these urban states who do not demonstrate the same characteristics as do the lifelong residents of São Paulo and Rio de Janeiro. The stereotype also better fits the Paulistanos, residents of the great metropolis, than the inhabitants of the interior of the premier state.

To the typical Mineiro (from Minas Gerais), Paulistas are pushy and often ob-noxiously domineering, and Cariocas are apt to be lazy and unreliable, even shift-less. Mineiros tend to be thoughtful, taciturn, and conciliatory—but also inclined to be moody. Their reputation for being wily and sagacious is, in the eyes of

Paulistas and Cariocas, often carried to the point of frustrating inscrutability. Bahianos reflect an Afro-Portuguese synthesis relatively free from other ethnic roots and are considered sensuous and preoccupied with food. In contrast, Gaúchos (from Rio Grande do Sul) seem to be displaced Europeans demonstrating traits identified with Mediterranean peoples, particularly Italians. To Mineiros they appear loud, direct to the point of rudeness, and unduly intransigent—veritable "Argentines." For their part Gaúchos prefer to interpret what others see as boisterous and belligerent as energetic, active, and productive.

To a high degree, a person in Brazil is important more for his relationships and ties than for himself. An observation forcefully portrayed by Roberto da Matta is that individuals without links to a person or institution of prestige in Brazilian society are treated as inferiors.[3] Faced with a situation in which a North American might expect the law to be applied in a straightforward manner, Brazilians will resort to the classic "do you know to whom you are speaking?" This is intended to point out the status the individual wishes to invoke as justification for contending that the law was not intended for a special person such as he or she should be perceived as being. For most Brazilians the law may be appropriate for others, but theirs is an exceptional case to be resolved on a personal basis. This projects onto the political scene with the famous dictum "for my friends everything; for my enemies the law."

Parentela is a fundamental characteristic of Brazilian life, and understanding it aids comprehending why certain things happen and how many things get done. Essentially this is rooted in the importance of the extended family to Brazilians. As perceptively described by Charles Wagley, this type of kinship group (at times approaching a small clan in extension and inclusiveness) has traditionally been the "most important single institution in Brazil."[4] Involving relatives plus a full array of in-laws, the *parentela* has on its fringes an assortment of informally adopted individuals and even family retainers. Its range is extended by the importance still given to *comadres* and *copadres* (godparents) by *afilhados* (godchildren) and their families. Even today in traditional areas, *parentelas* are a critical political factor, much more profound than the conventional North American or European concept of nepotism.

Even among members of modern urban society for whom *parentela* is less key because of physical distance from the bulk of their kinfolk, family remains crucial. As da Matta has shown, the domain of the home is important for Brazilians at all social levels. There the individual finds love, harmony, tolerance, decency, generosity, and hospitality often lacking in the outside world.[5] Within the home everyone is unique and irreplaceable, enjoying rights and position independent of accomplishment along with a safe haven from the perils and frustrations of life outside its purview. In the dog-eat-dog domain of the street, individuals are unable to control their lives. These two spheres of life interact with the transcendental or supernatural, which calls into play sentiments of universal love, altruism, and collectivism.[6] This approach holds strong appeal to the poor and unsuccessful, since at its core is the idea that in the world after death they may finally receive the justice and equality denied them in this difficult existence. *Umbanda* and popular Catholicism provide these persons with a taste of this reward on earth, as within them the individual has a chance to rise above his workaday status.

Da Matta stresses that lines of power within the value spheres represented by Carnival, Holy Week, and Independence Day converge in the recurrent search for the perfect leader/messianic figure.[7] When the complementarity of these domains is not seriously questioned, integration is through personal relationships and patronage; when it is challenged, there is a proclivity to call in the providential man who will unite them in an absolutist manner—an explanation congruent with the nonideological and largely nonclass basis of Brazilian electoral politics.

The brokering, clientelistic nature of the Brazilian political-governmental system reflects the pervasive role of the *panelinha,* an informal group of a closed nature bound together by common interests and personal ties. Its essence lies in having members in a variety of complementary positions in the sociopolitical-economic structure, and in its negative manifestations it may give rise to a kind of amoral cronyism. One of the most important of the types of personal links that maintain connections among interests, organizations, and agencies, *panelinha* is difficult to identify and trace, since there is no formal record of its existence.[8] Many of the mysteries and most of the odd bedfellows of Brazilian politics are not at all mysterious or odd once the intersecting *panelinhas* and *parentelas* involved are known.

The famous Brazilian *jeitinho* (the talent for mixing a good deal of ingenuity with a dash—or more—of bending the rules) is founded in the deeply felt need to reconcile a personal problem or convenience with the bothersome impersonality of the laws and rules. Thus in the face of a bureaucratic response that something cannot be done, or at least not at that time or in the way that the solicitant desires, the impasse is broken by invoking some factor that makes the functionary inclined to see this as a special case to be resolved within the spirit of the law rather than its inflexible letter. *Pistolão,* resort to influence and connections, may be involved, but the typical *jeitinho* approach is more likely to involve a common tie that enables the two parties to relate more as equals. A mutual friend, preference for the same soccer team or samba school, or origins in the same state are catalysts often invoked.[9] Together with the interacting spheres of existence and values, *parentela, panelinha,* and *jeitinho* serve as means for reconciling the modern and the traditional, certainly a continuing need for citizens of changing but not yet transformed Brazil. To understand Brazil, it helps to realize that there remains a degree of admiration for the *malandro,* seeker of the good life through craftiness and sharp dealing with the minimum expenditure of regular or disciplined effort. This distinctive type—of which a large proportion of Brazilians incorporate at least a few traits—has been enshrined in Brazilian literature.

A Word on the Media

Mass media have become very important in Brazil; there are 900 magazines, 1,650 newspapers (300 dailys), 3,000 radio stations, and 315 television stations.[10] Brazilian homes contain 40 million television sets and twice as many radios. Some

$3.35 billion is spent yearly on television advertising—dwarfing the amount for the print media—and nearly half goes to the dominant Globo network.[11] A distant second is SBT, headed by popular master of ceremonies Sílvio Santos, with nearly 15 percent of advertising revenues. Whereas SBT concentrates on lower-income groups, Manchete, a network in dire financial straits, aims at the upper strata of "discriminating viewers," and Bandeirantes emphasizes sports. As television viewing has risen, moviegoing has fallen from 275 million paid tickets in 1975 to but 75 million by 1992, rising with economic recovery to 85 million in 1995 as new movie houses opened.

On the print side, 360 million books are sold annually. The leading newsweekly *Veja* has a circulation surpassing 1 million, twice that of its chief competitor, *IstoÉ*, which is followed by the heavily pictorial *Manchete* at 130,000. São Paulo-based *Folha de S. Paulo* leads daily newspapers in circulation at 700,000 rising to 1.7 million on Sundays, followed by Rio de Janeiro's *O Globo* (370,000 and 1 million) and conservative *O Estado de S. Paulo*. As the second of these is part of a media empire including the country's nearly hegemonic television network, it is extremely influential, which makes its owner, octogenarian Roberto Marinho, one of the nation's leading movers and shakers. The Editora Abril group of magazines, with *Veja* as its flagship, has attributed its inability to break into the electronic media to a close relationship between Marinho and former communications minister and PFL strongman Antônio Carlos Magalhães. These individuals are part of a *panelinha* in which lack of change in the vast Bahian hinterlands is a requisite to retaining control of the state. On the other hand, cultural change is crucial to the political projects of other actors on the Brazilian scene, especially those of a progressive inclination.

The Written Word

Brazil has developed a rich literary tradition, particularly in fiction, reflective of its complex culture and society. Indeed, deepened understanding of critical aspects of Brazilian society and politics—class and race relations, regionalism, patronage populism, and co-optative clientelism—emerges from literary works. Hence separation of literature from other published fruits of intellectual endeavor inhibits understanding of the country and its people. The writers discussed here are important creative intellectuals who have had lasting influence in the hemisphere, and several are notable on the wider global scene.[12]

The Empire and Old Republic

Forebears of the broad and deep body of writings reflecting Brazilian character and concerns developed the themes of Indianism and regionalism. Brazil's first truly great international figure, Joaquim María Machado de Assis (1839–1908), catalyzed the early years of the republic as a period of intellectual explosion and affirmation of Brazilian culture. This upwardly mobile mulatto demonstrated profound insights into human nature in poetry, short stories, and novels. His masterpieces include *Memórias Postúmas de Bras Cubas* (1881, translated as *Epitaph of a Small Winner*, 1952); *Quincas Borba* (1891, in English as *Philosopher or Dog?* 1953); and *Dom Casmurro* (1900, in English in 1954). Set in the Rio de Janeiro of his times, these magnificent novels probe the relationship of individuals to society with a basic pessimism relieved by brilliant flashes of wit and humor tinged with irony.

Brazil's nineteenth-century intellectual life extended beyond literature. Joaquim Nabuco (1849–1910) was a distinguished politician and diplomat from Pernambuco best remembered as the articulate and fiery advocate of abolition. Bahia produced the even larger figure of Ruy Barbosa (1849–1923), orator and essayist par excellence, who would nearly be elected president. The opening decades of the twentieth century were graced by Alberto Tôrres (1865–1917), who laid a foundation for a search for Brazil's identity and destiny. His sociological probings were followed up by Francisco José de Oliveira Vianna (1885–1951), who continued the call for introspection rather than imitation well into the 1930s.

By the 1920s and 1930s São Paulo's versatile Mário de Andrade (1895–1945) captained the tardy arrival of Brazil's economic and industrial egine on the literary scene. In 1928 his masterful prose poem *Macunaíma: O herói sem nenhuma caráter* (Macunaíma: Hero Without Any Character) propelled the quest for truly Brazilian themes and more original styles of expression. Deeply steeped in Brazilian folk culture, Andrade created in Macunaíma a figure embodying all the strengths and weaknesses of Brazilian character.[13] The first of Brazil's great twentieth-century regionalists was Graciliano Ramos (1892–1953) from the northeastern state of Alagoas, whose most famous work was the highly moving *Vidas Secas*(1938, translated as *Barren Lives*, 1965).

The Contemporary Literary Scene

There was a greater talent developing in the shadow of Andrade and Ramos— Jorge Amado (b. 1912).[14] In *Jubiabá* (1935, in English in 1984) Amado demonstrated signs of the great writer he was soon to become, and *Capitães da Areia* (*The Beach Waifs*, 1937) gave him six novels by the age of twenty-five. These were surpassed in 1943 by his powerful *Terras do Sem Fim* (translated as *The Violent Land* in 1945). From this point on political insight was gradually subordinated to a deepening appreciation of human nature and an extraordinary ability to develop memorable characters, as apparent in 1958 with a work destined to become a major international success in three media—*Gabriela: Cravo e Canela* (*Gabriela: Clove and Cinnamon* in English in 1962). In 1966 came *Dona Flor e Seus Dois Maridos* (1966, in English as *Dona Flor and Her Two Husbands* in 1969). Later came the evocative *Tieta do Agreste* (English title *Tieta: the Goat Girl*, 1979) and *Tocaia Grande* (translated in 1988 as *Showdown*), followed in 1988 by *O Sumiço da Santa* (in English as *The War of the Saints* in 1993).

Just as Machado de Assis was Brazil's—and possibly the Portuguese-speaking world's—greatest writer of the 1800s, Amado earned this distinction in the rigorous competition of the twentieth century as he developed from a powerful portrayer of social protest to a magnificent purveyor of Bahia's culture and character, then on to a profound student of human nature. Yet two other major Brazilian novelists managed not to be eclipsed by the Bahia master. João Guimarães Rosa (1908–1967) wrote powerfully and often movingly of life in the vast interior region of southern Bahia and northern Minas Gerais, most notably in his 1956 novel of survival and violence, *Grande Sertão: Veredas* (translated in 1963 as *The Devil to Pay in the Backlands*). The Brazilian south gave rise to Érico Verissimo (1905–1975), whose masterwork was the five-volume *O Tempo e O Vento* (Time and Wind, 1950). Also overlapping the Amado era were Brazil's first notable female writers. On the strength of novels written in her youth, Ceará's Rachel de Queiróz (b. 1910) would be the first woman elected to the Brazilian Academy of Letters. Clarice Lispector (1920–1977) made her mark in 1961 with *A Maça no Escuro* (translated in 1967 as *The Apple in the Dark*. The space left by her untimely death was partially filled by Nélida Piñon (b. 1937) best known for her 1984 novel *A República dos Sonos* (The Dream Republic).

The intellectual tradition of Nabuco, Barbosa, Tôrres, and Oliveira Vianna remained alive in mid- and late-twentieth-century Brazil. Gilberto de Mello Freyre (1900–1987) was as faithful to his Pernambuco roots as Amado to Bahian origins. His monumental work on Brazilian social history, enriched by broad anthropological training, includes *Casa Grande e Senzala* (1933, translated as *The Masters and the Slaves* in 1946). Afonso (also spelled Affonso) Arinos de Mello Franco (1905–1990)—statesman, politician, and constitutional lawyer—may well be the greatest intellectual produced by Minas Gerais.[15] Of most lasting value among his many books is the multivolume *Um Estadista da República* (A Statesman of the Republic, 1955).

The Brazilian social sciences continue to produce a diversity of intellectuals. Florestan Fernandes (1920-1995), mentor of many Brazilian sociologists, is the radical Left's leading interpreter of Brazilian society.[16] One of his students, Fernando Henrique Cardoso (b. 1931), was a world-renowned sociologist before entering politics and being elected president. Hélio Jaguaribe Gomes do Mattos (b. 1923) has authored trenchant contemporary analyses of Brazil's sociopolitical conditions, and Celso Furtado (b. 1920) gained international renown with his ideas on development and dependency.

Music and Theater

In the musical realm development of distinctively Brazilian compositions and performing styles came later than in literature. The major achievement is a creative synthesis of the music of Brazilian Indians, African slaves, and that introduced by European immigrants—accompanied by absorption of external influences such as jazz.[17] Although there have been notable Brazilians in the field of classical music—including the hemisphere's most important operatic composer of the nineteenth century and Latin America's greatest composer of this century—popular music has been the sector of greatest relative development, and a talented generation of songwriters and singers rose in the 1960s on the foundations laid by many distinguished precursors. In the theater realm Brazil's tradition is more respectable than distinguished but has established a foundation for notable performance in television and film.

Composers and Performers

The first Brazilian in the music field to earn international recognition was operatic composer Antônio Carlos Gomes (1836–1896). His *Il Guarany* was an overnight success in Milan in 1870. Heitor Villa-Lobos (1887–1959) is the towering figure of Brazilian music. With a hundred compositions to his credit, Villa-Lobos played a major role in the modernism movement during the 1920s. Blending technical sophistication, great originality, and typical Brazilian themes, he climbed in the 1920s and 1930s to the pinnacle of international fame and national adulation. His "Chôros" and "Bachianas Brasileiras"—composed between 1930 and 1945 and successfully bringing Bachian procedures to Brazilian folk and popular music—stand out along with his seven operas, dozen symphonies, chamber music, and piano pieces. Villa-Lobos considered composing a "biological necessity," and his prodigious output that reached over a thousand works across well more than half a century did much to put Brazil on the global cultural scene.[18]

In the field of popular music Chiquinha Gonzaga (Francisca Edwiges Neves Gonzaga, 1847–1935) in 1899 composed "Abre Alas" (Open Wings), a pathbreaker in developing the samba as a song form. The 1930s and 1940s witnessed further sophistication of the samba at the hands of Ari Evangelista Barroso (1903–1964), composer of the unforgettable "Aquarela do Brasil." Portuguese-born Carmen Miranda (Maria do Carmo Miranda da Cunha, 1909–1955), was a multifaceted performer whose greatest international fame came through Hollywood films. The 1960s were the heyday of the bossa nova and launching pad for many great talents of Brazilian popular music.[19] Dean of this movement was composer-performer Antônio Carlos "Tom" Jobim (1927–1994), best known for his international hit "A Garota de Ipanema" (The Girl from Ipanema). On his heels came two towering talents: Roberto Carlos (Braga, b. 1943) and Chico Buarque (Francisco Buarque de Holanda, b. 1944). The former, Brazil's answer to Elvis Presley, established himself as a star in 1963 with his recording of "Calhambeque" (The Jalopy). He continued into the 1990s with his popularity and earnings undiminished. Like many other Brazilian entertainers, he has recorded also in Spanish, and his following has spread throughout South America.

The most complete Brazilian musical talent of this extraordinary generation is Chico Buarque, a singer of note but more famous as a composer. With a solid musical background gained in Europe, this São Paulo resident burst on the Brazilian scene in 1965 with "Pedro Pedreiro" (Pete the Stonemason). He became internationally known the next year for his "A Banda" (The Band). Through the 1970s he was responsible for a large share of the country's musical events—including his 1979 musical "Ópera do Malandro" (The Rascal's Opera). Many of his recent compositions fall into the category of socially relevant light opera.

Another extraordinary talent who had a profound impact upon Brazilian popular music from the 1950s through the 1970s was Vinícius de Moraes (Marcus Vinícius da Cruz de Melo Moraes, 1913–1980). Poet, lyricist, and composer, he used music to reach the masses with his poetic vision and in the process enriched and elevated their literary tastes. In the mid-1950s he had Tom Jobim compose music for his poem "Orfeu do Carneval," which was filmed by French director Marcel Camus as *Orfeu Negro* (Black Orpheus); the film won first place at Cannes in 1957 as well as the Oscar for best foreign film—in the process bringing Brazil to the attention of the cinema world. "Vinícius," as he was known, remained at his death Brazil's people's poet, beloved both for his talent and his irrepressible Bohemian lifestyle that embodied the Brazilian lust for life.

The Stage

The theater remained essentially derivative of Portuguese and other European models even past the intellectual and artistic ferment of the 1920s. The 1940s witnessed the arrival on the scene of Brazil's one truly major author for the theater, Nelson Rodrigues (1913–1980). Beginning with *Vestido de Noiva* (The Wedding Dress) in 1943, Rodrigues developed his fascination with sin and guilt, particularly their impact upon the family, in over a dozen plays. *Album da Família* (Family Album, 1946) and *A Falecida* (The Dead Woman, 1953) clearly earned him a place among the hemisphere's leading playwrights.[20] Rodrigues's death left Alfredo Dias Gomes (b. 1923) as Brazil's premier playwright. Author in 1959 of *O Pagador de Promessas* (The Given Word), which as a film won first place at Cannes in 1962, he is best known for *O Bem Amado* (The Beloved). Written as a play at the beginning of the 1960s, it enjoyed a long television run beginning in 1973. Together with poet-playwright Ferreira Gullar (b. 1930 as José Ribamar Ferreira) in 1968 he wrote *Dr. Getúlio*, a greater hit as a musical in 1983 with a score by Chico Buarque and Edu Lobo.

On the acting side, Cacilda Becker (Yaconis, b. 1922), Tônia Carrero (b. 1923), and Fernanda Montenegro (b. 1926) initiated long and distinguished stage careers in the 1940s. Procópio Ferreira (1898–1979), in his prime perhaps Latin American theater's most versatile actor, was followed by a series of major male performers who gained greater prominence through movies and television.

Cinema and Electronic Media

Brazil enjoyed a one-generation blossoming in the realm of film and has made great strides in television. Indeed, its *novelas*, a cross between shows like *Dallas* or *Dynasty* and afternoon soap operas but generally better written and acted, are avidly watched in countries as diverse as Italy and China. Because of its greater economic viability, television has become the sustenance of most Brazilian actors and actresses. They can earn a living in the electronic media, doing occasional movies and stagework between stints in *novelas* or miniseries. Television, much more than film and theater, reaches the vast majority of the Brazilian population—even in interior hamlets—and for better or worse has a cultural impact far beyond that of the print media. Millions of Brazilians are familiar with the country's literary works through their television adaptations and see movies only on television, which has become even a lower-class household necessity.

Film and Filmmakers

Brazil's film industry exploded to international attention in the 1950s and 1960s. It first awakened attention abroad in the mid-1950s with Victor Lima Barreto's *O Cangaceiro* (The Bandit, 1953), winner of the 1954 best adventure film award at Cannes, and Nelson Pereira dos Santos's 1955 *Rio Quarenta Graus* (Rio, Heatwave). The real explosion came in the following decade: Ruy Guerra (b. 1931 Ruy Alexandre Guerra Coelho), an immigrant from Mozambique working in Brazil since 1958, directed *Os Cafajestes* (The Hustlers) in 1961. Anselmo Duarte (b. 1920) won the best film award at Cannes in 1962 with *O Pagador de Promessas* (The Given Word); the same year Roberto Farias (b. 1932) directed *Assalto ao Trem Pagador* (The Paytrain Robbery). In 1964 Leon Hirszman (1937–1987) made Nelson Rodrigues's *A Falecida* into a film, Nelson Pereira dos Santos showed that his earlier triumph was no fluke with a critically acclaimed adaptation of Graciliano Ramos's masterpiece, *Vidas Secas*. In 1969 Joaquim Pedro de Andrade (1932–1988) pulled off the difficult challenge of bringing Mário de Andrade's *Macunaíma* to the big screen. Brazil's new cinema was well under way.

This impressive forward surge of the Brazilian cinema was soon all but overshadowed by the emergence of the country's true filmmaking genius. Coming out of Bahia, Gláuber Rocha (1938–1981) made an impact upon the international cinematic world before his premature death. In 1964 he unveiled his masterpiece, *Deus e o Diabo na Terra do Sol* (God and the Devil in the Scorching Land, titled in English *Black God, White Devil*). *Terra em Transe* (Anguished Land) followed in 1966 with the highly controversial *Cabeças Cortadas* (Severed Heads) in 1970. His production then fell off sharply until his ambitious *Idade da Terra* (Earth's Age) in 1980. This highly symbolic film did not gain the critical accolades Rocha was expecting—he had won the Cannes best director award in 1969—and the frustration of being misunderstood added to the emotional travail that preceded his untimely death. Yet his legacy was more than just his films, as many of his varied writings on films and filmmaking were subsequently brought together in *O Século da Cinema* (The Cinema Century, 1983).[21]

Brazilian moviemaking did not die with Rocha. In 1982 Bruno Barreto (b. 1954) brought out Amado's *Gabriela,* a follow-up to his 1976 success with

Amado's *Dona Flor*. Argentine-born Hector Babenco (b. 1946), in Brazil since 1967, gained international attention for his deeply moving 1980 film of the tragedy of São Paulo street urchins, *Pixote: A Lei dos Mais Fracos* (Pixote: Law of the Weakest). This success, which included the New York Film Critics best picture award, enabled him to get William Hurt and Raul Julia to star in *Kiss of the Spiderwoman*, filmed in São Paulo in 1983. Its success included an Oscar for Hurt. Alongside Babenco stands the innovative Tizuka Yamasaki (b. 1948), whose 1980 film *Gajin: Os Caminhos da Liberdade* (Gajin: The Ways of Liberty) probed the life of Japanese immigrants in the early 1900s. Her 1983 film *Parahyba, Mulher Macho* (Paraíba, Macho Woman) passionately explores the dilemmas of a liberated woman in the male-dominated ferment of the 1920s in Brazil's northeast.

On the performing side, following Carmen Miranda, Sonia Braga (b. 1950) went on to international fame through *Dona Flor* and *Gabriela*. Maríla Pêra (b. 1943) won the New York Film Critics award in 1981 as the year's best actress for her role in *Pixote*. Fernanda Tôrres (b. 1962), daughter of Fernanda Montenegro, emerged in the 1980s as the leading new serious movie actress, winning the Cannes best actress award in 1986 for the title role in Arnaldo Jabor's *Eu Sei que Vou Te Amar* (I Know That I Am Going to Love You).

Television

The television *novela* has become an integral part of the Brazilian way of life, from the presidential palace and corporate boardrooms down into the urban slums and out to the small towns of the interior. Running six days a week, they dominate prime-time programming; the Globo network—fourth largest in the world behind the U.S. big three—is accustomed to its eight P.M. show being the keystone of Brazil's viewing habits. Creations of proven authors are likely to be stretched out for nine months before winding up the complex affairs of their characters to the public's satisfaction. Often the basic theme is chosen to correspond to topics recently capturing public attention.

With television as a serious medium in Brazil, the country's top actors and actresses appear regularly. Established stage and screen stars have found a much wider audience and popular recognition through these vehicles; a new generation made the *novelas* the foundation of their careers. Then there are other types of television personalities such as mega-impresario Sílvio Santos (b. 1930 as Senor Abravanel), owner of the SBT network and the continent's most popular game-show host; comedy kings Chico Anísio (b. 1931 Francisco Anísio de Oliveira Paulo Filho) and Jô Soares (b. 1937 José Eugênio Soares); and Renato "Didi" Aragão (b. 1935), key to the eternally popular *Os Trapalhões* (The Bumblers). "Xuxa" (Maria da Graça Meneghel, b. 1963) is a show-business phenomenon who has progressed from emcee of a wildly popular children's show to international recording star with a $19 million annual gross. In 1993 she moved into the U.S. market.

Art and Architecture

Brazil's older cities abound with magnificent churches filled with beautiful sacred art from the colonial period—Portuguese in inspiration in most of the country but profoundly Dutch in Recife and certain other areas of the northeast. Salvador, Ouro Prêto, and Olinda are cities in which colonial architecture has best been preserved, though Rio de Janeiro has its share. Then, too, native arts and handicrafts abound, including marvelous wood carvings, soapstone sculptures, and delicate lacework. There is also a modern European-oriented tradition in the fine arts embracing two great twentieth-century painters and several highly creative architects. Even a quick trip along Rio de Janeiro's Ipanema, São Paulo's Avenida Paulista, or Brasília's central axis will bring this home with great visual impact.

Painting and Sculpture

Unlike the boom in Brazilian music, there has not been a resurgence in the present generation to substitute for the disappearance from the scene of the great painters who so advanced Brazil's art world from the 1930s through the 1950s. In sculpture no one in the last 180 years has remotely compared with Anônio Francisco Lisbôa, known as "Aleijadinho" (Little Cripple, c. 1738–1814), who was not only the greatest Brazilian artistic talent of the colonial period but very likely the most important the country has yet produced. Working largely with Brazilian soapstone—particularly after his leprosy forced him to use tools tied to his wrist stumps—he turned out an incredible number of statues, the most famous of which are the strong yet enormously sensitive Twelve Apostles outside the church of Bom Jesus de Matosinhos in Congonhas do Campo, Minas Gerais.[22]

Brazilian painting, the art form most highly developed in the national period, was highly derivative of European styles until well into the twentieth century. Lazar Segall (1891–1957), a Lithuanian immigrant with a solid background of study in Germany, was followed by two artistic talents of unquestioned global significance. Di Cavalcanti (Emiliano Augusto Cavalcanti de Albuquerque Melo, 1897–1976) is renowned for paintings of people and Brazilian landscapes, and Cândido Torquato Portinari (1903–1962) ranks with the century's great muralists. His *War and Peace* graces the United Nations in New York, and another stunning work adorns the walls of the Library of Congress in Washington.

Architecture and Landscape Artistry

It may be that Aleijadinho's true successors are not to be found in the field of sculpture, though Victor Brecheret (1894–1956) with his imposing *Monument to the Pioneers,* carved into a granite block 167 feet long, is of major note. They might better be sought in architecture, the modern era of which began in the 1920s with the visit to Brazil of Charles-Édouard Jeanneret "Le Corbusier" (1887–1965), who became the high priest of Brazilian architecture. The key figures of this explosion of new ideas and buildings during the 1930s through the 1960s were Oscar Neimeyer (Soares Filho, b. 1907) and Lúcio Costa (b. 1902, France).[23] The former became famous in the early 1940s for his highly imaginative church and restaurant buildings on the outskirts of Belo Horizonte; Costa built an outstanding reputation in both restoration of old cities and design of modern residences. In the late 1950s the former as architect and the latter as urban planner collaborated in the design of Brasília, built in the middle of an interior plateau.[24] Costa's plan of the city as a large airplane with its wings extending along the shores of an artificial lake and its body including governmental buildings blended with Niemeyer's striking architecture—ranging between modern and futuristic—as exemplified in the Congress, presidential palace, and supreme court.

A uniquely Brazilian talent, equal in his own way to Neimeyer and Costa, was Roberto Burle Marx (1909–1994), who was much more than a landscape artist. As illustrated by his mid-1991 exhibit at New York's Museum of Modern Art, he can well be considered an artist whose paintings were large, alive, and done with flowers and plants instead of oils and canvas. Colors, textures, materials, levels, and space were all blended by this genius in true manifestations of the Brazilian spirit.

9

BRAZIL IN THE WORLD

T HE INTERNATIONAL ROLE of Brazil has grown and changed with its development from a sparsely populated and economically backward country to a quasi-industrial nation today. Congruent with this incomplete transition, Brazil is at midstream between a past of being acted upon by international forces and a new era in which it will be among the globe's movers and shakers. At this intermediate juncture it possesses the capacity to shape significantly the course of its own affairs, exercise heavy weight in South American matters, exert substantial influence upon hemispheric issues, and have some impact on worldwide questions. From extreme dependency it has progressed to be a regional major power that is at the same time an upwardly mobile global middle power in the process of displacing Canada as the number two international actor in the Western Hemisphere. This rapid and continuing rise has made Brazil the most important nation among all countries lying below the equator—a somewhat dubious distinction in a Northern Hemisphere–dominated world.[1]

Much relevant ground concerning Brazil's place on the world scene has already been covered. In Chapter 2 the weight of British tutelage through the middle of the nineteenth century was depicted, as was the historical tension with Argentina. Britain's role in Brazil's international finances well into the twentieth century was outlined in Chapter 6. Coverage of U.S.-Brazilian relations during the 1940s to 1960s appeared in Chapter 3. Since there is no need to replow these fields, attention can be focused upon (1) the implications of Brazil's increasingly important role in international affairs; (2) the course and nature of U.S.-Brazilian relations; (3) changes in Brazil's relationships with its fellow Latin American nations; (4) Brazilian policy elites' worldviews; and (5) probable future foreign policy developments.

From Object to Actor

Only during the past generation has Brazil become a significant factor in international affairs beyond the South American continent. As capsuled by Frank D. McCann:

> Throughout the imperial period (1822–1889) European monarchies looked upon the Brazilian empire as a tropical oddity, while American republics regarded it with either suspicion or indifference. In the [early] twentieth century suspicion became paramount among its neighbors, while the powers tended to treat Brazil as an economic or political pawn that could be dealt with according to their needs.[2]

This contrasts sharply with the situation prevailing by the early 1980s, which Alvin A. Rubinstein distilled this way: "The era when Brazil was internationally passive and satisfied to follow in America's wake is over. The mood is now one of determination to plot an independent course in hemispheric and world affairs, with or without U.S. cooperation."[3] Troubles of the 1980s and early 1990s merely set back the timetable.

Coping with Dependency

Brazil began its life as a formally sovereign and independent nation in an international system in which Britain was hegemonic. With Napoleonic France's defeat, the British lion's global paramountcy was without challenge. The 1703 Treaty of Methuen, by which Portugal accepted a marginal position in a British-dominated mercantilist system, had ushered in what can be described as a prolonged period of "double dependency." Subsequently Brazil paid dearly for the recognition of its independence through a long-term treaty according the United Kingdom a marked commercial ascendancy.

Well aware of its limited international capabilities, imperial Brazil contented itself with efforts to keep its neighbors from ganging up on it. Subsequent stress on attracting Italian immigration and delimiting the country's borders were also initiatives falling within the scope of a state still far down in the international pecking order. Indeed, only the facts that other Latin American countries were even weaker and that almost all the Afro-Asian world was still the possession of one European power or another saved Brazil from being even more of a fragile raft tossed about by rough international seas. Britain's gradual withdrawal from a tutelary role in Latin America in favor of its junior ally, the United States, coincided with establishment of Brazil's republic. Although this development did not significantly alter Brazil's fundamental dependency, it did provide opportunity to be a more important quasi-client to the rising North American power than Brazil had been for Britain with its much wider and fuller global agenda. Latching on to the meteoric rise of the United States after the turn of the century, Brazil managed to become a regional actor accorded a modicum of respect by non–Latin American nations (particularly European ones) at the expense of loyally supporting the hemispheric paramount power in all international arenas and on almost every issue. This role of respectable client led Brazil both to function as the staunchest ally of Washington in Pan American affairs and to be the only Latin American country to join against the Central Powers during World War I. The 1920s were marked by a shifting of Brazil's debt away from Britain and toward the United States, a move accompanied by congruent trends in trade and investment; the latter part of the 1930s brought Brazil under Vargas to an improved bargaining position, wooed by Germany as well as by Britain and the United States.[4] These opportunities to play one side against the other, exploited with skill in the 1930s, disappeared with the entrance of the United States into World War II, and Brazil made the best of the situation by obtaining financing for a steel industry and military training and equipment as the price for use of the northeast as ferrying base and sending an expeditionary force to Italy.

In the bipolar world of the early postwar years, the superpower position of the United States left Brazil with little room for even limited independence—a fact brought home by repeated heavy-handed U.S. arm-twisting. Brazil was undergoing economic and social change that would have provided a base for increased nationalist sentiment under any circumstances; the mood was intensified by these constant reminders to Brazil that it should accept its place as a recipient of external pressures and not aspire to have an autonomous voice in international affairs. The result was an independent foreign policy by the Quadros administration in 1961 and its intermittent escalation under Goulart.

Although the coming to power of the military in 1964 led to a brief era of closer relations with the United States, fundamental differences in national interests were recognized by the Costa e Silva government. Still far from an immediate candidate for major power status, Brazil had definitely outgrown the secondary role assigned to it by U.S. policy. Moreover, it was clear that the international system had undergone substantial modifications bordering on transformation, as Cold War superpower bipolarity no longer prevailed—and with Castro ensconced in Cuba, the United States was no longer hegemonic in the hemisphere.[5]

Building the Launching Pad

The turning point, albeit with roots in the brief flourishing of independent foreign policy in the early 1960s, came during the 1970s as the confidence gained from the economic miracle interacted with the exigencies of adapting to the energy crisis. Its precepts are codified in the writings of the late João Augusto de Araújo Castro. The concepts of responsible pragmatism, no automatic alignments, and other options enunciated by subsequent foreign ministers were in large part derived from the views of this individual who bridged the 1964 watershed by serving as foreign minister under Goulart and later as ambassador to the United States. Concerned with the excessive weight of force and naked power in international affairs, Araújo Castro lamented that the major industrial nations held that the less-developed countries should accept curbs on utilization of their natural resources without a commitment on the part of the major industrialized nations to a truly effective system of collective security.[6] Brazil's most active negotiator of the 1970s, Paulo Cabral de Mello, picked up on this theme:

> The interdependence of nations in the present-day world is an irreversible process, but there exist two possible forms of interdependence: that which today governs the relations between central and peripheral economies, based on institutionalization of inequalities and serving as an instrument of dependency; and that which supposes equity and marks the road to independence.[7]

This outlook reflected realization that Brazil was far from having a place near the aristocratic nations of the global stratification system and indicated impatience with a low-level seat. Congruent with it, Brazil began to diversify its bilateral relationships and to strengthen ties with its South American neighbors.

The Once-Special U.S.-Brazilian Relationship

The most persistent myth concerning U.S.-Brazilian relations is that until recently they were consistently warm and close. If they ever approximated such an idyllic state, this was temporary and largely owing to the enormous disparity in terms of power and level of economic development. The vaunted "special relationship" or "unwritten alliance" was essentially one in which Brazil was subordinate to the United States, and its continuation was an obstacle to Brazil's playing a significant role in international affairs. Although the acrimonious confrontation of 1977–1978 triggered its demise, fundamental causes lay much deeper.[8]

Never a Marriage but an
Intermittent and One-Sided Affair

Owing to great differences in priorities and decision processes, Brazilian foreign policy elites have a well-defined view of the course of bilateral relations, but such historical perspective is generally missing on the U.S. side. This has repeatedly led to unnecessary problems between Washington and Brasília. As I once wrote:

> In many ways it is quite surprising that U.S.-Brazilian relations during the present generation have been as close as has generally been the case. . . . [T]he dominant power in this relationship has repeatedly taken actions which in hindsight appear almost to have been calculated to test how much strain the unequal "partnership" could bear. . . . New governments in Washington, believing strongly—at times with religious fervor—in certain values and goals, have brought these to bear in our relations with Brazil, often in a rather heavy-handed manner.[9]

Until the 1950s relations between Brazil and the United States were generally conflict-free and often even harmonious. Although this relationship was of the utmost importance to Brazil, it was well down the priority list of a United States on its way to becoming the world's top-ranking power. Minimal for the first century of U.S. independence and nearly three-quarters of a century of Brazil's national life, relations between the United States and Brazil began to flower in the last years of the nineteenth century and deepened during the decade that the baron of Rio Branco directed Brazil's foreign policy (1902–1912). The Brazilian foreign minister correctly perceived the increasing sway of the United States within Latin America and wisely decided that Brazil's interests lay in a close relationship. What Brazil had to offer Washington was primarily a staunch ally within the Pan-American forum, where U.S. imperialism would be certain to come under heavy attack by some Spanish-American countries.

Brazil's key need was U.S. support of its program of advantageously resolving pending border disputes and thus consolidating its land frontiers. In a situation that had parallels to how Texas had become part of the United States a half century earlier, Brazilian rubber gatherers in Acre revolted against Bolivian authority in 1899 and 1902. Following military occupation by Brazil, some 73,000 acres were annexed to Brazil (in return for a pledge to construct a railroad and to guarantee Bolivia river access to the Atlantic).[10] With acquisition of a net 53,000 square miles over which Peru relinquished its claims by 1909, Brazil was on its way to the total of 342,000 square miles over which its claims were legitimized by 1912.

Despite the era of cooperation that extended through World War II, the unwritten alliance proved to be a far from permanent feature of U.S.-Brazilian relations. At most it covered two-thirds of a century, and its heyday stretched only from 1910 through the 1940s—less than a full generation. It could not survive the double strain of its senior partner diversifying its interests to embrace the entire world while the junior one moved toward a policy of active, if still selective, international engagement. Not surprisingly, it flourished only while the United States was more concerned with hemispheric hegemony than global paramountcy and Brazil still depended upon coffee exports, chiefly to the United States, for at least 70 percent of its export earnings. Even then the alliance was generally more special in rhetoric than in deeds.

By the late 1930s U.S. concern with Brazil's orientation toward the impending conflict in Europe led to wooing the Vargas regime with substantial success; the result was Brazil's participation as an ally in World War II. From the early days of the Estado Novo, Foreign Minister Oswaldo Aranha worked assiduously to bring Vargas around to the side of the United States in the intense competition for Brazil's cooperation. Ability to deliver concrete benefits and basic geopolitical realities won out, and in September 1940 agreement was finally reached on an Export-Import Bank loan of $45 million to build the Volta Redonda steel mill of the government's National Steel Company. With the war raging in Europe and the Allies in control of the Atlantic, there was little chance of receiving further shipments of the $55 million in armaments ordered from Germany under a 1938 contract with Krupp industries.[11]

From Reconciliation to Estrangement

Entry into the war brought concessions by the United States on military hardware and economic assistance. This aid along with German torpedoing of Brazilian ships beginning in March 1942 led to Brazil's declaration of war in August.[12] With Dutra's endorsement, the idea of an army corps to be trained for combat in the European theater was discussed between Vargas and Roosevelt. This was scaled down to a reinforced division, and the close relations that developed between its officers and their U.S. counterparts became the key aspect of the special relationship.

Truman did not demonstrate significant appreciation for what Brazil under Vargas had done. Rather he was viewed as a dictator whose departure from power should be hastened, and U.S. backing went to those who brought this about in October 1945. Ironically, Dutra, originally much more pro-German than Vargas, reaped the benefits of the Truman administration's cooperative attitude toward Brazil, particularly as his government came quickly into line with U.S. recommendations once the Cold War was a reality. Thus, the Joint Brazil–United States Technical Commission issued an unspectacular set of recommendations in 1949.

This was not immediately affected by Vargas' return to power near the beginning of 1951. The Joint Brazil–United States Economic Development Commission began work in mid-1951, but a serious crisis in bilateral relations came after the change of administrations in the United States in early 1953. Whereas Truman had used Brazil as an ally against Perón's ambitions to displace U.S. influence in South America, Eisenhower almost reversed this arrangement. Petroleum policy was the chief factor with the creation of Petrobrás to be combated with single-minded determination, but Vargas's unwillingness to send troops to Korea was also held against him. Notice was served that the new U.S. administration felt no obligation to help implement the projects drawn up by the joint development planning body. More than sufficient private capital would be forthcoming, Brazilians were told, if only conditions were made sufficiently attractive, and the critical measure of this would be in the petroleum field.

A major jolt came as Milton Eisenhower traveled to Argentina to patch up relations with Perón. The visit resulted in substantial loans to the regime that had most hampered Allied efforts during World War II—and that was still effectively working to undercut U.S. influence in South America—and this linkage could only be interpreted by Brazil as a slap in the face and crude arm-twisting. The Argentine strongman was willing to modify his nationalist petroleum policy in exchange for financial assistance, which in Washington's view would put increased pressure on Brazil to abandon the idea of a state petroleum monopoly.

But Brazil held out, although Vargas did not survive, and after the implications of his August 1954 suicide note with its reference to irresistible pressures from foreign economic and financial groups, interim governments could not repudiate Petrobrás even had they wished to—for this would have made them appear more interested in pleasing Washington than in preserving Brazil's national interests. Hence, U.S. private investment did not get into the politically most sensitive area of petroleum extraction, and as a result the noisy, high-profile ultranationalist campaigns of the mid-1950s lacked a dramatic target upon which they could focus mass emotions. It subsequently proved important for the preservation of U.S.-Brazilian relations in the 1960s that the volatile issue of oil was not present when other strains appeared.

U.S. hostility to Petrobrás was an important factor in the decision to react negatively to Kubitschek's 1958 proposal for Operation Pan America as a cooperative attack upon Latin America's underdevelopment. Brazil's greatest democratic president was ridiculed in Washington for his pretensions to set what J. F. Dulles called the world's largest banana republic on the path to becoming a modern industrial nation. By mid-1959 this hostility manifested itself in proposals to put Brazil on a short leash. A large proportion of U.S. policymakers were surprised when Kubitschek refused to curtail his ambitious development projects and rejected adoption of an economic stabilization program the like of which many economists have come to believe contributed to prolonged stagnation in Bolivia, Chile, and Argentina. In any event, vigorous and sustained use of economic pressures did not bring about the policy result desired by the U.S. government but instead seriously aggravated the negative—especially inflationary—ramifications of Kubitschek's all-out development drive. Belatedly in 1960, after the departure of Dulles and George Humphrey from the policy scene, the Eisenhower government came around to embracing some of the policies championed by Kubitschek since mid-1958, and bilateral relations started back on the upswing.

Outliving Its Usefulness

Early 1961 saw new governments come into office in both Washington and Brasília, with the former inclined to maintain good relations with what President Kennedy recognized as a key developing country. But Quadros soon tripped himself up in his poorly executed scheme to gain extraordinary powers. By the time Lincoln Gordon, hand-picked by John F. Kennedy to deal with Quadros, could wind up his academic obligations and get down to Brazil, Goulart was in the presidency. A cooperative relationship with his government could not be achieved, and confrontation began with the 1962 elections in which Brazilian government resources were funneled to left-wing candidates and heavy U.S. backing went to their (hence Goulart's) opponents. This policy prevented major electoral gains by the Left, but one of its costs was a deepening of regime hostility toward the United States. Goulart and his advisers were not fooled by efforts to maintain security (later revealed by renegade CIA agent Phillip Agee) and knew U.S. government funds were the source of the several million dollars reaching right-wing candidates.[13] With the polarization of late 1963, relations deteriorated as Goulart was seen by Washington as demagogically associating with radical nationalists while distancing himself from the more responsible elements in his administration.

The policy relevance of these developments subsided with Goulart's ouster, but awareness of the extent of U.S. covert action in 1962 disposed many Brazilians to believe that Johnson administration involvement in 1964 was larger and more direct than was the case. Although the U.S. government was fully informed of plans to remove Goulart, wanted for them to succeed, and even had standby plans to assist the anti-Goulart forces should the coup degenerate into a protracted power struggle, none of this proved essential to a movement that had more than adequate capabilities to overthrow the regime rapidly and with a minimum of bloodshed. Yet many analysts still ascribe a more crucial role to the United States, and the question remains how far Washington might have gone if more far-reaching measures had proved necessary.[14]

The 1964–1976 period did not have episodes of crisis in U.S.-Brazilian relations. There was Brazilian disappointment that U.S. aid was not on a more generous scale, and this was followed by a somewhat less automatically pro-U.S. stance on the Foreign Ministry's part under Costa e Silva. The return of Republicans to power in early 1969 coincided with the authoritarian period in Brazil ushered in by the December 1968 Fifth Institutional Act. During the Médici and Geisel and Nixon-Ford administrations, relations were even if unbalanced. Under the baton of Henry Kissinger, Washington recognized Brazil's increasing importance and sought to reaffirm symbolically the special nature of the bilateral relationship while minimizing divergences within multinational arenas.

However, 1977 proved much more than another low point in the no longer special relationship, which was coming closer to formal burial. Carter administration officials were unconcerned that Brazilians might view their initiatives as another piece in a pattern perceived as one of concerted U.S. efforts to maintain or even reinforce Brazil's dependence. For many Brazilian players this contrasted with signals discerned during the immediately preceding years that the United States sympathized with Brazil's aspirations to play a more important and independent role in international affairs. The net effect was to heighten Brazilian feelings of disillusionment and even betrayal when the Carter administration immediately resorted to a Wilsonian diplomacy of self-righteous high-handedness rooted in a Dulles-like assumption that Brazil was only a somewhat larger Latin American country rather than either a longtime ally or a potential power.

An ill-conceived and poorly executed policy of linking pressures on the human rights and nuclear proliferation issues resulted in Brazil's abrogation of bilateral military agreements and increased determination to reject U.S. interference in Brazil's affairs. Although President Carter displayed a conciliatory attitude during a 1978 state visit to Brazil, this failed to stem the increasingly widespread view in Brazil that the United States could not be counted upon to provide adequate leadership to the Western alliance—yet another compelling reason for Brazil to act independently on many international issues.[15]

During the Reagan administration, deterioration in Brazil's relations with the United States was stemmed in many areas, but disputes in the trade field became more frequent and acrimonious, threatening to obscure areas in which cooperation continued and agreement was possible. Hence shortly before Brazil's return to civilian government its foreign minister pointed out that "it is perfectly natural

that on specific points of the international agenda, the United States, a superpower with a global projection, and Brazil, a developing country with global interests, may face the world in different ways and find areas of disagreement."[16] His
successor stressed that Brazilian "national interests on the political, economic,
technological, and cultural levels will be best met by the option that, without ideological connotations, opens all doors to us, closing none."[17]

The Recent Record

The situation in the late 1980s was aptly depicted in the report of a high-level
working group that pointed out that "both the U.S. foreign policy elite and the
general public pay less attention to Brazil than to any comparable geopolitical entity" and concluded that "opposition, challenge and discord" had come to mark
U.S.-Brazilian relations.[18] The panel recalled Brazil's determination in the 1960s to
maintain its nuclear options in the face of heavy U.S. pressure and its subsequent
development of a substantial arms industry in reaction to U.S. refusal to give Brazil
access to sophisticated weapons; panel members, who were experienced government and business Brazil hands, advised treating Brazil much more as an equal.[19]

These views had no visible impact upon the Bush administration as it took over in
1989. Brazilian officials and informed public opinion doubted the sincerity of
abruptly manifested U.S. and West European concerns for the Amazon environment
and the plight of Brazil's Indians. At only 246,000 (0.16 percent of the country's population), the latter have fared poorly by absolute standards but not in comparison to
the historical record with respect to indigenous populations of the United States or
the former colonies of European nations. Moreover, the controversial role of the
Amazon as the "lungs of the world" is important primarily because of the enormous
atmospheric pollution generated by the industrialized nations of the Northern
Hemisphere. Hence from the Brazilian point of view the pious positions assumed by
the United States and EEC countries fell between cynical and hypocritical. Skepticism
concerning motives also applied to the drug war, as articulated by a senior diplomat:

> Protecting the environment and combating drug traffic are current illustrations of
> these hegemonic notions. . . . The South is used as the scapegoat to prolong the eco-
> nomic and political status quo in the industrialized world. . . . Emphasizing rigorous
> attack against production in the South, while adopting lenient policies for combating
> drug marketing in the North, is a sure way of prolonging real solutions to the human
> tragedy of drug consumption.[20]

In short, an upwardly mobile middle power cannot be dealt with through pressure and bullying. Indeed, this has generally bolstered Brazil's determination to
push ahead on the path from which outside powers are seeking to divert it. The
tendency to react negatively to hard ball pressure tactics is reinforced by realization that in the past such efforts on the part of the United States were proved by
subsequent developments to have been wrongheaded as well as contrary to
Brazil's interests. Moreover, in the case of bilateral relations with the United States
cooperation consistently went unrewarded.

Neither Partners Nor Enemies:
The Prospects for a Friendly Rivalry

Brazil's most important bilateral relations are still with the United States—albeit by a reduced margin—and this country remains for Brazil the most influential actor within multilateral arenas. The relationship between the Western Hemisphere's two most important countries lacks the intimacy, flawed as it is by bitter memories on the part of the weaker nation of past aggressions and injustices, that characterizes relations between Mexico and the United States. Also missing is the fundamental realization of the need to cooperate engendered by the inescapable proximity of Mexico to the contiguous North American superpower. Rather than "so far from God and so near the United States"—the basic predicament for Mexico—Brazil is at a very comfortable distance from the formerly hegemonic nation of the New World. Thus, problems involving this pair of jumbo-sized countries—containing nearly three-fifths of the hemisphere's population—are strongly conditioned by the factor of geographic remoteness. Although there would be costs entailed, perhaps so high as to call into question the rationality of such an option, the two largest federal systems in the world could essentially go their separate ways, allowing unresolved differences to dictate a policy of minimizing contact. At the other extreme, there is no real policy alternative of rebuilding the "special relationship," for this is not in a state of disrepair or decay but rather is dead; it existed only as a transitory form of marked inequality. Not being close allies would not mean that Brazil and the United States must be antagonists. The disparity of power may be eventually reduced to a point at which a more constructive relationship becomes feasible. The faster Brazil develops and comes to grips with its social problems, the sooner this will be; the less acrimonious the discord until that time, the more easily it may come about.

Brazil's Neighbors Become More Special

In contrast to the relative deterioration in Brazil's relationship with the United States, relations with other Latin American nations have improved markedly.[21] The Brazilian diplomatic agenda in the mid-1970s reflected priority on consolidation of good relations within Latin America, both as a goal itself and as a means toward eventual potency in world affairs. Although closer ties with Western European nations and Japan were to be pursued, Latin America was to remain the center of a series of concentric rings of increasingly less intense diplomatic concern. Over a decade later, this doctrine of "close concern with the close at hand" would be reflected in this formulation: "We are a country with 10 contiguous neighbors. In what form can Brazil be a positive dynamizing factor within this panorama of little hope in which certain Latin American nations seem even to be heading toward dropping out of the world economy?"[22] Just as they are aware that Brazil's future international influence will largely depend upon the country's growth and modernization, Brazilian foreign policy elites realize that it would be difficult for Brazil to be an effective actor on the global stage if its neighbors were in turmoil, especially if this threatened to spill over into Brazil.

The energy crisis and the subsequent imperative need to generate large trade surpluses to handle the exploding foreign debt problem caused Brazil to concentrate heavily on trade with other areas of the world, but commerce with its financially strapped Latin American partners actually decreased in the 1980s. Yet through all this, significant diplomatic priority was focused upon its home region, and solidifying good relations with traditional rival Argentina was the central concern. Not only was initially vehement Argentine opposition to the construction of the Itaipu dam neutralized and the potential nuclear arms race brought under control during the Figueiredo administration, but special trade and economic cooperation relations were subsequently put into effect by the Sarney government. This was carried forward under Collor to the point of a joint nuclear project and formation of a Southern Common Market (Mercosul), including also Uruguay and Paraguay. Congruent with this was the 1992 decision to bring Bolivia into a closer relationship through a multibillion-dollar gas pipeline (to carry Bolivian natural gas to the industrial heart of Brazil), iron mining facilities, a steel mill, and thermoelectric plant centering on Puerto Suarez, Bolivia, and Corumbá, Brazil.

Brazil has been highly successful in dispelling the suspicion concerning possible hegemonic designs that threatened in the 1970s to thwart efforts toward closer relationships. To this end it has skillfully utilized subregional arrangements to reinforce bilateral ties. In addition to being the linchpin of both the Amazon and La Plata basin pacts, it has even managed to become a valued partner of the Andean pact—which was originally in large part directed against Brazil. It also made good use of collective concerns with the debt problem to stress being one of the Latin American contingent rather than a Portuguese outsider in a Hispanic continent. Support for the work of the Contadora group in finding a peaceful solution to the U.S.-Nicaraguan dispute and the Salvadorean conflict also strengthened Brazil's bona fides—as did reestablishment of diplomatic relations with Cuba. Relations with Venezuela center on border areas, and there is special attention to the activities of Brazilian prospectors and the problems posed by the Yanomani Indian nation extending on both sides of the international boundary. Drug traffic is, of course, crucial in Brazil's relations with Colombia and Peru.

Worldview and Foreign Policy Making

Brazilian foreign policy through the 1990s will be made in large part by those shaping it at present. Fundamental change in the constellation of forces determining Brazil's actions and a consequent basic reorientation of international ties and policies would require more than a single presidential term.[23] Adjustment to formulating foreign policy in a democratic system with a variety of competing interests after a long period of military hegemony has largely been completed.

Moreover, Cardoso demonstrated a reasoned and moderate stance during his stint as Franco's foreign minister.

Continuity of Goals in a Changing Context

A changing of the guard in terms of individuals and generations has taken place in the foreign service, and the cohort consolidating leadership within the ranks of Brazil's highly professional diplomatic service will be heading Itamaraty (as the ministry is generally termed) for some years yet. Already occupying key posts is a group of prestigious ambassadors still in their fifties, personified by former Finance Minister Ricupero and Strategic Affairs Secretary Ronaldo Sardenberg, as well as a slightly younger group experienced as heads of major departments and divisions of the ministry (exemplified by Foreign Minister Lampréia and his predecessor, Celso Amorim). Despite already holding ambassadorial rank for some years now, most of this cohort may be on active duty to the end of the century.

The mark of this generation was already evident on the international policies of the Sarney government, and as a whole they are not likely to change their views materially in the years ahead—either in terms of perceptions of national interest or of the basic need to consolidate cooperation among countries of Latin America in order to deal effectively with the challenges ahead. Although they may hold differing views on where Brazil's interests ultimately lie and how best to serve them, they are accustomed to working together with considerable give-and-take within the cooperative tradition—including the conciliation-facilitating dictum that it is sometimes necessary to "go along in order to get along." Moreover, compared to the past generation they generally have a much greater familiarity with and understanding of economic affairs.

Similarly within the armed forces, whose abiding interest in national security broadly defined still gives them a major voice in international policy, no drastic change in orientation is likely through the 1990s, since the prospective senior flag officers of that period have already earned their first stars (see Chapter 5). Many of them have attended the War College or will do so in the near future, and recent general staff and command school graduates will take their place during the mid-1990s as strategically placed colonels.[24] Brazil's military promotion system works so that generals, admirals, and air force brigadiers are in their late fifties to mid-sixties—an age at which significant changes in values, priorities, and worldview are most unlikely. Few of these officers or civilian officials dealing with foreign policy would sharply disagree with a well-known writer on military and geopolitical topics (who had served as deputy chief of the armed forces general staff) when he declared in the mid-1970s that "we possess all the conditions that enable us to aspire to a place among the world's great powers."[25]

The 1986 symposium "Brazil at the Turn of the Century" that brought together representatives of political groups and ranking governmental cadres affords a good window into their thinking.[26] The international session included the cream of the foreign service's intellectual elite, including Ricupero, Jerônimo Moscardo de Souza, 1994 deputy foreign minister Roberto Pinto Ferreira Abdenur, and four other young ambassadors serving in Brasília. All expressed a realistic degree of pessimism regarding unfavorable conditions prevailing in Brazil's external environment and determination to confront these as challenges to be overcome. Provocative positions were posed by future foreign minister Celso Lafer (an Ivy League Ph.D.) and Hélio Jaguaribe, former professor at Harvard, MIT, and Stanford. In response, these potential candidates for the post of foreign minister agreed that Brazil must deal energetically with the contradiction between being nearly developed in strictly economic terms but remaining at a Third World stage with respect to social indicators and quality of life. They viewed the rising importance of Japan and increasing international participation of China largely in the context of the economic realm—marked by considerable uncertainty over such critical matters as the impact of complete West European integration and the prospects for a significant new approach by the industrial powers to the debt question. They generally manifested confidence in a gradual increase in the importance and effectiveness of Brazil's international actions but expected that this would be reflected chiefly in a strengthened bargaining position rather than lead to a dramatically different role. They expressed determination to gradually assume a more conspicuous leadership position in hemispheric and global affairs. No longer viewed by their neighbors as an outsider—even a stalking horse for the United States—Brazil could emerge from a low international profile to assume formal leadership positions such as secretary general of the Organization of American States and membership in the U.N. Security Council, where it would like to gain a permanent seat. One elite gave this widely held opinion: "Brazil is seen as a useful partner, a necessary partner, and even one without which no [South American] country could thinkingly establish a valid medium- or long-range development strategy."[27]

First World, Like It or Not

For the cream of Brazil's diplomatic profession, continued economic development in Brazil will cause it to move closer to the industrial powers and decrease its ability to act as a Third World leader. This trend results from a perception on the part of the less developed countries that Brazil has advanced too far to remain in the same crowded boat with them. A major challenge stemming from this situation is to adapt Brazilian diplomacy to the new reality of graduation to First World candidate status, but the task is complicated by the fact that the core of the Brazilian foreign policy elite do not perceive a fundamental community of interests with the United States. Indeed, the recent record suggests that many of them view U.S. policy as at the heart of Brazil's most intractable international problems:

> The proliferation of protectionist trade policies lets the developed countries solve their internal crises by exporting their unemployment to the weaker trade partners, generally the developing countries; we see also that the international financial crisis is

the result of the ease with which the United States of America can avoid the budgetary adjustment of its economy, forcing the other countries to themselves adopt measures of rigorous readjustment.[28]

Policy elites view the primary task of Brazilian diplomacy as being to use every possible forum to increase their limited power to "further the international changes that permit Brazilian growth."[29] There is a consensus that Brazil must internationalize its economy but that this should stop short of the neoliberal model as implemented in the Asian tigers. Predominantly they are neither advocates of doctrinaire privatization nor ideologically wedded to statism but range across the spectrum between these two extremes. This broad, albeit incomplete, foreign policy consensus is premised on the belief that major changes in the international economic order will come in the years ahead. They intend to be active, even in the forefront, of bringing this about and harbor no illusions as to the extent of opposition they will encounter from the United States and the EEC. As cogently expressed by a bellwether figure, "The Nation needs to be psychologically prepared for evolution within a conflictive environment that is not necessarily one of rupture. It is an environment of confrontation, of opposing sides, of legitimate interests in shock within Brazil's quest for [foreign policy] space."[30] Such thinking brings them back to the touchstone of close cooperation with other Latin American countries reinforced by conviction that Brazilian growth would be very difficult in a stagnant Latin America.

Convinced that there is extreme fragility to the still incomplete consensus on minimum rules of international coexistence, Brazil's foreign policy elites wish to see an orderly transformation that would decrease tensions between North and South as has occurred between East and West. They no longer have to concern themselves with strategies for avoiding being drawn into the rivalry between the United States and the Soviet Union, and they are assessing how to maintain maximum freedom of action in a world with a single superpower—one whose control over their destiny they have been working long and hard to reduce. As articulated by a fast-rising ambassador, the 1990s have seen the emergence of an "asystemic, diverse world, tending to regionalize" and marked by a trend toward intense, even conflictual competition.[31] Deeply immersed in intense integration projects, the Northern Hemisphere powers demonstrate an "accelerated exclusion and increasing rejection of the peoples and nations of the South." Brazil's intellectually inclined professional diplomats will continue to be engaged in assessing implications of the end of the Cold War and disaggregation of the Soviet Union.[32]

Brazil has increasingly come to see association with its neighbors and strengthening of ties to Europe and Japan as the best road to the First World. Mexico has tied its fate to integration through the North American Free Trade Agreement, and thus Brazil, both for its unilateral interests and leading role in the Southern Cone Common Market, has little choice but to forge strong links with the other two pillars of the First World.

Future Trends and Uncertainties

As shown in the preceding chapters, Brazil has demonstrated a growing ability to overcome the obstacles placed in its path by the international system of which it is increasingly an active member. Just as the energy crisis of the 1970s pushed Brazil to expand its own petroleum production and augment this with alcohol and other nontraditional fuel sources, the upside of the ensuing debt burden was growth and diversification of exports as well as reduced dependence on imports. In the realm of international politics, Brazil has learned that it need not shy from confrontation with the United States or the industrialized nations of Western Europe on those occasions when defense of its legitimate interests is at stake. Never before has Brazil enjoyed such close relationships with its South American neighbors or found itself in as good repute in the more distant parts of Latin America.

In 1995 as a highly competent administration moved through its first year in office under favorable circumstances, Brazil's thoroughly professional diplomats were concerned with positioning their country for the challenges and opportunities the new century will bring. New challenges lie ahead, and some of them will likely be taxing and thorny, but Brazil's upward mobility will not only continue but even pick up further speed and momentum. No longer is the question whether Brazil will some day rank with the world's major powers; rather doubts center on how soon and to what effect. In this regard, the scope and pace of internal development and satisfactory disposition of domestic problems loom as more important than foreign policy initiatives. Although it seems painfully slow to those living through it, history will view Brazil's evolution from a clientlike junior and often ignored partner of the United States to major power status as having been remarkably rapid. In working its way up through the stratified and hierarchical world system, Brazil continues to be aided by factors I pointed out nearly two decades ago. "Brazil has been largely unhampered by the needs to organize massive military forces to provide for its security in global affairs, to seek the protection of exclusive military alliances, or to make other confining political commitments. Brazil can also escape military strategic pressures and keep military expenditures low."[33] As put recently by one of Brazil's diplomats, "By exercising the correct political will, the 'fortuna' of the South American position off the centers and axes of power has all the conditions to change into a value, to be transformed from a liability to an important asset."[34]

With the rise of the United States the world had its first non–West European world power; with the emergence of the Soviet Union its first partially Asian one; with Japan's ascendance its first Far Eastern and Pacific power. Just as these international system-changing developments occurred from the end of the nineteenth century through the first third of the twentieth, Brazil's continued evolution into a modern industrial nation will break the Northern Hemisphere monopoly on major power status a hundred years later—most likely to the advantage of the other nations that have had the misfortune of being on the "wrong side" of the equator.

Notes

Chapter 1

1. On Brazil's topography, see Celeste Rodrigues Maio, *Geomorfologia de Brasil: Fotos e Comentários*, 3d ed. (Rio de Janeiro: Fundação Instituto Brasileiro de Geográfia e Estatística, 1987).

2. The official Brazilian classification for urban is (1) any seat of a *município* (of which there are nearly 5,000) or (2) other district within it that has over 10,000 inhabitants. *Municípios* are created by law and have no minimum population requirement.

3. The classic study of this great city is Richard M. Morse, *From Community to Metropolis: A Biography of São Paulo, Brazil* (Gainesville: University of Florida Press, 1958).

4. On Rio de Janeiro, consult Janice E. Perlman, *The Myth of Marginality: Urban Poverty and Politics in Rio de Janeiro* (Berkeley: University of California Press, 1976).

5. The Federal District, the basic governmental and census unit, is composed of Brasília proper plus eleven satellite cities.

6. See Joe Foweraker, *The Struggle for Land: A Political Economy of the Pioneer Frontier in Brazil from 1930 to the Present Day* (New York: Cambridge University Press, 1981); and Norman Gall, "Letter from Rondônia: A Report on the Brazilian Frontier," *American Universities Field Staff Reports,* South America 1978, Nos. 9, 10, 11, 12, and 13 (Hanover, NH, April 1978).

7. A useful text on rubber and the Amazon is Warren Dean, *Brazil and the Struggle for Rubber: A Study in Environmental History* (Cambridge: Cambridge University Press, 1987).

8. Balanced works on the region include Juan de Onis, *The Green Cathedral: Sustainable Development of Amazonia* (New York: Oxford University Press, 1985); Ronald A. Foresta, *Amazon Conservation in the Age of Development: The Limits of Providence* (Gainesville: University of Florida Press, 1991); and David Goodman and Anthony Hill, eds., *The Future of Amazonia: Destruction or Sustainable Development* (London: Macmillan, 1991).

9. The early struggles to build railroads in the interior are recounted in Francisco Foot Hardman, *Trem Fantasma* (São Paulo: Companhia das Letras, 1988).

10. A reasoned approach is Carlos de Meira Mattos, *Uma Geopolítica Pan-Amazônica* (Rio de Janeiro: Biblioteca do Exército Editora, 1980).

11. See Lúcio Flávio Pinto, *Jari: Toda a Verdade sobre o Projecto de Ludwig: As relações entre estado e multinacional na Amazônia* (São Paulo: Editora Marco Zero, 1986); and Jerry Shields, *The Invisible Billionaire, Daniel Ludwig* (Boston: Houghton Mifflin, 1986).

12. On this region, see Riordan J. A. Roett, *The Politics of Foreign Aid in the Brazilian Northeast* (Nashville, Tenn: Vanderbilt University Press, 1972); and Manuel Correia de Andrade, *Estado, Capital e Indústria do Nordeste* (Rio de Janeiro: Jorge Zahar Editora, 1981), and *O Nordeste e a Nova República* (Recife: Editora ASA, 1987).

Chapter 2

1. Discussion of relevant literature is contained in Ronald M. Schneider, *"Order and Progress": A Political History of Brazil* (Boulder: Westview Press, 1991), pp. 390–408.

2. The grants were termed *capitanias,* and the recipient was called a *donitário.*

3. E. Bradford Burns, *A History of Modern Brazil,* 2d ed. (New York: Columbia University Press, 1980), is a more than serviceable survey of Brazilian history.

4. On the native population, see Manuela Carneiro da Cunha, ed., *História dos Índios do Brasil* (São Paulo: Companhia das Letras, 1992).

5. Ivan Alves Filho, *Memorial dos Palmares* (Rio de Janeiro: Xenon Editora e Produtora Cultural, 1987); and Clóvis Moura, *Rebeliões da Senzala* (Rio de Janeiro: Mercado Aberto, 1988).

6. Consult Tomo 1, Vol. 2, of *História Geral da Civilização Brasileira (hereafter HGCB), A Época Colonial: Administração, Economia, Sociedade* (São Paulo: Difusão Européia do Livro, 1960).

7. See Kenneth Maxwell, *Conflicts and Conspiracies: Brazil and Portugal, 1750–1808* (Cambridge: Cambridge University Press, 1973); and Maxwell, *Pombal: Paradox of the Enlightenment* (Cambridge: Cambridge University Press, 1995).

8. Key is Roderick J. Barman, *Brazil: The Forging of a Nation, 1798–1852* (Stanford: Stanford University Press, 1988).

9. Neil Macaulay, *Dom Pedro: The Struggle for Liberty in Brazil and Portugal, 1798–1834* (Durham, N.C.: Duke University Press, 1986), is the most important work on this controversial figure.

10. Pedro's decision was to exchange a crown in an out-of-the-way continent for a throne near the center of world affairs.

11. The slave population in the mid-1860s, although declining, was still over 1.7 million. The number that had arrived from Africa between 1781 and 1852 was just over 2.1 million.

12. Essential are Richard Graham, *Patronage and Politics in Nineteenth-Century Brazil* (Stanford: Stanford University Press, 1990); and José Murilo de Carvalho, "Sistemas Eleitorais e Partidos do Império," in Olavo Brasil de Lima Jr., ed., *O Balanço do Poder: Formas de Dominação e Representação* (Rio de Janeiro: Rio Fundo Editora, 1990), pp. 15–34.

13. See Robert A. Hayes, *The Armed Nation: The Brazilian Corporate Mystique* (Tempe: Arizona State University, 1989), pp. 11–77.

14. June E. Hahner, *Poverty and Politics: The Urban Poor in Brazil, 1870–1920* (Albuquerque: University of New Mexico Press, 1986), p. 40.

15. Estimates in Raymond W. Goldsmith, *Brazil 1850–1984: Desenvolvimento Financeiro sob um Século de Inflação* (São Paulo: Harper and Row do Brasil, 1986), pp. 20–27.

16. Joseph L. Love, "Political Participation in Brazil, 1881–1969," *Luso-Brazilian Review* 7, no. 2 (December 1970):3–24.

17. June E. Hahner, *Civilian-Military Relations in Brazil, 1889–1898* (Columbia: University of South Carolina Press, 1969), p. 10n, discusses the ratios of civilian to army heroes as war ministers.

18. Goldsmith, *Brazil 1850–1984,* pp. 27ff.

19. The republic's essentially elite nature is shown in José Murilo de Carvalho, *Os bestializados: O Rio de Janeiro e a República que não foi* (São Paulo: Companhia das Letras, 1987).

20. Consult Aspásia de Alcântara Camargo, "A Questão Agrária: Crise do Poder e Reformas de Base (1930–1964)," in *HGCB*, Tomo 3, Vol. 3, *Sociedade e Política, 1930–1964,* 3d ed. (São Paulo: Difusão Editorial, 1986), p. 130.

21. A useful source on the economy is Anníbal Villanova Villela and Wilson Suzigan, *Política do Governo e Crescimento da Economia Brasileira, 1889–1945* (Rio de Janeiro: Instituto de Planejamento Econômico e Social, 1973).

22. In Rio de Janeiro only 28,585 voted out of 109,421 literate males over twenty-one not serving as soldiers or priests. See Murilo de Carvalho, *Os bestializados*, p. 85.

23. See Joseph L. Love, *Rio Grande do Sul and Brazilian Regionalism: 1882–1930* (Palo Alto: Stanford University Press, 1971), pp. 47–75.

24. Amado Luiz Cervo and Clodoaldo Bueno, *História da Política Exterior do Brasil* (São Paulo: Editora Ática, 1992), pp. 157–160.

25. See Robert M. Levine, *Vale of Tears: Revisiting the Canudos Massacre in Northeastern Brazil, 1893–1897* (Berkeley: University of California Press, 1992).

26. See Frank D. McCann, "The Military," in Michael L. Conniff and Frank D. McCann, eds., *Modern Brazil: Elites and Masses in Historical Perspective* (Lincoln: University of Nebraska Press, 1989), pp. 50–51. This is developed further in his *History of the Brazilian Army, 1889–1930* (forthcoming).

27. Consult Steven Topik, *The Political Economy of the Brazilian State, 1889–1930* (Austin: University of Texas Press, 1987).

28. Quite insightful is Ralph della Cava, *Miracle at Joazeiro* (New York: Columbia University Press, 1970).

29. See Todd A. Diacon, *Millenarian Vision, Capitalist Reality: Brazil's Contestado Rebellion, 1912–1916* (Durham, N.C.: Duke University Press, 1991).

30. An important work is José Augusto Drummond, *O Movimento Tenentista: Intervenção Militar e Conflito Hieráquico (1922–1935)* (Rio de Janeiro: Edições Graal, 1986).

31. Mauricio Font makes a strong case that dissatisfied large coffee planters played a key if not dominant role in the PD. See his *Coffee, Contention, and Change: In the Politics of Modern Brazil* (London: Basil Blackwell, 1990).

32. A massive literature exists on Vargas; J.F.W. Dulles, *Vargas of Brazil* (Austin: University of Texas Press, 1967) is the place to begin.

Chapter 3

1. Relevant literature is discussed in Ronald M. Schneider, *"Order and Progress": A Political History of Brazil* (Boulder: Westview Press, 1991), pp. 410–438.

2. See Frank C. McCann, *A History of the Brazilian Army: 1889–1930* (forthcoming); and Robert A. Hayes, *The Armed Nation: The Brazilian Corporate Mystique* (Tempe: Arizona State University, 1989).

3. See Paulo Sérgio Pinheiro, *Estratégias da Ilusão: A Revolução Mundial e o Brasil, 1922–1935* (São Paulo: Companhia das Letras, 1991).

4. Consult Ernani do Amaral Peixoto with Aspásia Camargo, Lucia Hippolito, Maria Celína Soares D'Araújo, and Dora Flaksman, *Artes da Política: Diálogo com Amaral Peixoto* (Rio de Janeiro: Editora Nova Fronteira, 1986), pp. 69–82 and 97–139.

5. See Carlos E. Cortes, *Gaúcho Politics in Brazil: The Politics of Rio Grande do Sul, 1930–1964* (Albuquerque: University of New Mexico Press, 1974), pp. 24–67.

6. The best analysis is Robert Levine, *The Vargas Regime: The Critical Years, 1934–1938* (New York: Columbia University Press, 1970).

7. On the middle years of the Vargas era, see Aspásia Camargo, Dulce Chaves Pandolfi, Eduardo Rodrigues Gomes, Maria Celina Soares D'Araújo, and Mario Grynszpan, *O Golpe Silencioso: As Origens da República Corporativa* (Rio de Janeiro: Rio Fundo Editora, 1989); J.F.W. Dulles, *Brazilian Communism, 1935–1945: Repression During World Upheaval* (Austin: University of Texas Press, 1983); and Thomas E. Skidmore, *Politics in Brazil, 1930–1964: An Experiment in Democracy* (Oxford: Oxford University Press, 1967).

8. Eli Diniz, "O Estado Novo: Estrutura de Poder, Relações de Classes," in *HGCB*, Tomo 3, Vol. 3, p. 114; and Eli Diniz, *Empresário, Estado e Capitalismo no Brasil: 1930–1945* (Rio de Janeiro: Editora Paz e Terra, 1978).

9. See Frank D. McCann, *The Brazilian-American Alliance, 1937–1945* (Princeton: Princeton University Press, 1973).

10. Maria Victoria de Mesquita Benevides, *A UDN e o Udenismo: Ambigüidades de Liberalismo Brasileiro, 1945–1965* (Rio de Janeiro: Editora Paz e Terra, 1981), pp. 23–61.

11. For comparison with the previous presidential balloting, see Ronald M. Schneider, *Brazil Election Factbook* (Washington, D.C.: Institute for the Comparative Study of Political Systems, 1965), pp. 53–61.

12. In 1964 Lacerda continued to exploit this issue.

13. See John F.W. Dulles, *Carlos Lacerda: Brazilian Crusader*, Vol. 1, *The Years 1914–1960* (Austin: University of Texas Press, 1991), pp. 135–172.

14. Key is J.F.W. Dulles, *Unrest in Brazil: Political Military Crises, 1955–1964* (Austin: University of Texas Press, 1970).

15. Consult Maria Victoria Benevides, *O Governo Kubitschek: Desenvolvimento Econômico e Estabilidade Política, 1956–1961* (Rio de Janeiro: Editora Paz e Terra, 1976).

16. See Schneider, *Brazil Election Factbook*, pp. 43–46 and 58–61. Dulles, *Carlos Lacerda*, pp. 278–319, treats Lacerda's role in Quadros's rise.

17. In 1950 agriculture accounted for 26.7 percent of GDP and industry but 23.5 percent according to Raymond Goldsmith, *Brazil 1850–1984: Desenvolvimento Financeiro sob um Século de Inflação* (São Paulo: Harper and Row do Brasil, 1986), p. 225.

18. Quadros died in February 1992 following a comeback that led him to the São Paulo mayor's chair.

19. The most comprehensive study of IPES is René Armand Dreifuss, *1964: A Conquista do Estado, Ação Política, Poder e Golpe de Classe* (Petrópolis: Editora Vozes, 1981).

20. The Chamber of Deputies had been enlarged from 326 to 409. Turnout at 14.7 million was nearly two and a half times that of 1945.

21. Dulles, *Carlos Lacerda*, blends a portrait of Goulart's leading enemy with a feel for the times.

22. See Dênis de Moraes, *A Esquerda e o Golpe de 64: Vinte e cinco anos depois, as forças populares repensam seus mitos, sonhos, e ilusões* (Rio de Janeiro: Editora Espaço e Tempo, 1989).

23. The PCB was aligned with Goulart; the PCdoB favored Brizola's side.

24. The best case in point was Brizola's clandestine "Groups of 11." See Moraes, *A Esquerda,* p. 353.

Chapter 4

1. See sources in Ronald M. Schneider, *"Order and Progress": A Political History of Brazil* (Boulder: Westview Press), pp. 438–455, and in Schneider, *The Political System of Brazil: Emergence of a "Modernizing" Authoritarian Regime, 1964–1970* (New York: Columbia University Press, 1971), pp. 108–145; J.F.W. Dulles, *President Castello Branco: Brazilian Reformer* (College Station: Texas A&M University Press, 1980), pp. 1–63; and Thomas E. Skidmore, *The Politics of Military Rule in Brazil, 1964–1985* (New York: Oxford University Press, 1988), pp. 18–45.

2. Luíz Vianna Filho, *O Governo Castelo Branco* (Rio de Janeiro: Livraria José Olympio Editora, 1975).

3. About 1,200 were purged from the services. See Maria Helena Moreira Alves, *State and Opposition in Military Brazil* (Austin: University of Texas Press, 1985), p. 42.

4. Campaign issues, strategies, and results are analyzed in Schneider, *The Political System of Brazil,* pp. 163–169.

5. See Maria D'Alva G. Kinzo, *Legal Opposition Politics under Authoritarian Rule in Brazil: The Case of the MDB, 1966–1979* (New York: St. Martin's Press, 1988).

6. See Schneider, *The Political System of Brazil,* pp. 178–195.

7. On the student movement, consult João Roberto Martins Filho, *Movimento Estudantil e Ditadura Militar, 1964–1968* (Campinas: Papirus Livraria Editor, 1987), pp. 75–109.

8. Text in *Visão* of December 20, 1968, pp. 21–23 as well as in the daily papers of December 14.

9. On soccer, see Robert M. Levine, "The Burden of Success: Futebol and Brazilian Society through the 1970s," *Journal of Popular Culture* 14, no. 3 (Winter 1980):453–464.

10. A fuller discussion is in Schneider, *The Political System of Brazil,* pp. 319–324.

11. Works by leftist intellectuals include Paul Singer, *O "Milagre Brasileiro" Causas e Consequências* (São Paulo: CEBRAP, 1972), pp. 57–77; and Maria da Conceição Tavares, *Da substituição de importações ao capitalismo financeiro: Ensaios sôbre economia Brasileira* (Rio de Janeiro: Zahar Editores, 1973).

12. The Geisel period is treated in Thomas E. Skidmore, *The Politics of Military Rule in Brazil, 1964–1985,* pp. 160–209.

13. On the views of Geisel and Golbery, see Alfred Stepan, *Rethinking Military Politics: Brazil and the Southern Cone* (Princeton: Princeton University Press, 1988), pp. 33–44.

14. See Velloso's *O Último Trem Para Paris: De Getúlio a Sarney: "milagres", choques e crises do Brasil Moderno* (Rio de Janeiro: Editora Nova Fronteira, 1986).

15. On these elections, see Margaret J. Sarles, "Maintaining Control Through Political Parties: The Brazilian Strategy," *Comparative Politics* 15, no. 1 (1982):41–72.

16. Dionísio Dias Carneiro, "Crise e Esperança: 1974–1980," in Marcelo de Paiva Abreu, ed., *A Ordem do Progresso: Cem Anos de Política Econômica Republicana, 1889–1989* (Rio de Janeiro: Editora Campus, 1989), pp. 295–322; and Albert Fishlow, "A Tale of Two Presidents: The Political Economy of Crisis Management," in Alfred Stepan, ed.,

Democratizing Brazil: Problems of Transition and Consolidation (New York: Oxford University Press, 1989), pp. 83–119.

17. See Getúlio Bittencourt, *A Quinta Estrela: Como se tenta fazer um presidente no Brasil* (São Paulo: Livraria Editora Ciências Humanas, 1978); and Carlos Chagas, *A Guerra das Estrelas (1964/1984): Os Bastidores das Sucessões Presidenciais* (Porto Alegre, Brazil: L & M Editores, 1985).

18. Bolívar Lamounier and Fernando Henrique Cardoso, eds., *Os Partidos e as Eleições no Brasil* (Rio de Janeiro: Editora Paz e Terra, 1975).

19. Margaret E. Keck, *The Workers Party and Democratization in Brazil* (New Haven: Yale University Press, 1992).

20. My observations are detailed in reports issued through the Center for Strategic and International Studies in 1982.

21. See *Brazil Political Report* by Ronald M. Schneider and William Perry published by the Center for Strategic and International Studies (monthly July 1984 through January 1985).

22. This section draws on Ronald M. Schneider, "Brazil's Political Future" in Wayne A. Selcher, ed., *Political Liberalization in Brazil: Dynamics, Dilemmas, and Future Prospects* (Boulder: Westview Press, 1986), pp. 217–260; and Schneider, "Transition Without Rupture: Parties, Politicians, and the Sarney Government," in Julian Chacel, Pamela Falk, and David V. Fleischer, eds., *Brazil's Economic and Political Future* (Boulder: Westview Press, 1988), pp. 188–198.

23. Works explaining why the transition did not lead to a new order free of clientelism, populism, and military influence include Aspásia Camargo and Eli Diniz, eds., *Continuidade e Mudança no Brasil da Nova República* (São Paulo: Edições Vértice, 1989); Eli Diniz, Renato Boschi, and Renato Lessa, *Modernização e Consolidação Democrática no Brasil: Dilemas da Nova República* (São Paulo: Edições Vértice, 1989); and Fábio Wanderley Reis and Guillermo O'Donnell, eds., *A Democracia no Brasil: Dilemas e Perspectivas* (São Paulo: Ediçõess Vértice, 1988).

24. Best on the Cruzado Plan is Werner Baer and Paul Beckerman, "The Decline and Fall of Brazil's Cruzado," *Latin American Research Review* 34, no. 1 (1989):35–64.

25. See Ronald M. Schneider, *Brazil's 1986 Elections,* (Washington, D.C.: Center for Strategic and International Studies, December 1986).

26. João Gilberto Lucas Coelho and Antônio Carlos Nantes de Oliveira, *A Nova Constitução: Avaliação do Texto e Perfil dos Constituentes* (Rio de Janeiro: Editora Revan, 1989); David V. Fleischer and João Gilberto Lucas Coelho, *O Processo Constituente 1987–1988* (Brasília: Centro de Estudos e Acompanhamento da Constituente da Universidade de Brasília, 1988); Leôncio Martins Rodrigues, *Quem é Quem na Constituente: Uma Análise Socio-Político dos Partidos e Deputados* (São Paulo: O Estado de S. Paulo/Maltese, 1987); and Maria D'Alva Gil Kinzo, "O quadro partidário e a constituinte," in Bolívar Lamounier, ed., *De Geisel a Collor: O balanço da transição* (São Paulo: IDESP/Sumaré, 1990), pp. 105–134.

27. The text of the constitution is in *IstoÉSenhor* of October 12, 1988. See also Amaury de Souza and Bolívar Lamounier, "A feitura da nova constituição: Um resume da cultura política brasileira," in Lamounier, ed., *De Geisel a Collor,* pp. 81–104.

28. On electoral behavior, see Eli Diniz, "O Ciclo Autoritário: A Lógica Partidário Eleitoral e a Erosão do Regime," in Olavo Brasil de Lima Jr., ed., *O Balanço do Poder:*

Formas de Dominção e Representação (Rio de Janeiro: Rio Fundo Editora, 1990), pp. 73–86; and Marcus Faria Figueiredo, "O eleitor brasileiro sabe o que quer: Democracia e comportamento eleitoral estratégico," in João Paulo dos Reis Velloso, ed., *A Crise Brasileira e a Modernização de Sociedade* (Rio de Janeiro: José Olympio Editora, 1990), pp. 103–129.

29. See various reports by Ronald M. Schneider and William Perry, *The 1989 Brazilian Elections*, published by the Center for Strategic and International Studies (Washington, D.C.), including No. 1, "Background" (September 1989); No. 2, "The Campaign at Midstream" (September 1989); No. 3, "The Stretch Drive" (November 1989); and No. 4, "The First Round and the Campaign for the Second" (November 1989).

30. Ibid., Report No. 5, "The Final Tally" (January 1990).

Chapter 5

1. See Bolívar Lamounier, "Antecedentes, riscos e possibilidades do governo Collor," in Bolívar Lamounier, ed., *De Geisel a Collor: O balanço da transição* (São Paulo: IDESP/Sumaré, 1990), pp. 13–35.

2. Marcelo de Paiva Abreu, ed., *A Ordem do Progresso: Cem Anos de Política Econômica Republicana, 1889–1989* (Rio de Janeiro: Editora Campus, 1989), pp. 7–9.

3. See Ronald M. Schneider and William Perry, *The 1989 Brazilian Elections*, Report No. 6, "The Collor Government: A New Team Charts a New Course" (Washington, D.C.: Center for Strategic and International Studies, May 1990).

4. Consult Mário Henrique Simonsen, "A inflação e nove meses do Plano Collor," in João Paulo dos Reis Velloso, ed., *A Crise Brasileira e a Modernização da Sociedade* (Rio de Janeiro: José Olympio Editora, 1990), pp. 57–68.

5. See William Perry, *The 1989 Brazilian Elections*, Special Report, "The Collor Government's First Six Months: Forging a New Brazil" (Washington, D.C.: Center for Strategic and International Studies, September 1990).

6. See analyses by Ronald M. Schneider and William Perry, *The 1990 Brazilian Elections*, published by the Center for Strategic and International Studies (Washington, D.C.), especially No. 1, "Pre-Election Analysis: The Setting" (September 1990); No. 2, "Pre-Election Analysis: Into the Homestretch" (September 1990); and No. 3, "Post-Election Analysis" (December 1990).

7. Of the 11 governors elected on October 3, 6 were returnees as were 6 of the runoff losers and 10 new senators.

8. The text of the investigatory committee's report is in *Jornal do Brasil*, August 23, 1992. A thoughtful interpretation is Peter Flynn, "Collor, Corruption and Crisis: Time for Reflection" *Journal of Latin American Studies*, 25, no. 2 (May 1993):351–371.

9. See *O Globo*, November 22, 1992.

10. Warren Dean, *With Broadax and Firebrand: The Destruction of the Brazilian Coastal Forest* (Berkeley: University of California Press, 1995).

11. *Veja*, January 26, 1994, pp. 28–35; and *IstoÉ*, January 26, 1994, pp. 39–53.

12. In the United States only some governorship elections coincide with that for president, and but one-third of the Senate is chosen at the same time.

13. See *Veja*, January 18, 1995, pp. 78–80; and *IstoÉ*, January 11, 1995, pp. 56–65.

14. Cardoso's Hands to Work, Brazil program focused upon improving an unjust society through growth and job opportunities.

15. See Ronald M. Schneider, *"Order and Progress": A Political History of Brazil* (Boulder: Westview Press, 1991), pp. 12–14.

16. Olávo Brasil de Lima Júnior, "A Experiência Brasileira com Partidos e Eleições" in Lima Júnior, ed., *O balanço do Poder: Formas de Dominação e Representação* (Rio de Janeiro: Rio Fundo Editora, 1990), pp. 9–14.

17. See Abdo I. Baaklini, *The Brazilian Legislature and Political System* (Westport, Conn.: Greenwood Press, 1992).

18. PSDB views are in Maurício Dias David, ed., *Economia e Política da Crise Brasileira: A Perspectiva Social-Democrata* (Rio de Janeiro: Rio Fundo Editora, 1991).

19. Aspásia Camargo,"As duas faces de Janus: Os paradoxos da modernidade incompleta," in Velloso, *A Crise Brasileira e a Modernização da Sociedade*, pp. 49–77.

20. Eli Diniz and Renato R. Boschi, "A Consolidação Democrática no Brasil: Atores Políticos, Processos Sociais e Intermediação de Interesses," in Eli Diniz, Renato Boschi, and Renato Lessa, *Modernização e Consolidação Democrática no Brasil: Dilemas da Nova República* (São Paulo: Edições Vértice), pp. 58–59.

21. Aspásia Camargo and Eli Diniz, "Introdução: Dilemas da Consolidação Democrática no Brasil," in Camargo and Diniz, eds., *Continuidade e Mudança no Brasil da Nova República* (São Paulo: Edições Vértice, 1989), p. 12.

22. Guillermo O'Donnell, "Hiatos, Instituições e Perspectivas Democráticas," in Fábio Wanderley Reis and Guillermo O'Donnell, eds., *A Democracia no Brasil: Dilemas e Perspectivas* (São Paulo: Edições Vértice, 1988), p. 81. Also see Frances Hagopian, "The Compromised Consolidation: The Political Class in the Brazilian Transition," in Scott Mainwaring, Guillermo O'Donnell, and J. Samuel Valenzuela, eds., *Issues in Democratic Consolidation: The New South American Democracies in Comparative Perspective* (Notre Dame, Ind.: University of Notre Dame Press, 1992), pp. 243–293. A broader perspective is Samuel P. Huntington, *The Third Wave: Democratization in the Late Twentieth Century* (Norman: University of Oklahoma Press, 1991).

23. Hélio Jaguaribe, *Alternativas do Brasil* (Rio de Janeiro: Livraria José Olympio Editora, 1989), p. 123.

24. Wilfred A. Bacchus, *Mission in Mufti: Brazil's Military Regimes, 1964–1985* (New York: Greenwood Press, 1990); and Robert A. Hayes, *The Armed Nation: The Brazilian Corporate Mystique* (Tempe: Arizona State University, 1989), pp. 221–246.

25. See Alfred Stepan, *Rethinking Military Politics: Brazil and the Southern Cone* (Princeton: Princeton University Press, 1988).

26. Eli Diniz and Renato R. Boschi, "Empresarios e Constituente: Continuidades e Rupturas no Modelo de Desenvolvimento Capitalista no Brasil," in Camargo and Diniz, *Continuidade e Mudança no Brasil da Nova República*, pp. 133–134. See also René Dreifuss, *O Jogo da Direita na Nova República* (Petrópolis: Editora Vozes, 1989).

27. Camargo and Diniz, "Introdução: Dilemas da Consolidação Democrática no Brasil," in Camargo and Diniz, eds., *Continuidade e Mudança no Brasil da Nova República*, p. 16.

28. On labor through the 1960s, consult John D. French, *The Brazilian Workers' ABC: Class Conflict & Alliances in Modern São Paulo* (Chapel Hill: University of North Carolina Press, 1992); and Kenneth P. Erickson, *The Brazilian Corporative State and Working-Class Politics* (Berkeley: University of California Press, 1977).

29. See Leôncio Martins Rodrigues, *A CUT: Os Militantes e a Ideologia* (Rio de Janeiro: Editora Paz e Terra, 1990).

30. Sound analyses include Margaret E. Keck, "The New Unionism in the Brazilian Transition" in Stepan, *Democratizing Brazil,* pp. 252–296; Maria Hermínia Tavares de Almeida, "Novo Sindicalismo and Politics in Brazil," in John D. Wirth, Edson de Oliveira Nunes, and Thomas E. Bogenschild, *State and Society in Brazil: Continuity and Change,* (Boulder: Westview Press, 1988), pp. 147–178; and Tavares de Almeida, "Difícil caminho: Sindicatos e política na construção da democracia," in Reis and O'Donnell, *A Democracia no Brasil,* pp. 327–367.

31. Leôncio Martins Rodriques, "Novo cenário para o sindicalismo brasileiro," in João Paulo dos Reis Velloso, ed., *Condições Para a Retomada do Desenvolvimento* (São Paulo: Livraria Nobel, 1991), pp. 185–196; and Amaury de Souza, "Do corporativismo ao (neo) corporativismo: Dilemas da reforma sindical no Brasil," in Velloso, *A Crise Brasileira e a Modernização da Sociedade,* pp. 99–115.

32. See Bjorn Henning Maybury-Lewis, "The Politics of the Possible: The Growth and Political Development of the Brazilian Rural Workers' Trade Union Movement, 1964–1985" (Ph.D. dissertation, Department of Political Science, Columbia University, 1991). Works on agrarian reform include Cândido Grzybowski, *Caminhos e Descaminhos dos Movimentos Sociais do Campo* (Petrópolis: Editora Vozes, 1987).

Chapter 6

1. Many figures come from *Anuário Estatístico do Brasil 1993* (Rio de Janeiro: Fundação Instituto Brasileiro de Geografia e Estatística, 1994) and *Estatísticas Históricas do Brasil* (Rio de Janeiro: Fundação Instituto Brasileiro de Geografia e Estatística, 1987), pp. 17–50.

2. This is the average of the total number of live births for each adult woman.

3. Maria Judith de Brito Muszynski, *O impacto político das migrações internas* (São Paulo: Instituto de Estudos Econômicos, Sociais e Políticos de São Paulo, 1986).

4. I have calculated the populations for urban areas from the 1991 census figures adjusted for four years further change.

5. The best source is Werner Baer, *The Brazilian Economy: Growth and Development,* 3d ed. (New York: Praeger Publishers, 1989). For perspective, see Angus Maddison, "Desempenho da Economia Mundial Desde 1870," in Norman Gall, ed., *Nova Era da Economia Mundial* (São Paulo: Livraria Pioneira Editora, 1987), pp. 19–36. Growth is in terms of Brazilian currency adjusted for inflation translated into dollars by adjusted long-term exchange rate.

6. Relevant data are found in *Estatísticas Históricas do Brasil,* pp. 319–398.

7. Industrial growth is from *Anuário Estatístico do Brasil 1993,* Tables 4.1–4.49 and 4.63–4.88.

8. For the early stages of this industry, see Werner Baer, *The Development of the Brazilian Steel Industry* (Nashville, Tenn.: Vanderbilt University Press, 1969). Also valuable is Nathaniel H. Leff, *The Brazilian Capital Goods Industry, 1920–1964* (Cambridge: Harvard University Press, 1968).

9. See Patrice Franko Jones, *The Brazilian Defense Industry* (Boulder: Westview Press, 1991).

10. Consult Antônio Botelho and Peter H. Smith, eds., *The Computer Question in Brazil: High Technology in a Developing Society* (Cambridge: Massachusetts Institute of Technology Center of International Studies, 1985).

11. Census information on agriculture is in *Anuário Estatística do Brasil 1993*, pp. 267–365. For background, see José Francisco Graziano da Silva, *A Modernização Dolorosa: Estrutura agrária, fronteira agricultural, e trabalhadores rurais no Brasil* (Rio de Janeiro: Zahar Editores, 1982); and Otávio Guilherme Velho, *Sociedade e Agricultura* (Rio de Janeiro: Zahar Editores, 1982).

12. São Paulo dominates with respect to sugarcane with 143 million tons in 1993–1994 and leads refined sugar production with 1.6 million tons as well as the largest part of the 479 *usinas* and distilleries valued at $2.5 billion. Although producing far less cane—an average of under 25 million tons annually—Pernambuco follows closely in refined sugar with 1.5 million tons, then Alagoas at 1.3 million tons. The $6 billion annual industry has 50,000 suppliers of cane and employment of near 1 million. On the alcohol program, see F. Joseph Demetrius, *Brazil's National Alcohol Program: Technology and Development in an Authoritarian Regime* (New York: Praeger Publishers, 1990); and Michael Barzelay, *The Politicized Market Economy: Alcohol in Brazil's Energy Strategy* (Berkeley: University of California Press, 1986).

13. For background, see Kenneth P. Erickson, "The Energy Profile of Brasil," in Kenneth R. Stunkel, ed., *National Energy Profiles* (New York: Praeger Publishers, 1981), pp. 219–269.

14. See Francis A. Lees, James M. Botts, and Rubens Penha Cysne, *Banking and Financial Deepening in Brazil* (London: Macmillan, 1990); and Ary César Minella, *Banqueiros: Organização e poder político no Brasil* (Rio de Janeiro: Editora Espaço e Tempo, 1988).

15. On inflation, see João Paulo dos Reis Velloso, *Hiperinflação, Crescimento e Reformas* (Rio de Janeiro: Editora Campus, 1990); and Mário Henrique Simonsen, "A inflação e o pensamento econômico brasileira," in João Paulo dos Reis Velloso, ed., *Brasil: Agenda Para Sair da Crise—Inflação e Déficit Pública* (Rio de Janeiro: José Olympio Editora, 1990), pp. 15–25.

16. Useful are João Paulo dos Reis Velloso, *A Dívida Externa Tem Solução?* (Rio de Janeiro: Editora Campus, 1990); and Ernesto Lozardo, ed., *Déficit Público Brasileiro: Política Econômica e Ajuste Estrutural* (Rio de Janeiro: Editora Paz e Terra, 1988).

17. Baer's essay in his *The Brazilian Economy* remains the best brief analysis of the Brazilian public sector; Peter Evans, *Dependent Development: The Alliance of Multinational, State and Local Capital in Brazil* (Princeton: Princeton University Press, 1979), probes the subject of its social and political ramifications.

18. João Paulo dos Reis Velloso, "Um pais sem projecto: A crise brasileira e a modernização da sociedade—primeiras ideas," in Velloso, *A Crise Brasileira e a Modernização da Sociedade*, pp. 3–48.

19. See Barbara Stallings and Robert Kaufman, eds., *Debt and Democracy in Latin America* (Boulder: Westview Press, 1989); and Howard Handelman and Werner Baer, eds., *Paying the Cost of Austerity in Latin America* (Boulder: Westview Press, 1988).

20. Calculations are based on data in *Estatísticas Históricas do Brasil*, pp. 540–541, 551–553, and 570. Useful perspective is provided by Winston Fritsch, *External Constraints on Economic Policy in Brazil, 1889–1930* (Pittsburgh: University of Pittsburgh Press, 1988); and Frank Griffith Dawson, *The First Latin American Debt Crisis* (New Haven: Yale University Press, 1990).

21. Getulio Bittencourt, *Brazil in the Euromarket* (São Paulo: Gebam Editora, 1993), pp. 3–10.

22. Sérgio Goldenstein, *A Dívida Externa Brasileira: 1964–1982, Evolução e Crise* (Rio de Janeiro: Editora Guanabara, 1986); and Paulo Davidoff Cruz, *Dívida Externa e Política Econômica: A Experiência Brasileira nos Anos 70* (São Paulo: Editora Brasiliense, 1984).

23. Consult Jeffry A. Frieden, "The Brazilian Borrowing Experience from Miracle to Debacle and Back," *Latin American Research Review* 22, no. 1 (1987):95–131.

24. See Paulo Nogueira Batista Júnior, *Mito e Realidade na Dívida Externa Brasileira* (Rio de Janeiro: Editora Paz e Terra, 1983); and Marcílio Marques Moreira, *The Brazilian Quandary* (New York: Priority Press, 1986).

25. Paulo Roberto Souza, *Quem Paga a Conta: Dívida, Déficit, e Inflação nos Anos 80* (São Paulo: Editora Brasiliense, 1989), pp. 115–160; Regis Bonelli and Pedro S. Malan, "Industrialization, Economic Growth, and Balance of Payments: Brazil, 1970–1984," in John D. Wirth, Edson de Oliveira Nunes, and Thomas E. Bogenschild, eds., *State and Society in Brazil: Continuity and Change* (Boulder: Westview Press, 1988), pp. 13–47; and Edmar L. Bacha and Pedro S. Malan, "Brazil's Debt: From the Miracle to the Fund," in Alfred Stepan, ed., *Democratizing Brazil: Problems of Transition and Consolidation* (New York: Oxford University Press, 1989), pp. 120–140.

26. Wilson Sidney Lobato, *Comércio Exterior do Brasil: Dívidas e Dúvidas* (Rio de Janeiro: Editora Civilização Brasileira, 1977). A perceptive view of Brazil's relationship to the world economy is João Paulo dos Reis Velloso, "A inserção na economia internacional: Oportunidades e riscos," in João Paulo dos Reis Velloso, ed. *Dívida Externa e Desenvolvimento* (Rio de Janeiro: José Olympio Editora, 1991), pp. 3–14. Figures through 1992 are from *Anuário Estatístico do Brasil 1993*, Tables 7.38–7.51.

27. Susan Kaufman Purcell and Robert M. Immerman, eds., *Japan and Latin America in the New Global Order* (Boulder: Lynne Rienner Publishers, 1992), p. 15.

Chapter 7

1. On social conditions, see Hélio Jaguaribe, Wanderley Guilherme dos Santos, Marcel de Paiva Abreu, Winston Fritsch, and Fernando Bastos de Avila, *Brasil, 2000: Para um novo Pacto Social* (Rio de Janeiro: Editora Paz e Terra, 1986).

2. Vilmar Faria, "Mudanças na Composição do Emprego e na Estrutura das Ocupações," in Edmar Bacha and Herbert S. Klein, eds., *A Transição Incompléta: Brasil desde 1945* (Rio de Janeiro: Editora Paz e Terra, 1986), Vol. 1, pp. 73–109; and Charles H. Wood and José Alberto Magno de Carvalho, *The Demography of Inequality in Brazil* (New York: Cambridge University Press, 1988).

3. José Pastore, "Desegualidade e Mobilidade Social: Dez Anos Depois," in Bacha and Klein, *A Transformação Incompléta*, Vol. 2, pp. 31–60.

4. *Estatísticas Históricas do Brasil* (Rio de Janeiro: Instituto Brasileiro de Geografia e Estatística, 1987), pp. 72–78; and *Anuário Estatístico do Brasil 1993*, (Rio de Janeiro: Instituto Brasileiro de Geografia e Estatística, 1994), Table 2.65. A relevant essay is Carlos A. Hasenbalg and Nelson do Valle Silva, "Industrialization, Employment, and Stratification in Brazil," in John D. Wirth, Edson de Oliveira Nunes, and Thomas E. Bogenschild, eds., *State and Society in Brazil: Continuity and Change* (Boulder: Westview Press, 1988), pp. 59–102.

5. See Eva Alterman Blay, "Women, Redemocratization, and Political Alternatives," in Julian M. Chacel, Pamela S. Falk, and David V. Fleischer, eds., *Brazil's Economic and Political*

Future (Boulder: Westview Press, 1988), pp. 199–213; Sonia E. Alvarez, *Engendering Democracy in Brazil: Women's Movements in Transition Politics* (Princeton: Princeton University Press, 1990); and June E. Hahner, *Emancipating the Female Sex: The Struggle for Women's Rights in Brazil, 1850–1940* (Durham, N.C.: Duke University Press, 1990).

6. Pastore, "Desegualidade e Mobilidade Social," pp. 45–51.

7. See "Deu Zebra, Aliás Denise," *IstoÉ*, May 3, 1993, pp. 51–57; and "Cassino no vídeo," *Veja*, April 28, 1993, pp. 66–73.

8. Instituto Brasileiro de Geografia e Estatística, *Indicadores Sociais*, Vol. 2 (Rio de Janeiro: IBGE, 1984), p. 145; and Jane Souto de Oliveira, ed., *O Traço da Desegualidade Social no Brasil* (Rio de Janeiro: IBGE, 1993).

9. Figures are calculated from data in *Anuário Estatístico do Brasil 1993*, Tables 2.182–2.192.

10. Helga Hoffman, "Pobreza e Prosperiedade no Brasil: O que está mudando?" in Bacha and Klein, *A Transformação Incompléta*, p. 85.

11. *Anuário Estatístico do Brasil 1993*, Tables 2.83–2.112.

12. "Eu tenho Aids," *IstoÉ*, August 25, 1993, pp. 66–68.

13. See Amélia Cohn, *Previdência Social e Processo Político no Brasil* (São Paulo: Editora Moderna, 1981).

14. Calculated from data in *Anuário Estatística do Brasil 1993*, Tables 2.62 and 2.63.

15. See Claúdio de Moura Castro, "O Que Está Acontecendo com a Educação no Brasil," in Bacha and Klein, *A Transição Incompléta*, pp. 103–161; and *Anuário Estatístico do Brasil 1993*, Tables 2.125–2.137.

16. Consult Nathaniel H. Leff, *Development and Underdevelopment in Brazil* (Boston: Allen & Unwin, 1982), Vol. 1, p. 214, and Vol. 2, p. 57; and Fay Haussman and Jerry Haar, *Education in Brazil* (Hamden, Conn: Archon Books, 1978).

17. Pastore, "Desegualidade e Mobilidade Social," p. 41; and Rosa Maria Ribeira da Silva, *Sistema de Acompanhamento da Situação da Criança e de Adolescente* (Rio de Janeiro: Instituto Brasileiro de Geografia e Estatística, 1989).

18. A scathing criticism is Edmund Campos Coelho, *A sinecura académica: A ética universitária em questão* (São Paulo: Edições Vértice, 1988).

19. Lúcia Elena Garcia de Oliveira, Rosa Maria Porcano, and Tereza Cristina Araújo Costa, *O Lugar do Negro na Força de Trabalho* (Rio de Janeiro: Instituto Brasileiro de Geografia e Estatística, 1985), pp. 30–58.

20. Michel Bergmann, *Nasce um povo: Estudo antropológico da população Brasileira: Como surgiu, composição racial, evolução futuro* (Petrópolis: Editora Vozes, 1977).

21. Carlos A. Hasenbalg, "Race and Socioeconomic Inequalities in Brazil," in Pierre-Michel Fontaine, ed., *Race, Class and Power in Brazil* (Los Angeles: University of California at Los Angeles Center for Afro-American Studies, 1985), p. 31. On the double disadvantage of black women, see Sueli Carneiro, *Mulher negra: Política governmental e a mulher* (São Paulo: Conselho Estadual da Condição Feminina, 1985).

22. See Katia M. de Queiros Mattoso, *To Be a Slave in Brazil, 1550–1888* (New Brunswick, N.J.: Rutgers University Press, 1986); Thomas Flory, "Race and Social Control in Independent Brazil," *Journal of Latin American Studies* 9, no. 2 (November 1977):199–224; and Stuart B. Schwartz, "Recent Trends in the Study of Slavery in Brazil," *Luso-Brazilian Review* 25, no. 1 (Summer 1988):1–25.

23. Supplementing his *Black into White: Race and Nationality in Brazilian Thought* (New York: Oxford University Press, 1974) is Thomas E. Skidmore, "Biracial U.S. vs. Multiracial Brazil: Is the Contrast Still Valid?" *Journal of Latin American Studies* 25, no. 2 (May 1993):373–386.

24. UNESCO-sponsored studies that demolished scholarly bases for this myth include Charles Wagley, ed., *Race and Class in Rural Brazil* (Paris: UNESCO, 1952); and Roger Bastide and Florestan Fernandes, eds., *Relações raciais entre negroes e brancos em São Paulo* (São Paulo: Companhia Editora Nacional, 1953). These pioneering works led to Fernandes's monumental 1965 study, available in English as *The Negro in Brazilian Society* (New York: Columbia University Press, 1969).

25. Lélia Gonzalez and Carlos Hasenbalg, *Lugar do negro* (Rio de Janeiro: Editora Marco Zero, 1982); and Ana Lucia E.F. Valente *Ser Negro no Brasil Hoje* (São Paulo: Editora Moderna, 1987). See also George Reid Andrews, *Blacks and Whites in São Paulo, Brazil, 1888–1988* (Madison: University of Wisconsin Press, 1991).

26. See Nelson do Valle Silva and Carlos A. Hasenbalg, *Relações raciais no Brasil contemporâneo* (Rio de Janeiro: Rio Fundo Editora, 1992)

27. See Amaury de Souza and Bolívar Lamounier, "A feitura da nova constituição: Um reexame da cultura política brasileira," in Bolívar Lamounier, ed., *De Geisel a Collor: A balanço da transisão* (São Paulo: IDESP/Sumaré, 1990), pp. 81–104.

28. Fontaine, "Blacks and the Search for Power in Brazil" in Fontaine, ed., *Race, Class and Power in Brazil*, pp. 56–72.

29. Engaged literature includes Abdias do Nascimento, ed., *O Negro Revoltado* (Rio de Janeiro: Edições GRD, 1968); and Clóvis Moura, *Brasil: As Raízes do Protesto Negro* (São Paulo: Global Editora, 1983).

30. The 1984 class of the Military Academy was 6 percent blacks and mulattoes, up from 2.3 percent in 1962. Frank McCann, "The Military," in Michael L. Conniff and Frank D. McCann, eds., *Modern Brazil: Elites and Masses in Historical Perspective* (Lincoln: University of Nebraska Press, 1989), p. 72.

31. Centro de Estudos Nipo-Brasileiros, *Pesquisa de População de descendentes de Japoneses residentes no Brasil* (São Paulo: São Paulo Jinbun Kagaku Kenkyûsho, 1990).

32. See Instituto Superior Brasileiro-Italiano de Estudos e Pesquisas, *Imigrção Italiana* (Porto Alegre, Brazil: Universidade de Caxias do Sul, 1979).

33. Consult Claude Fahd Hajjar, *Imigração Arabe: Cem anos de reflexão* (São Paulo: Icone Editora, 1985).

34. See Jeff H. Lesser, "Continuity and Change Within an Immigrant Community: The Jews of São Paulo, 1924–1945," *Luso-Brazilian Review* 25, no. 2 (Winter 1988):45–58; and Lesser, "From Peddlers to Proprietors: Lebanese, Syrian, and Jewish Immigrants in Brazil, 1930–1945," in Albert Hourani and Nadim Shehadi, eds., *The Lebanese in the World: A Century of Emigration* (New York: St. Martin's Press, 1991).

35. See "Fé en desencanto," *Veja*, December 25, 1991, pp. 32–38, which gives the ratio of priests to potential parishioners as 7,100 to 1 in 1970 and 10,600 to 1 in the early 1990s.

36. On the Church's history, see Paulo Krischke, *A Igreja e as Crises Políticas no Brasil* (Petrópolis: Editora Vozes, 1979); Thomas C. Bruneau, *The Political Transformation of the Brazilian Catholic Church* (London: Cambridge University Press, 1974); Bruneau, *The Church in Brazil: The Politics of Religion* (Austin: University of Texas Press, 1982); and Scott

Mainwaring, *The Catholic Church and Politics in Brazil, 1916–1985* (Stanford: Stanford University Press, 1986).

37. Essential are Ralph della Cava, ed., *A Igreja em Flagrante: Catolicismo e Sociedade na Imprensa Brasileira, 1964–1980* (Rio de Janeiro: Editora Marco Zero, 1985); and his "Catholicism and Society in Twentieth-Century Brazil," *Latin American Research Review* 11, no. 2 (1976):7–50. See also Ralph della Cava and Paula Montero, *E O Verbo Se Faz Imagen: A Igreja Católica e os Meios de Comunicação no Brasil, 1962–1989* (Petrópolis: Editora Vozes, 1990); and Warren Edward Hewitt, *Base Christian Communities and Social Change in Brazil* (Lincoln: University of Nebraska Press, 1991).

38. See Ralph della Cava, "The Vatican and the Roman Catholic Church in Brazil, Policy, 1985–1990" (New York: Columbia University Institute of Iberian and Latin American Studies, 1991) and Paulo Krischke and Scott Mainwaring, eds., *A igreja nas bases em tempo de transisão* (Porto Alegre: L & PM Editores, 1986).

39. The division of São Paulo left Cardinal Arns with 241 parishes in an area embracing a population of 7.6 billion.

40. Consult Ralph della Cava, "The Ten-Year Crusade Towards the Third Christian Millennium: An Account of Evangelization 2000 and Lumen 2000" (New York: Columbia University and New York University Consortium on Latin American Studies, 1990).

41. See Eduardo Hoornaert, *O Cristianismo Moreno do Brasil* (Petrópolis: Editora Vozes, 1991); and Rowan Ireland, *Kingdoms Come: Religion and Politics in Brazil* (Pittsburgh: University of Pittsburgh Press, 1991).

42. Consult Francesco Cartaxo Rohm, *Penecostais no Brasil: Uma interpretação Sócio-religiosa* (Petrópolis: Editora Vozes, 1985).

43. Basic is Diana D. Brown, *Umbanda: Religion and Politics in Urban Brazil* (Ann Arbor: University of Michigan Research Press, 1985).

44. Especially useful is David Hess, *Spirits and Scientists: Ideology, Spiritism, and Brazilian Culture* (University Park: Pennsylvania State University Press, 1991).

Chapter 8

1. The place to begin on Brazil's culture is with Charles Wagley, *An Introduction to Brazil*, rev. ed. (New York: Columbia University Press, 1971); for greater detail, see Fernando de Azevedo, *A Cultura Brasileira* 4th ed. (São Paulo, Edições Melhoramento, 1964).

2. See Renato Ortiz, *Cultura Brasileira e Identidade Nacional* (São Paulo: Editora Brasiliense, 1985); and Ortiz, *A Moderna Tradição Brasileira* (São Paulo: Editora Brasiliense, 1988).

3. See Roberto da Matta, "The Quest for Citizenship in a Relational Universe," in John D. Wirth, Edson de Oliveira Nunes, and Thomas E. Bogenschild, eds., *State and Society in Brazil: Continuity and Change* (Boulder: Westview Press, 1987), pp. 307–335, especially p. 315.

4. Wagley, *An Introduction to Brazil*, pp. 167–185. Also see Linda Lewin, *Politics and Parentela in Paraíba: A Case Study of Family-Based Oligarchy in Brazil* (Princeton: Princeton University Press, 1987).

5. Roberto da Matta, *O que faz o brasil, Brasil?* (Rio de Janeiro: Editora Rocco, 1984), pp. 23–33. These ideas are expanded upon in Roberto DaMatta, *A Casa e a Rua: Espaço, cidadania, mulher e morte no Brazil* (São Paulo: Editora Brasiliense, 1985).

6. Roberto da Matta, "The Ethic of Umbanda and the Spirit of Messianism: Reflections on the Brazilian Model," in Thomas C. Bruneau and Philippe Faucher, eds., *Authoritarian Capitalism: Brazil's Contemporary Economic and Political Development* (Boulder: Westview Press, 1981), pp. 239–264.

7. Ibid., p. 251.

8. See Anthony Leeds, "Brazilian Careers and Social Structure," *American Anthropologist* 66, no. 6 (December 1964):1321–1347.

9. Consult da Matta, *O que faz o brasil, Brasil?* pp. 97–101; and Lívia Barbosa, *Jeitinho brasileiro ou a arte de ser mais igual que os outros* (Rio de Janeiro: Editora Campus, 1992).

10. See Joseph Dean Straubhaar, "Mass Communications and the Elites," in Michael L. Conniff and Frank D. McCann, eds., *Modern Brazil: Elites and Masses in Historical Perspective* (Lincoln: University of Nebraska Press, 1989), pp. 225–245. Renato Ortiz argues in *A Moderna Tradição Brasileira* that Brazilian intellectuals have become co-opted into the commercialization of culture because "popular" has become equated with mass consumption through the influence of electronic media.

11. In 1991 Globo had revenues of $650 million compared to $140 million for SBT, $96 million for Bandeirantes, and $72 million for Manchete. By 1994 Globo's revenues exceeded $1.4 billion.

12. One can begin exploration of Brazilian literature with Claude L. Hulet, *Brazilian Literature* (Washington, D.C.: Georgetown University Press, 1974); and Afrânio Coutinho, *An Introduction to Literature of Brazil* (New York: Columbia University Press, 1969).

13. Consult Mário de Andrade, *A Imagem de Mário: Textos extraídos da obra* (Rio de Janeiro: Edições Alumbramento, 1984).

14. Alfredo Wagner Berno de Almeida, *Jorge Amado: Política e Literatura: Um estudo sobre a trajectoria intelectual de Jorge Amado* (Rio de Janeiro: Editora Campus, 1979); and Paulo Tavares, *O Baiano Jorge Amado e sua Obra* (Rio de Janeiro: Editora Record, 1980).

15. Affonso Arinos de Mello Franco, *Um Estadista da República*, 3 vols. (Rio de Janeiro: Livraria José Olympio Editora, 1955); and his *Evolução da Crise Brasileira* (São Paulo: Companhia Editora Nacional, 1965).

16. Consult Maria Ángela D'Incar, ed., *O Saber Militante* (Rio de Janeiro: Editora Paz e Terra, 1988).

17. In English a place to begin is David P. Appleby, *The Music of Brazil* (Austin: University of Texas Press, 1963); and Gerard Béhague, *Music in Latin America: an Introduction* (Englewood Cliffs, N.J.: Prentice-Hall, 1979). On more recent periods, see Charles A. Perrone, *Masters of Contemporary Brazilian Song* (Austin: University of Texas Press, 1989).

18. Eduardo Storni, *Villa-Lobos* (Madrid: Espasa-Calpe S.A., 1988), is useful, as are Bruno Kiefer, *Villa-Lobos e o Modernismo na Música Brasileira* (Porto Alegre: Editora Movimento, 1986); and Museu Villa-Lobos, *Villa-Lobos, sua Obra* (Rio de Janeiro: Museu Villa-Lobos, 1987), the third edition of a very detailed work.

19. Fundamental are Ruy Castro, *Chega de Saudade* (São Paulo: Companhia das Letras, 1990); and Almir Chediak, ed., *Songbook da Bossa Nova*, 4 vols. (Rio de Janeiro: Editora Lumiar, 1990).

20. Consult Ruy Castro, *O Anjo Pornográfico* (São Paulo: Companhia das Letras, 1992); and Sabato Magaldi, *Nelson Rodrigues: Dramaturgia e encenações* (São Paulo: Editora Perspectiva, 1987).

21. Gláuber Rocha, *O século da cinema* (Rio de Janeiro: Editorial Alhambra, 1983).

22. Beautiful plates of his extraordinary works are in Carlos Alberto Cerqueira Lemos, *The Art of Brazil* (New York: Harper and Row, 1983), pp. 110–135.

23. Consult Sylvia Ficher and Marlene Milan Acayaba, *Arquitetura Moderna Brasileira* (São Paulo: Editora Projeto, 1987).

24. See pictures of Neimeyer's works in Lemos, *The Art of Brazil*, pp. 260–263; Brasília is treated in Alex Shoumatoff, *The Capital of Hope* (New York: Coward, McCann and Geoghegen, 1980).

Chapter 9

1. The first serious systematic studies beyond article length were William Perry, *Contemporary Brazilian Foreign Policy: The International Strategy of an Emerging Power, Foreign Policy Papers,* Vol. 2, No. 6 (Beverly Hills, Calif.: Sage Publications, 1976); Ronald M. Schneider, *Brazil: Foreign Policy of a Future World Power* (Boulder: Westview Press, 1977); and Wayne A. Selcher, *Brazil's Multilateral Relations: Between First and Third Worlds* (Boulder: Westview Press, 1978). Brazilian writers joined in with Hélio Jaguaribe et al., *Leituras de Política Internacional: A Nova Orden Internacional* (Brasília: Editora Universidade de Brasília, 1982); and Celso Lafer, *Paradoxos e Possibilidades: Estudos sobre a ordem mundial e sobre a política exterior do Brasil num sistema internacional em transformação* (Rio de Janeiro: Editora Nova Fronteira, 1982). A useful historical survey is Amado Luiz Cervo and Clodoaldo Bueno, *História da Política Exterior do Brasil* (São Paulo: Editora Ática, 1992).

2. Frank McCann, "Brazilian Foreign Relations in the Twentieth Century," in Wayne A. Selcher, ed., *Brazil in the International System: The Rise of a Middle Power* (Boulder: Westview Press, 1981), p. 1.

3. Alvin Rubenstein, "Editor's Preface," in Robert Wesson, *The United States and Brazil: The Limits of Influence* (New York: Praeger Publishers, 1981), p. vi.

4. Most useful are Frank D. McCann, *The Brazilian-American Alliance, 1937–1945* (Princeton: Princeton University Press, 1973); and Stanley E. Hilton, *Brazil and the Great Powers, 1930–1939* (Austin: University of Texas Press, 1975).

5. A sound work on U.S.–Latin American relations is Abraham F. Lowenthal, *Partners in Conflict: The United States and Latin America* (Baltimore: Johns Hopkins University Press, 1987).

6. João Augusto de Araújo Castro, "A Brazilian View of a Changing World," lecture at Temple University, Philadelphia, November 17, 1973.

7. Paulo Cabral de Mello, "O Brasil e os Problemas Econômicos Mundiais," *Revista Brasileira de Estudos Políticos* 42 (January 1976):155–156.

8. Albert Fishlow, "Flying Down to Rio: Perspectives on U.S.-Brazil Relations," *Foreign Affairs* 57, no. 2 (Winter 1978–1979):387–405; Fishlow, "The United States and Brazil: The Case of the Missing Relationship," *Foreign Affairs* 60, no. 4 (Spring 1982):904–923; and Roger W. Fontaine, "The End of a Beautiful Relationship," *Foreign Policy* 28 (Fall 1977):166–174.

9. Ronald M. Schneider, memorandum letter to Acting Assistant Secretary of State for Inter-American Affairs Charles Bray, "Notes on Winning Battles but Losing a War," February 18, 1977.

10. Best on this period is E. Bradford Burns, *The Unwritten Alliance: Rio Branco and Brazilian-American Relations* (New York: Columbia University Press, 1966).

11. See Stanley E. Hilton, *O Brasil e a Crise Internacional* (Rio de Janeiro: Editora Civilização Brasileira, 1977).

12. João Mascarenhas de Moraes, *Memórias* (Rio de Janeiro: Livraria José Olympio Editora, 1969).

13. Phillip Agee, *Inside the Company: CIA Diary* (New York: Stonehill Press, 1975), esp. p. 362.

14. Jan Knippers Black, *United States Penetration of Brazil* (Philadelphia: University of Pennsylvania Press, 1977); Phyllis R. Parker, *Brazil and the Quiet Intervention, 1964* (Austin: University of Texas Press, 1979); and Robert Wesson, *The United States and Brazil: Limits of Influence* (New York: Praeger, *1982)*, pp. 33–48. Ruth Leacock, *Requiem for Revolution: The United States and Brazil, 1961–1969* (Kent, Ohio: Kent State University Press, 1990), is refuted by Lincoln A. Gordon in a book review in *Journal of International Studies and World Affairs*, 32, no. 2 (Summer 1990):165–178.

15. See Robert Wesson, *The United States and Brazil*, pp. 75–103; and Scott D. Tollefson, "Brazilian Arms Transfers, Ballistic Missiles, and Foreign Policy: The Search for Autonomy" (unpublished Ph.D. dissertation, Paul H. Nitze School of Advanced International Studies, The Johns Hopkins University, 1991).

16. Ramiro Saraiva Guerreiro, "Brazilian-U.S. Relations" in Julien M. Chacel, Pamela S. Falk, and David V. Fleischer, eds., *Brazil's Economic and Political Future* (Boulder: Westview Press, 1988), p. 255.

17. Olavo Egydio Setubal, "Brazil's Foreign Policy in the New Republic," in ibid., p. 241.

18. The Panel on U.S.-Brazil Relations, *The United States and Brazil: Structuring a Mature Relationship* (Washington, D.C.: Center for Strategic and International Studies, 1988), pp. 9–10.

19. Ibid., pp. 27, 37. Also of interest is Abraham F. Lowenthal, *Brazil and the United States* (New York: Foreign Policy Headline Series, May–June 1986).

20. Carlos Augusto R. Santos-Neves, "The South and the New World Order: A Personal View" (Durham: University of New Hampshire, Center for International Perspectives, November 12, 1990), p. 12.

21. Consult Wayne A. Selcher, "Brazil and the Southern Cone Subsystem," in Pope Atkins, ed., *South America in the 1990s* (Boulder: Westview Press, 1990), pp. 87–120.

22. Rubens Ricupero in Gabinete Civil (presidential staff), *III Encontro Governo-Sociedade: O Brasil na virada de século* (cited hereafter by short title) (Brasília: Presidência da República, 1986), p. 26.

23. See Alexandre de S.C. Barros, "The Formation and Implementation of Brazilian Foreign Policy: Itamaraty and the New Actors," in Heraldo Muñoz and Joseph S. Tulchin, eds., *Latin American Nations in World Politics* (Boulder: Westview Press, 1984), pp. 30–44.

24. Consult Schneider, *Brazil: Foreign Policy of a Future World Power,* pp. 68–77, and 149–153.

25. Carlos de Meira Mattos, *Brasil: Geopolítica e Destino* (Rio de Janeiro: Livraria José Olympio Editora, 1975), p. 72.

26. *III Encontro Governo-Sociedade;* and Gabinete Civil, *Cenário Internacional, Textos* (Brasília: Presidência da República, 1986).

27. Ambassador Paulo Tarso Flecha de Lima in *III Encontro Governo-Sociedade*, p. 28.

28. Flecha de Lima, "Condicionantes da Ação Externa do Brasil," *in Cenário Internacional*, p. 60.

29. Rubens Ricupero in *III Encontro Governo-Sociedade*, p. 23. See also his "O Brasil e o Futuro do Comércio Internacional," in Norman Gall, ed., *Nova Era da Economia Mundial* (São Paulo: Livraria Pioneira Editora, 1987), pp. 87–110.

30. Flecha de Lima in *III Encontro Governo-Sociedade*, p. 28.

31. Carlos Augusto R. Santos Neves, "South America and North America: Prospects for the 1990s" (New Orleans: Tulane University, Forty-seventh Congress of Americanists, July 9, 1991), pp. 2–9.

32. For suggested implications, see Ambassador Carlos Augusto R. Santos-Neves, "O Brasil e o Futuro: Linhas para um Presença do Brasil na Vida Internacional" (Rio de Janeiro: Finep, December 1992); and his "South America and the Emerging Blocks" (New York, Columbia University Seminar on Brazil, March 26, 1992), pp. 8–10.

33. Schneider, *Brazil: Foreign Policy of a Future World Power*, p. 3.

34. Santos Neves, "South America and North America," p. 18. Compare with Marcos Castrioto de Azambuja, "Conjuntura Internacional: Centros Mundiais do Poder," *Revista da Escola Superior de Guerra* 7, no. 17 (July 1991):9–29, decrying the tendency of the major powers to undertake collective interventionist actions to push their versions of democracy, human rights, and environmental preservation.

About the Book and Author

Myths and misconceptions about Brazil, the world's fifth largest and most populous country, are long-standing. Far from a sleeping giant, Brazil is the southern hemisphere's most important country. Entering its second decade of civilian constitutional government after a protracted period of military rule, it has also recently achieved sustained economic growth. Nevertheless, the nation's population of 157 million is divided by huge inequities in income and education, which are largely correlated with race, and crime rates have spiraled as a result of conflicts over land and resources.

Ronald Schneider, a close observer of Brazilian society and politics for many decades, provides a comprehensive multidimensional portrait of this, Latin America's most complex country. He begins with an insightful description of its diverse regions and then analyzes the historical processes of Brazil's development from the European encounter in 1500 to independence in 1822, the middle-class revolution in 1930, the military takeover in 1964, and the return to democracy after 1984. Schneider goes on to offer a detailed treatment of contemporary government and politics, including the 1994 elections. His closing chapters analyze the economy and society, and explore Brazil's rich cultural heritage and assess Brazil's place in the international arena.

Ronald M. Schneider is professor of political science at Queens College–the City University of New York.

Index

"A Banda" (The Band) (Buarque), 199
Abdenur, Roberto Pinto Ferreira, 215
Abertura (political opening), 95, 99, 103, 135
"Abre Alas" (Open Wings) (Gonzaga), 198
Acre, 23
  representation for, 131
  revolt in, 208
Additional Act (1834), 39
ADEP. *See* Democratic Parliamentary Action; Popular Democratic Action
A Falecida (The Dead Woman) (Rodrigues), 199, 200
Affonso, Paulo, 34, 148
Afilhados, 193
Afro-Brazilians, xi
  Catholic Church and, 185, 189
  education for, 183, 184
  illiteracy rate for, 183
  life expectancy for, 183
  number of, 183–184, 184–185
  status of, 169–170, 184, 185
  voting by, 116
"A Garota de Ipanema" (The Girl from Ipanema) (Jobim), 198
Agee, Philip, 210
Agreste, 28, 32
Agriculture, 12–14, 119, 222(n17)
  diversification in, 65
  employment in, 79, 98, 171, 174
  exports from, 46
  modernization of, 137, 141–145, 147
  potential for, 144–145, 147
Agulhas Negras (Black Needles), 11
AIDS, problems with, 177
AI–5. *See* Institutional Act No. 5
Aircraft industry, 142
AL. *See* Liberal Alliance

Alagoas, 33
Album da Família (*Family Album*) (Rodrigues), 199
Albuquerque Lima, Afonso de, 92
Alcoa, Alumar project of, 30
Alcohol program, development of, 149–150
Alencar, Marcello, 124
Almeida, José Américo de, 63, 64, 66
Alta Floresta, 20
Alumar project, 30
A Maça no Escuro (*The Apple in the Dark*) (Lispector), 197
Amado, Jorge, 34, 191, 196–197
Amapá, 27–28
  representation for, 131
Amazon River, xi, 1, 4, 21, 23 (photo)
  deforestation along, 24 (photo)
  development along, 25–26
  environmentalists and, 148
Amin, Espiridão, 124
Amorim, Celso, 215
Anápolis, 18
Andrada, Antônio Carlos Ribeiro da, 56, 57
Andrada e Silva, José Bonifácio, 38
Andrade, Joaquim Pedro de, 200
Andrade, Mário de, 196, 200
Andrade Vieira, José Eduardo, 129
Angra plants, 148
Anísio, Chico (Francisco Aníso de Oliveira Paulo Filho), 201
ANL. *See* National Liberating Alliance
Anti-Communists, 63, 84
"Aquarela do Brasil" (Barroso), 198
Aracajú, 33
Aracruz, 144
Aragão, Renato "Didi," 201
Araguaia, 25

Aranha, Oswaldo, foreign policy and, 208
Arapiraca, 33
Araújo Castro, João Augusto de, 206–207
Araújo Lima, Pedro de, 39
Arbiter-ruler dilemma, 88–91
Architecture, 202–203
ARENA. *See* National Renovating Alliance
A República dos Sonos (*The Dream
Republic*) (Piñon), 197
Argentina
relations with, 204, 214
stagnation in, 210
trade with, 168
Arida, Pérsio, 129
Arinos de Mello Franco, Afonso (Affonso),
197
Ariquemes, 20–21
Armaments industry, 142
Armed forces. *See* Military
Arns, Paulo Evaristo, 187, 188, 232(n39)
Arraes, Miguel, 83, 125
Art, xiii, 202–203
Articulation faction, 118
Assalto ao Trem Pagador (*The Paytrain
Robbery*) (Farias), 200
Authoritarianism, 60, 88, 96
Automobile industry, 142, 142 (photo)
foreign investment in, 167
Autonomous agencies/foundations,
employment in, 156
Azeredo, Eduardo, 124

Babaçu region, 28, 30
Babenco, Hector, 201
Bacha, Edmar, 129
"Bachianas Brasileiras" (Villa-Lobos), 198
Baer, Werner, 155
Bahia, 33–34, 35
conspiracy in, 37
population of, 139
Bahianos, characteristics of, 193
Balance of payments, 157–161, 164–168
Bandeirante planes, 142
Bandeirantes, 36, 195
Bandeiras, 36
Baníwa Indians, 26
Bank of Brazil, 151, 157

Bank of Guanabara, 118
Barbalho, Jader, 125
Barbosa, Ruy, 46, 47, 52–54, 196, 197
Barra Mansa, 11
Barreto, Bruno, 200–201
Barros, Adhemar de, 69, 70, 74, 75, 77, 80
Barroso, Ari Evangelista, 198
Bauru, 8
Becker Yaconis, Cacilda, 199
Belchior Marques, João, 82
Belgo-Mineiro, 9
Belo Horizonte, 9
Bernardes, Artur da Silva, 54, 55
Bico de Papagaio (Parrot's Beak), 27
Birth control, misinformation about, 177
Blacks. *See* Afro-Brazilians
Blancos (Liberals), 42
Blumenau, 15, 15 (photo)
BNDE. *See* National Economic
Development Bank
BNDES. *See* National Economic and Social
Development Bank
Boa Viagem district, 32
Boa Vista, 26
Boias frias, number of, 145
Bolivia
relations with, 208, 214
stagnation in, 210
Bom Jesús de Lapa, pilgrimages to, 189
Borborema Plateau, 31, 32
Borges de Medeiros, Antônio Augusto, 53,
54, 57
Botofogo District, 10 (photo)
Braga, Roberto Carlos, 198
Braga, Sonia, 201
Brasília, 77
Brasília planes, 142
"Brazil at the Turn of the Century,"
215–216
Brazilian Center of Analysis and Planning
(CEBRAP), 128
Brazilian Communist Party (PCB), 62, 70,
73, 108, 119, 135, 223(n23)
ANL and, 63
support for, 115, 116
See also Communist Party of Brazil

Brazilian Democratic Movement (MDB), 90, 91, 93, 97
support for, 96, 99, 111
Brazilian Expeditionary Force (FEB), 66
Brazilian Institute of Democratic Action (IBAD), 83
Brazilian Labor Party (PTB), 67, 71, 82, 85, 100, 119, 129, 135
potential of, 69–70
PSD and, 68, 75, 79, 84, 86
support for, 107, 115, 116–117, 122, 124, 125, 126
Brazilian Social Democracy Party (PSDB), 109, 119, 128, 129
support for, 116, 122, 124, 126
Brazilian Socialist Party (PSB), 119
support for, 115, 116, 125, 126
Brazilian Workers' Confederation (CTB), 70
Bráz Pereira Gomez, Wenceslau, 52, 53
Bresser Pereira, Luíz Carlos, 108, 109, 129
Bresser Plan, 108
Britto, Antônio, 121, 124
Brizola, Leonel, 77, 102, 110, 111, 116, 118, 120, 124
Goulart and, 87
National Liberation Front and, 83
support for, 84, 85, 86
trabalhista and, 74
Buaiz, Vitor, 125
Buarque, Chico (Francisco Buarque de Holanda), 198–199
Burle Marx, Roberto, 203

Cabeças Cortadas (Severed Heads) (Rocha), 200
Caboclos, 36
Cabo São Roque, 32
Cabral, Bernardo, 115, 125
Cabral, Pedro Álvares, 35
Cabral de Mello, Paulo, 207
Cachoeira de Itapemirim, 12
Café Filho, João, government of, 74–77
Caixa Econômico Federal, 151
Caldas, Eduardo Jorge, 129
"Calhambeque" (The Jalopy) (Buarque), 198
Camaçari, 33

Camaçari Petrochemical Pole, 143
Camargo Neto, Affonso, 112
Camelôs (street vendors), 172
Campina Grande, 32
Campinas, 7
Campista, Ary, 135
Campo Grande, 19
Campos, 11
Campos, Roberto, 90
Campos Salles, Manuel Ferraz de, 45, 50
Camus, Marcel, 199
Candomblé, 190
Canudos, destruction of, 49–50
Capitães de Areia (*The Beach Waifs*) (Amado), 196
Carajás, 25
mineral deposits in, 26
Cardoso, Fernando Henrique, xii, 23, 109, 113, 121, 123, 132, 197
economic growth and, 129
foreign investment and, 167
foreign relations and, 215
government by, 127–128
inauguration of, 127 (photo)
internal debt and, 155
PMDB and, 128
privatization and, 152
support for, 124, 126, 130
Cardoso de Melo, Zélia, 115, 117–118
Cardoso Plan. *See* Real Plan
Cariocas, characteristics of, 192, 193
Carnaúba, 30, 32
Carrero, Tônia, 199
Cartorial state, 41, 48, 58, 69, 80, 132
Caruaru, 32
Carvalho, Clóvis, 129
Carvalho e Mello, Sebastião José de, 37
Casa-Grande e Senzala (*The Masters and the Slaves*) (Freyre), 183, 197
Cascavel, 14
Castelo Branco, Humberto de Alencar, 70, 86, 95
arbiter-ruler dilemma and, 88–91
direct elections and, 90
foreign debt and, 160–161
Kubitschek and, 89
Castro, Fidel, 77, 206

Catholic Church, 92, 170
  Afro-Brazilians and, 185, 189
  colonization and, 35
  dominance of, 187–188
  human rights violations and, 93
  politics and, 63, 86, 91, 134, 187–188
  understaffing of, 189
Catholicism
  dissident strains of, 187–188
  folk, 189
  Umbanda and, 194
Caxias, 40, 41, 42, 43, 44
Caxias do Sul, 16
Ceará, 30–31, 32
  population of, 139
CEBRAP. *See* Brazilian Center of Analysis
  and Planning
CEBs. *See* Ecclesial base communities
Center-Right alliance, 108–109, 116
Center-West, 17–21, 17 (map)
Central Bank, 151, 154, 165, 166
CGT. *See* General Workers Center; General
  Workers Confederation
Chamber of Deputies, 47, 50, 62, 77, 82, 84,
  91, 93
  Collor and, 120
  election to, 96
  reapportionment of, 131
  seats in, 126, 222(n20)
Chapada de Araipe, 31
Chapada Diamantina, 9
Chaves, Aureliano, 103, 111, 112
Children, 174 (photo), 181 (photo)
  street, xi–xii, 176 (photo)
Chile, stagnation in, 210
China, relations with, 216
Chlorochemical Pole, 143
"Chôros" (Villa-Lobos), 198
Christian Democratic Party (PDC), 75,
  108, 119
  PDS and, 122
  support for, 115, 117, 122
Cinta Larga Indians, 21
Cities, population of, 3 (table)
Clientelism, 65, 74, 80, 156, 188, 195
Clothing industry, 144
CNBB. *See* National Conference of
  Brazilian Bishops

CNI. *See* National Confederation of
  Industries
CNTI. *See* National Confederation of
  Industrial Workers
Coal, production of, 149
Coffee, 54
  export of, 45, 51, 137
  immigrants and, 7
  prices of, 56–57
  production of, 40–41, 145
Cohen Plan, 63
Coimbra, Marcos, 115
Collor de Melo, Fernando, 123, 127, 214
  commerce and, 168
  external debt and, 159, 166
  government by, 117–119
  inflation and, 153
  internal debt and, 154
  priorities of, 114–115
  privatization and, 152
  problems for, 113, 119, 120–122
  rise of, 110–112, 114
Collor Plan, 115, 117, 154
Colombia, relations with, 214
Colorado Party (Conservatives), 42
Comadres, 193
Communications, 147–151, 191–192
  government monopoly on, 156
Communist Party of Brazil (PCdoB), 62,
  108, 223(n23)
  support for, 115, 116, 126
  See also Brazilian Communist Party
Communists, 70, 72, 77, 78
  armed forces and, 133
  problems with, 73
  threat from, 64, 84
Computer industry, growth in, 143
CONCLAT. *See* National Conference of the
  Working Class
Confederation of the Equator, 39
Congress, reapportionment of, 131
Congressional building, 76 (photo) 121
  (photo)
Conselheiro, Antônio, 49
Conservative Party, 41, 42, 44
Conservative Republican Party (PRC),
  52, 53

Constant, Benjamin, 44
Constitutional reform, 123–127, 130
Contadora group, 214
Copadres, 193
Coronelismo, 36, 48
Correia de Melo, Francisco de Assis, 89
Corruption, 89, 156
Corumbá, thermoelectric plant at, 19, 214
Costa, Lúcio, 203
Costa e Silva, Artur da, 90, 95, 206
    foreign debt and, 160
    humanization and, 91–92
    Revolutionary Supreme Command and,
        89
    U.S.-Brazilian relations and, 211
Council of Ministers, 82
Council of the Republic, 109
Couto e Silva, Golbrey do, 86, 99, 100
Covas, Mário, 108, 109, 112, 124, 128
Crato, 31
Criciúma, 15
Cruzado Plan, 106, 110, 126, 165, 167
    collapse of, 135–136
    inflation and, 153
CSN. *See* National Steel Company
CTB. *See* Brazilian Workers' Confederation
Cuba, relations with, 214
Cuiabá, 20
Culture, xiii, 191
    commercialization of, 233(n10)
    media and, 192–195
    written word and, 195–197
Curitiba, 13
CUT. *See* Single Workers Center
CVRD. *See* Vale do Rio Doce Company

Da Matta, Roberto, 193, 194
Dantas, Francisco Clementino de San
    Thiago, 85, 86
D'Avila Mello, Ednardo, 97
Death squads, xi, 93
Decompression (*distensão*), 95–97, 99
Deforestation, 21, 23, 24 (photo)
De Gaulle, Charles, 82
Delfim Netto, Antônio, 91, 99, 100
De Melo, Custódio: revolt by, 47
Democracy, 67–73, 86–87, 97, 99, 236(n34)
    institutionalized, 130

liberal, 66, 70–71
    promotion of, xii, 73–80
    representative, 131
    resistance to, 132–133, 134
    transition to, 104, 105–106, 109–112
Democratic Alliance, 103–104, 105, 107
Democratic Parliamentary Action (ADEP),
    83
Democratic Party, 56, 61
Democratic Social Party (PDS), 104, 119
    ARENA and, 100
    Maluf and, 103
    PDC and, 122
    support for, 100, 102, 107, 110, 115, 116,
        121–122
Democratic Workers' Party (PDT), 100,
    102, 106, 119
    support for, 107, 110, 115, 116, 122, 125,
        126
Demographics, shifts in, 137–140
Deodoro da Fonseca, Manuel, 44, 47, 52,
    55, 61
Deus e o Diabo na Terra do Sol (God and the
    Devil in the Scorching Land) (*Black
    God, White Devil*) (Rocha), 200
Development. *See* Economic development
Developmentalism, 67, 74
Devil's Throat (Garganta de Diabo), 14
Dias Gomes, Alfredo, 199
Di Cavalcanti (Emiliano Augusto
    Cavalcanti de Albuquerque Melo),
    191, 202
Discrimination, 182–187, 184–185
Divinópolis, 9
Docenave, 144
Dr. Getúlio (Gullar), 199
Doin Vieira, Paulo Afonso, 125
Dom Casmurro (Machado de Assis), 196
Domingos, Guilherme Afif, 112
Dona Flor e Seus Dois Maridos (*Dona Flor
    and Her Two Husbands*) (Amado),
    196, 201
Drug traffic, 214
Drug war, 212
Duarte, Anselmo, 200
Dulles, J. F., 210
Duros, dominance by, 91–95

Dutra, Eurico Gaspar, 63, 67, 71, 80, 209
  conservative republic and, 68–70
  liberal democracy and, 66

EAP. *See* Economically active population
Ecclesial base communities (CEBs), 188
Economically active population (EAP), 98, 170–174
Economic development, xii–xiii, 85, 93, 94, 119, 126–127, 130, 162–163 (table), 170, 206
  financing, 72, 158
  foreign debt and, 159
  foreign policy and, 216–217
  industrialization and, 182
  inflation and, 123, 129
  patterns of, 137–140, 141
  quest for, 73–80, 167–168
  race relations and, 182
Economic problems, 99–100, 102–104, 137, 152–157
Editora Abril group, 195
Education, 46
  Afro-Brazilians and, 183, 184
  income and, 170, 177–178
  opportunities for, 180–182
  problems with, 178–182
  race and, 182–183
  social mobility and, 169, 170
  spending on, 179
Eisenhower, Milton, 209
Elbrick, C. Burke, 92
Elections, 41, 43, 131, 194
  1860s, 42
  1870s, 43
  1880s, 44
  1890s, 45, 47, 49, 50
  1900s, 50–51, 52, 53
  1910s, 53
  1920s, 53, 55, 56, 57
  1930s, 61–62
  1940s, 68–69
  1950s, 71, 74–75, 77
  1960s, 80, 83–84, 90–91, 93
  1970s, 96, 97, 99
  1980s, 100, 102, 103–104, 106–112
  1990s, 116–117, 121–122, 123–126

direct, 104
  flaws in, 131
Electrobrás, 155
Electronic media, 191, 199–200, 233(n10)
Electronics industry, growth in, 143
Energy, 147–151
  crisis, 95, 218
  industrialization and, 147–148
Engenhos, 36
Environmental preservation, 23, 212, 236(n34)
ESG. *See* National War College
Espírito Santo, 8, 12
  population of, 4
Estado Novo, 63–64, 65, 67, 69, 70–71, 78, 134, 208
EU. *See* European Union
European Union (EU), 213
  trade with, 167–168
Eu Sei que Vou Te Amar (*I Know That I Am Going to Love You*) (Jabor), 201
Export-Import Bank, 208
Exports. *See* Trade
External debt. *See* Foreign debt

Family, 181 (photo)
  socialization and, 192
Farias, Paulo César, 120
Farias, Roberto, 200
Farroupilha Revolution, 40
Favelados, 174
Fazendas, 36
FEB. *See* Brazilian Expeditionary Force
Federal District, 219(n5)
  representation for, 131
  revolt in, 86
Federalism, 47, 68
Federal Railroad System (RFFSA), 151
Federal Republican Party (PRF), 49
Federal Savings Bank (Caixa Ecônomico Federal), 151
Feijó, Diogo Antônio, 39
Feira de Santana, 33
Fernandes, Florestan, 128, 197
Ferreira, Procópio, 199
Ferreira Carneiro, Enéas, 124
Ferreira da Nóbrega, Mailson, 109

Fiat, investment by, 142
Figueiredo, João Baptista, 95, 98, 105, 118, 214
 foreign debt and, 161, 164–165
 government of, 99–100, 102–104
 problems for, 102–103
Films, 191, 199–201
Financial institutions, 147–151, 158
Fishing, 175 (photo)
Fleury Filho, Luiz Antônio, 117
Flôres da Cunha, 61
Florianópolis, 14
FMP. *See* Popular Mobilization Front
Fogaça, José, 125
Folha de S. Paulo, 195
Folk art/music, 191, 196, 198
Fonseca, Euclides Hermes da, 55
Fonseca, Hermes Rodriques da, 44, 52, 53, 54
Força Sindical (FS), 136
Foreign debt, 48, 98, 106, 108, 115, 143, 157–161, 164–168, 216, 218
 Latin American relations and, 214
 moratorium on, 159–160
 perspectives on, 158–159
 petroleum imports and, 160
 renegotiating, 152
 service, 158, 161, 166
Foreign exchange, 94, 97–98, 161
Foreign policy
 developing, 204, 206–207, 208, 213–218
 economic development and, 216–217
Fortaleza, 31
Fort Copacabana, 55
Foz de Iguaçu, 14, 14 (photo)
FPN. *See* Nationalist Parliamentary Front
Franca, 8
Franco, Itamar Augusto Cauteiro, 113, 126, 127, 128
 foreign relations and, 215
 Real Plan and, 153
 rise of, 120–122
Franco Montoro, André, 128
Free Zone, 25, 143
Freire, Roberto, 125
French Revolution, 37
Freyre, Gilberto de Mello, 183, 197

Fronape, 144
Frota, Sylvio, 97, 98
FS. *See* Força Sindical
Fulnio Indians, 32
Funaro, Dilson, 106, 108
Furnas hydroelectric project, 9
Furtado, Celso, 85, 197

Gabriel, Almir, 125
Gabriela: Cravo e Canela (*Gabriela: Clove and Cinnamon*) (Amado), 196, 200, 201
Gajin: Os Caminhos da Liberdade (*Gajin: The Ways of Liberty*) (Yamasaki), 201
Gaúchos, characteristics of, 193
Geisel, Ernesto
 ARENA and, 95
 decompression and, 96
 foreign debt and, 160–161
 government of, 95–99
 U.S.-Brazil relations and, 211
Geisel, Orlando, 93, 95
General Assembly, 39
General Motors, investment by, 142
General Workers Center (CGT), 135, 136
General Workers Confederation (CGT), 135
Globo network, 195, 233(n11)
 novelas on, 201
Góes e Vasconcelos, Zacarias de, 42
Góes Monteiro, Pedro Aurélio de, 59, 63, 66, 67
Goiás, 18
Gomes, Antônio Carlos, 198
Gomes, Ciro, 124
Gomes, Eduardo, 55, 66, 68, 71
Gomes de Mattos, Hélio Jaguaribe, 132, 197, 216
Gomes Pinheiro, José, 51–52
Gonzaga, Chiquinha (Francisca Edwiges Neves Gonzaga), 198
Gordon, Lincoln, 210
Goulart, Belchior Marques João, 67, 71, 74, 75, 77, 80–82, 86, 88, 89, 135, 206
 Brizola and, 87
 foreign debt and, 160

opposition to, 84
Three-Year Plan and, 85
U.S.-Brazil relations and, 210–211
Vargas and, 83
Governor Valladares, 9
Grande Sertão: Verdas (*The Devil to Pay in the Backlands*) (Guimarães Rosa), 197
Great Britain, relations with, 204
Great Depression, 139
Guerra, Ruy (Ruy Alexandre Guerra Coelho), 200
Guiana Highlands, 1, 21
Guimarães, Ulysses, 105, 111, 112, 128
Guimarães Rosa, João, 197
Gullar, Ferreira (José Ribamar Ferreira), 199

Hands to Work, 225(n14)
Hargreaves, Henrique, 120–121
Health care, spending on, 177
Heartland, 4–5, 5 (map), 7–12
Herzog, Vladimir, 97
Hirszman, Leon, 200
Humaitá, 42
Human rights, 93, 211, 236(n34)
Humphrey, George, 210
Hurt, William, 201
Hydroelectric projects, 147, 148, 155

IADB. *See* Inter-American Development Bank
IBAD. *See* Brazilian Institute of Democratic Action
IBRD. *See* World Bank
Idade da Terra (Earth's Age) (Rocha), 200
Il Guarany (Gomes), 198
Ilhéus, 34
Illiteracy rate, 180, 183
IMF. *See* International Monetary Fund
Immigrant groups, 7, 186–187
Immigration, 51, 54
industrialization and, 45–46, 186
See also Migration
Imperatriz, 30
Income distribution, 170–173
education and, 170, 177–178
race and, 182–183
Inconfidência Mineira, 37

Independence Day, 38, 194
Indians, xii, 195
plight of, 185–186, 212
Industrialization, 8, 42, 64, 66, 70, 71, 75, 76, 94, 137, 141–145, 169
economic development and, 182
energy and, 147–148
foreign investment and, 166
growth of, 148–149
immigration and, 45–46, 186
import-substitution, 65, 143, 144, 156, 158, 167
income concentration and, 172
inflation and, 155
transportation and, 150
Industry
employment in, 79, 98, 143, 171, 174
GDP from, 222(n17)
modernization and, 141–142
Inflation, 48, 94, 98, 102, 106, 112, 115–116, 118, 119, 127, 130, 143, 152–157
attacking, 108–109, 114, 117, 153
deficits and, 155
economic growth and, 123, 129
problems with, 152–153
Informal sector, employment in, 171–172
Infrastructure, 147–151, 152
Institute for Social Research and Studies (IPES), 83, 86
Institutional Act No. 5 (AI–5), 92–93, 96–99, 211
Integralism, 63, 64, 124
Inter-American Development Bank (IADB), 160, 165, 166
Internal debt, 152, 155–156
privatization and, 157
problems with, 153–155
International Bank for Settlements, 164
International Monetary Fund (IMF), 78, 106, 119, 158
Brazil and, 102, 117, 152, 159, 160, 164, 165
Interpretive Law (1839), 39
Interventors, 59, 61, 62, 65, 67, 69
Investment, 157–161, 164–168
Ipatinga, 9

IPES. *See* Institute for Social Research and
    Studies
Istoé, 195
Itabuna, 34
Itaipu Dam, 14, 148, 149 (photo), 214
Itajaí, 15
Itamaraty, 215
Itaparica dam, 34, 148
Ivaí Valley, 14

Jabor, Arnaldo, 201
Jabotão, 32
Jaguaribe, Hélio Gomes de Mattos, 132,
    197, 216
Japan, relations with, 213, 216
Japanese-Brazilians, influence of, 186
Jari pulpwood-cellulose-mining-
    agricultural project, 27
Jatene, Adib, 129
Jeitinho, 194
Jereissati, Tasso, 125
Jewish-Brazilians, number of, 186–187
João VI, 37, 38
João Pessoa, 32
Jobim, Antônio Carlos "Tom," 198, 199
Jobim, Nelson, 129
Jogo de bicho, 171–172
John XXIII, Second Vatican Council and,
    187
John Paul II, doctrinal cleavages and, 188
Joint Brazil-United States Economic
    Development Commission, 209
Joint Brazil-United States Technical
    Commission, 209
Joinville, 15
Juazeiro, 34
Juazeiro do Norte, 31
Jubiabá (Amado), 196
Juiz da Fora, 9, 120, 121
Julia, Raul, 201
Julião, Francisco, 83, 136
Jundiaí, 8

Kaiwá Indians, 20
Kardac, Alan, followers of, 190
Kayapó Indians, 20, 27
Kennedy, John F., 210
Kissinger, Henry, 211

Kiss of the Spiderwoman, 201
Klein, Odacir, 129
Kleinubing, Vilson, 125
Krause, Gustavo, 129
Krupp industries, armaments from, 208
Kubitschek de Oliveira, Juscelino, 74, 80,
    81, 82, 87
    Castelo Branco and, 89
    economic growth and, 76, 139, 210
    foreign debt and, 159
    IMF and, 78
    industrialization and, 79
    nationalism of, 77
    Program of Goals of, 75–76
    U.S.-Brazilian relations and, 210

Labor, 170–172
    political clout of, 134–136
Lacerda, Carlos, 72, 73, 74, 81, 82, 85
Lafer, Celso, foreign relations and, 216
Lages, 15
Lagoa dos Patos, 16
Lampréia, Luiz Felipe, 129, 215
Land law (1850), 43
Landowners
    agriculture and, 145
    control by, 134
Latin America
    relations with, 213–214, 217
    trade with, 168
Lebanese-Brazilians, influence of, 186
Lerner, Jaime, 125
Liberal Alliance (AL), 57, 59, 60
Liberal Front Party (PFL), 103, 104, 105,
    119, 129
    support for, 107, 110, 116, 122, 124, 125,
        126
Liberal Party (PL), 41, 42, 56, 107, 119
    reform manifesto of, 43
    support for, 115, 117, 122, 125, 126
Liberationist Alliance, 56
Liberation theology, 187
Libertadores, 57
LIBOR. *See* London interbank offered rate
Lima Barreto, Victor, 200
Lima e Silva, Francisco de, 39
Lima e Silva, Luís Alves de, 39
Linha dura faction, 89

Linhares, José, 67
Lins de Barros, João Alberto, 60–61
Lisbôa, Antônio Francisco ("Aleijadinho"),
    202
Lispector, Clarice, 197
Literacy rates, 46, 180
Lobo, Edu, 199
London interbank offered rate (LIBOR),
    161
Londrina, 13
Lorscheider, Aloísio, 187
Lorscheiter, Ivo, 188
Lott, Henrique Duffles Teixeira, 70, 74, 75,
    79, 80
Lucena Boavista, Miguel, 53
Ludwig, Daniel, 27
Lula da Silva, Luís Inácio, 101 (photo), 110,
    123, 128, 135, 136
  Articulation faction of, 118
  PT and, 100
  support for, 111–112, 124
"Luso-tropical" man, 183
Lutfalla-Maluf family, Maluf campaign
    and, 186
Luz, Carlos, 75

Maceió, 33
Machado, Pinheiro, PRC and, 52
Machado de Assis, Joaquim María, 191,
    195, 196
Maciel, Marco, 129
Macumba, 190
Macunaíma: O herói sem nenhuma caráter
    (Macunaíma: Hero Without Any
    Character) (Andrade), 196, 200
Macuxi, 26
Magalhães, Antônio Carlos, 118, 128, 129,
    130, 195
  support for, 124, 125
Magalhães, Luiz Eduardo, 129
Magazines
  dissemination of, 191
  number of, 194
Magri, Antônio Rogério: CGT and, 136
Maia, César, 122
Maksouds, 186
Malan, Pedro Sampaio, 129

Malandro, 192
Maluf, Paulo Salim, 98, 111, 112, 121–122
  family support for, 186
  PDS and, 103
  PDS-PDC merger and, 122
Mamelucos, 36, 37
Manaus, 25
Manaus Free Zone, 25, 143
Manchete (network), 195
Manchete (pictorial), 195, 233(n11)
Mannesmann, 9
Marabá, 27
Maranhão, 26, 28, 30, 40
  pacifying, 39
  population of, 139
March 31 Movement, 88
Marighella, Carlos, 93
Maringá, 13
Marinho, Roberto, 118, 195
Mato Grosso, 20, 21
Mato Grosso do Sul, 18–19
McCann, Frank D., on Brazil/international
    affairs, 205
MDB. *See* Brazilian Democratic Movement
Medeiros, Luíz Antônio, 136
Medeiros, Octávio, 100
Media
  cultural traits and, 192–195
  migration and, 192
Médici, Emílio Garrastazu, 92
  foreign debt and, 160
  government of, 93–95
  security apparatus and, 96
  U.S.-Brazil relations and, 211
Mekragnote reservation, 27
Memórias Postúmas de Bras Cubas (*Epitaph
    of a Small Winner*) (Machado de
    Assis), 196
Mendes, Chico, 25
Mendes de Almeida, Luciano, 188
Meneguelli, Jair, 135, 136
Mercosul. *See* Southern Common Market
Metropolitan regions, population of, 3
    (table)
Mexico
  bankruptcy for, 102
  debt moratorium by, 164

North American Free Trade Agreement
and, 217
relations with, 213
Solidarity Program of, 130
Middle class, 58, 72
income for, 172
spiritism and, 190
Migration
internal, 138–139
media and, 192
See also Immigration
Military
Communists and, 133
employment in, 156
foreign relations and, 215
Paraguayan War and, 42
politics and, 133–134
Military Club, 44, 47, 70, 83
tribunal of honor and, 54
Minas Gerais, 8–10, 12, 18, 19, 36
coffee from, 51
conspiracy in, 37
economy of, 10
growth of, 46, 52
mining in, 141
population of, 4, 139
representation for, 131
Mineiros, characteristics of, 192, 193
Minimum wages, 173, 174, 178
Mining, potential of, 147
Ministry of Health, expenditures by, 177
Miranda, Carmen (Maria do Carmo
Miranda da Cunha), 198, 201
Modernization, 169, 213
agricultural, 141–145, 147
industrial, 141–142
resistance to, 132
social, 130
women and, 171
Montenegro, Fernanda, 199, 201
Montes Claros, 10
Moraes, Vinícius de (Marcus Vinícius da
Cruz de Melo Moraes), 199
Morais Barrios, Prudente José de, 45, 47, 49
Moreira, Delfim, 53
Moreira, Marcílio Marques, 117–118, 120
Moreira Alves, Márcio, 92

Moreira Neves, Lucas, 188
Morumbí, 5
Moscardo de Souza, Jerônimo, 215
Mossoró, 32
Motta, Sérgio Vieira de, 129
Mount Roraima, 26
Multinational companies, 155, 167
Muslims, 186

Nabuco, Joaquim, 196, 197
Napoleão, Hugo, 125
Napoleon, 37
Natal, 32
National Confederation of Industrial
Workers (CNTI), 135
National Confederation of Industries
(CNI), 134
National Conference of Brazilian Bishops
(CNBB), 187, 188
National Conference of the Working Class
(CONCLAT), 135. *See also* General
Workers Center
National Constituent Assembly, 61
National Defense Council, 109
National Democratic Union (UDN), 67,
69, 75, 76, 77, 80, 84, 85, 86, 88
Vargas and, 73
National Economic and Social
Development Bank (BNDES), 129,
151
National Economic Development Bank
(BNDE), 155
Nationalism, 67, 72, 73, 74, 76, 77, 78, 206
economic, 70
Nationalist Parliamentary Front (FPN), 77,
86
National Liberating Alliance (ANL), 62, 63,
82
National Liberation Front, 83
National Pro-CUT (Single Workers
Center) Commission, 135
National Reconstruction of Order Party
(PRONA), 124
National Renovating Alliance (ARENA),
90, 91, 93, 95, 98, 105
support for, 96–97, 99, 111
National Renovation Party (PRN), 115,
117, 119

National Steel Company (CSN), 11, 143, 155, 208
National War College (ESG), 73, 86, 87
foreign relations and, 215
Natural gas, 25, 149, 150
Natural resources, 141–145, 147
Neimeyer Soares Filho, Oscar, 191, 203
Neoliberalism, 128, 217
Neves, Tancredo de Almeida, 82, 100, 103, 104–105, 120
Newspapers, number of, 194
New State. *See Estado Novo*
North, 21–23, 22 (map), 25–28
North American Free Trade Agreement, Mexico and, 217
Northeast, 28–34, 29 (map)
Nossa Senhora da Aparicida, pilgrimages to, 189
Nosso Senhor do Bonfim, ceremonies at, 189
Nova República, 105
Novelas, 192, 199–200, 201
Nuclear proliferation, 211
Numbers game, 171–172

O Bem Amado (The Beloved) (Dias Gomes), 199
Obstructionism, 78, 81
O Cangaceiro (The Bandit) (Lima Barreto), 200
O Estado de S. Paulo, 195
O Globo, 195
Oil. *See* Petroleum
Old Republic, 65
breakdown of, 55–57, 60
written word in, 195–196
Olinda, 32
Oliveira, Dante de, 125
Oliveira Vianna, Francisco José de, 196, 197
O Pagador de Promessas (The Given Word) (Dias Gomes), 199, 200
"Ópera do Malandro" (The Rascal's Opera), 199
Operation Pan America, 78, 210
"Orfeu do Carneval" (Moraes), 199
Orfeu Negro (Black Orpheus) (Camus), 199
Organization of American States, 216
Orixás, 190

Os Cafajestes (The Hustlers) (Guerra), 200
O Século da Cinema (The Cinema Century) (Rocha), 200
Osório, Manuel Luíz, 44
Os Trapalhões (The Bumblers), 201
O Sumiço da Santa (The War of the Saints) (Amado), 196
O Tempo e O Vento (Time and Wind) (Verissimo), 197

Paankotō-Tiriyós, 27
Pact of Pedra Altas (1923), 55
PAEG. *See* Program of Government Economic Action
Paiva, Paulo, 129
Panelinha, 194, 195
Pankararú Indians, 32
Pantanal, 19, 19 (photo), 20
Pará, 26–28
mining in, 141
population of, 139
transformation of, 27
Paraguay
relations with, 214
trade with, 168
Paraguayan War, 42–43, 159
Parahyba, Mulher Macho (Paraíba, Macho Woman) (Yamasaki), 201
Paraíba, 32
Paraíba Valley, 8, 11
Paraná, 25
population of, 139
Paranaguá, port of, 13–14
Paranapanema River, 8
Paraná River, 12
Parastatal enterprises, employment in, 156, 157
Pardo, number of, 183
Parentela, understanding, 193–194
Paris Club, 117, 165, 166
Parliamentary system, 48, 82–84, 109
Parnaíba, 30
Party of the Brazilian Democratic Movement (PMDB), 100, 102, 103, 104, 105, 106, 119, 124, 128, 129, 135
support for, 107–111, 115, 116, 121–122, 125, 126
Parukotó-Charúmas, 27

Passo Fundo, 16
Patronage, 48, 80, 132, 156–157
Paulista Republican Party, 56
Paulistas, characteristics of, 192, 193
PCB. *See* Brazilian Communist Party
PCdoB. *See* Communist Party of Brazil
PDC. *See* Christian Democratic Party
PDS. *See* Democratic Social Party
PDT. *See* Democratic Workers' Party
Pedro II, 38–39, 220(n10)
    industrialization and, 43
    reign of, 39–40, 41
"Pedro Pedreiro" (Pete the Stonemason)
    (Buarque), 198–199
Peixoto, Floriàno, 44, 47, 48, 50, 52, 90
    civil war and, 49
Pelotas, 16
Pelourinho, 33
Pena, Afonso Angusto Moreira, 49, 51, 52
Pentecostal sects, 94, 189
Pereira, Francelino, 125
Pereira dos Santos, Nelson, 200
Pereira dos Souza, Washington Luís, 55, 57,
    59
Pernambuco, 32, 34
    conspiracy in, 37
    population of, 139
    settlement of, 36
Pernambuco Alcohol-Chemical Pole, 143
Perón, Juan, 72, 209
Peru, relations with, 208, 214
Pessoa, Epitácio, 53
Pessoa, João, 59
Petrobrás, 72, 143, 144, 155, 157, 209
    alcohol development by, 149
    energy self-sufficiency and, 150
    U.S. hostility for, 210
Petrochemical industry, 143
Petroleum, 147, 161, 209, 210, 218
    debate about, 72
    development of, 149, 150
    foreign debt and, 160
    government monopoly on, 156
    import of, 156
    offshore, 11, 149, 150
    reducing need for, 164, 165
Petrópolis, 11
Petroquisa, 143

PFL. *See* Liberal Front Party
Pico de Bandeira, 9
Pico de Neblina, 26
Pindaré, 30
Piñon, Nélida, 197
Pinto, Edmundo, murder of, 25
Pires, José Maria, 189
Pires, Olavo, 21
Piricicaba, 8
Pistolão, 194
Pixote: A Lei dos Mais Fracos (Pixote: Law
    of the Weakest) (Babenco), 201
PL. *See* Liberal Party
Plano Verão, 110
PMDB. *See* Party of the Brazilian
    Democratic Movement
Poços de Caldas, 9
Political divisions, 2 (map)
Politics, xii
    radicalization of, 72–73
Pollution, 4, 7, 212
Ponta Grossa, 14
Popular Democratic Action (ADEP), 83
Popular Mobilization Front (FMP), 86
Popular Party (PP), 100, 126
Popular Socialist Party (PPS), 119, 125
Population, xi, xii
    economic growth and, 140
    growth of, 78–79, 99, 138–139
    rural/urban, 139
Populism, 64, 67, 74, 85, 121, 188, 195
Portinari, Cândido Torquato, 191, 202
Porto Alegre, 16
Porto Velho, 20
Portugal, colonization by, 35–36
Postal service, 151, 156
PP. *See* Popular Party
PPR. *See* Progressive Renovating Party
PPS. *See* Popular Socialist Party
PRC. *See* Conservative Republican Party
Presidentialism, 78–79, 83, 84, 109, 122
Presidents, choosing, 110–112, 123–127
Prestes, Júlio, 57
Prestes, Luís Carlos, 55, 62
Prestes Column, 55, 59
Preto, number of, 183
PRF. *See* Federal Republican Party

Privatization, 115, 117, 118, 119, 130, 152,
    154, 156, 157
PRN. *See* National Renovation Party
Program of Goals (Programa de Metas),
    75–76
Program of Government Economic Action
    (PAEG), 90
Progressive Renovating Party (PPR), 122,
    124, 130
    support for, 125, 126
"Project Brazil: Great Power," 93
PRONA. *See* National Reconstruction of
    Order Party
Property owners, control by, 134
Protectionism, 70, 115, 118, 143, 167
Protestantism, 170
    growth of, 187, 189
PSB. *See* Brazilian Socialist Party
PSD. *See* Social Democratic Party
PSDB. *See* Brazilian Social Democracy
    Party
PSP. *See* Social Progressive Party
PT. *See* Workers' Party
PTB. *See* Brazilian Labor Party
Public sector, 152–157
Puerto Suarez, Bolivia, thermoelectric
    plant at, 19, 214

Quadros, Jânio, 74, 79, 80, 110, 128,
    222(n18)
    foreign debt and, 160
    government of, 81–82
    U.S.-Brazil relations and, 210
Queiróz, Rachel de, 197
Quércia, Orestes, 117, 118, 124, 125
Quincas Borba (Philosopher or Dog?)
    (Machado de Assis), 196

Race relations, xiii, 182–187
Rademaker Grünewald, Augusto, 89, 93
Radicalization, 80–84, 91
Radio stations, number of, 194
Railroads, 41, 150–151
Rain forests, 1, 21, 23, 122
Ramos, Graciliano, 196, 200
Ramos, Nereu, 75
Real Plan (Cardoso Plan), 123, 126, 127,
    153

Recife, 32
    revolt in, 40
    settlement of, 36
Recôncavo, 33
Reforestation, 24 (photo)
Reis Velloso, João Paulo dos, 95
Religion, 44, 187–190
    Afro-Brazilian, 170, 185, 187
Republicanism, 45–46
Republican Party, 46, 53, 55, 57
    armed forces and, 45
    liberals and, 43
Republican Reaction, 54
Requião, Roberto, 125
Resende, Iris, 125
Revolt of 1922, 55
Revolt of 1924, 55
Revolt of 1930, 58–62
Revolution, 54–57, 58–62, 90–91
Revolutionary Legion, 61
Revolutionary Supreme Command, 89
RFFSA. *See* Federal Railroad System
Ribeirão Preto, 8
Ricupero, Rubens, 122, 123, 124
    foreign relations and, 215
Rio Branco, 23
Riocell, 144
Riocentro incident, 100
Rio de Janeiro, xi, 10–12, 40
    Botofogo District of, 10 (photo)
    conspiracy in, 37
    population of, 2, 4, 56, 64–65, 139
    port of, 151
Rio Grande do Norte, 31–32
Rio Grande do Sul, 16, 51
    population of, 139
    revolt in, 47, 55
Rio Negro, 21, 25–26
Rio Quarenta Graus (Rio, Heatwave)
    (Pereira dos Santos), 200
Rocha, Glauber, 191, 200
Rodrigues, Nelson, 199, 200
Rodrigues Alves, Francisco de Paula, 50
    economic development under, 51
    election of, 53
Rondônia, 20, 21
Roosevelt, Franklin D., 66, 209

Roraima, 26
  representation for, 131
Rubinstein, Alvin A., 205

Sales Oliveira, Armando de, 61–62, 63, 67
Salgado, Plínio, 62
Salvador, 33
  chemical industry in, 143
San Francisco River, 34
  hydroelectric potential of, 148
Santa Catarina, 14–15, 16
Santa Maria, 16
Santarém, 27
Santos, 7, 11, 151
Santos, Sílvio, 195, 201
Santos Andrade, Joaquim dos, 135, 136
São Bernardo do Campo, 8
São José de Rio Preto, 8
São José dos Campos, 8
São Luis, 30
São Mateus do Sul, 14
São Paulo, xi, 4–5, 7–8, 7 (photo)
  population of, 2, 4, 56, 64–65
  representation for, xii, 131
  revolt in, 60–61
São Paulo Church, 188
São Paulo dynasty, 49–51
São Paulo Federation of Industries, 111
São Paulo state, population of, 139
Saraiva law (1881), 43–44
Sardenberg, Ronaldo Mota, foreign
  relations and, 129, 215
Sarney, José, 111, 118, 121, 124, 127, 128,
  129, 130
  armed forces and, 133
  Catholic Church and, 188
  foreign debt and, 165–166
  government by, 104–109
  inflation and, 114, 153
  unpopularity of, 110
Sarney, Roseana, 125
SBT network, 195, 201, 233(n11)
Schooling. *See* Education
Second National Development Plan:
  1975–1979, 97
Second Vatican Council, 187
Segall, Lazar, 202

Sem terras, number of, 145
Senate
  curbing of, 62
  election to, 96
  seats in, 99, 131
Sepetiba, 11
Sergipe, 33
Sergipe Fertilizer Pole, 143
Serra, José, 129
Serra da Mantiqueira, 8, 9, 11
Serra do Mar, 11, 12, 15
Serra do Navio, 27
Serra do Orgãos, 11–12
Serra dos Cariris Novos, 31
Serra Geral, 15
Serra Grande, 31
Serra Pelada, 26
Sertão, 28–29, 31, 33
Shell, Alumar project of, 30
Shipbuilding, 11, 144
Siderbrás, 155
Silva, Benedita da, 122, 125
Silva, Ozires, 115
Silva, Vicente Paulo da, 136
Silva Xavier, Joaquim José da, 37
Simões de Moura, Emílson, 136
Simonsen, Mário Henrique, 95, 99, 100
Single Workers Center (CUT), 135, 136
  Catholic Church and, 188
Siqueira Campos, Antônio de, 55
Slaves, 44, 46
  population of, 37, 40, 43, 220(n11)
Soap operas, 199–200
Soares, Jô (José Eugênio Soares), 201
Sobradinho dam, 34, 148
Social change, xiii, 80, 173–174, 177–178,
  206
  dealing with, 169–170
  urbanization and, 169
Social Democratic Party (PSD), 67, 69, 71,
  74, 76, 80
  PTB and, 68, 75, 79, 84, 86
Social mobility, 170–173
  education and, 169, 170
Social problems, 174–177, 213
Social Progressive Party (PSP), 69
Social security system, 118, 119, 130, 177

Social welfare, 64, 71, 76
Solano López, Francisco, 42
Solidarity Program (Mexico), 130
Solimões, 21
Sorocaba, 8
South, 12–16, 13 (map)
Southern Common Market (Mercosul),
214, 217
Souto, Paulo, 124
Souza, Paulo Renato de, 129
Souza, Tomé de, 35, 129
Soybean fields, 146 (photo)
Spiritism, 170, 187, 190
States, characteristics/rank of, 6 (table)
Statism, 155–157
Steel, 141–142
Stephanes, Reinhold, 129
Student demonstrations, 94 (photo)
Suapé, 33
Sugar, 40
    export of, 36, 37
    production of, 145, 228(n12)
Sumaré/Americana, 8
SUMOC. *See* Superintendency of Money
    and Credit
Superintendency of Money and Credit
    (SUMOC), 151
Suruagy, Divaldo, 125
Syrians, 186

Tapajós, 20, 25
Tariána Indians, 26
Taubaté pact, coffee sector and, 54
Taulipáng, 27
Távola, Arthur da, 125
Tavora, Juarez do Nascimento Fernandez,
75
Technology, diversification and, 143–144
Telebrás, 157
Telephone system, 151
Television, 191, 192, 201
    stations, 194
Tenentes, 59–60, 63, 66, 87
    opposition by, 56, 61, 62, 70
Tenentismo, 54–57, 60
Terêna Indians, 20
Teresinha, 30
Terra em Transe (Anguished Land)

(Rocha), 200
Terras do Sem Fim (*The Violent Land*)
    (Amado), 196
Terrorism, 91–92
Three-Year Plan, 85
Tieta do Agreste (*Tieta: the Goat Girl*)
    (Amado), 196
Tietê, pollution of, 7
Tocaia Grande (*Showdown*) (Amado), 196
Tocantins, 18, 25
Tôrres, Alberto, 196, 197
Tôrres, Fernanda, 201
Trabalhista, modernization of, 74
Trade, 151
    deficit, 97, 160–161, 164–165, 168
    diversification of, 218
    earnings from, 137
    surplus, 123, 158, 164, 166, 167, 168
Transportation, 147–151
Treaty of Methuen (1703), 205
Treaty of Tordesillas (1494), 35
Tres Marias hydroelectric project, 9
Trombetas, 27
Truman, Harry S., 209
Tuberão, port of, 151
Tucuruí hydroelectric facility, 27, 148
Tukúno Indians, 26

Uamué Indians, 32
Uberaba, 9
Uberlândia, 9
UDN. *See* National Democratic Union
Umbanda, 94, 190
    Catholicism and, 194
Um Estadista da República (*A Statesman of
    the Republic*) (Arinos de Mello
    Franco), 197
Unemployment, 102, 170
Unibanco, 118
Unions, 151
    political clout of, 134–136
United Provinces of the Rio de La Plata, 39
United States
    funds from, 72, 117, 164
    relations with, 77–78, 204, 205, 207–213,
        216, 217, 218
    trade with, 168
U.N. Security Council, 216

Urbanization, 2–3, 4, 45, 48, 64, 65,
    219(n2), 227(n4)
  social changes and, 169, 173–174
Uruguaiana, 16
Uruguay
  relations with, 214
  trade with, 168
Usiminas steel company, 9, 118, 157

Vale do Rio Doce Company (CVRD), 144,
    155, 157
Vargas, Getúlio Dornelles, 57, 80, 81, 82,
    85, 128, 134, 155, 206
  Estado Novo and, 64, 66, 67, 70–71
  foreign policy and, 208
  paternalism of, 60
  rise of, 58–62
  rule of, 62–73
  social/economic change under, 64–66
  suicide of, 73, 209
  World War II and, 66–67
Veja, 140, 195
Venezuela, relations with, 214
Verissimo, Érico, 197
Vestido de Noiva (The Wedding Dress)
    (Rodrigues), 199
Vidas Secas (*Barren Lives*) (Ramos), 196,
    200
Villa-Lobos, Heitor, 191, 198
Vitória, 12
Vitória da Conquista, 34
Volkswagen, investment by, 142
Volta Redonda, 11, 208

Wagley, Charles, on *parentela*, 193
War and Peace (Portinari), 202
War of the Farrapos, 40
Wealth, distribution of, 138, 172–173
Weffort, Francisco, 129
Werneck, Dorothéa, 129
Westinghouse, Angra I plant and, 148
Women
  Afro-Brazilian, 171
  social role of, 169, 171
  voting by, 116
Workers' Party (PT), 100, 102, 106, 118,
    119, 136
  Catholic Church and, 188
  support for, 107, 110, 115, 116, 122, 124,
    125, 126, 135
Working class, 68
  income for, 172
  political clout of, 134–136
World Bank (IBRD), 160, 165, 166
World Cup soccer, 93, 124

Xavántes, 20
Xingô dam, 33, 148
Xingu National Park, 20, 25, 27
Xukurú Indians, 32
"Xuxa" (Maria da Graça Meneghel), 201

Yamasaki, Tizuka, 201
Yanomanıs, 26, 214

Zona da Matta, 28, 32